Diffractive Reading

New Critical Humanities

Series Editors: Birgit Kaiser, Associate Professor of Comparative Literature, Utrecht University, Timothy O'Leary, Professor of Philosophy, University of Hong Kong, and Kathrin Thiele, Associate Professor of Gender Studies and Critical Theory, Utrecht University

In this time of global crises, from the COVID pandemic and climate change to transnational inequalities and persistent racial injustices, the value of the critical humanities and their intervention into public discourse is once again of central concern. This Series publishes books that demonstrate an understanding of critique in action, while also questioning and redefining its inherited methodologies and perspectives. The books in this series contribute to a re-imagination of critique; its powers, its strengths, and its transformative potential. Grounded in the core humanities disciplines (including philosophy, literature, gender and cultural studies), the series challenges and sharpens the question of critique itself, thus situating the critical humanities at the centre of envisioned collective responses to the fundamental demands of the twenty-first century.

The series is linked to the international research network *Terra Critica: Interdisciplinary Network for the Critical Humanities*, which the editors Birgit M. Kaiser and Kathrin Thiele founded and coordinate since 2012 (www.terracritica.net), and of which Timothy O'Leary is a member.

Untranslating Machines: A Genealogy for the Ends of Global Thought
    Jacques Lezra
Naturally Late: Synchronisation in Socially Constructed Times
    Will Johncock
Urban Arabesques: Philosophy, Hong Kong, Transversality
    Gray Kochhar-Lindgren
Revolts in Cultural Critique
    Rosemarie Buikema
Diffractive Reading: New Materialism, Theory, Critique
    Edited by Kai Merten

Diffractive Reading

New Materialism, Theory, Critique

Edited by
Kai Merten

ROWMAN & LITTLEFIELD
Lanham • Boulder • New York • London

Published by Rowman & Littlefield
An imprint of The Rowman & Littlefield Publishing Group, Inc.
4501 Forbes Boulevard, Suite 200, Lanham, Maryland 20706
www.rowman.com

6 Tinworth Street, London SE11 5AL, United Kingdom

Selection and editorial matter copyright © Kai Merten 2021. Copyright in individual chapters is held by the respective chapter authors.

All rights reserved. No part of this book may be reproduced in any form or by any electronic or mechanical means, including information storage and retrieval systems, without written permission from the publisher, except by a reviewer who may quote passages in a review.

British Library Cataloguing in Publication Information Available

Library of Congress Cataloging-in-Publication Data

Names: Merten, Kai (Professor of English literature), editor.
Title: Diffractive reading : new materialism, theory, critique / edited by Kai Merten.
Description: Lanham : Rowman & Littlefield, [2021] | Series: New critical Humanities |
    Includes bibliographical references and index.
Identifiers: LCCN 2021007277 (print) | LCCN 2021007278 (ebook) |
    ISBN 9781786613967 (Cloth) | ISBN 9781786613974 (ePub) |
ISBN 9781538155677 (Pbk)
Subjects: LCSH: Reading. | Difference (Philosophy) | Diffraction—Philosophy. |
    Critical theory.
Classification: LCC LB1050 .D52 2021 (print) | LCC LB1050 (ebook) |
    DDC 372.4—dc23
LC record available at https://lccn.loc.gov/2021007277
LC ebook record available at https://lccn.loc.gov/2021007278

Contents

1 Introduction: Diffraction, Reading, and (New) Materialism ... 1
   Kai Merten

PART I: DIFFRACTIVE READING: GROUNDWORK ... 29

2 On the Politics of Diffractive Reading ... 31
   Birgit Mara Kaiser

3 Heraclitus's Onto-stories: Impossible Appointments and the Importance of the Encounter ... 51
   Max Walther

4 Decoherent Reading: On the Constitutive Exclusions of Diffractive Reading ... 71
   Stacey Moran

5 Reading Speculative Horror Readings Diffractively ... 93
   Peter Schuck

PART II: DIFFRACTING LITERATURE: DIFFRACTIONS OF THE WORLD-TEXT-READER ENTANGLEMENT ... 115

6 Diffractive Poetics in William Carlos Williams's *Paterson* ... 117
   Brendan Johnston

7 Sauron's Sliding Door: The Diffraction of Mythological and Intimate "Evil" in Tolkien ... 135
   Bo Kampmann Walther

8	Sensing I and Eyes in Ali Smith's *How to Be Both* Daniela Keller	153
9	Practices of Entanglement: Unreading the Genre in China Miéville's *The Scar* Agnieszka Kotwasińska	175
10	The Entanglements of Harry Burden: A Diffractive Reading of Siri Hustvedt Matthias Stephan	193
11	Surfacing: A Diffractive Reading Experiment with Books and Houses in Walter Benjamin's *Ich packe meine Bibliothek aus* and Carlos María Domínguez' *Casa de papel* Annina Klappert	211

PART III: DIFFRACTING (IN) MUSIC, VISUAL, AND DIGITAL MEDIA   233

12	Diffractive Aesthetics and Holographic Literacies: Transcoding the Gigaton Volume Detector [A Diffracted Photo-Essay] Jol Thoms	235
13	Diffracting Maternal and Female Midlife Sexual Assemblages in Postfeminist Popular Culture Susan Yi Sencindiver	249
14	Ontoflecting through U2 Nathan D. Frank	269
15	Reprogramming Rhetoric: Toward a Diffractive Epistemology of Computer Composition Sean McCullough	287

Bibliography   307

Index   331

About the Contributors   343

Chapter 1

Introduction[*]
Diffraction, Reading, and (New) Materialism
Kai Merten

The main aim of the present volume is to both discuss and practise a new methodology of *reading*, inspired by recent discussions of how matter (and matter beyond culture in particular) could be integrated more strongly into theories and methods within the Humanities and the Social Sciences. The volume has benefited greatly from these discussions; however, it does not want to contribute to the basic debate if and how a new materialist turn is necessary or feasible. Instead, it has started from a very hands-on idea that came up in the Erfurt Network on New Materialism a while ago after we had read and discussed Karen Barad's *Meeting the Universe Halfway* in a round of sessions. Inspired by Barad's notion of an onto-epistemological entanglement of discourse and matter, we, a group of mainly Literary Studies scholars, were wondering if a mode of reading was thinkable, usable, theorizable that interfered much more directly with what was being read—regardless whether what was read was a text or a physical phenomenon—and that by doing so, influenced and changed what was read. We were fascinated by the term "diffraction" that Barad suggests in this context. If reading could, or even: must, be seen as interfering in this way, we thought, wouldn't that make for a much more involved and also politically interventionist grasp of what reading really meant? That by reading we create and change the things we read, that reading is not some kind of tinkering with a cultural code at a great remove from the world, but that, instead, reading is part and parcel of the text, of the world, of the matter that is read.[1]

The theory and the actual readings that this collection unfolds are in this spirit. Both started out from Barad's concept of diffractive reading that she takes from Donna Haraway and develops on (as, in turn, Barad's concept

---

[*] I would like to thank Chaniga Chaipan for her invaluable help in preparing this volume.

has been worked on by Kathrin Thiele and Birgit Kaiser in their volume *Diffracted Worlds—Diffractive Readings*[2]), and both—my methodological considerations in this introduction and the incredibly versatile range of diffractive reading in practice that follows—move on from there into directions/diffractions of their own. This is not to say that this introduction is not some kind of starting point to the collection, but this is to insist that my own chapter and the chapters that follow have come into existence in an exchange, diffraction, with each other: the readings done in this volume developed out of abstracts that reacted to a short abstract of mine that was merely suggestive of a notion of diffractive reading, and while I sketched out this introduction in more detail, I kept reading all the wonderful draft chapters coming in, and these chapters finally reacted to, and made changes to, my draft introduction (as well as to each other in some cases) in the further revision process. We were all diffracted/diffracting with each other all the time. This also means that all our chapters have a Baradian starting point from which we move on, both theoretically (and, in my case, only theoretically) and practically.

What interests me most by way of introduction to this project is to bring together the *two* notions of diffractive reading that I consider to be available from Barad's book: a diffractive reading of *text* and a diffractive reading of *matter*. To arrive at this junction, I have to travel a somewhat long distance, through a range of already existing "materialist" reading theories, that is, mainly approaches that concern themselves with the reading of *matter* and some of which have already compared text reading to matter reading in a more explicit way than Barad. By doing so, I also want to connect the actual diffractive readings I received from the other contributors more closely with each other, both in the sense of suggesting a common, overarching theoretical concern with participating, contributive, interacting reading in these chapters and in the sense of making these texts (and indeed all texts) diffract(able) with each other.

DIFFRACTION AND DIFFRACTIVE READING IN BARAD

An often-asked question during the preparation and discussion of this volume was why interfering, participatory reading should be called *diffractive* reading, and what "diffraction" actually means when it comes to modify the verb "read." Karen Barad, who coined the term "diffractive reading," actually takes the trouble to deduce the term from physics and then use it for a hermeneutic methodology, so it is worth looking at this deduction in some more detail. Barad starts from (macro-)physical standard definitions of diffraction but moves on from there into the quantum sphere. "[D]iffraction has to do with the way waves combine when they overlap and the apparent bending and spreading of waves that occurs when waves encounter an obstruction. Diffraction can occur with any kind of wave: for example, water waves, sound waves, and light waves all exhibit diffraction under the right conditions."[3] At first, diffraction is described here as a phenomenon of wave interference but it is more commonly connected to the "obstructions" that Barad mentions in the second place, that is, obstacles that bend and spread the waves that pass through them. In an experimental context, such processes are instigated by the so-called diffraction gratings. The phenomenon coming up against the obstacle is diffracted into showing the behaviour of a (regularly) bent wave when having passed through an opening in the grating. When there are two or more openings of similar size in the (diffraction) grating, two or more waves will interfere in a regular pattern after passing through. Diffraction in this sense creates both differences (waves of different amplitudes) and a complex interference of these differences.

In quantum physics, the scientific approach that Barad is most strongly concerned with, diffraction is present in a double manner, at least in Barad's extension of the term. First, there are important quantum-physical experiments that prove that not only light but also "electrons, neutrons, atoms and other forms of matter"[4] show wave behaviour, that is, diffraction, when sent through a special diffraction grating. In other experiments (using the same grating!), however, particle behaviour can be observed in the same elements. What is more, it is the experimental set-up, together with the arranging human experimenter as a part of this set-up, that proves to be decisive for the behaviour of the electron as wave or particle: the nature of the observed is dependent on the pre-arranged set-up of the experiment[5]—for Barad, a prime example of an onto-epistemological entanglement. Barad calls this particular entanglement "diffraction" because it is centred around the physical phenomenon of real diffraction. For Barad, the quantum-physical set-up therefore produces two diffractions—a real one in the observed phenomenon and a (more or less) metaphorical one on the side of the observer, in the shape of the observer's onto-epistemological entanglement with the observed phenomenon.[6]

In her contribution to the present volume, Stacey Moran argues that the wave behaviour of particles only exists in the quantum realm and is lost when confronted with the so-called "classical realm," so that it is problematic to extend the wave nature of particles into the realm of macroscopic matter. She therefore suggests that on the macro level, diffraction is partially a "fictive" model, itself charged with the entanglement of different contradictive physical states and their interpretations.[7] I would also hold that diffractive entanglement of the world at large in Barad is rather to be taken as a metaphor—but one that is based on real diffraction of matter on the quantum level. By being onto-epistemologically entangled with the experimental set-up, the quantum experimenter is metaphorically diffracted with(in) a constellation that leads to real diffraction of matter on the quantum level. Metaphorical diffraction creates real diffraction, so to say.

For Barad, these (partially metaphorical) diffractive onto-epistemological entanglements are not stable "objects" but, apart from being inextricable configurations of "subject" and/with "object," they are *momentary* situations. To convey both these aspects, entanglement and eventness, Barad has coined the felicitous term "intra-action": "In fact it is not so much that [entanglements] change from one moment to the next or from one place to another, but that space, time, and matter do not exist prior to the intra-actions that reconstitute entanglements."[8] Intra-actions in turn are created by "agential cuts" within "apparatuses."

> Apparatuses enact agential cuts that produce determinate boundaries and properties of "entities" within phenomena, where "phenomena" are the ontological inseparability of agentially intra-acting components ... It is only through specific agential intra-actions that the boundaries and properties of "components" of phenomena become determinate and that particular articulations become meaningful.[9]

Onto-epistemological diffraction, therefore, is a highly situational and performative activity and creates different results that belong to entirely different moments of producing "boundaries" and "properties" of entangled phenomena. Entanglement appears to be different in every new situation, while these situations are not available to each other because each of them is an alternative realization in a different (moment in) time. Logically, therefore, agential cuts produce entanglements but are not entangled/entangleable with *each other*. This suggests that "agential cut" could be seen as a complement or alternative to the concept of entanglement, in that it stands for the diverse, even mutually exclusive moments of entanglement produced in different situations. Even if Barad nowhere states this explicitly, the idea of mutually exclusive agential cuts allows for a radicalization and widening of the notion of diffraction and the—quite impossible, but therefore radical and attractive—idea of diffraction as the encounter of the contrary, the mutually exclusive, the temporarily different. This frictional, paradoxical (notion of) diffraction is suggested in Stacey Moran's, Nathan Frank's, and Agnieszka Kotwasińska's contribution to this volume among others. In my own discussion of the concept of diffractive reading throughout this chapter, I will also think through an entanglement of diverse onto-epistemological situations.

As has become clear, diffraction is not only a physical phenomenon for Barad, but also a prime example of any agential, and, as I will argue, particularly human, encounter with the world, an encounter that is always both analytical and participatory, as well as situationally differentiated. In an apt synecdoche, diffraction becomes Barad's term for any analytical method in general. Referring to the physical difference between diffraction and (optical) reflection, she establishes an anti-reflexive notion of analysis, one that creates differences rather than identical representations. In doing so, she starts from Donna Haraway:

> Haraway's point is that the methodology of reflexivity mirrors the geometrical optics of reflection, and that for all of the recent emphasis on reflexivity as a critical method of self-positioning it remains caught up in geometries of sameness; by contrast, diffractions are attuned to differences—differences that our knowledge-making practices make and the effects they have on the world.[10]

"[K]nowledge-making practice" refers to any method of scholarly world approach. However, as Barad is both a physicist and a Cultural Studies scholar, she focuses on physics and Literary/Cultural Studies when it comes to exemplifying diffractive methodology. It is in this context that she refers to reading—surprisingly regarding *both* fields, as we shall see.

For Literary and Cultural Studies, a diffractive reading as proposed by Haraway/Barad would be a kind of reading that is both entangled with what is read and brings out the differences and entanglements in and of the read phenomenon itself. Barad proposes this kind of diffractive reading to be "reading through (the diffraction grating)" as opposed to reflexive reading, which is "reading against (some fixed target/mirror)."[11] Throughout her book, she mainly characterizes her own diffractive method as "reading insights [of two authors or theoretical approaches] through one another."[12] Reading in this sense interrelates "insights from different disciplines" with each other, so that, for example, the terminology of one approach is (re-)defined by using definitions of the other or so that one argument is recast in the different argumentative structure of the other. The two approaches become entangled like two waves in a diffractive phenomenon. Importantly, none of the two texts (or theorists) is meant to be the stable foil against which (as in a mirror) the other text, just as static, is read simply to be better understood. The two rather create a nonhierarchical network of irreducible differences.

This notion of diffractive reading has already proved fruitful in the field that Barad proposes: in *Diffracted Worlds - Diffractive Readings*[13], diffractive reading is theorized with, and practised on, both literary and theoretical/philosophical texts. Existing interventionist literary-critical approaches, such as deconstruction[14] and intertextuality,[15] are interrelated (diffracted exactly in Barad's sense) and, by doing so, further radicalized—diffracting them, as it were, makes them (more) diffractive themselves. Diffractive intertextuality would be one that leaves behind any notion of contact-giving and contact-taking text and instead sees (and reads) texts as always already entangled with each other, without any priorities or hierarchies. What is more, Birgit Kaiser extends this kind of intertextuality to a nonhierarchizing interculturality, performed by literary and theoretical texts alike.[16] Other contributions perform sample diffractive readings of literary texts, where these texts are either diffracted with other literary texts[17]—exactly in the spirit of diffractive intertextuality—or seen as diffracted within themselves, for example, in the writing process or in their textual appearance.[18] The philosophical contributions, by Barad and Thiele as well as Melanie Seghal and Iris van der Tuin, while considering more general philosophical issues, also practise this kind of interlacing diffraction of texts.[19]

Valuable as this work on—and with—diffractive reading clearly is, I think that Barad's own notion of diffractive reading goes even deeper than that. To be sure, Barad also suggests reading *matter* diffractively, moving in the direction of a scientific notion of diffractive reading. If the scientific observer is seen to be diffracted with the observed phenomenon as in Barad's wider sense of diffraction, then diffractive reading is really the entangled (co-)creation of matter[20] by observing, or *reading* it. Arguably, this notion of reading actually comes closer to what Barad sees as "reading through the diffraction grating" than just the interlacing of two texts/theorists as suggested by Barad herself. Diffractive reading in this stronger sense emerges when diffractive entanglement in physics is connected with reading in the sense of taking the results of a *scientific measurement*.

Reading as taking measurements is strongly present in Barad's text, and is routinely seen as interfering with or (co-)creating what is measured, even if this kind of reading is nowhere explicitly called "diffractive" by Barad. Consider the following quote:

> Measurements, then, are causal intra-actions, physical processes. What we usually call a "measurement" is a correlation or entanglement between component parts of a phenomenon, between the "measured object" and the "measuring device," where the measuring device is explicitly taken to be macroscopic so that we can *read* the pattern of [e.g. diffraction] marks that the measured object leaves on it.[21]

The measuring device (together with the observer) co-creates the measured phenomenon, in this (quantum) case not least because this device is designed in such a way as to make the phenomenon produce particular traces which are then read by the observer. Measuring-cum-reading the phenomenon co-creates it by entanglement. This is diffractive reading in the wider sense of working out the entangled/wave-like nature of something, while at the same time partaking in the very creation of this entanglement. In her notion of (diffractive) reading, therefore, Barad addresses both what could be called a "humanities," or: hermeneutic, sense of reading (deciphering code), as with the interlacing of two texts/theorists, and a scientific sense of reading as taking the results of measurements.[22] She relates both these kinds of reading to her notion of onto-epistemological entanglement: diffractive reading is either the nonhierarchizing entangling of two texts/theorists or the (co-)creating of matter by making it readable.

Diffractive reading in Barad turns out to be a kind of reading that is always already entangled either with other texts or with the material "referent." Diffractive reading is not a reflection of the represented in an ideal summary or copy but rather the (situational) creation of something new next to it, entangled with it. To make the Baradian approach really fruitful for Literary and Cultural Studies, the two angles of Barad's approach, reading text and reading matter diffractively, should be united. This will be done in the following section by considering materialist reading theories[23] already existing in Literary/Cultural Studies, and by studying, among other things, how these approaches combine diffracting text(s) with diffracting matter. These approaches will be from Material Culture Studies, Science Studies, and Material(ist) Ecocriticism. I will sketch out some of the most important arguments and approaches on reading from the three mentioned fields before delineating in which ways Barad's notion of diffractive reading profits from them, because they bring language/text and matter closer together under the notion of "reading," so that Barad's two angles can be increasingly merged. To my mind, however, diffractive reading, enriched and charged in these ways, must be confronted with the human diffractive agent and his/her responsibility, by considering the tradition of theorizing human specificity in anthropology. Even if this means forgoing the decentralizing of the human in Barad to a certain extent, I think this is necessary because it gives diffractive reading, seen as a particularly human activity, both an important ethical responsibility and a timely political edge.

DIFFRACTIVE READING IN THE LIGHT OF OTHER (NEO)MATERIALIST READING THEORIES

Reading matter has first been theorized within the fields of Material Culture Studies and adjacent fields of Cultural Studies. While both fields have different origins and connections (Material Culture to, among other fields, archaeology; Cultural Studies has one of its roots in the study of popular culture), they come together where they posit culture—cultural objects and cultural practices, respectively—to be readable like texts. Christopher Tilley, an archaeologist and theorist of material culture, writes: "Material culture is 'written' through a practice of spacing and differentiation in just the manner as phonetic writing. . . . [T]he text of material culture is like an edited book, sentences written by different authors within a text constituting a larger overall text."[24] In a wider sense, culture as a whole is considered to be something we can read, as is, for example, claimed by the title of a wide-ranging and influential Cultural Studies anthology of German origin.[25] There are, of course, extended further suggestions of reading culture and cultural matter like texts, such as the later work by Tilley[26] or *The Oxford Handbook of Material Culture Studies*.[27] Reading cultural matter, however, becomes particularly interesting for us where it considers reading matter *together with* (literary) texts. The work on material culture *and* literature, represented in such recent work as the handbook edited by Scholz and Vedder,[28] is pointedly summarized in Bertschik's claim that in literary texts *on* material objects, these objects become textualized while the texts' language becomes more material.[29] To a certain extent, objects and literary/linguistic texts are seen as entangled, *diffracted*, influencing each other with their respective dominant quality as matter or sign. While this indeed goes in the direction of reading text and matter together diffractively, it is still only cultured matter that is considered, matter that is made readable and therefore always already (like) a text and always already diffracted as/with text. What is not considered in these approaches is matter *as such*, so to speak, matter—or the question of matter—in its sheer physical givenness. While of course, physical matter can also be seen as *cultural* to some extent, it is a kind of matter less, or at least differently, entangled with culture than cultural objects, as we will see. From the perspective of Baradian diffraction, the notion of (the reading of) matter should be expanded to include physical matter and to therefore entangle cultural reading and extra-cultural, physical matter much more strongly. The potential sign power, and therefore readability, of extra-cultural matter is considered in Science Studies.

While in Barad's notion of diffractive reading, extra-cultural, physical matter is more an implicit presence, reading theories from Science Studies openly consider scientific and hermeneutic notions of reading together. A prime example where human reading is studied in this complexity is genetics. A large body of work on questions of reading and writing the so-called "genome" has come out of Science Studies recently but has largely been ignored in Literary and Cultural Studies when it comes to extending the notion of reading. The important Science Studies scholar and theorist Hans-Jörg Rheinberger explores the advent of the genome as a so-called "epistemtic thing," which in his argument is the co-creation of a scientific object by the (often completely coincidental) discovery of certain natural phenomena on the one hand and the "graphematic articulations" used to turn these discoveries into a phenomenon representable to human perception on the other hand.[30] The genome is read (and written) into existence diffractively, so to say; science makes nature readable for the human observer just like a cultural object. However, the genome goes beyond the material objects considered in Cultural Studies as, even if it is written into human culture, it comes from the outside, so to speak. Nature and culture intra-act in this reading/writing, Barad would say.

Consequently, many Science Studies scholars explore a wide-ranging notion of (what could be called) diffractive reading when it comes to the field of the so-called gene editing. The genome has routinely been seen as a readable text and, concomitantly, analyzing and modifying it, as practised in genetic technology, has been conceptualized as *writing* this text. This kind of diffractive reading/writing of matter not only lies outside culture/Cultural Studies. What is more, it also moves beyond the (co-)creative reading of wave or particle in quantum experiments as explored by Barad. Humans "find" a language-like structure in nature, decode it and learn how to write it back into nature. The body of work on this kind of reading/writing is large[31] as is the critical consciousness concerning this kind of human interference into nature. I am interested in these analyses and in this critique because I want to charge the notion of diffractive reading practised in this collection with its critical and political edge.

One of the earliest and at the same time most incisive and wide-ranging proponents of this kind of critique is philosophical anthropologist Hans Blumenberg. In his book *Die Lesbarkeit der Welt*, he explores reading/writing the genome within his notion of the "legibility of the world."[32] For Blumenberg, the legibility of the world is a double metaphorical complex of "book" and "world." Reality is made available for human beings as readable like a book against the horizon of a meaningful totality, "the world." In other words, reading is world understanding, that is: metaphorical world creation, before a meaningful totality which is either a total book, such as the Bible, or the "world" (made) *like* a total book. Therefore, Blumenberg analyses the medieval and early modern notions of the Book of the World or the Book of Nature, among others. In the last chapter of *Die Lesbarkeit*, he considers modern science and scientific reading in the sense also explored by Barad. For Blumenberg, with the advent of modern science, a new notion of reading (nature) emerged that conceived of reading not as the reception of a coherent text, a unified whole, anymore, but rather as the deciphering of discreet units, whose totality is not (yet) known to the reader and can therefore not provide the horizon for the reading process.[33] It is in this context that he considers the genome: not only does it epitomize the new kind of "discreet" reading; it also implies, in a kind of new materialist moment rare in Blumenberg, superseding the status of reading the world as a metaphor and the advent of reading/writing nature "for real": the world is read and written diffractively by the human reader, not *like*, but *as* a text.[34] The hermeneutic and the scientific notion of diffractive reading as explored by Barad are unified at this point.

Reading-cum-writing in nature as exemplified by genetics is an important aspect of diffractive reading not really considered in any depth by Barad.[35] However, to make the idea available to the interests of this collection (also in a self-critical manner), it needs to be brought into contact more closely with what could be called cultural textuality. We will do that in the next section. What needs to be done before that, however, is to reconcile—or rather diffract—Barad's central notion of onto-epistemological entanglement with the equally important premise of human distance to the world in philosophical anthropology. Blumenberg insists that the very idea to interfere with cell development by modifying the underlying genetic structure must be related to an original distance that humans have to the world. Science is an activity, he writes, "based on a tremendous [human] distance to any immediacy of nature,"[36] which means reversely that "[a]s [merely] natural beings, we would stand no chance to know about nature what theory allows us to know about nature."[37] It is from this *distance* that any possibility to arrange a scientific set-up that subsequently facilitates an onto-epistemological diffractive reading, to use our terminology, only arises. By contrast, Barad insists on the very opposite of this, that is, that any dimension of the human only emerges within the (scientific) onto-epistemological intra-action:

> There are no preexisting, separately determinate entities called "humans" that are either *detached spectators* or necessary components of all intra-actions. Rather, to the extent that "humans" emerge as having a role to play in the constitution of specific phenomena, they do so as part of the larger material configuration, or rather the ongoing reconfiguring, of the world. Thus no *a priori* privileged status is given to the human—and this is precisely the point. "Humans" are emergent phenomena like all other physical systems.[38]

As I have already suggested, I find it important to consider human agency when it comes to diffractive reading. In this context, it is ultimately not important for me whether human episteme, that is, the dimension of human thought and the concomitant aspect of extensive human sign usage are before/beyond the matter they come to work on or not, if it is only clear that human interference with nature is extremely strong, and stronger than the interference of other biological species. Blumenberg speaks of a "fatal [human] urge for biotechnical control" in genetics,[39] implying both that humans want to control what they experience as fundamentally uncontrollable for them and that this dream of control is ultimately both dangerous and futile. From this perspective, Blumenberg and Barad can be brought together if we consider that human world intrusion, whether based on distance or not, leads to a particularly strong onto-epistemological entanglement, as can be seen in genetics[40] for example, that is to a large extent uncontrollable in its consequences for humanity and tremendously harmful to the whole planet.

What is more, as we will see in the following section, an epistemic relation to the surrounding material processes can be posited for any organism's entanglement with the world. It is in the field of new materialist ecocriticism that human reading is considered as one organic world access among others and consequently set in relation to the world accesses of other species. In biosemiotics, largely based on the early twentieth-century work of Baltic-German biologist Jakob Johann von Uexküll, reading is studied as a participation in, or shaping of, the world of any organism. Uexküll's biosemiotical theory has been advocated by various ecocritical and media scholars in Literary/Cultural Studies, among them Wendy Wheeler, Inga Pollmann, and Timo Maran.[41] Using it as a concept of intrusive/diffractive reading has been suggested by both Wheeler and Hayley Zertuche,[42] and it is these suggestions which are going to be expanded into a notion of diffractive reading that takes its origin from Barad but is heedful both of Science Studies and of biosemiotics itself, in the remainder of this chapter. Uexküll is famous for being the first scholar to have theorized the notion of environment (*Umwelt*). According to Uexküll, every organism, down to the single cell, creates a subjective world (*Umwelt*) for itself, based on signs which are both received and created by the organism.[43] These signs are impulses taken as meaningful by the receiving organism and therefore endowed with meaning by it—this meaning can only be given by living organisms and it separates both the sign from the impulse and the organism from the machine. Each organism's sign structure is different (or at least specific to the species) and fully available/perceptible only to that organism itself; it is in this sense that *Umwelten* are seen as both intrinsically semiotic and intrinsically subjective. *Umwelten* are also, as Uexküll insists, "epistemological"; he provocatively speaks of the "ego-qualities" (already) of the single cell.[44]

In this context, Uexküll has theorized a functional circle[45] according to which an organism, in the so-called "perceptual dimension," receives innumerable impulses some of which it actively transforms into signs, thereby creating its environment. The reading of the impulse as/into a sign by the organism is already part and parcel of the "operational" dimension, to which a reaction to the sign, for example, its incorporation, by the organism also belongs. The impulse's sign function is usually exhausted after having been read by the organism. The circle therefore consists of a perceptual vector that leads from the impulse giver and potential "meaning carrier" to the "utilizing" organism, and an operational vector from the organism to the impulse utilized as a sign. In terms of diffractive reading, the organism both creates and modifies its *Umwelt* by making it legible. In turn, however, the organism is also deeply shaped by its *Umwelt*; every sign, so to speak, is echoed in the organism's body shape. The body creates the signs and is at the same time affected by the signs[46]; diffractive readers of the world are in turn read/diffracted into the world.

There are surprising parallels between Barad's notion of diffraction and biosemiotics: both posit a diffractive creation of matter by "grasping" it, and both see this activity as a situational agential cut. Since they depend on a reading performed by the organism, *Umwelten* are highly individual, self-contained, and situational – something that is reminiscent of the mutual exclusivity of different agential cuts as discussed above.[47] What is more, Uexküll posits an epistemological dimension as virtually indispensable to organic processes of world-making. It is the individual assignment of meaning which constitutes an *Umwelt* by filling it with matter turned sign. Sign grasping creates the matter of the organism's world, including its own body, in what can absolutely aptly be named an onto-epistemological entanglement. Zertuche therefore rightly links biosemiotics both to Baradian entanglement and to Baradian diffraction.[48]

To be sure, Barad insists on a mutual creating of all elements in the encounter, whereas Uexküll posits a certain priority of the grasping organism, the utilizing subject—even if he has organic body and *Umwelt* ultimately shape each other. Also, Uexküll's model is absolutely focused on organisms—there is no world(-making) outside the organic sphere for him. Whereas he therefore explicitly denies machines any participation in processes of diffractive *Umwelt* creation, Barad speaks of "apparatuses" as the entangled operators in world-making, agencies definitely comprising both the organic and the inorganic, for example, technical, sphere. It is beyond the scope of this introduction to discuss whether diffractive *Umwelt* creation could and should be made to include inorganic agents as *Umwelt* makers. However, as I am most interested in theorizing diffractive reading as a human activity, this discussion may be dispensed with in the context of this chapter. What should be noted is that Barad's concept of diffractive reading is valuably expanded by being confronted with Uexküll's semiotics: biosemiotics suggests a deeply entrenched and expanded notion of diffractive reading, that comprises all organic processes and activities and therefore, as we will see in the following, also includes language and the textual. What is more, onto-epistemological entanglement can now be conceptualized more thoroughly: the organism's active assigning of meaning to exterior impulses is the epistemological element but both this episteme and the organism's own shape get inseparably entangled with an *umwelt* that is both continuously (re)created and actively shaping.

What is particularly intriguing about biosemiotics is that it integrates the notion of diffractive matter reading-cum-creation into a semiotic model and makes it therefore connectable to any other signification process. Biosemiotics has been an integral part of semiotics and semiotic theory virtually from the beginning of the field[49] and is therefore longstanding if somewhat ignored offer to bridge the distance between the cultural and the natural, a New Materialism *avant la lettre*. In Literary and Cultural Studies, this approach has been neglected until very recently, when Ecocriticism developed an interest in biosemiotics and started working on a biosemiotical criticism.[50] Biosemiotical criticism considers the sign usage, of all organisms together with the much more thoroughly researched semiotic activities specific to human beings. It is in this context that reading appears as something done by all organisms and that human reading is seen as only a (species-) specific form of this.

Human-related semiotics has often used the concept of modelling, for example, in Yuri Lotman's work that has proved highly relevant for Literary and Cultural Studies/Theory. "Modelling" describes the (human) world construction by sign usage, organized in complex sign systems, such as culture, and therefore seems to be in line with the anthropological understanding of human world access and world constitution as being at a remove from nature and from the world access of more "natural" organisms. However, with Uexküll's *Umwelt* concept in mind, it becomes clear that human semiosis/modelling is just another form of *Umwelt* constitution,[51] that may be specific to the human species (and is therefore perhaps specifically complex) but is by the same token deeply onto-epistemologically entangled, as I have already argued above. I am therefore wary of the idea of rising abstraction in semiotic processes, that would lead from more primitive to more sophisticated signs, such as language, even if this idea is already laid out in the semiotic theory of Charles Peirce.[52] Rather, I would take up Wendy Wheeler's suggestion that one reading leads to further readings, one *Umwelt* becomes the basis for further *Umwelten* and so on: "[The] readings of signs [undertaken by living things] which constitute their world are also always interpretations which are, ipso facto, recursively led back into that world where further readings and interpretations go on producing newer layers or strata of understanding."[53] Reading creates new, further matter, which is always already readable and hence expandable. Where Wheeler seems to refer to an organism's self-development ("recursively"), I would expand her metaphor of "layers and strata" as to suggest the development of an ever-increasing "geological formation" of further, mutually entangled organisms and their *Umwelten*. Diffractive readings/constitutions of matter are the basis for further diffractions and so on: there is perhaps a rising horizontal complexity (increasingly expanded onto-epistemological entanglements of different "worldings") but not a vertical one. This suggestion also tackles the problem of the exclusiveness of *Umwelten* in Uexküll—or indeed of agential cuts in Barad. *Umwelten*, alias agential cuts, are also world readings ready to be taken up (partially at least), and therefore to be entangled with, further world readings.[54] Diffractive reading(s) of nonhuman organisms are taken up by human diffractions, which are usually linguistic and hence textual. And these diffractions are taken up by further diffractions, both human (textual) and nonhuman. It is in this spirit that I want to connect diffractive world reading more fully to diffractive text reading in the final section.

DIFFRACTIVE READING AND BIOSEMIOTICS: HUMAN INTERVENTION, LANGUAGE, AND TEXT

In my opinion, human-specific *Umwelt* building is itself more complex than the *Umwelten* of nonhuman species; not, however, in the sense of vertical, hierarchical complexity but in the sense of horizontal expansion: human *Umwelten* are particularly, and dangerously, expanded.[55] As Blumenberg has already shown, the human notion of the "legible world" has traditionally been a concept, or: *model*, of totality, some kind of vision, or attempted mental prehension, of the given as a whole. That is why humans "naturally" strive to extend both their sensorial and their semiotic scope. In the German language, in its most common usage the word *Umwelt* has even come to stand for planetary nature altogether.

In this context, language, in the linguistic sense of an abstract and self-enclosed sign system, is a specificity of human *Umwelt* building, quite unique to the human species—or at least, so it seems to us.[56] Human language strives for totality by giving a word to each and everything known/knowable. Seen through the eyes of Uexküll's theory, it becomes even clearer now why human language is part and parcel of the particularly momentous and consequential onto-epistemological entanglement of the human species. Humans make signs out of/for *everything*, so they end up, so to say, entangled into the world to a much larger extent than other species.[57] What is more, this restlessly thorough linguistic take-in of the world is also an expression of the human idea to make the "world" better and better (only for themselves!)—to (human-)optimize it by relentless enquiries for (further) options of interference into natural processes. As has already been discussed with reference to genetics, human "readers" both agentially cut, and hence get entangled with, nature as no other species.

To be sure, linguistic activity often entails analyzing an already existing language; discursive activity is prone to lead to further discourse. Therefore, and quite helpfully, human semiosis, due to its thoroughness, not only tends to want to change the world but also to intervene in, in the sense of both reflection and critique, already existing human semiosis as insistently as possible. This can now be reformulated in a biosemiotical/diffractive way. The use of linguistic language is a human-specific mode of diffractive reading that leads to ever-expanding worldings with a strongly interventionist tendency. As worldings are prone to diffract with already existing worldings, as I have argued following Wheeler, this also entails diffractive readings into/of already existing human diffractions. Diffraction is prone to diffract with earlier diffraction, at infinite regress, with "interpretations [being] recursively led back into [the *Umwelt*/text]" but also creating "further readings and interpretations" with "newer layers or strata of understanding." Texts will (critically) refer to, read, other texts, endlessly, and potentially more and more critically.

Taking up the already-mentioned notion of semiotic world modelling, reflexively and critically myself, I now want to turn to literary and cultural texts as diffractive reading. Lotman conceives of literature, and indeed of any artistic/cultural activity, as a secondary world model—a cultural/linguistic system reproducing existing human world models on a higher, more complex level.[58] It is tempting to connect this idea of modelling with the general tendency of language to interact with existing language. However, as I have said, I do not see semiotic complexity as a hierarchical, vertical process, culminating in human literature as the summit of worlding and reading— but rather as a horizontal development of expanding onto-epistemological entanglement: literature's diffraction is always both textual and material. Still, it would be fascinating to theorize what Lotman sees as artistic world modelling as a particular—and particularly intensive—form of diffraction: literary and other cultural texts are texts particularly capable of intervening into earlier texts and other language usages, and of thereby creating more and more complex layers/entanglement of interventions. From this perspective, literary criticism is another form of diffractive reading, namely of literature, simply (and naturally) on a further "plateau"[59] of diffraction. The expansive entangling of diffractive readings is endless. Altogether, biosemiotics is able to integrate literature and other cultural practices into diffractive reading, so that diffractive reading now really both encompasses and politicizes all reading processes from organic world perception-as-creation to (reading) literary/ cultural texts. And in that cosmos, literary (and other cultural) texts have the potential to be both diffractive participants in and diffractive analysts of, world/matter diffraction.

Conclusively, we can differentiate between several forms/plateaux of (human) diffractive reading, and they relentlessly refer to/diffract each other:

1. diffractive onto-epistemological entanglement of human discourses with matter, that is, reading matter into the/a world, for example, in the

form of "participating" cultural texts; connected to that, the diffraction/ entanglement of the reader with the world thus read;
2. (diffractively) analyzing/criticizing textual world modelling (world intervention), particularly by "analytic" cultural texts;
3. (diffractively) analyzing literary texts (and other artefacts), which relate to all these forms of diffraction *and so on, potentially endlessly.*[60]

As this overview shows, both notions of diffractive reading suggested by Barad, of texts and of matter, are now combined in one model, just as the particular "intrusiveness" of diffractive reading, both into the "world" and into other texts/diffractions, is thought through. Diffractive reading has come to stand, or has the potential to come to stand, for both our dangerous(ly) endless "Anthropocenic" meddling with the world and our helpful(ly) incessant readiness to (not only reflect but) *diffract* on this meddling further and further.

CHAPTER OVERVIEW

As should have become clear, I am not suggesting that diffractive reading is a narrowly (bio-)semiotic method, which explores its objects of study solely for their signs and the latter's embeddedness into nature. Biosemiotics simply bespeaks a particular proximity, and mutual constitution, of reading/reader and read, as well as a very general, and wide-ranging, activity of reading, which implies any organism and its constitution of a material world. Therefore, diffractive reading is not a particular method of literary analysis but rather a wholly new understanding of reading in general (text, matter, etc.), which sees reading/reader as participating in, not representing, what is read. Not only can any existing notion of interventive reading be turned to be diffractive.[61] As the articles particularly by Agnieszka Kotwasińska, Brendan Johnston, and Birgit Kaiser in the present volume will show, any academic reading (method) can be perspectivized as diffractive, with its reflexive/representational(ist) character consequently toned down or superseded. In general, texts can be read as not reflexive but invasive, world-constituting, *diffractive.* To see the code-matter boundary in texts as fluent or permeable is a matter of perspective on *any* text. Reader and "read" can always be seen as constituting each other along the lines of onto-epistemological entanglement and the biosemiotical circle.

In the same vein, the notion of diffraction/diffractive reading is open to any kind of cultural text. Images and music may be just as diffractive of the world or of other texts as linguistic texts (or arguably even more so, as we will see). Although Lotman's approach to the "artistic text" is both language and literature based, it may be, and has been, expanded to any kind of cultural text, just as semiotics was expanded to include theatre, film, and painting: all of these texts may be just as complex and incisive diffractions of matter or of other texts.[62] So, just as my concept of diffractive reading is not narrowly semiotic, it is not narrowly language or literature focused either. This book is therefore divided into three sections. The first section offers (more) theoretical groundwork on diffraction and diffractive reading. The second develops a range of diffractive readings of literary texts. Literature has traditionally been the starting point of many reading theories, so it's apt to first intervene diffractively into literary texts, readings, and reading theories. Moving on from there, however, the diffractions of visual and acoustic media must be considered, so as to do justice to—and to field-test—the scope and potential of the idea of diffractive reading developed in this introduction. This will be done in the third section. While visual and acoustic media can be seen as arguably more diffractive than literary texts both semiotically and physically, what we will finally see in digital culture is also a return to the diffraction of/ with written language.

Under the title "Diffractive Reading: Groundwork," the first section deepens (but also diffracts) our theoretical considerations into various directions, so that the eponymous "groundwork" comes to stand not only for a foundational expansion but also for an undermining,[63] that means complicating and problematizing, of my concepts of diffraction and diffractive reading.

In the first contribution to this section, by Birgit Kaiser, diffractive reading is positively distinguished from further recent reading theories, such as distant reading or surface reading. The chapter first examines how reading a text by Etel Adnan, who is both a writer and a visual artist, performs entanglement and diffractive patterning and how the text thereby gets into view a diffractive reading *polis* (comprising both the text and its readers among others) hitherto invisibilized. In a second step, the chapter shows how this conception of pattern(ing) differs from the term's use in distant and surface reading, thus also engaging the *politics* of the field of Literary Studies, which is currently played out especially around methods of reading. While an ethics of reading (Derek Attridge) stresses our exposure to (textual) otherness, a *politics* of diffractive reading rather trains our perception of co-implication and entanglement. Ever wary of any sense of human prioritization in the entanglements of diffractive reading(s), even (particularly!) in theorizing Anthropocenic responsibility, Kaiser's notion of a poli(tic)s of entanglement both complicates and deepens my own (human-centred) considerations of the politics of ("incisive") diffractive reading and human responsibility therein. And while her contribution engages diffractive reading in an aptly foundational manner, therefore belonging in the first section, it also lays some of the ground for diffractive reading of literary texts in the second section.

Max Walther's contribution both explores and widens the *philosophical* reverberations of Barad's theorizing, thus pointing in the direction of various strands of a philosophy of diffraction: starting from different theoretical conceptions of relational thinking (net and meshworks, assemblage and encounter), developed mainly within recent philosophy and Literary/Cultural Theory, Walther's entanglement (of) theory culminates in Heraclitus. This "ancient" philosopher epitomizes entangled thinking both in his texts and by his texts. The essay therefore performs a diffraction of and with the philosophical "tradition" (also in its chronology) while also considering literature (diffracting philosophy and literature): borrowing Jane Bennett's term "onto-story," Walther discusses the fundamental relationship between writing about fluidity—in a diffracting/diffracted fashion—and the result of such a writing, that is, texts/fragments. In this sense, diffractive reading of the world is always both philosophical and literary, equally pointing to our fluidity in/with the world and itself floating.

Stacey Moran proposes the confrontation of diffraction with the non-homogenous and the in-coherent. In her chapter, diffraction is connected to the "mysterious interactions" between actually incompatible systems (called "decoherence"). For Moran, in both Barad and the existing usage of diffractive reading, onto-epistemological entanglement is seen as the creation of a more or less harmonious field, from which the irresolvable contradictions both of physical interpretations and of conflicting world views are excluded, and in which, therefore, differences can be positively but also rather peacefully considered, unlike contradictions. Moran advocates a more confrontational notion of diffraction, both on the level of the diffracted elements and on the level of the discussion of the term "diffraction" itself. She ultimately suggests a diffraction of the mutually exclusive—the deeply problematical encounter of "impossibly different" elements. A range of contributions to this volume, particularly by Peter Schuck, Nathan Frank, and Agnieszka Kotwasińska, also consider this kind of diffraction. In my own discussion of diffractive reading, I have tried to give weight to both "fusionist" and "frictional" aspects of diffraction.

Peter Schuck's paper both describes and performs a diffraction of a range of speculative texts, which combine philosophy, science, and readings of horror (horror as literature but also horror as philosophy). By being "speculative," they subscribe to the project of a renewed attempt to think the absolute, a real(ity) independent of human thought and cognition. This so-called speculative realism is strongly connected to Quentin Meillassoux's work and his attempt to sketch out a philosophy of the real/material, strictly beyond any notion of an entanglement of the human with nonhuman matter. Schuck, however, proceeds to prove how various speculative texts, mainly by Eugene Thacker and Reza Negarestani, can both be read as (about) entanglements and as in an entanglement with each other. The texts are connected by oil and ooze, which is both a topic for the texts and a materiality they conjure up as definitory for their own matter(s). While, of course, petrol can justifiably be seen as an uncanny outside to human culture, it is, similarly to the genome considered in the introduction to the present volume, also a matter of the deepest entanglement with "us," which we diffract/get diffracted with by analyzing, exploiting and manipulating beyond control. Oily texts can therefore be seen as texts about our deep and definite diffractions of/with physical reality and they just as strongly diffract with us and with each other. The bridging of Baradian diffraction with the neomaterialist notion of speculation in Schuck's paper is another mysterious (or decoherent) relation of the seemingly incompatible. While this bridging is also taken up in Jol Thom's photo essay in the present volume, it suggests future work, which would interlace diffraction with concepts from other directions of New Materialism. A strong and pertinently Anthropocenic New Materialism should be ready to explore the affiliations of speculation and diffraction, and of speculative and diffractive texts.

The second section "Diffracting Literature: Diffractions of the World-Text-Reader Entanglement" proceeds to relate diffraction to literary texts and their reading(s). As both Kaiser's contribution and my own introduction show, the literary world-text-reader relationship can be fruitfully re-perspectivized by seeing all elements of this constellation as *diffractions*: (1) the text itself is a diffraction with, and thereby creation of, the world; (2) texts create diffractions with (are diffractive readings of) other texts, co-creative of each other but also producing complex overlappings that problematize the notion of the unified and closed single text; (3) a similar kind of diffraction happens between the text and the reader: the reader diffracts the text but the text also diffracts the reader in a mutual entanglement. These literary diffractions are both analyzed and themselves created within the (diffractive) readings of literary texts in this section.

The section starts with Brendan Johnston's analysis of William Carlos Williams's long poem *Paterson*. Johnston explores the text's attempt at merging the particular with the general as well as the material with the discursive, thus working out *Paterson*'s diffraction with Paterson so to say. While the essay delineates both the capacities and limits of such poetics, it proposes as its own method a materialist reading that stays open to both "old," that is, Marxist, materialism, and the various discourse analytical approaches from Modernist Studies, new and old. Johnston refers to Moran's insistence that the concept of diffraction itself should remain diffractable/debatable to avoid what Johnston sees as the danger of a new methodological—this time materialist—totalitarianism. To the poem's own diffractive reading of Paterson, he therefore adds a localized, particularized, in this sense: *diffractive* reading of the text itself.

Bo Kampmann Walther's essay on some apocryphal texts of the Tolkien corpus also combines a diffractive reading of the text with a diffraction that the text itself undertakes. Kampmann Walther works out a Deleuzian materialism both in the analyzed texts and in Tolkien's own theorizing on the virtual materiality of his own fantasizing. What is more, both Deleuze's notion of virtuality and Tolkien's *phantazein* can be compared to Barad's onto-epistemology. Therefore, Tolkien's texts practise a deeply embedded diffraction of their signs with the "real" they conjure up. And Kampmann Walther's reading is itself diffractive where it entangles the marginal "particles" of Tolkien's post-Rings texts with the Tolkienian canon, and therefore performs both a text-world and a text-text diffraction.

In Annina Klappert's contribution, the entanglement of matter and sign in diffracted reading is also theorized by way of Deleuze's notion of the virtual. Klappert proceeds to connect this notion to her own concept of surface reading. As opposed to the recent suggestion of surface reading by Best and Marcus, Klappert conceives of surface as a Deleuzian virtuality for the actual emergence of forms. Surface reading for her is therefore the experimental constitution of a textual arrangement (in her case of texts by Walter Benjamin and Carlos María Domínguez), a surface of the virtual out of which forms can emerge as actualities (another Deleuzian term). In her own surface reading of these texts, forms of books and houses become visible, which on the surface (are made to) diffract with(in) each other. Along the way, Klappert traces Karen Barad's notion of the (reading) apparatus back to Michael Foucault, Bruno Latour, and again Deleuze. Klappert's concept of surface reading is therefore a diffractive/new materialist alternative to Best and Marcus's concept while also enriching diffraction itself with suggestions by further materialist thinkers.

Daniela Keller's chapter performs a diffractive reading of Ali Smith's *How to Be Both* and impressively shows this text to be itself an exemplary piece of diffractive literature. It argues that the novel epitomizes a "material-discursive phenomenon"[64] by working out how Smith's book entangles meaning with textual and, crucially, extra-textual materiality. Furthermore, by reading actual spaces and objects through the text, the analysis discloses an ingenious "twist in the tale"[65] that cuts agentially between the fictional world of the characters and the actual world of the readers. The essay therefore again both reads and *is* diffraction. What is more, by being available in two versions, *How to Be Both* is another example of a radical diffraction of the incompatible. Each version is an irreducibly different agential cut, while it is exactly the impossible interlacing of these two cuts that is considered, as the novel's title already suggests.

Like Kampmann Walther and Keller, Agnieszka Kotwasińska's essay also works out the diffractive structures (and sutures) of a literary text obsessed with its fantastic and virtual alternatives. China Miéville's novel *The Scar* is a continuous diffraction with what could have happened and therefore a defamiliarization of the continuity and also the ending of narration as such. In using Viktor Shklovsky's concept of *ostranenie*, Kotwasińska lays bare her own stance as a professional reader in an embattled and geopolitically biased academic market, using an enstranged version of Viktor Shklovsky's *ostranenie* that she sees itself as a marginalized analytical tool. The diffraction of her own method is thus also a revealing of her own entanglement, involvement, obsession with the text she reads, both privately and professionally.

Matthias Stephan's chapter presents a deep entanglement of writer Siri Hustvedt's poly-generic work: the texts diffract/are entangled with each other but also with the writer's own body, or, more exactly, her own mind-body entanglement. Stephan's reading(s) proceed(s) very much along the lines of the notion of "windows." This is a metaphor that Hustvedt herself suggests but that becomes expanded to the idea of different apertures which are opened upon these entanglements in Stephan's own diffractive procedure: like agential cuts seen as incompatible with each other, each diffractive window shows a different entanglement, so that Hustvedt's own textual windows/cuts are also much different from those opened by her reader Matthias Stephan.

The third section "Diffracting (in) Music, Visual and Digital Media" leaves literature and the linguistic sign behind to move into the different areas of the photographic image (still and moving), music, and finally digital culture. From a semiotic perspective, photographic images have both an iconic and an indexical quality. Arguably, they are therefore diffractive of extra-cultural matter to a stronger degree than linguistic signs, just as photographic light waves (or particles?) are closer to a Baradian physical materiality than the signifying matter of literary texts. The same pertains to the sound waves of music which are also (of) a matter seemingly more directly connected to physical diffraction. This is not to say that literary texts cannot be just as entangled with physical diffraction as visual or acoustic media (as is shown, for example, in Daniela Keller's contribution). And yet I think that both in their physico-material make-up and in their historical development, visual and acoustic media are perhaps more deeply onto-epistemologically entangled than print because they entangle more pronounced differences of the natural/physical and the cultural: Keller's paper, to be sure, diffracts literature most intensively where the latter is itself entangled with painting and the (admittedly both physical and linguistic!) question of eye/I-sight.

Jol Thoms's photo essay is a fascinating exploration of the "natural" diffractions of photography and other media. The contribution combines images with (linguistic) text, iconic/indexical signs with language. These media are shown to be diffractive, both with each other and with the extra-cultural matter they are confronted with. Still images taken from Thoms's experimental film *A Borderline Conception Lying at The Extreme Edge of the World of Appearances* from 2019 document the transformations of a lake as it is instrumented to become a telescope. Both Lake Baikal and the essay itself become (literally, physically) *brilliant* sites of diffractive apparatuses in which the strongly technology-based reading of nature by high-resolution cameras is met/diffracted with the even more illuminating reading of nature by itself. What is important, therefore, is that Thoms opens up the potential, and the necessity, of an entanglement that is beyond the human, and that humans can only speculate on in a way similar to Meillassoux's "Great Outdoors." Therefore, as also suggested in Peter Schuck's essay, Thoms's contribution considers diffraction together with speculation.

Susan Sencindiver's contribution is also concerned with images, in her case feature films and video clips about maternal and mature female sexualities. These sexualities are agential cuts, or: assemblages, of female bodies that are both discursively constructed and actually lived (in). And, what is more, in the particular case studies in Sencindiver's essay, these sexualities are diffracted with(in) postfeminist popular visual texts. As Sencindiver argues in a theoretical excursus on the diffractive quality of cultural texts in general, her cases studies are ontological agents within, not just reflections of, female sexual assemblages. They (intra-)actively participate in the assemblage constellation of female sexualities, which are both material and discursive as well as both generally institutionalized and individually embodied.

Nathan Frank's essay expands the range of cultural texts explored for their diffractions to include the music of famous rock band U2, music that is both sonic and sung, and (within Frank's text) written twice (as lyrics and as notes)—or even three times considering that it is of course also written *about* by Frank. He weighs all these diffractions, while combining this reading with important theoretical interests. Frank's notion of diffraction is reminiscent of Moran's radicalization, as it sees diffraction as the mutual interpenetration of opposites: minds and worlds, culture and nature, and ultimately, figures and grounds *diffract* each other, with the result that Frank's interpretations of U2 pluralize according to mutually exclusive agential cuts that act as gratings. In this contribution, popular culture, again, turns out as a particularly diffractive site, where media-technological diffractions are echoed by equally complex interactions with recipients' bodies, readings, and discourses.

Diffraction from a technological perspective is also strongly present in Sean McCullough's contribution to what he describes as (diffractive) Code Studies, an important if somewhat understudied field within Literary/Cultural Studies, particularly in Europe, that comprises "code" in the sense of both linguistics and informatics. In a persuasive and demanding argument, reminiscent of Karen Barad's forays into the complexities of quantum experiments, McCullough claims that not only has rhetoric to be considered as a characteristic of both the language used on the internet *and* of the programming of this language to be digitally communicable. What is more, this rhetoric does not exist *either* within the questions users ask *or* the software code; it rather exists in the intersections of *both*, diffractively. What is also fascinating about this contribution is that it returns from the issue of diffractions within the most elaborate cultural technology currently available to the question of written *language*, as rhetoric or code or rather as rhetoric/code diffraction. Written language is the starting point of this volume, both in its theoretical considerations and its concrete reading practices, and, fascinatingly, written language proves to be a diffractive cultural technique at the heart of the onto-epistemological entanglements within the hitherto most advanced media technology. McCullough's chapter is therefore an apt conclusion to this collection, in that it returns the book's topic of diffractive reading to the linguistic and literary origins of many reading theories while at the same time suggesting—and performing—the traversal that this volume undertakes toward (reading) many more medialities, their matters, and their politics. Diffractive reading, as this volume shows in many ways, celebrates and activates both these matters and these politics in a new and forward-looking way.

NOTES

1. This entails (but not only) the notion of academic reading in the sense of "producing a scholarly analysis of," which actually always also includes *writing* (such readings). As we will see throughout this chapter, diffractive reading is reading (made, seen as) so productive that, "even" if nonacademic, it is always also writing, producing, making. Altogether, diffractive reading is not a particular new method of academic analysis but a suggestion for a new perspective on reading as such.

2. Birgit Mara Kaiser and Kathrin Thiele, eds, *Diffracted Worlds—Diffractive Readings: Onto-Epistemologies and the Critical Humanities* (London: Routledge, 2018). The volume is a republication of the 20, no. 3 (2014) issue of the Critical Theory journal *Parallax*. .

3. Karen Barad, *Meeting the Universe Halfway: Quantum Physics and the Entanglement of Matter and Meaning* (Durham: Duke University Press, 2007), 71.

4. Barad, *Meeting*, 83.

5. Barad, *Meeting*, 306–312.

6. Barad, *Meeting*, 83.

7. Moran speaks of the "the necessarily interpretive and fictional elements entangled with factual claims," 79.

8. Barad, *Meeting*, 74.

9. Barad, *Meeting*, 148.

10. Barad, *Meeting*, 72.

11. Barad, *Meeting*, 90.

12. Barad, *Meeting*, 71.

13. Kaiser and Thiele, *Diffracted Worlds*.

14. Derrida is discussed particularly in Barad's and Thiele's chapters; see *Diffracted Worlds*, 168–187 and 202–216. Beyond the volume, Derridaen deconstruction is explored as "reading as intervention" in Penelope Deutscher, *How to Read Derrida* (London: Granta Books), 15–26.

15. Even if the word "intertextuality" is not used in the volume, diffractive intertextuality is implicitly theorized and practised in many contributions to *Diffracted Worlds*.

16. Kaiser, "Worlding CompLit," in Kaiser and Thiele, *Diffracted Worlds* (London: Routledge, 2018), 284, sees reading as the "co-appearance [of patterns]" (e.g., of cultural values, theoretical approaches or of texts). "Readings are, in the strongest sense performative of 'world'." In the present introduction, I want to take up Kaiser's notion of world(ing) and expand it first into physical and then into organic world-making by (diffractive) reading.

17. Jacob Edmond, "Diffracted Waves and World Literature," in Kaiser and Thiele, *Diffracted Worlds*, 81–93.

18. Kiene Brillenburg Wurth, "Diffraction, Handwriting and Intra-Mediality in Louise Paille's *Livres-livres*," in Kaiser and Thiele, *Diffracted Worlds*, 94–109.

19. Melanie Sehgal, "Diffractive Propositions: Reading Alfred North Whitehead with Donna Haraway and Karen Barad," in Kaiser and Thiele, *Diffracted Worlds*, 24–37; and Iris van der Tuin, "Diffraction as a Methodology for Feminist Onto-Epistemology: On Encountering Chantal Chawaf and Posthuman Interpellation," in Kaiser and Thiele, *Diffracted Worlds*, 67–80.

20. "Matter" here in the general sense of the realm of the available/observable in physics as opposed to the textual.

21. Barad, *Meeting*, 337; italics mine.

22. Arguably, reading as measuring is closer to the original meaning of the word. In the *OED*, to be sure, reading appears as related to German "raten" and means among other things "consider, interpret, discern." "Reading," therefore, has no automatic connotation to letters or code. The scientific meaning considered by Barad is *OED* II 11c: "To take a measurement" (German "ablesen"). See *Oxford English Dictionary Online*, s.v. "measure, v."

23. As will become clear in the following, by materialism I do not imply the Marxist tradition, which is focused on socially and politically coded matter, but those approaches that are either concerned with matter in culture in a more general sense or move in the direction of matter beyond culture.

24. Christopher Tilley, *Material Culture and Text: The Art of Ambiguity* (London: Routledge, 1991), 17 and 20.

25. Gerhard Neumann and Sigrid Weigel, eds, *Die Lesbarkeit der Kultur: Literaturwissenschaften zwischen Kulturtechnik und Ethnographie* (München: Fink Verlag, 2000).

26. Such as *Metaphor and Material Culture* (Oxford: Blackwell, 2000) or *Interpreting Landscapes: Geologies, Topographies, Identities* (Walnut Creek: Left Coast Press, 2012).

27. Dan Hicks and Mary C. Beaudry, eds, *The Oxford Handbook of Material Culture Studies* (Oxford: Oxford University Press, 2010).
28. Susanne Scholz and Ulrike Vedder, eds, *Handbuch Literatur & Materielle Kultur* (Berlin: De Gruyter, 2019).
29. Julia Bertschik, "Literatur als Gehäuse der 'nächsten Dinge' im 19. Jahrhundert," in *Magie der Geschichten: Weltverkehr, Literatur und Anthropologie in der zweiten Hälfte des 19. Jahrhunderts*, ed. Michael Neumann und Kerstin Stüssel (Constance: Konstanz University Press, 2011), 326.
30. Hans-Jörg Rheinberger, *Toward a History of Epistemic Things: Synthesizing Proteins in the Test Tube* (Stanford: University of Stanford Press, 1997), 106.
31. Cf. Evelyn Fox Keller, *Refiguring Life: Metaphors of Twentieth-century Biology* (Columbia: Columbia University Press, 1995); Lily E. Kay, *Who Wrote the Book of Life? A History of the Genetic Code* (Stanford: Stanford University Press, 2000); Judith Roof, *The Poetics of DNA* (Minneapolis: University of Minnesota Press, 2007); Bettina Bock von Wülfingen, "Das Genom als Text: Die Schriftmetapher Revisited." *Metaphorik* 26 (2016): 117–153, https://www.metaphorik.de/de/journal/26/das-genom-als-text-die-schriftmetapher-revisited.html.
32. Hans Blumenberg, *Die Lesbarkeit der Welt* (Frankfurt am Main: Suhrkamp, 1981).
33. Blumenberg, *Lesbarkeit*, 373.
34. Blumenberg speaks of an "unexpected and disturbing turn of the metaphor," by which he implies its turn into the (diffracted) real. This move outside the notion of a culturally constructed reality at the very end of one of Blumenberg's key "metaphorological" works is an impressive and tremendously forward-looking moment. Cf. *Lesbarkeit*, 398; translation mine.
35. Cf. Barad, *Meeting*, 219, on human interference in genetic activity but without the notion of reading the genome.
36. Blumenberg, *Lesbarkeit*, 373; translation mine.
37. Blumenberg, *Lesbarkeit*, 374; translation mine.
38. Barad, *Meeting*, 338; first italics mine.
39. Blumenberg, *Lesbarkeit*, 399; translation mine.
40. Human interference in genetic processes is increasingly seen as uncontrollable in its consequences. The CRISPR technology notwithstanding, completing the Human Genome Project has shown that humans are absolutely in the dark about the function of large sections of the DNA and that the actual decision which of these sections are activated in the process of a cell development is subject to a varying, situational process scattered across the cell—an intra-action of cell and genome without any controlling "subject."
41. Wendy Wheeler, "Postscript on Biosemiotics: Reading Beyond Words—and Ecocritcism," *New Formations* 64 (2008): 137–154 and Wheeler, "The Lightest Burden: The Aesthetic Abductions of Biosemiotics," in *Handbook of Ecocriticism and Cultural Ecology*, ed. Hubert Zapf (Berlin: De Gruyter, 2016), 19–44; Inga Pollmann, "Invisible Worlds, Visible: Uexküll's *Umwelt*, Film and Film Theory," *Critiqual*

Inquiry 39, no. 4 (2013): 777–816; Timothy Maran, "Biosemiotic Criticism," in *The Oxford Handbook of Ecocriticism* (Oxford: Oxford University Press, 2014), 260–275.

42. Hayley Zertuche, "A Humanimal Rhetorics of Biological Materiality," in *Rhetorical Animals: Boundaries of the Human in the Study of Persuation*, ed. Kristian Bjørkdahl and Alex C. Parrish (Lanham: Lexington Books, 2018), 23–40.

43. Thure von Uexküll, "The Sign Theory of Jakob von Uexküll," in *Classics of Semiotics*, ed. Martin Krampen et al. (New York, London: Plenum Press, 1987), 155f.

44. Uexküll, "Uexküll," 155.

45. Uexküll, "Uexküll," 166–169.

46. Jakob von Uexküll and Georg Kriszat, *Streifzüge durch die Umwelten von Tieren und Menschen: Ein Bilderbuch unsichtbarer Welten—Bedeutungslehre* (Reinbek: Rowohlt, 1951), 158.

47. Significantly, Barad calls intra-actions also "worlding,"—a concept that is similar to the notion of *Umwelt*. Barad, *Meeting*, 181.

48. Zertuche, "Humanimal Rhetorics," 25, 36, 28.

49. Cf. its inclusion into the *Classics of Semiotics* together with Thomas Sebeok's similar approach as one (resp. two) of only eight approaches discussed at length.

50. Cf. in particular Timo Maran's work.

51. Sebeok even sees modelling as characteristic of any organic *Umwelt* process and not at all specific to humans. Cf. *A Sign Is Just a Sign* (Bloomington: Indiana University Press 1991).

52. Cf. Wheeler, "Postscript," 143–145. Peirce posits a developmental semiotics that ranges from iconic signs over indexical signs to symbolic signs—with increasing complexity in usage and sign structure.

53. Wheeler, "Postscript," 154.

54. An organism's *Umwelt* gets entangled with another *Umwelt*, for example, if that organism becomes a sign in that other *Umwelt*.

55. To be sure, my notion of human *Umwelt* is a species-specific application of the Uexküllian notion of *Umwelt*, not an alternative to it as anthropologists routinely strive: Pollmann ("Invisible Worlds," 797f.) refers to a range of anthropologists who try to limit the (Ueküllian) *Umwelt* idea to nonhuman animals, positing for humans an "openness to the world" or "*Umweltfrei[heit]*" (both Max Scheler) or a "world-forming" capacity against the "*weltarm[ut]*" (Martin Heidegger) of animals.

56. Human language seems to be a particularly ambitious and dynamic semiotic project. I am not saying at all, however, that it is unique to the human species. Other animals may have similarly expanded languages.

57. To substantiate this claim linguistically any further is beyond the scope of this chapter. See, however, for example, Sebeok's considerations of language in relation to Uexküll's notion of *Umwelt* in *Just a Sign*, 49–59: verbal signs are special cases of *Umwelt* signs, that is, exterior impulses endowed with special meaning by/within the (human) organism; in that sense, for humans, *every* perceptual impulse becomes a sign/has sign quality, with a tendency toward increasing extension and complexity of this process. Taken together with the sense of (human) *Umwelt* as entanglement, human must be seen as world-entangled particularly *by* language.

58. Jurij Lotman, *The Structure of the Artistic Text,* trans. Ronald Vroon (Ann Arbor: Michigan University, 1977); Cf. also Timo Maran, "Biosemiotic Criticism: Modelling the Environment in Literature," *Green Letters* 18, no. 3 (2014): 300.

59. Cf. Gilles Deleuze and Félix Guattari, *A Thousand Plateaus,* trans. Brian Massumi (London: Continuum, 2004), 24: "We call a '*plateau*' any multiplicity connected to other multiplicities." I use this splendid term to avoid the word "level," which again denotes a hierarchically higher status.

60. This endlessness also pertains to the potential "number" of diffractions that can be taken up in a "single" cultural text or that the cultural text may enter into with other texts: true to the origin of diffraction in the study of waves, cultural diffractions are multiple like wave encounters.

61. See Kaiser and Thiele, *Diffracted Worlds* passim.

62. Cf. Erika Fischer-Lichte, *The Semiotics of the Theater* (Bloomington: Indiana University Press, 1994); Christian Metz, *Film Language: A Semiotics of the Cinema* (Chicago: University of Chicago Press, 1974); and Göran Sonesson, "Methods and Models in Pictorial Semiotics," Report 3 from the Project *Pictorial Meanings in the Society of Information,* Lund University, 1988.

63. For a double use of "undermining" as weakening and "providing a substructure to," see my "Undermining Masculinity: Psychoanalysis, the 'Weak Man' and the 'Caring Woman', in Rebecca West's *The Return of the Soldier* and Willa Muir's *Imagined Corners,*" in *Psychoanalyticism: Uses of Psychoanalysis in Novels, Poems, Plays and Films,* ed. Anton Kirchhofer and Ingrid Hotz-Davis (Trier: WVT, 2000): 32–52.

64. Barad, *Meeting,* 381.

65. Ali Smith, *How to be Both* (London: Penguin, 2015), 182.

Part I

DIFFRACTIVE READING

GROUNDWORK

Chapter 2

On the Politics of Diffractive Reading

Birgit Mara Kaiser

In May 2019, the *Guardian* reported that more than 50 percent of Antarctica's Thwaites glacier basin has thinned considerably.[1] If the West Antarctic Ice Sheet alone were to melt, which is the smaller part of Antarctica's ice mass to which Thwaites belongs, sea levels are estimated to rise by about five meters. Among other things, this would likely mean the flooding of two-thirds of the Netherlands, despite excellent coastal engineering. As a resident of the Netherlands, this concerns me. At the same time, over the course of 2019, this chapter gestated in the form of several talks that I gave at different locations across Europe, to each of which I travelled by plane or train. In total, those travels produced about 0.8t of CO_2 emissions, as I could easily calculate on the application *myclimate*.[2] To limit global heating, *myclimate* tells me that each of us would need to reduce carbon spending annually to 0.6t, which giving those talks already exceeded by 0.2t—not to mention the average annual carbon footprint of an EU citizen, which currently lies at 8.4t. Thus, not only is this chapter intertwined with the rising temperatures and the melting of the poles, which most of us are aware of, presenting it at conferences has also already consumed more than my annual allowance of CO_2 emissions. And I still went to give the talks.

In what follows, I would like to reflect on this predicament, in which "mere" knowledge of the links between travel and global heating seems not enough to deter me from producing excessive CO_2 emissions. I will do so first and foremost as a literary scholar, not only because I also worry about the future of literature and literary studies in times of global heating and the exhaustion of planetary life when other than poetic engagements often seem more pressing, but also because it seems that a certain type of reading, which literary texts can demand, might train readers toward viscerally realizing these implications of travel, academic papers, and melting poles. Obviously, I am not considering this from any moral high-ground, as can be seen above, but with the sincere question of how to learn to sense the entanglement of planetary life, including academic papers, to modify habits of consumption and spending. Against the background of these larger concerns, the chapter concretely engages with the poetic essay *Journey to Mount Tamalpais* by Beirut-born writer and artist Etel Adnan,[3] and examines what diffractive reading might imply—a question this volume invites—and if it might offer food for thought in view of the above quandary. As we will see in detail, *Journey to Mount Tamalpais* is composed of loosely linked paragraphs, with recurring themes and imagery that present us with the entangled lives of Mount Tamalpais, the narrator, the lasting legacies of settler colonialism and the nationalist, belligerent space race of the 1960s. The text presents us, I argue, with a diffraction pattern that manifests around Mount Tamalpais and at the same time also challenges the reader to pursue these often implicit layers and patterns of difference. It demands a certain attention from the reader, for which diffractive reading might be a suitable term. As we will see, such textual engagement cannot be separated from readings of location and situation, from the *stakes* implicated in the reading of text and the patterns formed in reading. In that regard, the chapter also engages diffractive reading in contrast to other modes of reading—especially distant and surface reading—which have recently been proposed as necessary methodological changes to the field of literary study.

The chapter moves in three steps. It will first examine how *Journey to Mount Tamalpais* ensnares us in an experience of reading that demands tracing entanglement and diffractive patterning, and thereby gets into view a *polis* hitherto invisibilized and of which the reader forms part. In a second step, I will show how this conception of pattern(ing) differs considerably from the term's understanding in distant and surface reading—and thereby also engage the *politics* of the field of literary studies, which in recent years have played out especially around methods of reading. In a last step, the chapter then returns to the specific practice of reading *Journey to Mount Tamalpais* invites and asks how it might differ from an *ethics* of reading. How a politics of diffractive reading (doubly understood as reading the diffraction pattern *Journey to Mount Tamalpais* harbors and as actualizing a reading's diffraction pattern here-now) might not only practice our exposure to otherness, which the aesthetic training of an ethics of reading (Attridge, Spivak) stresses, but especially train our perception of co-implication and entanglement. Given that Western habits of mobility and consumption are implicated in the thinning of Antarctica's ice, such a reading engagement with literary texts might offer trainings for a renewed *polis* of co-in-habitation. This at least is the wager here.[4]

READING JOURNEY TO MOUNT TAMALPAIS

According to the OED, reading means to "consider, interpret, discern . . . scan or study writing silently"—in the conventional sense of the word as discerning something eyes on page. In a slightly broader understanding, reading also means "to assess precisely any indications or clues given out by (a location, situation, etc.) in order to decide on a course of action" (OED). Reading here is not so much the endeavor to determine truth or excavate meaning, but part of a pragmatics of living. Also "[a] face and body, a figure, is a cipher, to be deciphered, read,"[5] as Spivak notes. In what follows, reading will be used not only as a direct encounter with texts, but in these multiple senses. But let me begin with a textual engagement and take a first look at *Journey to Mount Tamalpais*, which opens as follows:

SOMETIMES, THEY OPEN A NEW HIGHWAY, AND LET IT ROLL, OPEN WIDE the earth, shake trees from their roots. The Old Woman suffers once more. Birds leave the edges of the forest, abandon the highway. They go up to mountain tops and from the highest peaks they take in the widest landscapes, they even foresee the space age.

The condor is dying. He used to live on the top of Tamalpais. His square wings used to carry him all over the area: the hills were moving beneath him with silent pride. He used to cut through the clouds like a fearful knife. At certain seasons he used to carry the moon between his claws. Now we took over his purpose. We are the ones to go to the Mountain.

This morning I took the card table and put it out on the deck, under the pine trees. On a piece of paper shadows fell. I tried to catch their contours but they were slowly moving, all the time. They made me think of sidewalks on which people pass, swiftly. And the big mountain sent a wild smell of crushed herbs into the air making everything feel slightly off.[6]

The essay's ensuing sixty pages are composed, like the opening here, in short stanza-like paragraphs of poetic prose, interspersed with drawings by Adnan herself of Mount Tamalpais, a mountain near her former home in Sausalito, California (see fig. 2.1, 2.2, and 2.3). The structure of the essay itself is not progressive, but, as we will see, rather diffractive, of which this opening might give a hint.

I encountered *Journey to Mount Tamalpais* by chance at dOCUMENTA (13) in 2012, whose curator Carolyn Christov-Bakargiev decided to include some of Adnan's paintings in the exhibition. Struck by her visual work, I found *Journey to Mount Tamalpais* later in the dOCUMENTA bookshop, which attracted me more than the catalog with her paintings. Thus, in a way,

Figure 2.1 Etel Adnan, Mount Tamalpais, in *Journey to Mount Tamalpais*, 36.

Figure 2.2 Etel Adnan, Mount Tamalpais, in *Journey to Mount Tamalpais*, 45

contingency and appetition, inclination and chance were at the basis of my engagement with Adnan's text here and reading *Journey to Mount Tamalpais* was from the start not merely an individual experience. My encounter with the text was already implicated in Christov-Bakargiev's curatorial decision, which not only brought Adnan to my attention but also massively increased her wider visibility and appreciation.[7] Surely, generally speaking, texts come to us within specific distributions of power/knowledge and we get to read

Figure 2.3 Etel Adnan, Mount Tamalpais, in *Journey to Mount Tamalpais*, 56.

only what the cultural archives hold. The archives' enabling violence (to use Spivak's term)[8] is part of any reading event so that from the start more forces are at work than the couple of reading *subject* and *object* of study. Reading events exceed the bilateral, silent interaction between reader and text and rather always already involve a *polis* of some sort: my reading encounter with *Journey to Mount Tamalpais* involves Christov-Bakargiev's decision to involve Adnan in dOCUMENTA (13). It is crucial to consider these elements that enable, shape, and precede textual encounters, but given the limits of space here, this chapter can merely acknowledge these constitutive conditions of reading events and will focus on the engagement of reading itself that ensues. It asks what might come into view if we attended to reading events not as sites of ethical reappraisals of a reading subject, which reception aesthetics, but especially Attridge's ethics of reading has proposed, but as (a politics of) diffractive pattern formation. While agreeing with Attridge that responsible engagements with texts affirm an exposure to difference, to textual difference as an otherness, which a subject cannot incorporate or dominate, and affirming this as a starting point, I would like to see how diffractive reading encounters might engage not so much difference (as otherness), but "differencing: differences-in-the(re)making"[9] and permit getting implicatedness and readerly entanglement into view in new ways. If, as Karen Barad's work has argued, the world is spacetimemattering—that is onto-epistemologically in-the-making—then author/reader/text apparatuses are also sites of radical entangledness.[10] The diffraction pattern which a reading onto-epistemologically produces fabricates a *polis*, more than just rearrange myself vis-à-vis a non-appropriable other. Could diffractive reading, on the one hand, wrestle with the politics that go into the event of any reading before we even start (e.g., the curatorial decisions, the institutional powers); and could it, on the other hand, implicate readers more radically in a production of worlding than the ethical reappraisal of our stances vis-à-vis otherness might permit? Might other matters become more widely shared *public* affairs—in the sense of the classical Greek *politiká* (τὰ πολιτικά) meaning public matters? Given that this chapter is entangled with the future of Thwaites glacier, making perceptible a new sense of *polis*—of which Thwaites is part, as am I, as is the paper on which this chapter is printed and the trains and planes getting me around to talks—might be a crucial lesson for the twenty-first century.

With these questions in mind, we can return to *Journey to Mount Tamalpais*, which reflects on the relation of art to nature and on painterly and poetic ways of making perceptible. The narrative voice dwells on her multisensory, affective relation to Mount Tamalpais, a mountain close enough to her home in Sausalito, CA to—as we saw earlier—send over "a wild smell of crushed herbs."[11] In word and image, the essay sketches that mountain, its geological changes from active to now "silenced volcano,"[12] its transforming environment from condor-habitat to recreational site, but also its continuous transformations depending on light, time of day, season, or distance, position, perspective, and mood of its interlocutor. Some mornings, Tamalpais is "lost amid clouds," then covered by smoke from "huge fires erupted all over Marin County"[13]; indeed a county prone to wild fires due to its charrapal shrubland and oak savannahs, which at times turn Tamalpais "jungle-green,"[14] then again make it "fume."[15] From "Throckmorton Avenue, it resembles Ramses II of Egypt or, perhaps, the Sphinx."[16] Pursuing its metamorphoses, the text does not present Tamalpais as a hitherto overlooked object that can now come to light independent of human interference, but dwells on it as a phenomenon which is profoundly relational, in multiple ways.[17] The reference to one of Sausalito's central avenues marks Tamalpais as part of the town's everyday life, as a companion who keeps the narrator company and who "looks back at me."[18] Tamalpais is also, she notes, "the first of the mountains that constitute the convulsive spine of the American continent" and thus the Andes's "peaceful kin," connecting the Californian coast with land "all the way to Tierra del Fuego." *Journey to Mount Tamalpais* portrays "this Mountain that looks like an elephant and feeds on green grass"[19] as a habitat shared, albeit unequally, by humans and nonhumans alike and subterraneously extending as far as the most southern tip of the Americas.

Keeping Tamalpais as its focal point, the essay weaves other aspects into what I suggest becomes a diffraction pattern. We already saw the reference to the space age (the leaving birds "take in the widest landscapes, they even foresee the space age") and—more cryptically in the opening quote—a reference to native culture in the smell of crushed herbs. These two allusions are explicitly related later in the essay, when Tamalpais is said to be a "space-launch" and the narrator notes:

> The Tamal Indians knew it: they are still living on it, transformed into trees. Some of them are madrones, others are oaks. The Old Creator had told them: "Your spirit power will be discovered and will be brought back to earth to be of great use to the human race. The power to soar."[20]

Their spiritual soaring reminds us of the condor's "square wings" in the opening lines, an association that invites questioning the opposition of human and animal, or culture and nature, which the "new highway" in those opening lines precisely appeared to reinforce. For sure, the narrator does not repeat the colonial attribution of "nature" to native peoples, as she herself affirms kinship to the mountain. Asked after the most important person in her life, she notes that she realized that it was "[a] mountain;" that "Tamalpais was at the very center of my being."[21] That former indigenous inhabitants are said to live on as trees rather marks their violent displacement and deaths resulting from settler colonialism as well as their continued strategies of survival, and gestures toward a cosmology, in which the mountain is a sacred being.[22] Earlier, a paragraph had even Tamalpais' very name mark the colonial layers of this place.

> The Indian called the Mountain Tamal-Pa, "the One close to the Sea." The Spaniard called it Mal-Pais, "Bad Country!" The difference between the native and the conqueror is readable in these two different perceptions of the same reality. Let us be the Indian and let be! What is close to the sea shall remain close to the sea.[23]

Early Spanish settler colonialism, which started near Tamalpais around 1775, is intersected with millennia-old native inhabitance, and in turn both subsist in the paratactic arrangement of the text alongside—and on—Mount Tamalpais and its contemporary Sausalito habitats. *Journey to Mount Tamalpais* renders these multiple layers as superposed and Adnan's interweaving of Tamal and Spanish settlement, of condor and car, of Tamalpais and herself reminds us that, as Barad notes, "[l]and is not property or territory; it is a time-being marked by its own wounds and vitality, a layered material geo-neuro-biography of bones and bodies, ashes and earth, where death and life meet."[24] Adnan renders Tamalpais as such a layered time-being, a superposition of several significant vectors—a superposition it also carries in its name, as Adnan's short excursion to its etymology highlights; "[e]tymological entanglements" that, as Barad adds to her observations about land, "already hint at a troubling of assumed boundaries between allegedly different kinds."[25] And Noura Wedell remarks that in Adnan's text the "superposition of the *mal pais* over its ancient form has left that old form still alive, if necessarily transformed, transparent in the sense of possessing greater power to affect those who perceive it."[26]

Journey to Mount Tamalpais then—although not in linear succession—adjoins to these colonial-historical layers memories of the space launches of the 1960s, which the very first paragraph already evoked in the birds' flights foreseeing the space age. Later, space travel returns more directly when the narrator recalls watching the Cape Kennedy NASA launches on TV with "members of the Perception Workshop,"[27] a workshop run by artist Ann O'Hanlon, in which Adnan participated with sculptor Dick O'Hanlon and curator John Humphrey among others. After noting that from Throckmorton Avenue Tamalpais "resembles Ramses II of Egypt or, perhaps, the Sphinx" and standing on its summit "one wants to keep going, out into space," the next paragraph jumps again to the Perception Workshop. The paratactic contiguity of paragraphs typical of *Journey to Mount Tamalpais* produces a sudden shift of focus; it requires that we move our attention again, in this case to the space race.

> From their very beginnings, we followed the space travels of America, from the Mountain. Ann, Dick, John Humphrey and I spent hours, days, years in front of the television screen. We tried to figure out the color of outer space, the speed of the rockets, the landscapes seen by the astronauts, their thoughts, their feelings, their mutations.

In line with the workshop's concern for perception, its members wonder about the colors of outer space and lunar landscapes as they watched the launches on TV. In particular, the narrator notes that she "will always remember the day Ranger 8 hit the moon. It was a Saturday, in February."[28] Although the text does not explicate it for us, we might remember—or find out on the internet—that NASA's Ranger series prepared the later Apollo program and was itself a project of perception, equipped with cameras that transmitted high-resolution photographs of the lunar surface.[29]

> It [Ranger 8] sent back the first close-ups of the craters and of a face with was pocked, rubbery, like burning milk breaking up in bubbles, and stretching its skin. We felt like we were sitting within that strange lunar smile making fun of earth-bound creatures.[30]

Journey to Mount Tamalpais in turn makes the moon launches tangible by means of language, including figurative language (simile ["like burning milk"] or metaphor ["spine"]), but thereby also seems to challenge and destabilize what one takes as immediately evident on these photographic images. A few lines down, the exhaust of Ranger 9's engines, launched a month later, looks "like a gigantic white beard," an image that in turn triggers a memory. "When I was 9 years old I had seen that beard in a dream, that waterfall of pure energy under a semblance of a face, and I had thought that I had seen God. I believed then in what I saw."[31] By association, the number 9 recalls a childhood dream at age nine, whose relevance is not so much the resemblance between the white exhaust and the face of God, but the statement that—in the past (in 1965 or at age nine, we are not sure)—the narrator believed in what she saw. By the time of writing, questions of perception have become trickier and the face has now become the *semblance* of a face. To the same extent that we have seen the essay interlace, in a strange simultaneity, the mountain's geology with native heritage and Spanish settlement, it also brings in the space race of the 1950s and 1960s, interlinked with personal memories from earlier days, possibly childhood days passed in Beirut. As we proceed from paragraph to paragraph, times and places thicken through and around Mount Tamalpais.[32]

Other vectors could be traced in this pattern that Adnan's text weaves, but I believe that its key interlacing elements are art, perception, Mount Tamalpais, native California, settler colonialism, migration, and the space race. *Journey to Mount Tamalpais* does not unfold their relations for us explicitly or establish causal links between them but proceeds rather by diffraction. "[A] diffraction pattern is a manifestation of a superposition,"[33] Barad notes. Adnan's text writes (and reads) these different elements through each other, traces their entanglement and performs their superposition. It does what Barad notes for diffraction, namely "(re)configuring . . . patterns of differentiating -entangling"—demonstrating that "[t]here is no absolute boundary between here-now and there-then. There is nothing that is new; there is nothing that is not new."[34] On this mountain, we might say, 1492 lives inside 1986 lives inside 1965 lives inside Tamalpais's folding in the Pliocene lives inside 1775 lives inside Miwok Tolay lake settlements 4000BC. Troubling the boundaries of chronological time, such a superposition does not conflate or unduly flatten all these times into one. Rather, intersecting the ecological, colonial, geological, cosmological, scientific, and nationalist vectors that subsist on and around this mountain, Adnan's essayistic dwelling on Mount Tamalpais puts the thickness of time and place before us. In the formal arrangement of loosely connected paragraphs as well as the organization of its subject-matters, the text performs a diffraction of times and perspectives and does the "hard work of tracing the quantum entanglements"[35] so that such a pattern emerges. Therefore, Adnan offers a perceptive reading of Tamalpais; one that is, it seems to me, not so much an archaeological attempt at excavating the mountain as object or giving one true account of this mountain, which would, as an appropriative move, also be at odds with the native cosmologies the text respectfully acknowledges. Rather, what *Journey to Mount Tamalpais* unearths is the diffraction pattern "Mount Tamalpais" of which the mentioned elements of native California, settler colonialism, Mount Tamalpais, migration, the space race as well as the narrator are all part. As such a *polis* of human and nonhuman forces, "Mount Tamalpais" (as much as the essay itself) makes it impossible to neatly separate and keep separate ecology, coloniality, geology, science, and nationalism (to just name the realms the essay engages). What Adnan brings into view is "Mount Tamalpais" as instantiating entanglement, not as an object or "nature" and in that sense her text does "the hard work of tracing the quantum entanglements."[36]

So far, I have treated Adnan as a perceptive reader of Mount Tamalpais and the essay as the (per)form(ance) of her reading. Now, from an agential realist perspective, diffraction as a methodological lens surely also requires thinking about the essay's reader in different ways. Diffractive reading complicates the entire author/reader/text apparatus, because one key point of quantum diffraction is that "human subjects are neither outside observers of apparatuses, nor independent subjects that intervene in the workings of an apparatus, nor the products of social technologies that produce them." Rather, they are—as elements of the apparatus—also "part of the larger material configuration of the world"[37] and speaking of diffractive reading entails more than "merely" tracing a diffraction pattern *in* the world or *in* a text. The pattern my reading tried to trace was not there *in* the world before Adnan begins her reading/writing, nor was it there *in Journey to Mount Tamalpais* before I read the text. So, stopping at pointing to what a text does—which is what I have done up to this point—is not yet sufficient; diffractive reading would also require thinking about which polis matters forth in each reading event, about how reader/author/text/world emerge always in new ways.[38] The entanglements performed in *Journey to Mount Tamalpais* emerge *as* we pursue them and resonate according to the echoes of their subject-matters in our own time. We are only alive to the work the text does if we ourselves put work into it again. Hinting as how native and Spanish life came to be enmeshed with Tamalpais and the space race; how the colonial appropriation of land resonates in lunar expeditions, the essay involves us into concrete text work that requires (re-)membering (as in reassembling) the vectors that the text offers so as to perceive their pattern. Reading *Journey to Mount Tamalpais* here and now involves that type of work, and my engagement with the essay is therefore undeniably (in)formed also by the current frenzy of new nationalisms that appear to fuel a new space race; by years of raging wild fires in California; by the climate emergency and its asymmetrical effects on different peoples, with the continued global inequalities we inherit from settler colonialism and the imperial project. My account of Adnan's essay is reading work done in now-time (to evoke Walter Benjamin),[39] (in)formed by the news of wild fires and Thwaites' continuous melting and implicated—even if almost imperceptibly—in the *polis* the essay evokes. It seems to me that the work required for producing such diffraction patterns—on Adnan's as much as on the reader's end and for which a text like Adnan's lends itself exceptionally well—demands of us to viscerally grapple with echoes and entanglements, with what being entangled with 1986, 1492, 1775, the Pliocene, distant and near places, and 1965 means. Such grappling might train not primarily an ethos of otherness, but a politics of sensing the tangle of terran existence, of attending to the *polis* that each reading event makes possible (at the expense of other unrealized *poleis*). Given that this chapter is enmeshed with the future of Thwaites glacier, sensing the tangle of terran existence or how Thwaites implicates us, and we her, seems a condition that is worth physically realizing. Literary texts (weaves by name) might be suitable training fields for the indispensable new arts of living "on a damaged planet" (to evoke Anna Tsing).[40]

PATTERN DOES NOT EQUAL PATTERN

If what has been said so far holds, then *Journey to Mount Tamalpais* ensnares us in an experience of reading that differs from some of the reading practices that have been put forward in recent years as necessary changes to the field, either as distant reading or as surface reading, but also from the ethics of reading. In a second step, I want to now turn to the debates concerning the future of the field of literary studies, which in recent years have played out especially around methods of reading.[41] These methodological debates have seen defenses of close reading; renewed attention to reading in translation; the digital humanities' proposition of distant reading; post-critical approaches such as surface reading; and now also diffractive reading, of which the volume gives proof.[42] Especially in these last three propositions, patterns play a considerable role in grappling with what reading does or means. However, pattern does not equal pattern and given this chapter's attention to diffraction patterns, the differences between the notion of pattern for distant reading and surface reading, on the one hand, and diffractive reading, on the other, are informative. The differences in the use of patterns stem precisely, it seems to me, from the status given to the human subject or reader and to meaning-making.

In "Surface Reading: An Introduction" (2009), Stephen Best and Sharon Marcus propose a new way of "just" *reading on the surface* to move away from notions of interpretation that seek the deeper meaning of a text in what remains unsaid. They identify the latter as prevalent in symptomatic reading, which according to Best and Marcus is "an interpretive method that argues that the most interesting aspect of a text is what it represses" and that seeks "a latent meaning behind a manifest one."[43] Jameson is referenced as one prominent representative of this tradition and against this somewhat myopically chosen foil—for, surely, there are other prominent modes of reading— Best and Marcus propose reading on the surface. Striving to leave behind the implicit political agendas they detect in symptomatic reading (which seems to know what it is looking for before starting), they propose taking "texts at face value" in an allegedly neutral position of "just reading."[44] Rather than suspiciously searching for unspoken, deeper truths, and ideological machinations, readers should expose themselves "simply" to "what is evident, perceptible, apprehensible in texts."[45] As we have seen in Adnan, what is perceptible and evident might not be so straightforward, and evidence and face value precisely emerge out of (dis)entanglements and work, rather than being factual givens. Regardless, Best and Marcus suggest that surface readers "locate narrative structures and abstract patterns on the surface, as aggregates of what is manifest in multiple texts" so that the "critic becomes an anatomist breaking down texts or discourses into their components, or a taxonomist arranging and categorizing texts into larger groups."[46] The problem with such an assertion is not the scientific lexicon, but that surface readers are said to be "relatively neutral about their objects of study," "free from having a political agenda,"[47] and able to "recognize without judging." The political is equated with the "distortions of ideology"[48] and to guarantee neutrality, the analyzing subject must remain detached from the object of study to arrive at abstractions. The entire disposition to patterning (and/as reading) is different from a diffraction pattern. For Barad "[d]iffraction is not a set pattern, but rather an iterative (re)configuring of patterns of differentiating-entangling,"[49] and for Adnan, as we saw, the narrator is anything but detached from the "object" of study. The value of pursuing the diffraction pattern Adnan's text produces around Tamalpais lies, as I suggested, precisely in perceiving our (including the author's) readerly implications in it. Patterns in that sense are not evident, lying either in deep structure or on the surface, but they mark and emerge from material-semiotic entanglements, which thus thwarts any innocent anatomic or taxonomic description from the start. In his recent "Patterns and Interpretation" (2017), Franco Moretti, one of the original proponents of distant reading, makes a similar move. Given the new procedures of computational criticism, which the advent of digital tools permits, literary scholars are called to engage "[i]nstead of reading, [in] pattern recognition."[50] While pattern had been, according to Moretti, a "normative concept" that designated a model imposed on the world, the term shifted around 1900 to designating a "relationship of elements" and patterns are now no longer said to be brought into the world (as normative models tied to masters), but to have become "empirical, independent existence[s]."[51] We can detect patterns from among the "chaos of empirical data."[52] The logic is close to that of surface reading: where normative models seem to indicate ideology or unwanted interventions (a hidden political agenda), such an involvement that puts patterns *onto* the world (or deep meaning into texts) is seen as no longer valid (or even a politically invested distortion) and instead patterns are now said to be *in* the world and there to be "found."[53] Readers are called to "explain . . . why patterns are there."[54]

My discomfort with these propositions of computational criticism, distant reading, and surface reading does not stem from an old humanist concern about the loss of hermeneutic suspicion. Rather, from a diffractive perspective the worry is that these propositions precisely re-instate a scientific subject who seems to merely recognize what is out there. From an agential realist perspective, the ontological claim that patterns "are there" and the epistemological aim of recognition raises suspicions, since a familiar gesture from modern, humanist science returns here: modest objectivity coming from nowhere, merely recognizing what is given. Donna Haraway termed this figure that pitches the "scientist" in the position of the "witness whose account mirrors reality"[55] the *modest witness*—a position of detachment that both Moretti and Best and Marcus for sure present as an *advance* over earlier, normative political agendas, rather than a return.[56] The modest witness, however, is a traditional position of Western science and inhabits "the potent 'unmarked category', which is constructed by the extraordinary conventions of self-invisibility . . . the space perceived by its inhabitants to be the 'culture of no culture'." From a position of self-invisibility, patterns are declared to be *there* making the modest witness "the legitimate and authorized ventriloquist for the object world, adding nothing from his mere opinions, from his biasing embodiment." Finding patterns and taking texts at face value falls into that tradition, as it keeps the observer or reader again modestly out of the picture. Thus, I also worry from a feminist perspective that such self-invisibilization returns us to "the specifically modern, European, masculine, scientific form of the virtue of modesty ... one of the founding virtues of what we call modernity."[57] For one, Bohr's quantum thought had complicated that assertion profoundly. His innovation, which Barad draws out for us, was precisely to stress the entanglement of measured and measurer. "We" are not outside the world looking in, since from a Bohrian-Baradian quantum perspective "[t]here is no 'I' that exists outside of the diffraction pattern, observing it, telling its story . . . 'I' am neither outside nor inside; 'I' am *of* the diffraction pattern."[58] Diffraction patterns are therefore "patterns of difference that make a difference"[59]—agential, but neither merely human or willful, nor "there" before "we" look. "We" are agentially cutting together apart as world; we are not in or on the world, but of it, which also means that the subject (reader) "is not 'me' alone and never was," that it is "always already multiply dispersed and diffracted throughout spacetime(mattering), including (in) this paper, (in) its ongoing being-becoming is *of* the diffraction pattern."[60] Including (in) Adnan's reading-writing of Mount Tamalpais, including (in) our reading of Adnan today. The underlying conventional realism of a given world repeats a gesture of modern science that not only becomes questionable from the perspective of agential realism, but also obscures the decisive question that both postcolonial and feminist (literary) critique have insisted on for a long time, namely: who reads what for-with-through-by whom, where, when, and with which stakes? Thus, a politics of diffractive reading then would attend to this question and thereby also tackle these recent claims of distant and surface reading to merely apply new technological tools or stay on the surface. What these latter pitch as eschewing political agendas that allegedly distort criticism is rather an attempted re-negotiation of the methodology of literary studies. While they claim to merely make use of new machinic possibilities or revalued neutrality, what returns with a vengeance in pattern *recognition* is Man.

A POLITICS OF DIFFRACTIVE READING

Within this current tangle of the field of literary studies, the task of a politics of diffractive reading is then also to challenge the currently hegemonic use of "pattern" as order abstracted from chaos and to insert itself into the current politics of the field, to repattern it. Now, the tangle of that field includes yet another interlocutor, and one that is much closer to the concerns of this chapter: the ethics of reading mentioned earlier. I hope we can now see, how speaking of a *politics* of reading aligns with, but also slightly differs from the *ethics* of reading that scholars committed to close reading—prominently Attridge, but also Spivak and others—have suggested. This will be the last step of my argument.

In his book on *Coetzee and the Ethics of Reading*, Attridge argues that reading a literary text requires responsiveness to what one encounters. Reading is an act of responding to a text whereby the "reader—not as free-floating subject but as the nexus of a number of specific histories and contextual formations . . . brings the work into being, differently each time" so that reading gains the quality of an act or event. Although conventionally seen as being about "meaning of a literary work . . . carried away when we have finished reading it," reading literature for Attridge is rather "a singular performance of the work."[61] Each time anew, this performance is guided by the textual material, its compositions, and poetics (Wolfgang Iser's textual repertoire and horizon of expectations), but the densities of the textual material precisely also demand from readers an openness to the text as something that is not immediately accessible.

> Reading a work of literature entails opening oneself to the unpredictable, the future, the other, and thereby accepting the responsibility laid upon one by the work's singularity and difference. There is also abundant evidence that *writing* a literary work is often a similar experience. In a sense, the "literary" is the ethical.[62]

The ethical allows Attridge to move beyond one-sided attention to a work's content and a direct focus on its political implications—as representation of otherness and critique of oppressive structures—and, at the same time, to get beyond a formal aestheticism that had traditionally tended to remove the literary text from worldly concerns.[63] Edward Said's contrapuntal reading makes a similar move.[64] Certainly, the ethical for Attridge is not a set of moral directives, but the injunction to enter "a process of constant reappraisal and self-redefinition,"[65] in which readers test their own assumptions and blindspots. In *The Singularity of Literature*, he notes that:

> To respond to the demand of the literary work as the demand of the other is to attend to it as a unique event whose happening is a call, a challenge, an obligation: understand how little you understand me, translate my untranslatability . . . It means suspending all those carefully applied codes and conventions and reinventing them.[66]

The inaccessibility of Mount Tamalpais—its otherness and the otherness of Adnan's poetic text—might be focal points of an ethics of reading; wrestling with the text can teach us to "understand how little you understand me." Such a bet on ethics as an experience of non-appropriable alterity is highly valuable and desirable, as it demonstrates the limits of the cognizing subject, but in more worldly ways, we might say, than Kant's free play of the faculties in aesthetic judgment, and in ways that do not confirm *us* in the exercise of our faculties, but ideally train us toward greater respect for otherness. As a keen reader of Attridge, I fully subscribe to this. It is an important wager for the value of literature and a sophisticated engagement with it—missing neither literature's poetic densities nor its worldly conditions and our involvement in them—and I affirm Attridge's commitment to reading as event, to textual density and the attentive, close labor of reading it requires. But while a focus on the ethical alerts us to encounters with difference and otherness, it dwells mainly on the silent, bilateral interaction of a reader with a text and pays less attention to the worlding that matters forth in/as reading events. If practices of reading partake in spacetime-mattering, then they are also more radically productive of world, I would venture, than the self-assessment of a reader responding to a text. What I have suggested here tentatively as a politics of diffractive reading might emphasize how such reading encounters are indeed also "part of the larger material configuration of the world"[67]—how they/we are singular-collective encounters with-in textured materiality that include texts, the fields of relations that constitute "us," current times, past times, the "world," as well as the in/exclusions and ghosts that permeate and co-generate reading encounters. If world is intra-active, reading is too. It does not occur at a *reflexive* distance from world or text but is one form of *diffractive* intra-action with/in it. Thus, if it warrants saying, the term "politics" in such a politics of reading does not reference a political agenda imposed on texts. Rather, it asks what *polis* already inheres in a reading encounter, what *polis* matters forth in each reading anew, in excess of the silent experience of our limits of understanding. It might enable perceiving more thoroughly *how/what/when/where/with whom* we read and *which* patterns get generated. If world is the ongoing co-appearance of all "relata/entities" (a diffraction in principle), practices of reading are *radically* performative. Less interested in drawing out patterns across texts or finding them in the world, a politics of diffractive reading then stresses its own performativity of world—always in localized, specified, errant span—and thus, as one case in point, also intra-acts with the current methodological debates in the field of literary studies. Concretely, it affirms reading encounters as *producing* patterns and sites of experiencing the entanglement of reader/author/text/world. Again, given that Western habits of mobility and consumption are implicated in the thinning of Antarctica's ice and much more, we might have to practice not only our exposure to otherness, but train precisely our perception of entanglement. Reading in the way Adnan demands of us might retrain our habits of detachment and objectivity toward viscerally realizing what co-implication requires of "us" with and for a renewed *polis* of planetary co-in-habitation.[68]

NOTES

1. Damian, Carrington. "'Extraordinary thinning' of ice sheets revealed deep inside Antarctica," *The Guardian (US)*, May 16, 2019, https://www.theguardian.com/environment/2019/may/16/thinning-of-antarctic-ice-sheets-spreading-inland-rapidly-study.

2. Myclimate (website), Foundation MyClimate, accessed September 16, 2019, https://www.myclimate.org/.

3. Etel Adnan, *Journey to Mount Tamalpais* (Sausalito: The Post-Apollo Press, 1986).

4. Surely, *polis* refers first and foremost to ancient Greek city-states; see H.D.F. Kitto, "The Polis," in *The City Reader*, eds Richard T. LeGates and Frederic Stout (London: Routledge, 1996), 40–45. I am using the term here not to evoke Greek-Latinized political legacies, but to highlight the etymological link of politics to *politeia* and *polis*, that is the formation of a body politic or a commons.

5. Gayatri Ch. Spivak, *An Aesthetic Education in the Era of Globalization* (Cambridge: Harvard University Press, 2012), 271.

6. Adnan, *Journey*, 9.

7. Before dOCUMENTA (13), Adnan had primarily been known for her writing, especially her prize-winning novel *Sitt Marie Rose* (1977) and her poetry collections. dOCUMENTA (13) triggered a much wider reception of her work, bringing also her paintings, drawings and leporellos to larger audiences; see Klaudia Ruschowski, "The Many Worlds of Etel Adnan," *PAJ: A Journal of Performance & Art* 117 (2017): 77–81 for an overview of Adnan's artistic œuvre; also Gareth Harris, "Etel Adnan: 'This is the summit of my career'," *The Art Newspaper*, June 13, 2018, https://www.theartnewspaper.com/interview/etel-adnan-this-is-the-summit-of-my-career.

8. see Gayatri Ch. Spivak, "Bonding in Difference. Interview with Alfred Arteaga," in *The Spivak Reader*, eds Donna Landry and Gerald Maclean (London: Routledge, 1996), 15–28.

9. Karen Barad, "Diffracting Diffraction: Cutting Together-Apart," *Parallax* 20, no. 3 (2014): 175, https://doi.org/10.1080/13534645.2014.927623.

10. See Karen Barad, *Meeting the Universe Halfway: Quantum Physics and the Entanglement of Matter and Meaning* (Durham: Duke University Press, 2007).

11. Adnan, *Journey*, 9.

12. Adnan, *Journey*, 40.

13. Both quotations from Adnan, *Journey*, 11.

14. Adnan, *Journey*, 17.

15. Adnan, *Journey*, 18. Tamalpais owes it ever-changing velvety green to its vegetation, which consists of Maritime Charrpal, an evergreen oak scrubland unique to the wet-hot coastal climate of California. Maritime Charrpal is also extremely prone to wild fires and dependent upon them for regeneration.

16. Adnan, *Journey*, 40.

17. In *Journey to Mount Tamalpais*, the mountain is not an object, but a phenomenon in Bohr's sense. "[P]henomena do not merely mark the epistemological inseparability of 'observer' and 'observed'; rather, *phenomena are the ontological inseparability of agentially intra-acting 'components'*. That is, phenomena are ontologically primitive relations—relations without preexisting relata." Karen Barad, "Posthumanist Performativity: Toward an Understanding of How Matter Comes to Matter," *Signs: Journal of Women in Culture and Society* 28, no. 3 (2003): 815; see also Barad, *Meeting*, 97–132.

18. Adnan, *Journey*, 17. In "The Cost of Love We Are Not Willing to Pay," in *The Book of Books*, dOCUMENTA (13) Catalogue 1/3 (Ostfildern: Hatje Cantz, 2012), Adnan notes: "Living north of San Francisco, near the other side of the Golden Gate Bridge, I developed a familiarity with Mount Tamalpais . . . Gradually, the mountain

became a reference point . . . It became a companion . . . To observe its constant changes became my major preoccupation."

19. All Adnan, *Journey*, 17.

20. Adnan, *Journey*, 40.

21. Adnan, *Journey*, 10.

22. For a wonderful account of the mutual entanglements of indigenous and nonindigenous worlds in the Andes and mountains as spiritual earth beings, see Marisol de la Cadena, *Earth Beings: Ecologies of Practice Across Andean Worlds* (Durham: Duke University Press, 2015).

23. Adnan, *Journey*, 16–17.

24. Karen Barad, "Troubling Time/s and Ecologies of Nothingness: Re-turning, Re-membering, and Facing the Incalculable," *New Formations* 92 (2017): 83.

25. Barad, "Troubling Time/s," 83.

26. Noura Wetdell, "Etel Adnan: Responsibility to That Green," *Flash Art* 324, no. 52 (2019): 89.

27. Adnan, *Journey*, 21.

28. All preceding quotations are from Adnan, *Journey*, 40.

29. See Wikipedia, s.v. "Ranger Program," last modified September 10, 2019, 12:03, https://en.wikipedia.org/wiki/Ranger_program/.

30. Adnan, *Journey*, 40.

31. All preceding quotations are from Adnan, *Journey*, 41

32. Even when the text suddenly gives a precise date, seemingly referring to a NASA launch—"if you like numbers, I will tell you that here on earth it was February 14th, and it was spring: flowers were all around and a warm breeze was mixing my fever with the clouds" (for the dream, for the launch?)—that precision does not dissolve the density of time and place that has been generated. February 14 is Valentine's day, but neither Ranger 8 (February 17, 1965) nor Ranger 9 (March 21, 1965) were launched on February 14.

33. Barad, "Troubling Time/s," 68.

34. Both Barad, "Diffracting Diffraction," 168.

35. Barad "Diffracting Diffraction," 180–81.

36. Barad "Diffracting Diffraction," 181.

37. Both Barad, *Meeting*, 171.

38. Complicating the author/reader/text apparatus also entails that we mean more by diffractive reading than "merely" reading texts with and through each other, which is not all too far removed from classical comparatist procedures. Unless we destabilize the thought images of either representing a phenomenon *in* the world/text (depicting diffraction) or impartially enabling an unforeseen encounter of texts (facilitating diffraction), we run the risk of leaving largely in place our well-known critical distance, as if a reader or critic were merely the one giving room to the textual encounter.

39. For Walter Benjamin's *Jetztzeit* [now-time], see his "Theses on the Philosophy of History," in Benjamin, *Illuminations*, ed. Hannah Arendt (New York: Schocken, 1968), 261.

40. Anna Lowenhaupt Tsing, Heather Anne Swanson, Elaine Gan, and Nils Bubandt, eds, *Arts of Living on a Damaged Planet: Ghosts and Monsters of the Anthropocene* (Minneapolis: University of Minnesota Press, 2017).

41. Surely, there is good reason to reexamine how we read. On the one hand, digitalization indeed makes more data accessible much faster. On the other hand, close reading has run into practical challenges of linguistic skill. With increased critical awareness that especially the discipline of Comparative Literature is based on a very narrow, Eurocentric linguistic canon the practice of close linguistic engagement with texts bears the risk of structurally excluding non-European literatures. For a discussion of the latter, see Gayatri Ch. Spivak, *Death of a Discipline* (New York: Columbia University Press, 2003), especially her suggestion of stronger collaboration between literary studies and area studies in chapter one.

42. For defenses of close reading, the method inherited from the new critics' attention to the internal organization of literary texts, rhetorical composition, and aesthetic strategies, see for example, Gayatri Ch. Spivak, *Readings* (London: Seagull Books, 2014); for reading in translation resp. attending to untranslatability (David Damrosch, *How to Read World Literature?* (Hoboken: Wiley-Blackwell, 2008); Emily Apter, *The Translation Zone* (Princeton: Princeton University Press, 2004); Jacques Lezra, *Untranslating Machines: A Genealogy for the Ends of Global Thought* (London: Rowman & Littlefield International, 2017); for distant reading, affirming big data and machines' capacity to get larger sections of the archive into view and make palpable patterns in literary history, see Franco Moretti, *Distant Reading* (London: Verso, 2013); for surface reading, see Stephen Best and Sharon Marcus, "Surface Reading: An Introduction," *Representations* 108, no. 1 (2009): 1–21; for other post-critical propositions of reading aligned with surface reading, see Lucas Thompson, "Method Reading," *New Literary History* 50, no. 2 (2019): 293–321, and Annina Klappert in this volume for a diffractive attention to surface.

43. Both Best and Marcus, "Surface Reading," 3.
44. Best and Marcus, "Surface Reading," 12.
45. Best and Marcus, "Surface Reading," 9.
46. Best and Marcus, "Surface Reading," 11.
47. Both Best and Marcus, "Surface Reading," 16.
48. Both Best and Marcus, "Surface Reading," 18.
49. Barad "Diffracting Diffraction," 168.
50. Franco Moretti, "Patterns and Interpretation," *Stanford Literary Lab*, Pamphlet 15 (September 2017): 4, https://litlab.stanford.edu/pamphlets/.
51. Both Moretti, "Patterns," 4. Moretti notes that "pattern" derives etymologically from the French "*patron*" (master, owner, boss).
52. Moretti, "Patterns," 9.
53. Moretti, "Patterns," 4.
54. Moretti, "Patterns," 5.
55. Donna Haraway, "Modest_Witness@Second_Millennium," Chapter 7 in *The Haraway Reader* (New York: Routledge, 2004), 223.
56. The interventions are presented as advances in methodology and thus strive to make a difference; they are indeed patterning literary studies away from the (radical) hermeneutic traditions that championed close reading. Hence, my proposition that distant and surface reading's reassertion of the modest witness *returns* to the unmarked position of Man, which those critical traditions had questioned; see, for example, Jacques Derrida's 1967 essay "The Ends of Man," in *Margins Of Philosophy* (Chicago: Chicago University Press, 1982), 109–136.

57. All preceding Haraway, "Modest_Witness@Second_Millennium," 223–224.
58. Barad "Diffracting Diffraction," 181.
59. Barad, *Meeting*, 72.
60. Barad "Diffracting Diffraction," 181–182.
61. All quotations from Derek Attridge, *J.M. Coetzee and the Ethics of Reading: Literature in the Event* (Chicago: University of Chicago Press, 2004), 9.
62. Attridge, *Ethics of Reading*, 111.
63. Attridge calls this an "aestheticism . . . regarded as being defined precisely by the avoidance of political responsibility, by the vaunting of an artistic autonomy that has little interest in modes of otherness in cultural and political life." *Ethics of Reading*, 8.
64. Edward Said, *Culture & Imperialism* (London: Vintage, 1994), 78–80; see also Said, "Opponents, Audiences, Constituencies, and Community," in *The Politics of Interpretation*, ed. W. J. T. Mitchell, (Chicago: University of Chicago Press, 1982), 7–32.
65. Attridge, *Singularity*, 111.
66. Attridge, *Singularity*, 131. Gayatri Ch. Spivak has been making similar propositions for the *ethical* dimensions of a literary education and the praxis of reading. In *Readings*, she notes that what "training in literary reading offers beyond the conventional definition of literature" is "a painstaking learning of the language of the other." Furthermore, a literary education can thus also "direct one to noticing . . . otherwise ignored details," to pay attention to what has been marginalized. Spivak, *Readings*, 6 and 7.
67. Barad, *Meeting*, 171.
68. The term *co-in-habitation* is inspired by Kathrin Thiele's diffractive reading of Barad with Bracha L. Ettinger. Ettinger's "co/in-habit(u)ation" stresses, as Thiele highlights, the "superposition of habitat and habituation" and resonates with the "manifold entangled relations of Barad's quantum ontology." Thiele, "Ethos of Diffraction: New Paradigms for a (Post)humanist Ethics," *Parallax* 20, no. 3 (2014): 213, https://doi.org/10.1080/13534645.2014.927627.

Chapter 3

Heraclitus's Onto-stories

Impossible Appointments and the Importance of the Encounter

Max Walther

"Splashes in the water."

Kathrin Thiele and Birgit M. Kaiser, *Diffracted Worlds*

"What if this ghost were taken seriously? That is, what if it were understood that the point is not uncertainty after all—not man's knowledge measured against some present presence that is or some past-present that was—but rather, indeterminacy hauntological multiplicity—which, crucially, is not about Man once again, not about origins finally, nor the end of time?"

Karen Barad, "Quantum Entanglements"

GUIDELINES AND SEATBELTS

Heraclitus (520–460 BCE) is present-absent. His philosophical oeuvre,[1] presumed to have been compiled in a book that had no title, is missing. Fragments of his work were handed down through texts by Greek and Roman authors such as Plato, Aristotle, Hippolytus, Diogenes Laertius, in copy or quotes supposedly true to the original. Thus, his philosophy/theory, at the same time, does and does not exist. There is a long-standing and ongoing debate about the authenticity of this tradition, with which this chapter shall concern itself only in so far as the genesis of the corpus of Heraclitean words, that is, his philosophy as we are used to knowing and reading it, may usefully reflect on the questions discussed here.

Reading in and with, and through, an author/figure like Heraclitus, as well as writing encounters with and through texts from the inevitable view point of contemporaneity or *Zeitgenossenschaft*,[2] and, last, bringing together complex understandings of philosophies/philosophers across space and time always entails the risk of making the same mistake over and over again: stating origins, staging "father figures," reading as *stating* different scales. Enforced by bridging: effortlessly unreflectedly, bridges are constructed where there is neither water nor ditch. Reading and thinking with (or through) a certain notion of "history" and "historicity" by constantly simultaneously (re-)producing these constructs. Promoting linearity of time (and space), progress, finitude, or at least single points of a supposed—and therefore reassuring—finitude. Out of habit, or to simplify complex constellations like "life," "world," or "time" and "space." Theoretical seatbelts, which "we" should in fact cut loose.

And this cutting loose means reflecting on the quotation of Karen Barad above and on the (polemical) introduction: "we" do not need the idea of origins—because there is no such thing as *an/the* origin. Less do "we" need father figures. Even less *the* father figure. Twisting Whitehead's (in itself highly provocative) statement concerning the European history/making of philosophy, that is, "tradition," as "a series of footnotes to Plato"[3] turns the focus on a crucial point: it is not about a replacement. It is not about footnotes to Heraclitus. It is about a nonhierarchical, non-linear "reading insights through one another,"[4] without a somehow fixed and presupposed (spatial and chronological) constellation-thinking, that is, bridging. It is about *impossible appointments* and the/a *importance of the encounter*.

READING RELATA. RE-READING RELATIONALITY

To make my attempt comprehensible, I will draw attention to different concepts related to my understanding of *appointment* and *encounter* and by doing so address the inevitably arising questions concerning the relata that "meet" in an encounter. By highlighting the various ontological and epistemological implications of these concepts—especially: net(-work), meshwork, web, entanglement, and encounter [assemblage]—I will read them through, with and perhaps most importantly *against* the notion of diffraction, respectively, diffractive/-ed reading. By encountering them—the text(s), the reading, and the reader—my aim is neither to discredit these concepts nor to supersede or replace them in the sense of a new (truth-giving) paradigm, but to expose them, that is, encounter them through one another, to sharpen my/a possible definition for further diffractive investigation and intervention.

After working out these methodological groundings and the outlining of a reading practice, I will focus on Heraclitus's philosophy. Reading his fragments in the context of this chapter means highlighting the nexus between ontology and epistemology in discussing the in-forming of "our" relationship to "the" world—*in-forming* both in the sense of giving sense and giving shape. A short detour to the rivalry between Heraclitus and the atomists, especially Democritus, and the reception of both in a (new) materialist tradition is indispensable for an im/possible conclusion to the discussion of these concepts. Moving further, I will introduce my understanding of the "onto-story,"[5] which will lead to questions related to the fundamental relationship between writing about fluidity—in a diffracting/diffracted fashion—and the "result" of such a writing, that is, texts/fragments. At this point, it will be possible to foreground the becoming of text(s) by "specifying the apparatus"[6]—the text, the reading/translating/editing/commenting/picking up and the reader—to possibly move beyond both Roland Barthes's concept of the "birth of the reader"[7] and the Constance-school Reader-Response Criticism (aesthetics of reception).[8] The aim is to open up for intra-active reading insights through one another, for a diffractive/-ed reading. Hence, this moving beyond is to be understood as a chance both for literary criticism and (literary) intervention. Because, as one can state with Barad (moving through Derrida), "in an intra-active reading, not only texts" and the reader "are made to matter, but 'world' is also in the making."[9]

The (inter)relational concepts mentioned above all reflect the way "we" are *in* and *of* the world. In my opinion, they share some crucial similarities: first, they break with the idea of a given world, consisting of pure, silent, and inactive matter that is "there" to be reflected on by (Cartesian) subjects. Because, arguably, matter is not simply out there, to be observed and objectified or to be regarded as the other, waiting passively to be ruled by human subjects. Second, these concepts arouse in themselves questions related to what "we" call agency. They are set up to re-think and in a second step to shatter "our" understanding of human supremacy: it is not about isolated human subjects acting in and upon the material world that surrounds them, but about thinking subjectivity, matter, worlding in terms of relations. And in terms of active processes: of *becomings*. Therefore, they (also) break with the very idea of social constructivism that gives all power to the human subject, that is, the (human) mind, as the master of the universe.

In some respect, all of this is related to a tradition of materialist thinking—although I want to stress that "the/a tradition of materialistic thinking" is to be understood as an ongoing dialogue; these concepts foreground (inter-)

activity in the sense of (social) practices that in-form (our understandings of) the world(s). Stepping beyond the anthropocentrism that is inscribed in most lines of this tradition, the concepts under discussion offer a somehow different approach: by stating and reflecting on an active role of matter in the very processes of *worlding* they shift "our" attention to the relationality of these becomings. Reflecting upon relationality means—thinking especially through Bohr/Barad—to question the relata in relationality. To be precise: the link between (new) materialist conceptions and the atomistic thesis must be revised, at least be discussed. The atom, as in the reading of Louis Althusser or even Gilles Deleuze, to mention just two names, as the smallest, indivisible and disjunctive entity to be somehow traced back as the/a constituent and therefore as the/a relata of (contingent and/or accidental) encounters seems central to many (new) materialist conceptions, which must, however, really be read *against* an intra-active account. Thinking the pre-existence of entities that encounter—even by grasping the un/thinkable smallest unit—seems to fall back to the realm of (logocentric) distance-making and (*inter*active) disjunction.

A CRITICAL SURVEY: NETS, WEBS, AND MESHES

Impossible Appointments and the Importance of the Encounter

Stating and staging a relational ontology that cannot be separated from its epistemological dimensions, as Barad attempts, leads to a discussion of the in-forming of world(s) and necessitates a critical survey. As shown above, there are concepts, thinking patterns, and starting points that do not take the easy way out: not taking as a given the (ontological and epistemological) division of subject and object/matter, a powerful human mind reigning supremely, or a fixed, somehow transcendental order to be inhabited. Instead, relationality is thought differently and so is the notion of difference.

MESH(-WORK)

It was Bruno Latour who, in his Actor–network theory (ANT), offered a profound conceptualization of "networks."[10] It centres around, and foregrounds questions of agency and the relation between subject and object by focusing on the site of encounters (the laboratory, the experimental ground). His theoretical and methodological approach highlights the empirical observation of phenomena. These phenomena occur when objects, ideas, processes, subjects, and objects interact (at present) in networks, re-focusing the very perspective on observation and knowledge production as well as matter and materialization. His networks are nonhierarchical structures: they include rather than exclude; actors and actants are on the same level, there is no in- and outside, "everything" in the natural and social world interacts in constantly shifting networks. Instead of disjunctions and somehow given and fixed distinctions, relationality and interaction set the tone.

In ANT, meaning-making and knowledge production seem to overshadow the ontological dimension in some respect; instead, the focus is on the very nature of the inter-/intra-acting relata. Without doubt, ANT has had a huge impact on the so-called "neomaterialist debate" or "material turn" and therefore on the shift to a non-anthropocentric perspective toward the in-forming(s) of world. Latour's operative ontology is to be regarded as a great contribution to that ongoing debate and further investigation on the relationship between diffraction and ANT could be fruitful. In this spirit, I want to shortly focus on meshworks, read as a critical continuation of ANT.

British anthropologist Tim Ingold established the concept of meshworks, reading it against a particular notion of network, counterpointing the implicit and explicit implications of that concept. To define his concept, Ingold writes in *Making: Anthropology, Archaeology, Art and Architecture*:

> By this [a meshwork] I mean an entanglement of interwoven lines. These lines may loop or twist around one another or weave in and out. Crucially, however, they do not connect. This is what distinguishes the meshwork from the network. The lines of the network are connectors, each given as the relation between two points, independently and in advance of any movement from one toward the other ... the lines of a meshwork, by contrast, are of movement or growth. They are temporal "lines of becoming."[11]

Coming from Deleuze and Guattari, Ingold takes up the idea of becoming rather than that of "being," working on an ontology of becoming instead of being. In contrast to the notion of networks, Ingold proposes the idea that the relata, and therefore the relations of meshworks do not pre-exist, they are not "given ... independently and in advance [of any movement]." Further, Ingold claims that "where the network has nodes, the meshwork ... has knots" with "loose ends," "somewhere beyond the knot, where it is groping towards an entanglement with other lines, in other knots."[12]

To further distinguish Latour's network from Ingold's meshwork, it is helpful to have a look on knowledge production, that is, knowledge transferability and exchangeability. In *Point, Line, Counterpoint: From Environment to Fluid Space*,[13] Ingold re-reads Latour's concept of the "immutable and combinable mobiles"[14]—which Latour established in his discussion on how information, that is, knowledge, is passed between agents—confronting it with the concept of "liquid space" and/or "mutable mobiles."[15] Introduced by

Annemarie Mol and John Law, these two concepts question Latour's claim of the actant's invariability to make information/knowledge transmission possible and propose a different approach that focuses on the actant's/actor's (inevitable) transformation in the processes of transfers. Ingold takes up this idea to further develop his theory of relations and meshworks.

Clearly, Ingold's dynamic, processual, and highly temporal conception of the mesh(-work), and his highly productive speaking of "knots," "threads," and "loose ends" reaches beyond the realm of inter-activity. Still I suspect that his anthropological philosophy does not quite reach the field of intra-activity as suggested by the term "entanglement."

ENCOUNTER

"La rencontre" is a concept popularized by Deleuze and picked up among others by Jane Bennett. There seems to be a specific proximity to the concept of assemblages (agencements), denoting a complex constellation of objects, bodies, expressions, qualities, and territories "that come together for varying periods of time to ideally create new ways of functioning."[16] As it is understood as an important key to Deleuze's and Guattari's "philosophy of becoming," it seems worth to question the nature of the Deleuzian encounter, that is, to trace back the relata that encounter in "la rencontre."

Deleuze's and Guattari's philosophy of becoming is certainly relational: what "we" consider by thinking, seeing, grasping is not fixed or stable, not given (in a metaphysical or transcendental order) but assemblages in process, in which relations and relationality are foregrounded as "condition" for (the) becoming.

Hints concerning the underlying nature of the entities (human and nonhuman /material and nonmaterial) that encounter in assemblages can be found in Deleuze's reading of ancient atomism (Lucretius and Epicurus) in *Repetition and Difference*, *Lucretius and the Simulacrum* and in *What is Philosophy* where Deleuze "recognizes Epicurean atomism as an attempt to formalize a conception of problematic ideas," as Michael James Bennett puts it.[17] Reading Epicurus, Deleuze conceives of, by simultaneously problematizing, ideas as multiplicities of atoms: "atoms being the objective elements of thought."[18]

Deleuze is in line with a particular (materialist) tradition in which ontology is bound to the atomistic thesis. This tradition would define the relata as bundles of bits or atoms that (accidentally and/or contingently) met/encountered in falling into the void, to speak with Lucretius. In assuming these bundles, "we" are forced to think a pre-existence of the smallest unit, bit or atom, which exists independently even if there is nothing/anybody who could name, grasp or conceive it, as Louis Althusser puts it.[19] It is there without a "here-there-anywhere," it is before without a "then-now." But "there" in a specific sense of *everything's* origin. "There" as *everything's* part in advance. The most interesting and innovative part in Deleuze's reading of Epicurean atomism seems to me his reconceptualization of the role or function of the *clinamen*, that is, the swerve of atoms—understood as an encounter—that leads to emergencies. The swerve as the generative momentum, as put by Lucretius: "When theses bodies (atoms) are being drawn downwards by their own weight straight through the void, at totally uncertain times and uncertain places they turn aside a little in space, just so much that you could call their motion changed. Because if they were not accustomed to swerve, everything would fall downwards through the deep void, like drops of rain, no collision would occur and no blows be effected among the atoms: nature would not have created anything."[20] But against other, for example, Democritus's conception of "forced motion" or the Greek "theory of fate," Deleuze proposes a theory of the immanent self-determination of atoms that confronts a/the tradition of thinking and conceptualizing indeterminacy. Deleuze writes: "it is indeed essential that atoms be related to other atoms at the heart of structures that are actualized in sensible composites. In this regard, the clinamen (swerve) is by no means a change of direction in the movement of an atom, much less an indetermination testifying to the existence of a physical freedom. It is the original determination of the direction of movement, the synthesis of movement and its direction which relates one atom to another."[21] In emphasizing an original determination of the direction of movement, Deleuze proposes a specific principle for atomic collision that confronts the idea of contingency (in a complex way). By bringing together the speed (and their direction of movement) of atoms and the speed of thought (derived not at least from a re-reading of Epicurus's theory of *eidola*, as Bennett argues) in his re-configuration of the swerve (clinamen) as determined, or more precisely the determination of a relation among atoms, he is able to formulate a specific materialism of thought that topples both "our" understanding of materialism and thought, as well as a "our" approach to the idea of origins.

Despite the mentioned reservations concerning the pre-existing relata in an atomistic cosmology, following Deleuze's concept of the encounter brings a specific agency/motivation of any atom into discussion. Deleuze's approach, especially his sensibility for the principles (the "how" instead of a "why") of encounters or collisions seems to me an important step in the line of thinking a relational ontology, epistemology, and ethics and toward an intra-active account.

ENTANGLEMENT/(ENTANGLED) WEBS

Moving further in the field of relational ontology, two theoretically less-determined terms need to be considered: entanglement and the (entangled) web. Often used synonymously, the two concepts imply a theoretical standpoint in which the nature of the relata is explicitly addressed.

Frequently used by Karen Barad, Donna Haraway, and Vicky Kirby, entanglement expresses a specific multiplicity or superposition of "beings, becomings, here and there's,"[22] which won't melt into some kind of unity with erased or concealed differences. As Barad puts it: "entanglings entail differentiatings, differentiatings entail entanglings. One move—cutting together-apart."[23] Entanglement therefore allows us to think difference differently by disrupting the binary as well as the very idea of cutting apart as one (necessary cognitive) move and putting together as a second (necessary cognitive) move: two operations that are usually neatly separate but become fused in the notion of the entanglement. Furthermore, and most importantly, thinking in and with entanglements breaks with the idea of pre-existing entities. Instead, the ontology of entities relies on involvement(s) in (entangled) webs or entanglements. Relata emerge through relationality. To quote Thiele:

> Seeing entities emerging through intra-active relationality prioritize relations so fundamentally that this not only implies that each and everything is logically effectuated by relations that ontologically come first ... but that each and everything is necessarily the temporary and historical product of the most specific—always concrete and mattering—constellation.[24]

This shift in perspective, by considering entities as fundamentally relationally, processually, and asymmetrically produced, queers "our" (classical) understanding of relationality. And therefore, also our understanding of concepts like identity and difference that were/are based on this notion of relationality. A supposed pre-existence of the relata within entanglements, as in the atomic thesis, is made groundless. When we use the prefix *inter* "we" need to think given entities, for example, relata, that (inter-)act to form a "new" entity, for example, a network, meshwork, an assemblage. Stating and staging a fundamentally relational ontology makes it necessary to reconsider this prefix and to change it, in accordance with a profound change in conceptual thinking, from *inter-* to *intra*(-action)—a "profound connectional shift"[25] indeed!

Reading diffraction with Barad's concept of agential intra-activity in mind, which means to think "the" universe/"the" world as agential intra-activity in its becoming and therefore to consider not things (or atoms and bits) as the primary ontological units but "phenomena"—"dynamic topological reconfigurations/entanglements/relationalities/rearticulations"[26]—allows us to sharpen our notion of diffraction and its implications. Diffraction then "expresses these 'entangled relationalities', which includes the entanglement of the observers within any process of meaning-making."[27] Neither human bodies/subjects nor matter pre-exist as such. As parts *of* the world in its open-ended becoming and its ongoing materialization they emerge through intra-activity in entanglements. "[D]iffraction not only brings the reality of entanglements to light, it is itself an entangled phenomenon"[28]—a conceptual shift which marks both entanglement and diffraction off from the concepts discussed above, despite their family likeness. The degree of *involvement* (with implications both for the ontological as well as the epistemological dimension) could be read as an effective demarcation line in this marking off.

With this in mind—and the applicability of diffraction and entanglement for literary intervention and critique as a major concern—it becomes possible to think world itself as becoming diffraction pattern(s), "and with it 'knowing, thinking, measuring, theorizing, and observing'" as "material practices of intra-action within and as part of the world." "Things matter and theory never is a purely epistemological undertaking. Which cuts are made ... will make a difference—and necessarily so because these cuts constitute ('are') the very plane from-with everything emerges."[29]

"We do not obtain knowledge by standing outside of the world; we know because 'we' are of the world." The diffracted reading, which is proposed here, relies upon that "of," the very *of* in comparison to a more classical "in." As Kaiser puts it, "we" are of the world and not in the world. Always-already entangled, always-already part of the processes of worlding. Therefore, reading, thinking, theorizing does not take place in and from a distance to the world, but as a (material) practice it is to be understood as "one form of intra-action with/in it." The reader, the reading, the text[s] emerge in encountering; therefore, not only is the text "made to matter"—as, for example, already in reader-response-criticism—but "world is also in the making." Reading, thinking, and theorizing is worlding—considering *both* the epistemological and ontological dimension, which in thinking diffraction as a practice therefore remain inseparable.[30]

(HERACLITUS'S) ONTO-STORIES

Borrowed from Jane Bennett, and slightly removed out of its original context, the term "onto-story" or "onto-tale" denotes a type of writing that both writes "the" world as actor-networks, assemblages or ecologies and is itself a practice of intervention. In her book *Vibrant Matter*, she seeks to establish a "new" concept of ethical thinking, also including (ecological) responsibility. "One moral of the story," Bennett states right at the beginning, is "that we are also nonhuman and that things, too, are vital players in the world." The postulated aim of such a re-writing would then be, to "generate a more subtle awareness of the complicated web of dissonant connections between bodies" that "will enable wiser interventions into that ecology." And: "The story will highlight the extent to which human being and thinghood overlap, the extent to which the us and the it slip-slide into each other."[31] The aim of re-shaping the "it" and "we/us" and re-focusing interconnections and interactivities is to overcome the binary structure of s/Subject and o/Object. This re-orientation of perception, in which epistemology and ontology of subject and object are not separated, challenging the assumption that "we" are *in* the world with the suggestion that "we" are actually *of* the world. It makes us question the *how* and the *what* of writing. In-forming occurs again in its double meaning: as the "forming" in "informing" and the "informing" in "forming." Because in this understanding of the onto-story, it is not about a reading-writing of the entangled nature of world from high above, settled in an (impossible and therefore) artificial distance but about the grasping of a practise of reading-writing as always-already entangled: not in interactions but in intra-actions. Furthermore, it is not about a representation of the entanglement (or encounter) in writing but about the impossibility of such representations. The writer-reader is always-already part of the encounter, for example, entangled, and there is no outside (as a precondition for representation) where to stand and to observe from. Everything is inside. And being part of is to be understood as not pre-existing the encounter. Stepping in and out (again)—as in a more classical conception of participating in observing—is impossible. Onto-taling and diffracted/-ive reading come together at that point as an inseparable *ethico-onto-epistemological* operation.

The riddle as well as the fragment (fragmentary reading-writing) are to be considered as "the" (supposedly) most suitable form of expression for an intra-active onto-story, as *form* and *content* overlap/intra-act. Reading the fragmentary, starting with Maurice Blanchot and George Bataille, continuing with the conceptional re-workings and (theoretical) widening by Jacques Derrida and Paul de Man as a never-ending process of confrontations, shifts and transfers and as an open dialogue (which collapses the concept of linear time) is to open a discussion about the relationship between the fragmentary and the very idea of intra-action, for example, onto-taling and diffracted/-ive reading. The supposed endlessness of a text, its never-ceasing ongoing or movement correlates with the conception of unstable (but relational or operative) ontology in its entanglement with epistemology and ethics. The fragment as a specific and somehow necessary mode of expression seems to meet, by simultaneously exposing or staging, the challenge. Namely, the *how* to write (and read) diffractively.

This takes us back to Heraclitus and the discussions of his time and sheds some light onto my suggestion that his fragmentary texts and the concept of onto-story, even though applied out of its contemporary context, share a similar philosophical relevance.

In defiance of Heraclitus, the Riddler, Plato argued:

> Then if it never stays the same, how can it *be* something? ... for at the very instant the knower-to-be approaches, what he is approaching is becoming a different thing ... so that he can't yet come to know either what sort of thing it is or what it is like.[32]

HERACLITUS'S (ONTO-STORIES)

As I said earlier, Heraclitus is present-absent. His words, his philosophy/theory, both do and do not exist. Plato's *Cratylus* is probably the best witness to this: letting Heraclitus speak through Socrates in his dialogue with Hermogenes, Plato hands down supposedly authentic, philosophical quotes, simultaneously commenting on them to make his point. By reading his own philosophy (diverted in and by the very form of the dialogue) through Heraclitean theory, he produces or creates the latter in inter-/intra-activity.

One could now argue that, definitely since Roland Barthes' "birth of the reader" or the development of reader-response-criticism, there is no text without a reader/reading and therefore this remark may seem like a pointless repetition of long-established theoretical approaches. But I would argue that this particular case is different. Not least of all because I would argue that Heraclitus could be regarded as a/the theorist of diffraction *avant la lettre* and in some way a diffractive writer-philosopher whose philosophy should itself be read diffractively.

ONE: PANTHA RHEI'

Even if the provenance of the phrase *phanta rhei* as well as the comparison of things to the "stream of a river you cannot step twice into" is not verifiable, as argued earlier, the famous formula "all things flow" is connected to Heraclitus's ontology of becoming. Read as a paraphrase, or a chain of paraphrases, rather than as a quotation, this formula (both form and content considered) addresses exactly our questions: not only the problems concerning the/a becoming of text(s) through inter- versus intra-activity but also the questions concerning the nexus of epistemology and ontology, for example, the production or emergence of knowledge and/in the very practice of mattering in a broader sense. Focusing on the first set of questions, it seems clear that there is no (material) text but only reading(s). There are only encounters (to come) and, in a strict sense, no pre-existing relata. Relata in becoming, unstable in an "all things flow." Still becoming. Still flowing.

Focusing on the second part, and reading Heraclitus in an anti-Platonic way means to deny the assumption of stable being(s) to be observed—as in the quote by Plato above, marked by the very idea of an objective "observer" who "approaches" phenomena—and to highlight the very idea of becoming. As Clement of Alexandria rephrases Heraclitus: "Most men do not think things in the way they encounter them, nor do they recognize what they experience, but believe in their own opinions."[33] The testifying authority is not outside, but inside, always-already entangled in the very process of (impossible) "observation." It is entangled becoming/experience versus presupposed concepts/being, for example, therefore most explicitly versus Plato's theory of ideas. The insistence on "experience," of worldly and mattering intra-action in Heraclitus annuls all forms of metaphysics and/or transcendentalism underlying the idea of being. "Whatever comes from sight, hearing, learning from experience: this I prefer" "quotes" Hippolytus from Heraclitus.[34] Both the emphasis on experience as well as the highlighting of the chaos, the entangled chaotic state of the world (and cosmos) that Heraclitus does not seek to segregate (unlike Parmenides, Plato in his succession and continued by the theorists of the Deleuzian *major tradition*[35]) point toward a materialist commitment in Heraclitus philosophy. Even the very idea of "logos" is connected to everyday practice and not bound up with transcendental thought. As Theophrastus quotes Heraclitus on that: "The fairest order in the world is a heap of random sweepings."[36] The world (as well as the cosmos) is neither ordered nor structured. The very notion of "sweepings"—in other translations "manure" or "muck" or "midden"—refers to an anti-structure; therefore, it emphasizes the idea of becoming in an endless flowing.

TWO: LIGHTNING AND WATER

Whereas Parmenides, who is often regarded as Heraclitus' antipode, established a philosophy of segregation—the world of gods separated from the world of men, ideas separate from reality—Heraclitus' approach is less speculative. Orientated on empirical everyday life experience, he seeks to understand the un/ordered (chaos) by being involved. Involvement in this particular context stands in opposition to speculation and reflection as operations in which the idea as well as the practise of both inside and outside are posited. As Polybius quotes Heraclitus on knowledge production and wisdom, for example, on reflecting the state of the world: "In taking the poets as testimony for the things unknown, they are citing authorities that cannot be trusted."[37] As in ancient times, knowledge production and transfer was not, as we (think to) know it today, neatly separable from poetics, and poets were in fact a reference and source of "proper" philosophical insight, this Heraclitean fragment could be read as another hint to his unorthodox "everyday-life-philosophy."

Reading Heraclitus on knowledge production, on the inseparable entanglement and on "sweepings" as anti-principle of order leads to the question of origins. In examining being (einai), philosophy seeks to name *the* origin (of everything). Leaving the question of *the* or an origin aside, but highlighting the openness of becoming, as Heraclitus does, breaks with the notion of philosophical certainty. "Philosophia," the love of wisdom traditionally posits knowing the origin (of everything) as the greatest and most desirable wisdom: in Thales of Miletus' cosmological thesis it is water,[38] Anaximenes of Miletus proposes the (ambiguous substance) "apeiron" as "arche," the underlying material of the world,[39] and so on. In Heraclitus, "we" find neither approach nor explanation: It is *openness*, *becoming*, the *cyclic* and, not least, *contingency* "we" encounter.[40] "It rests by changing,"[41] Plotinus paraphrases the Heraclitean theory of becoming. But it does not change according to some hidden plan or (super-)natural law; rather, this conception of change implies contingency—expressed firstly in the idea of flowing water, second in Heraclitus's theorem of the "thunderbolt" that "pilots all things"[42] and, last, as Alexander Kluge in discussion with Oskar Negt puts it, in the Heraclitean notion of "war" and "conflict."[43]

THREE: RIVER READINGS

"As they step into the same river, other and still other waters flow upon them," Arius Didymus paraphrases the famous saying by Heraclitus. Interestingly, in this version, it reads like it is only the water[s] that change[s]. "Other and still other waters" supersedes in some regard the question of who and how things change by implicating that the prominently situated "they" stays the same, a stable and unquestioned entity in being. As opposed to that, reading the version in Plutarch makes a difference. "One cannot step twice into the same river, nor can one grasp any mortal substance in a stable condition, but it scatters and again gathers; it forms and dissolves, and approaches and departs."[44] In this version, which side is the active and which the passive one, that is, the source of agency, is not obvious anymore. One/they is not excluded from the principle of becoming at the very outset. *All* "things" flow. And it is, I would argue in the first place, not the "same river" because the "one" can never be the same. Second, I would argue that "river" as well as the "one" are emerging in the intra-action and not pre-existing (as such) the encounter or entanglement. There is ground left neither for constructivist perspectives nor for anthropo- or logo-centrism: the ontology *and* epistemology of the "one" *and* the river is bound to the stepping (in), for example, to the encounter through which the relata emerge—becoming in intra-action: "as relata-within-phenomena" emerging "through specific intra-actions." With that in mind, Heraclitus's river fragment could be read as a perfect (didactical) illustration of diffraction's idea: the emergence of relata-within-phenomena through (specific) intra-actions whereby matter comes to matter and knowledge is produced. In that, intra-action "enact[s]," as Barad formulates it, "an agential cut," which "effect[s] a separation between subject and object that allows a certain "agential separability."[45]

FOUR: DIFFERENT DIFFERENCE

Thinking and reading difference differently is at the heart of many feminist projects (Donna Haraway, Trinh Minh-ha, and others), in which (among other things) the ethical dimension of "becomings," for example, materializations thought of as processes and meaning-making considered as part of these processes, is discussed. With Haraway and Thiele, ethics are inscribed into the conceptualization of diffraction. "Taking diffraction as a possibility to move beyond the persisting binary logic of difference inherited from the history of Western philosophy"[46] brings up questions of a "new" way of thinking difference. Thinking and reading not the "apartheid type of difference," as Trinh Minh-ha belligerently put it, but a thinking and reading of difference that is neither "opposed to sameness, nor synonymous with separateness." A different difference, as a disruption of the binary, which accepts that there are "differences as well as similarities within the concept of difference."[47] Trinh Minh-ha's brilliant notion of the "apartheid type" exposes the hegemonic structure of this simplification of difference in Western philosophy, which, although it paved the way to racism, fascism or sexism, "we" still acknowledge everywhere-everytime. Stepping aside and (re-)focusing difference differently means giving up the easy way and earning to think again. Thinking (and reading) anew with a pre-Socratic philosopher like Heraclitus could be helpful in this. Branded as a Riddler or "the" Obscure, Heraclitus as a "Western philosopher" annuls (in a particular reading) the very idea of the given and fixed binary that prepared the ground for the "apartheid type of difference." By reading Nietzsche reading Heraclitus' fragments like "They do not comprehend how a thing agrees at variance with itself; it is an attunement turning back on itself [like that of a bow and the lyre]," "The way up and down is one and the same" or even "Graspings: wholes and not wholes, convergent divergent, consonant dissonant, from all things one and from one thing all."[48] And by reading Nietzsche reading Spinoza (while thinking Spinoza reading Heraclitus), then reading Deleuze reading Nietzsche, Spinoza and Heraclitus, and "finally" (in an improper sense) to read Barad reading Bohr with Bohr reading[49] ... one will slowly get attuned to a different thinking of difference, in which difference, and maybe contradiction, is to be affirmed and grasped in a more productive way—less destructive, to be sure, than most conceptions of difference in Western philosophy. A thinking in which "a wave" is queered, a thinking in which the "binary light-darkness story" is to be retold, a cat is dead and alive at the same time or the way up and down is one and the same. Difficult graspings which change the footing on which "we" meet, read and think. The Obscure encounters Derridean-Baradian ghosts: "Mystery is alive and well in physics ... Physics has always been spooked."[50]

RE-READING ENDS

There are many names, concepts, and illustrations for a simple fact: there is no end to and for a text. Polyp, rhizome, fragment, or mycelium . . . it all boils down to the one quotable phrase: a text has neither a beginning nor an end. There are surely texts that suggest having something like a beginning and something like an end, but the closer one looks, as deeper one dives, beginning and end fade and get loose. This is in some respect a twentieth-century agreement.

"Our" twenty-first-century challenge, adventure, and most importantly (ethical) responsibility is to move further and to diffract "us," "our" thinking habits as well as "our" reading practices. It is to intersect the maxims of "our" neoliberal, racist, biopolitical, and exclusive present. It is to read and write against tradition, understood both as a concept and as a multiplicity of implications, to "finally" (again in an improper sense) being able to grasp reading as an interventionalist practice "anew."

Reading Heraclitus's fragments through and with the readings and writings of "his" translators-, commentators-, or simply readers-to-become as proposed here, does not mean to follow chronological time as a specific politics of temporality in which one moment is superseded by the next and there is (a) past and (a) present but no future yet. Rather is it about a concept of (in-)folded time which breaks with the very idea of chronology and therefore with a conceptualization of causality as an inevitability of it. Time and temporality are queered, so that "Zeitgenossenschaft" is to be grasped differently: as a model of "thinking encounters" that operates in and with diachronic time and therefore intersects succession and sequentiality to foreground a certain coexistence. It is Deleuze's "philosophical time" that comes to mind, as a "static time that does not follow simple successive orders of before and after but "superimposes" before and after on coexisting planes that converge and diverge at different points,"[51] or as Deleuze puts it: "Philosophy is becoming, not history; it is the coexistence of planes, not the succession of systems."[52]

Thinking and reading "Zeitgenossenschaft" in that way allows not only to re-conceptualize the/a concept of "the" encounter and its im/possibilities but it also sheds a different light on the idea of "reading insights through one another" as one that is in the strict sense worlding: a co-creative and co-operative reading-writing understood as an act of both resistance and freedom. A step forwards to a rearranging ethical responsibility. Furthermore, this refocusing gives way to a re-thinking of the very notion of "distance" and "reflection." Distance is toppled by an including and entangling proximity in intra-action, and reflection as a model that is based on distance is superseded, too, in the toppling. The idea of a mirroring reflection as a form of "simple" dis- or replacement of the "s/Same" is superseded by diffraction—is diffracted itself. To apply these assumptions on readings and reading practices would then mean to grasp coexisting planes and superpositions as grounds for encountering texts. Not assumed to be somehow simply "there," fixed and stable but as to-be-emerging in the encounter by subject-readers that *are* not (by thinking or reading) but that are to come, for example, that emerge in intra-active reading(s), which is, as mentioned above, to be understood as intra-active worlding(s). Reading and worlding are not separable in a diffracted/ive reading: as "any diffractive reading involves inevitably the affirmation of a diffracted/ing world, and thereby also has to tackle what 'world' implies from within such a practice."[53]

Heraclitus's onto-stories, which would better be named *onto-epistem-ethico-stories*, and which model a diffractive reading in a diffracted world, read together and through—or dreamed with, to stretch a concept of ghostly intra-action by Hans Jürgen von der Wense[54]—the various reworkings (Marx, Plato, Heidegger, Nietzsche, Plutarch, and many more that coexist) puts into question what texts are and how to read them. Even more, it puts into question what and who and where this "I" is that speaks with and through, while the It-I worlds (It-I-self) are always-already entangled by being part of the endless flow. By being always-already in the river. As and with "splashes in the water" on a plane of (spooky) coexistence. To read and write means then to become aware of this very fact without getting haunted or, as Eve Sedgwick would put it, without getting paranoid.[55]

NOTES

1. For this chapter, I worked with Charles Kahn's book *The Art and Thought of Heraclitus* (Cambridge: Cambridge University Press, 2001), a translation and critical collection of Heraclitus's fragments with annotations, commentary, and many useful references that helps the reader to navigate through Heraclitus's thoughts as well as through the numerous philosophical and philological debates since 460 BCE.

2. My notion and understanding of *Zeitgenossenschaft* comes from reading Deleuze on history, philosophical time, and conceptual personae in his books *What is Philosophy*, trans. Hugh Tomilson and Graham Burchell (New York: Columbia University Press, 1991) and *Difference and Repetition*, trans. Paul Patton (London: Continuum, 2001).

3. Alfred North Whitehead, *Process and Reality: An Essay in Cosmology* (New York: The Free Press, 1978), 39.

4. Karen Barad, *Meeting the Universe Halfway: Quantum Physics and the Entanglement of Matter and Meaning* (Durham: Duke University Press, 2007), 71.

5. Jane Bennett, *Vibrant Matter: A Political Ecology of Things* (Durham: Duke University Press, 2010), 4.

6. Birgit Mara Kaiser, "Worlding CompLit: Diffractive Reading with Barad, Glissant and Nancy," *Parallax* 20, no. 3 (2014): 276, https://doi.org/10.1080/13534645.2014.927634.

7. Roland Barthes, "The Death of the Author," trans. Richard Howard, *Aspen: The Magazin in a Box*, no. 5+6 (Fall-Winter 1967): item 3 (web documentation), accessed August 7, 2019, http://www.ubu.com/aspen/aspen5and6/threeEssays.html#barthes.

8. My reference here is to Wolfgang Iser and Hans-Robert Jauss or the so-called *Konstanzer Rezeptionsästhetik*. For further readings, see Wolfgang Iser's *The Implied Reader: Patterns of Communication in Prose Fiction from Bunyan to Beckett* (Baltimore: John Hopkins University Press, 2011); Hans-Robert Jauss' *Toward an Aesthetic of Reception*, trans. Timothy Bahti (Minneapolis: University of Minnesota Press, 2013).

9. Kaiser, "Worldling CompLit," 276.

10. Bruno Latour, *Reassembling the Social: An Introduction to Actor-Network-Theory* (Oxford: Oxford University Press, 2005).

11. Tim Ingold, *Making: Anthropology, Archaeology, Art and Architecture* (London: Routledge, 2013), 132.

12. See note 11.

13. Tim Ingold, "Point, Line and Counterpoint: From Environment to Fluid Space," in *Neurobiology of "Umwelt," How Living Beings Perceive the World,* ed. A. Berthoz and Yves Christen (Berlin: Springer, 2009), 141–155.

14. Bruno Latour, *Science in Action: How to Follow Scientists and Engineers through Society* (Cambridge: Harvard University Press, 1987).

15. Annemarie Mol and John Law, "Regions, Networks and Fluids: Anaemia and Social Topology," *Social Studies of Science* 24, no. 4 (1994): 641–71.

16. Graham Livesey, "Assemblage," in *The Deleuze Dictionary*, ed. Adrian Parr (Edinburgh: Edinburgh University Press, 2010), 18.

17. Michael James Bennett, "Deleuze and the Epicurean Philosophy: Atomic Speed and Swerve Speed," *Journal of French and Francophone Philosophy – Revue de la philosophie française et de la langue française* XXI, no. 2 (2013): 131.

18. Deleuze, *Difference and Repetition*, 184. Gilles Deleuze's "theory of ideas" which he unfolds in *Difference and Repetition* is a complex re-reading of concepts such as difference, metaphysics, transcendence, and so on, which cannot be

summarized in one sentence here. Nor can the impact of ancient atomism on Deleuze – scholars who know Deleuze's philosophy better than me, may therefore forgive me for this (necessary) reduction and somewhat polemical demand to re-read Deleuze concerning "his" atomistic rooting.

19. Louis Althusser, "The Underground Current of the Materialism of the Encounter," in *Philosophy of the Encounter: Later Writings, 1978*-87, trans. G. M. Goshgarian (London: Verso, 2006).

20. Bennett, "Deleuze and the Epicurean Philosophy," 136.

21. Deleuze, *Difference and Repetition*, 185.

22. Karen Barad, "Diffracting Diffraction: Cutting Together-Apart," in *Diffracted Worlds – Diffractive Readings: Onto-Epistemologies and the Critical Humanities*, edited by Birgit Mara Kaiser and Kathrin Thiele (London: Routledge, 2018), 12.

23. Ibid.

24. Kathrin Thiele, "Ethos of Diffraction: New Paradigms for a (Post)humanist Ethics," in Kaiser and Thiele, *Diffracted Worlds*, 42.

25. Karen Barad, "Posthumanist Performativity: Toward an Understanding of How Matter Comes to Matter." *Signs: Journal of Women in Culture and Society* 28, no. 3 (2003): 815.

26. Barad, *Meeting the Universe Halfway*, 141.

27. Birgit Mara Kaiser and Kathrin Thiele, preface to Kaiser and Thiele, *Diffracted Worlds*, xiii.

28. Thiele, "Ethos of Diffraction," 41.

29. Ibid., 42, 40.

30. Quotations in this paragraph from Kaiser, "Worldling CompLit," 277, 282, 276.

31. All preceding quotations are from Bennett, *Vibrant Matter*, 4.

32. Plato, "Cratylus," in *Complete Works*, ed. John M. Cooper and trans. C.D.C. Reeve (Indianapolis: Hackett Publishing Company, 1997), 155, line 1440.

33. Kahn, *The Art and Thought*, 28.

34. Kahn, *The Art and Thought*, 35.

35. See Deleuze, Gilles, *What is Philosophy?* Further readings on the distinction between minor and major tradition, as well as of Deleuze's concept of "conceptual personae": see Ryan Johnson, "The Theory of Ideas in Ancient Atomism and Gilles Deleuze" (PhD diss., Duquesne University, 2013), https://dsc.duq.edu/etd/706/; and Jay Lampert, *Deleuze and Guattari's Philosophy of History* (New York: The Free Press, 1978).

36. Kahn, *The Art and Thought*, 85.

37. Kahn, *The Art and Thought*, 33.

38. Jaap Mansfeld, "Der Wegbereiter: Thales," in *Die Vorsokratiker I; Griechisch/Deutsch*, ed. Jaap Mansfeld (Stuttgart: Philipp Reclam, 1999), 39.

39. Jaap Mansfeld, "Der Systematiker: Anaximander," in *Die Vorsokratiker I; Griechisch/Deutsch*, ed. Jaap Mansfeld (Stuttgart: Philipp Reclam, 1999), 57.

40. Without doubt there are – most famously Martin Heidegger's transfer/translation of Heraclitean philosophy into a *Seinsgeschichte* – approaches which discuss Heraclitus in line with a classical ontology and as a philosophy of origins

that therefore differ from my reading. For Heidegger, see both "Der Anfang des abendländischen Denkens (Sommersemester 1943)," and "Logik: Heraklits Lehre vom Logos (Sommersemester 1944)," in *Heraklit*, by Martin Heidegger, Vol. 55 of *Gesamtausgabe* [In German], ed. Manfred S. Frings (Frankfurt am Main: Vittorio Klostermann, 1994).

41. Kahn, *The Art and Thought*, 53.

42. Kahn, *The Art and Thought,* 83.

43. Alexander Kluge, "Heraklit der Dunkle," interview by Oskar Negt, *Ten to Eleven*, Alexander Kluge: Kulturgeschichte im Dialog, April 1, 1996, https://kluge.library.cornell.edu/de/conversations/negt/film/2119.

44. All preceding citations are from Kahn, *The Art and Thought,* 53.

45. This and the preceding quotation are from Barad, "Posthumanist Performativity," 815.

46. Thiele, "Ethos of Diffraction," 39.

47. Trinh Minh-ha, "Not You/Like You: Post-Colonial Women and the Interlocking Question of Identity and Difference," *Inscriptions* 3-4 (1988), quoted in Karen Barad, "Diffracting Diffraction: Cutting Together-Apart," in Kaiser and Thiele, *Diffracted Worlds*, 5.

48. All from Kahn, *The Art and Thought,* 65.

49. The harsh distinction between Western and Eastern philosophy is an invention of Western philosophers, constructed as a demarcation line, to define where rational thinking begins and ends. In a particular philosophical tradition, Eastern philosophy is left aside, marginalized as spiritual, naïve thinking which is opposed to the 'rationality' of Western culture. That many of the theorists in that reading-line (Spinoza, Nietzsche, even Bohr) reflect upon ideas circulating in non-Western philosophy seems/is obvious. The influence and the impact is provable. Furthermore, the distinction itself has its historicity: in retrospective, it seems clear that these ancient cosmologies, as well as Heraclitus' "non-cosmology" are close to concepts known from Eastern philosophy.

50. Barad, "Diffracting Diffraction," 7, 10.

51. Johnson, "The Theory of Ideas," 9.

52. Deleuze, *What is Philosophy?*, 59.

53. Kaiser, "Worldling CompLit," 277.

54. See Jens Rücker, afterword to *Heraklit: Urworte,* ed. Jürgen von der Wense (Berlin: Blauwerke, 2016), 39–56.

55. Karen Barad, "Verschränkungen und Politik: Karen Barad im Gespräch mit Jennifer Sophia Theodor," in *Verschränkungen*, trans. Jennifer Sophia Theodor (Berlin: Merve Verlag, 2015), 200.

Chapter 4

Decoherent Reading

On the Constitutive Exclusions of Diffractive Reading

Stacey Moran

INTRODUCTION

To observe the behavior of the smallest objects in the universe is a delicate and complicated business. Because scientists cannot view the quantum universe directly, they have developed advanced technological tools to visualize quanta, tools that enable them to "see" what's going on at the quantum level. For example, the scanning tunneling microscope (STM) developed at IBM by Gerd Binning and Heinrich Rohrer in 1981 was conceived as an instrument capable of depicting atomic surfaces.[1] The STM microscope works differently than traditional optical microscopes. Rather than using magnification lenses to see very small things, the "optics" of the STM is created through touch, something akin to braille reading.[2] In the braille system, fingers glide over and detect the raised dots on a page that represent letters or words. Similarly, the STM uses a feeler probe, but instead of physically touching the objects, the STM uses a "tunneling current" that flows between an arrangement of atoms on a conducting surface and a hyper-fine stylus. As the tunneling flow glides across, it measures the levels of flow, and thus "feels" the arrangement of atoms. The data of these levels is then collected, mapped, and displayed on a computer screen. These different layers of technological intervention prepare the way for us to see what our eyes cannot.

In *Meeting the Universe Halfway*, Karen Barad breathlessly describes watching the operator of an STM develop images of carbon atoms. She expresses her gratitude for being part of this generation of scientists who have grown up with the privilege of "seeing" atoms.[3] Despite her exuberance over the seeing-power produced by the STM, Barad is more interested in what must be excluded from the visualizations to create the illusion that they depict reality. Barad draws attention to the optical illusions, as well as the bracketed techniques required to create them. She offers an "abbreviated" list of the complicated historical processes necessary to produce an image of atoms:

> STM microscopes and practices of microscopy, the history of microscopy, scientific and technological advances made possible by scanning tunneling microscopes, the quantum theory of tunneling, material sciences, IBM's corporate resources and research and development practices, scientific curiosity and imagination, scientific and cultural hopes for the manipulability of individual atoms, Feynman's dream of nanotechnologies, cultural iconography, capitalist modes of producing desires, advertising, the production and public recognition of corporate logos, the history of the atom, the assumption of metaphysical individualism, complex sets of visualizing and reading practices that make such images intelligible as pictures of words and things, and the intertwined histories of representationalism and scientific practice.[4]

Barad notes that successful images require not only multiple practices but also technical skills and "a good deal of practice."[5] For example,

> The specimen has to be prepared and carefully positioned on the scan head; a new tip has to be cut for each specimen; the tip has to be carefully positioned above the surface of the specimen; the specimen's tilt coordinates have to be adjusted properly; the system has to be isolated from direct light, vibrations, air currents, and temperature fluctuations during the scan, or else the image will be compromised; a scan range must be selected; and the operator must decide if the image produced constitutes a "good image."[6]

In painstaking detail, Barad demonstrates that microscopic images of the quantum realm are not created by simply "pushing a button" and capturing images of microscopic objects. Instead, the ability to see quanta "operates on very different physical principles than sight."[7] Barad uses the STM to show how scientific "proof" is not "discovered" through the observation of reality, but rather, is produced by condensing layered sets of practices that intra-vene to create the illusion that we could observe the quantum reality.[8] Barad reveals precisely how the "facts" of quantum mechanics are "made." Ultimately, the STM serves as a productive site for Barad's critique of the correspondence theory of representation, which she calls, "a practice of bracketing out the significance of practices," the result of which "marks a failure" to account for practices through which representations are produced.[9] The method of diffraction, then, operates for Barad as a corrective to the failure of representation, and "trains us to a more subtle vision."[10] Diffraction is a feminist "optics" that refuses to assume that seeing is a passive physico-sensorial act, and takes into account the multiple techniques required "to see." In this spirit, my essay provides an account of some techniques deployed in diffractive readings, active techniques that are necessary to render visible both quantum bodies and an affirmative approach, but which also must be excluded to enact their visibility.

To render these technologies visible, the essay begins by unpacking Barad's treatment of the measurement problem in physics. Despite the fact that it has been deemed controversial for over a century, and that physicists continue to debate possible solutions to the measurement problem, Barad claims to have "solved" it. I argue that Barad's theory of agential realism should thus be viewed not primarily as "scientific," but rather in light of Donna Haraway's notion of the artefactual. Artifactuality is both "fact and fiction," and revokes the (de)naturalization of entities and (re)places them in a context of "world-changing techno-scientific practices by particular collective of actors in particular times and places."[11] Barad entangles fact and fiction to declare the death of classical bodies. The trouble with her claim is not that it is "non-scientific," but that it poses as a scientific solution that renders classical bodies "obsolete" while rendering the quantum realm the condition of possibility for the classical; in doing so, she prioritizes the condition over the conditioned. Her diffractive reading does not account for what it must necessarily exclude to constitute the priority of quantum bodies: the controversy surrounding the measurement problem in physics. This reading renders visible the techniques required to enact such a constitutive exclusion.

Second, the essay shows how characterizations of these new quantum bodies and the affirmative ethics of care they represent also require a number of techniques to render visible, or "bring before the eyes,"[12] new ethical subjects. Such depictions rely on stereotypical feminine traits of classical (feminine) bodies: nonviolent, connected, gentle, generous, caring. What's interesting to me is not only the metaphors of (cultural) femininity imported to the science (this has been written about before),[13] but also, the demand to "unsee"[14] these stereotypes to bring the whole system into view: the quantum entanglement of bodies, affirmative critique, and ethics of care. To state it another way: reading diffractively is theorized as an affirmative practice that requires making measurement cuts and thus enacting certain constitutive exclusions, but those exclusions become "ethical" only when they are stereotypically feminine.

The essay concludes by proposing the concept of decoherence. Decoherence is the study of the transition between the quantum and classical realms. Although decoherence is another word for "collapse," it does not carry the etymological weight of a "lapse" (Latin, *labi* "to lose one's footing, fall, decline, go to ruin"). Barad's preference for the term "collapse" over "decoherence" in her descriptions of the double-slit diffraction experiment emphasizes "the fall" from wave to particle, and promotes the ontologically prior status of the quantum as "that from which" it falls. The moral undertones of the fall should not be ignored either, for they imply a chain of related binaries: quantum/classical, condition/conditioned, pure/impure, and so on. Using the terms coherence (Latin, *cohaerere*, "to cleave together"), decoherence (Latin *de-* prefix, which reverses the verb's action) and recoherence (prefix *re-* back, again) is more in line with Barad's ethico-onto-epistemological project because these terms reflect the mutual presupposition of entanglements, whereby neither quantum nor classical is presumed to come first, but mutually presuppose one another. As the study of their relations, a concept of decoherence refuses to let these binary relations in through the back door, and would complement diffractive readings by incorporating controversy and the mysterious interactions between seemingly incommensurate systems, rather than excluding them.

INVENTING THE MYTH OF QUANTUM BODIES

The discovery of quantum bodies—or rather, as I am arguing, their "in(ter) vention"—is vital to challenging the assumptions that, according to material feminisms, have dominated feminist discourses for decades: representationalism, individualism, and humanism.[15] Barad proposes a queer quantum world in which all matter is "fundamentally entangled and emergent" in an ongoing process of materialization,[16] thereby radically shifting the ontology of the body: "What is at issue is the nature of reality; not just how the body is positioned or understood *in* reality but the nature of materiality of the body *itself*. Matter entails entanglements—that is its nature."[17] Barad claims that entanglement is a normal operation of the physical world; the entanglement of bodies is not simply metaphorical or conceptual, but "real." And while she warns against reductionism, saying that "it would be wrong to simply assume that people are the analogues of atoms," nevertheless, her project equally "entangles" all manner of bodies-entities-phenomena as operations of the physical world: "Mattering and its possibilities and impossibilities for justice are integral parts of the universe in its becoming."[18] Moreover, Barad goes so far as to claim that, *qua* real, these entanglements are "inescapable." All entities are "inextricably fused together," such that "no event, no matter how energetic, can tear them asunder."[19] Barad forcefully states that quantum entangled bodies are fundamental to the universe, and that diffraction makes the "downfall of classical physics explicit."[20]

Proof for the existence of these quantum bodies is the "effects of difference" in observational settings, otherwise known as interference patterns. As an apt metaphor of this experimentation technique, diffractive reading practices "read insights through one another" and can be understood as produced through the layered sets of practices that intra-vene and create an illusion for seeing bodies in a particular way. In this way, Barad's diffractive reading provides the evidence for the quantum entanglements upon which classical bodies are declared dependent. By extension, feminist habits of thinking that remain hegemonically tethered to those classical bodies are also implicated. In other words, Barad's diffractive optics is artefactual: it invents a visualization that serves as the "discovery" (or proof) of the priority of the quantum realm, which then authorizes her strong claim that bodies no longer follow the logic of classical physics. And she is not alone in this: although Haraway does not use quantum vocabulary, she also insists that we have already leapt outside of the confines of bounded individualism, which "has finally become unavailable to think with, truly no longer thinkable."[21]

Here's the trouble with this origin story of quantum bodies: Richard Feynman called the diffraction experiments "the embodiment of the mystery" of quantum mechanics. He characterizes the situation of wave-particle duality as a "psychological torment" that makes us scratch our heads and ask, "But how can it be like that?"[22] While Barad zooms in on the concept of quantum entanglement to tell a tidy story that renders classical bodies "obsolete," quantum mechanics tells a much messier story. For physicists, making the leap from the classical to the quantum register is extremely difficult, if not impossible. The most distinctive feature about the quantum realm, according to Feynman, is that "no one really understands it."[23] More specifically, what he meant was, no one really understands the precise relationship between the classical and quantum realms.

The modern double-slit diffraction experiment has been well rehearsed in recent material feminist texts, but it bears repeating. Non-scientists often refer to the experiment as evidence of the wave behavior of matter. Quantum entanglements are presented as the condition of possibility for classical bodies, the "out of which" such bodies might emerge. However, in scientific texts, the diffraction experiment is not used as evidence, but rather, as a heuristic device, useful for demonstrating everything that is puzzling about quantum mechanics.[24] I repeat the experiment here to highlight the confusion surrounding what the double-slit diffraction actually proves.

The modern double-slit diffraction experiment looks like the following: when a laser is shot through two vertical slits cut out of a wall, waves of light show up on a back screen in the form of an interference pattern. Interference patterns have multiple bands, alternating light and dark, with the brightest band in the middle, and the lightest bands at the edges. Interference patterns always indicate wave behavior. When matter is sent through the slits, for example, grains of sand, they hit the screen behind the wall to leave a different pattern, that of two bright bands (or "double band" pattern), which reflect the shape of the slits. No interference pattern appears with matter. However, when the matter is scaled down to quantum size and electrons are shot through the same two slits in the wall, the normal double band pattern does not appear. Instead, what shows up is an interference pattern, indicating the wave behavior of matter. When it was discovered in the early twentieth century that light and matter each demonstrate both particle and wave behavior, it set off a flurry of excitement and controversy, and all manner of debates quickly formed around what is now referred to as "wave-particle duality."

There is no controversy over the fact that in an experimental situation, interference leads to the collapse of a wave into a particle. The debate centers on the nature of that "collapse" *means*: what is a "collapse," and in what sense can we understand it to be *real*? Is the wave fundamental and thus prior to the particle? Or is the wave function, just that: a mathematical tool that is predictable, but cannot tell us anything about the nature of the universe? These matters are highly contested in quantum mechanics. Modern philosophers of physics have dubbed this "The Measurement Problem in Quantum Physics." Historically, there are a number of theories offered for how to interpret the measurement problem, including Bohr's Copenhagen interpretation and Einstein's hidden variable interpretation, and the many developments that arose from those: De Broglie-Bohmian theory, Ghirardi-Rimini-Weber theory, the Many Worlds approach, and Quantum Bayesianism (QBism), and the Decoherence Program.[25] Today, physicists continue to develop more refined versions of the double-slit diffraction experiment, and are now able to send compound molecules containing 430 atoms through the slits and demonstrate quantum interference.[26] Even so, there is still no consensus on the measurement problem, and the notion of a "collapse" still remains controversial.

In the 1970s, the contested "collapse" of the wave into a particle was renamed "decoherence" by physicist Hans Dieter Zeh. Zeh defined decoherence as "the practically irreversible and practically unavoidable disappearance of certain phase relations from the states of local systems by interaction with their environment."[27] He adds that "the concept of decoherence does not contain any new physical laws or assumptions beyond the established framework of quantum theory."[28] Zeh calls entanglement "the norm" of the quantum realm, but remarks that although decoherence is also "a normal consequence of interacting systems," it is "remarkable" that physicists overlooked it for so long.[29] Although decoherence adds nothing new to physics, has been confirmed experimentally, and is universally accepted, Zeh says, "misunderstandings of its meaning seem to persist in the literature." Used as a general concept, decoherence refers not to the interfering action that causes the collapse of the wave, but to the study of the nature of the transition between the two systems. Without a theory of everything, the precise nature of the relation between the quantum and classical realms remains mysterious.

Barad uses the term, "decoherence," only four times in her very long book. Entanglement is the key player in Barad's story of diffraction: the word appears nearly 400 times in her text. She prefers to emphasize the powers of entanglement and she refines its meaning repeatedly: "entanglement" doesn't mean just any old kind of "connection, interweaving or enmeshment" in a complicated situation, entanglements are "dynamic and shifting," co-constituted and help to enact a super-correlation that is unlike any classical one. Entanglements, like superpositions, are uniquely quantum mechanical; there is no classical equivalent.[30] Like a single word-particle sent through the diffraction grating again and again, an interference pattern begins to appear along the back wall of Barad's text. Barad's repetition of the word, "entanglement" forms a kind of refrain that continually emphasizes the fundamental importance of this quantum concept. "Like a good magician," she illuminates the qualities of entanglement through her representations of it, as she has "us focus on what seems to be evidently given, hiding the very practices that produce the illusion of givenness."[31] Barad's quantum refrain builds up over the course of the book, drawing the reader deeper into the givenness of entanglement. Entanglement's repetition brings the quantum realm before our eyes; it is a rhetorical technology, part of the layered set of practices that produce visual evidence for the givenness of the quantum. This vision prepares us to accept Barad's strong claim that we have arrived at "the end of classical bodies."

Rather than engage with the more recent concept of decoherence, Barad prefers to use the older term, "collapse." She briefly outlines the various approaches to the measurement problem, and then promptly claims to have solved it, stating: "There is no physical collapse involved."[32] "*It's all a matter of where we make the cut. The solution to the measurement problem is recognizing that what is at stake is accountability to marks on bodies in their specificity by attending to how different cuts produce differences that matter.*"[33] Barad's solution to the measurement problem is to reject the collapse.[34]

Barad does not dismiss decoherence per se, that is, she does not dismiss the cutting action of the measurement apparatus. Quite the contrary, it becomes the key to her solution: "*what's at stake is accountability*" to those cuts. However, as a concept that studies the precise relation of the transition, Barad glides over it. She does not deal with the nature of the transition, but with the different arrangements of cuts and their effects. Barad's story of quantum emergent bodies focuses on their givenness, and hides the very practices that produced the illusion of their givenness. In other words, her story smooths over of the controversy among physicists regarding the precise relationship between the quantum and classical. She minimizes the *tension* among competing scientific interpretations; in resolving the controversy, she has brought an end to the tension. But let's be clear: this is not a critique of Barad. It is an account of Barad's reading and of the boundary-making move that matters in her text: the constitutive exclusion of the controversial measurement problem in physics is what produces quantum bodies as the real bodies that matter. The discovery of our quantum "bodies" is premised on "hiding the very practices that produce the illusion of givenness."[35]

Physicists continue to grapple with the question of the relation between the two systems; rather than disappearing, the classical realm stubbornly and repeatedly reinserts itself.[36] The question, therefore, for quantum mechanics is not how to render the classical "obsolete," but rather, how to explain the relationship between the classical and quantum realms. It is important to mention here that a tension exists between the experimental and theoretical sciences. Any given experiment can be examined through different theoretical lenses.[37] Experiments are not in the realm of the given; their meaning requires interpretation.[38]

Others have critiqued Barad's science. For example, Trevor Pinch claims that Barad seems completely uninterested in the history of physics, and finds her "failure to situate these experiments is one of the paradoxes of the book." Pinch says she excludes many key elements of quantum mechanics. S. S. Schweber calls Barad's book "imaginative" and "important," but argues that it "does not rest on a 'quantum mechanical' foundation." And Dorothea Olkowski claims that Barad unnecessarily privileges Bohr's interpretation and fails to adequately address the numerous other interpretations of the measurement problem.[39] Unlike these critiques, I do not highlight diffraction stories to argue that Barad's story about diffraction is incorrect. Instead, I find it more productive to view Barad's use of the double-slit diffraction experiment as an interpretation, specifically, one that supports the ontological priority of waves, and thus reveals her allegiance to one of the interpretations of the measurement problem. The erasure of the decoherence controversy should not be viewed as a reflection of "bad science," but rather, as first, highlighting the role of interpretation in science, and thereby supporting Barad's claim to the entanglement of matter and meaning; second, that her preference for the term "collapse" over "decoherence" is an integral part of the diffractive optics that envisions entities otherwise in a creative restaging of both sight and bodies. In Barad's text, diffraction does not operate as a heuristic device for revealing the puzzles of science. On the contrary, she weaves a tale about the sober certainty of entanglement, the givenness of quantum entities, and in so doing, privileges the condition of possibility over the conditioned. Her "scientific" evidence then supports a reformulation of both bodies and feminist critique.[40] I myself am not a scientist, and I cannot provide additional commentary about the disciplinary "facts" of science. I am concerned instead with paying close attention to the salient technologies that contribute to feminism's quantum story and the characters that bring it to life. As the study of the mysterious relations between the quantum and the classical, I am proposing that decoherence could serve as an interfering reminder in diffractive readings that the quantum mystery resists ready resolution. Or rather, that any resolution necessarily implies that an interpretation has always already been made. Holding onto this tension, or "staying with the trouble," as Haraway puts it, could stave off the desire to make hierarchizing moves that privilege the quantum over the classical, matter over meaning, science over storytelling (or their opposites).[41] The concept of decoherence serves as complement to diffractive reading practices by emphasizing the necessarily interpretive and fictional elements entangled with factual claims. It views all reading as an active rewriting, and insists on the importance of these feminist rewritings because they are contestants in the battle for what matters.

CONTESTING POSITIVITY

What makes stories stick is not their truth or falsity, but their capacity to satisfy certain (unseen) desires. What are the mechanisms operating in Barad's story that lead to the death of classical bodies? Sara Ahmed and Clare Hemmings have both argued that the new materialist approach legitimizes itself through various rhetorical strategies. In particular, they show how poststructuralism and its metonymic associations operate to construct a kind of academic common sense that assumes the material. Hemmings argues that generalizations and progress/loss narratives move the plot of the materialist story along, and she outlines the ways in which individual feminists emerge as "threshold" characters in the new materialist story.[42] If there is a "political grammar" to the stories we tell about feminism and its bodies,[43] then my concern is to pay attention to the mechanisms of constitutive exclusion that produce the quantum feminist story as specifically "affirmative." Barad admits that her diffractive story might have been told otherwise.[44]

Barad's quantum story lays the foundation for a feminist overcoming of the metaphysics of individualism. Barad excludes the controversy surrounding decoherence, but includes indeterminacy, connecting it to Bohr's concept of complementarity. Her story thus remains keenly focused on the variability of measurements that operate to produce a boundary. In Barad's dramatization, the measurement apparatus is capable of making "cuts," that is, interfering on the "dynamic relationality" and the "material-discursive nature of boundary-drawing practices." But that's not the end of the story. Barad's interpretation of the Stern-Gerlach experiment cleverly extends the measuring apparatus from the scientific laboratory out indefinitely, including gender, class, caste, community, and even the shop room floor.[45] In Barad's hands, the quantum concept of indeterminacy thus becomes the condition of possibility for the emergence of entangled entities that enjoy a privileged ontological status to bo(u)nded ones. The main characters in her story are quantum entanglement, quantum superposition, quantum indeterminacy, and the ontological intra-relations that all entities share. Her picture of the universe illuminates the quantum priority, and provides support to the claim that "individually determinate entities do not exist."[46] Here's another way to put it: in Barad's story of diffraction, the concept of indeterminacy operates as a measurement that cuts classical physics and its bo(u)nded entities out of the picture. Her interpretation of the Stern-Gerlach experiment creates an optical illusion; her diffractive apparatus invents an optics for seeing the quantum bodies that we real-ly are. And like all other quantum scientific images, hers relies on the bracketing out of constitutive practices. And at the end of the day, this exclusion is not accounted for, but obscured by the diffractive method's "affirmative" nature. This is the crux of my argument: diffraction is posited as affirmative, that is, a generous, caring, and polite alternative to the negative violence of critique. As an approach, then, affirmation is produced by the exclusion of negation it opposes. By excluding the controversy, contest, and debate over the nature of reality that are central to quantum mechanics (in short, Barad has one proposal and not *the* proposal), it is able to prioritize one version of reality that is stereotypically "feminine"—affirmative, caring, and nurturing.

Barad's diffractive method is part of the "reorientation" of feminist theory that, according to Maureen McNeil, has recently entered a "strikingly affirmative phase."[47] Indeed, many diffractive readings are characterized as "affirmative critique" or "affirmative engagement."[48] According to Barad, affirmative engagement is indebted to the critical tradition of Marx, Nietzsche, and Foucault, but excludes their traditional mode of "disclosure, exposure and demystification." As affirmative, diffraction supplements the earlier (masculine) critical tradition with a newer one, indebted to Elizabeth Grosz, Donna Haraway, Eve Kosofsky Sedgwick, and Melanie Klein,[49] and as such, is conceived of as "an iterative practice of reworking."

The destructive nature of critique is reworked by Bruno Latour, who characterizes critique as a weapon, and employs war metaphors throughout "Has Critique Run Out of Steam?": "Wars. So many wars. Wars outside and wars inside . . . My question is simple: Should we be at war, too, we, the scholars, the intellectuals?" He wonders whether we shouldn't "bring the sword of criticism to criticism itself," and he laments "the cruel treatment objects undergo in the hands of . . . *critical barbarity.*" Latour recognizes the difficulty of "dismantling" the "critical weaponry" because like "atomic silos," they remain "dangerous" long after being stored away. Invoking Whitehead,

Latour compares it to "throwing a match into a powder magazine. It blows up the whole arena." Latour's allegory of critique-as-war proposes a cease-fire: the problem we face is how "to associate the word *criticism* with a whole set of new positive metaphors, gestures, attitudes, knee-jerk reactions, habits of thoughts."[50]

Barad takes her cues from Latour, proposing diffraction as just such a positive gesture. As an alternative practice that contributes to the dismantling of the "the critical weaponry so uncritically built up,"[51] the diffractive method turns away from the negative tradition of critique and its violent metaphors, which Barad finds too "chilling and ominous" for feminist engagement.[52] The violent metaphors are replaced with more positive ones, and diffractive reading is characterized as an "affirmative engagement" that is "respectful, detailed and ethical."[53] Barad is committed to:

> the possibilities for making a better world, a more livable world, a world based on values of co-flourishing and mutuality, not fighting and diminishing one another, not closing one another down, but helping to open up our ideas and ourselves to each other and to new possibilities, which with any luck will have the potential to help us see our way through to a world that is more livable, not for some, but for the entangled wellbeing of all.[54]

Kathrin Thiele extends the affirmative method by outlining what a diffractive ethos might look like. This ethos requires "a change in attitude" and "an opening up of the whole engagements with difference(s) and differentiality" that "aims at the multiplication and dissemination of differential powers in order to produce other, unexpected, and (hopefully) *less violent interference patterns.*"[55] Echoes of Barad's rejection of violence combined with a renewed conceptual creativity run through new material discourse.[56] The "iterative reworking" process in diffractive readings is a part of a more general trend, I suggest, that operates through the rhetoric of wave metaphors. In the affirmative mode, the nonviolent metaphors in diffractive readings tend to smooth over the perceived violence of critique by reconciling difference and overlooking turbulence.

A couple of quick examples will serve to demonstrate this trend. Iris Van der Tuin characterizes her affirmative reading of Bergson as a reworking of the normative feminist critique of Bergson's "hypermasculine theory of life." Read as a "devaluation of matter as feminine,"[57] feminist readings often dismiss Bergson's work. Van der Tuin refuses to engage in such either/or dualisms. Her reading "assents to" rather than "dissents from" Bergson's primary text, and "reworks the concepts."[58] Reworking in this case means, "to affirm links between seemingly opposite schools of thought or scholars, thus breaking through the politics of negation."[59] Setting up any dualism between the two, she claims, would only result in "the underprivileged coming back with a vengeance."[60] In addition to the positive "assent," this reading also assents to what Bergson and Barad share: a philosophy of dynamism and a "similar ethics." Their relation is imagined to be two diffracted "waves" that "complement each other," and thereby "instantiates an affirmative relation between the two, wherein negation . . . does not play a role."[61] This reading thus "strengthens" Bergson's philosophy and frees it up to be "made to work for feminism and sexual difference theory."[62] The reading is characterized, finally, as the only form of critique capable of the "respectful engagement."[63] Respect and care are a common theme in affirmative readings. Elsewhere, Van der Tuin insists that her response comes from her exceptional "caring for feminism's past, present and future and for new materialism."[64] Theorist of education, Carol Taylor, reiterates this theme of care, referring to affirmative critique as "engaging critique as a close encounter of the generous kind." Diffraction, Taylor argues, is not meant to "be negative, hostile or destructive," but "a gentle holding."[65] Through the metaphorical mechanism of the classical superposition of water waves, waves interfere and are reconciled by canceling out violence while amplifying respect and care, which reflect the ethics of the affirmative mode.

Like Van der Tuin's diffractive reading, Thiele's reading of Bracha Ettinger and Barad seeks to find resonance in difference. This reading warns that "although Ettinger's psychic registers surely will introduce a difference that is not all too easily brought into harmony with the posthuman(ist) theorization of diffraction," nevertheless it hopes to "produce significant resonances amongst these two thought-universes."[66] The motif of resonance is explicitly tied to the critique of individualism, and is grounded in the politics of inclusivity. Thiele hopes "to keep open the currently stifling boundaries between what supposedly is or counts as posthuman(ism) and human(ism) respectively." The inclusivity is all-encompassing; although specific forms of exclusion need to be retroactively included (global politics, inequality, and xenophobia, etc.), the use of brackets indicates the ongoing inclusion of ever more bodies, including not only "othered" human bodies, but also nonhuman ones, and importantly, as well as the "-isms," or bodies of knowledge through which we come to know those in-/ex-cluded bodies *qua* "others." The radical openness of the diffractive ethos seeks only "the most respectful, the most grateful, and the most giving" methods of relating. Thiele's use of the word "resonance" here speaks to a double meaning: the two different texts are brought together like resonant sound waves that positively amplify each other, rather than the negative, "noisy" wave encounter that would cancel them out. This affirmative reworking of opposing ideas into harmonious ones should "strike a chord" with the reader. As an affirmative method of relating, diffraction promotes inclusivity, openness, and nonviolence. The implication is that ethical relations are harmonious, not dissonant.

Melanie Sehgal's reading of Whitehead, Haraway, and Barad opens with a reference to the physical phenomenon of diffraction, whereby a stone is dropped into the water and the ripples form amplifying circles where a diffraction pattern appears.[67] Sehgal uses the pattern of waves as a metaphor for the friction between the three different thinkers. She finds a "surprising convergence of these heterogeneous thinkers," however, the similarities are not the main point, she insists, but rather, the "possible entanglements" between them. In this reading, Barad and Whitehead "share a concern" for the philosophical consequences of physics, and share a refusal to criticize Newtonian physics. Although Whitehead seems to promote "the view from nowhere," this reading shows how his thinking can be "reconciled" with Haraway's. If there were frictions among the three thinkers, this reading ultimately finds "resonance" among them through the metaphor of waves that smooth over any potential textual turbulence.

Here, we have a number of examples in which diffraction operates as affirmative critique by "reworking" concepts. This reworking is indebted to the use of wave metaphors that "smooth over" the dichotomizing demands of dualisms and the violent waters of critique. It opens up new, more positive, that is, "feminist" versions of, in this case, Bergson, Whitehead, and psychoanalysis. These readings can be characterized as positive, according to Van der Tuin, precisely because they allow us to *overlook* certain unsavory elements; in the case of Bergson, we overlook his "hypermasculine" approach. In other words, diffractive readings are not only capable of producing visualizations of quantum objects, but can also be deployed for *"unseeing" undesirable elements*. In the examples here, we are allowed to unsee the masculinism and phallocentrism derived from outdated dualisms. This practice of "unseeing" dualisms is precisely what makes Bergson new and palatable for a materialist feminist ethics. Likewise, frictions between authors like Whitehead or Ettinger and Barad can be affirmatively overcome in "resonance," their amplification and "harmony." It is through the metaphor of diffracting and amplifying waves that various forms of negativity are constitutively excluded through techniques of "unseeing." Unsavory (and unethical) elements can be politely and discretely "washed away," like the tide washes away footprints in the sand.

CONCLUSION

Quantum physicists remain embroiled in controversy over the measurement problem in physics. Physicists do not have answers to the mysteries of the world. But they continue to take sides, and propose interpretations about what—for the moment—remains fundamentally unresolvable: the nature of the transition between classical and quantum phenomena. Contest, conflict, and irresolvable tension lie at the heart of our understanding of the nature of the universe. Feminism, too, remains caught in the ongoing contests for what counts as "feminist," as "experience," or as "political." In particular, material feminisms continue to endure despite mounting critiques lodged against them. For example, some argue that material feminisms are "post-millennial"/"post-gender,"[68] and have "abandoned" real political commitments;[69] that they reproduce a "non-innocent," "colonialist" discourse.[70] Others argue that the project cannot be considered properly "feminist" because it has dispensed with the critique of phallocentrism or patriarchy,[71] and contributes to the death of feminism as "the end of activism."[72] As part of the ontological turn, material feminisms are accused of being more interested in abstract questions of knowledge production than in concrete politics that address the lived experiences of real women.[73] Like physicists, feminists do not have the answers to these unresolvable problems. Unlike physicists—and please excuse me for stating the obvious—the problems that feminists work on are wicked, which is to say, inherently *unresolvable*.[74] Feminists therefore continually propose theories and interpretations, constitute new entities, approaches, and ethical positions, and continually rework them. These reworkings, or technologies of reading and writing, are contests for what counts in feminism. They should not be read as "scientific," or as though scientific rationalism could resolve them. These are the very contests that enact feminism, and are "fundamental to women's study practice."[75]

However, in material feminism's affirmative approach, the general tendency is to exclude controversy.[76] In this chapter, I have demonstrated some ways in which diffractive readings use wave metaphors to "smooth over" various controversies—Barad's solution of the measurement problem is like diffracted water waves canceling each other out. In the other examples, interpretive and rhetorical strategies are employed to exclude all notions of struggle, contest, and controversy, and then the act excluding these forms of violences are fashioned as positively ethical. The technological operations required to produce this diffractive optics necessarily brackets out acts of violence, transforming violence or oppression into politeness or resonance. These bracketing operations are the condition of possibility for the emergence of a conception of diffraction-as-affirmative engagement. The exclusion of the negative is viewed as a positive gesture, one that sidesteps critique, which is "a destructive practice, meant to dismiss, to turn aside, to put something or someone else down—another scholar, another feminist, a discipline, an approach."[77] Affirmative engagement, on the other hand, is rendered "political" because it is nonviolent, and therefore ethical.[78]

But make no mistake: by showcasing the exclusion of negativity, I am not critiquing diffractive readings. Quite the contrary, I am arguing that these technologies of reading and writing are part and parcel of the contest for what counts in feminism. They also constitute the creative action that visualizes quantum bodies, enacts the downfall of classical bodies, and introduces a new ethical program. I would therefore venture to say that the diffractive method extends far beyond critique, and should be viewed as a richly inventive practice. Diffractive readings "read insights through one another," which is to say, they produce creative visualizations by means of condensing layered sets of practices that intra-vene on the world to create the illusions of both seeing and unseeing. Through inventive technologies of seeing and unseeing, the diffractive readings analyzed here create the givenness and the priority of the quantum, which leads to the "discovery," or in(ter)vention of new quantum bodies and the restaging of ethical response-ability. Through inventive technologies of unseeing, diffraction makes a simultaneous double move, excluding controversy and investing in the ethics of affirmation. And herein lies the takeaway point: without these constitutive practices of visualization, material feminists could not tell the story that reveals how we came to be the quantum bodies we "real-ly" are. In other words, this story is an etiological myth for our quantum subjectivity. But here are the risks of such mythologies: Are affirmative gestures alone capable of composing an ethics, for those affirmative gestures that seek to exclude (some forms of) violence, nevertheless rely on (other forms of) violence? What we need to be questioning is not the fact that diffractive readings must include exclusionary practices—affirmative feminisms are ipso facto exclusionary—but what kind of ethical program it generates in its wake. Do we want to sanction a quantum feminism that silences controversy, that prefers politeness over contest?[79] Perhaps Rosi Braidotti recognizes the tendency when she warns against precisely this: "It is important that this fundamentally positive vision of the ethical subject does not deny conflicts, tension, or even violent disagreements between different subjects."[80] Instead of a peaceful, utopian story of quantum feminism, might we imagine one that, like decoherence and the study of relations, embraces controversy and studies the mysterious interactions between "impossibly different" systems?

Barad's story of the diffraction experiment catalyzes the role of indeterminacy to promote the dynamism of the universe. She claims to have solved the measurement problem in physics, and thus proclaims the death of the classical body. Her story achieves this through an optics that overlooks or "unsees" a controversy that physicists who, working under the burden of uncertainty, are still embroiled in. Her claim that entanglements are "inescapable," and all entities are "inextricably fused together," and that "no event, no matter how energetic, can tear them asunder," is less a scientific solution than an act of creative storytelling. As Haraway argues, "vision is always a question of the power to see—and perhaps of the *violence* implicit in our visualizing practices." She encourages us to ask, "With whose blood were my eyes crafted?"[81]

NOTES

1. On scanning tunneling microscopy, see G. Binning and H. Rohrer, "Scanning Tunneling Microscopy," *IBM Journal of Research and Development*, 2nd ser., 44, no. 1 (2000): 279–93; J. A. Golovchenko, "Tunneling Microscopy," in *Solvay Conference on Surface Science: Invited Lectures and Discussions*, ed. Frederik W. DeWette (Berlin: Springer, 1988), 198–215; Paul K. Hansma, and Jerry Tersoff, "Scanning Tunneling Microscopy." *Journal of Applied Physics* 61, no. 2 (1987): R1–R24.
2. Press Release for the 1986 Nobel Prize in Physics.
3. Karen Barad, *Meeting the Universe Halfway: Quantum Physics and the Entanglement of Matter and Meaning* (Durham: Duke University Press, 2007), 39.
4. Barad, *Meeting*, 360.
5. Barad, *Meeting*, 360
6. Barad, *Meeting*, 52.
7. Barad, *Meeting*, 53.
8. Barad relies on Ian Hacking's "don't just peer, interfere" from *Representing and Intervening: Introductory Topics in the Philosophy of Natural Science* (Cambridge: Cambridge University Press, 1983). See also, Michael Lynch and Steve Woolgar, eds, *Representation in Scientific Practice* (Cambridge: MIT, 1990) and Joseph Rouse, *Engaging Science: How to Understand its Practices Philosophically* (Ithaca: Cornell University Press, 2018).
9. Barad, *Meeting*, 53.
10. Donna Haraway, "The Promises of Monsters: A Regenerative Politics for Inappropriate/d Others," in *Cultural Studies*, ed. Lawrence Grossberg, Cary Nelson, and Paula A. Treichler (New York; Routledge, 1992), 300.
11. Haraway, "Promises of Monsters," 296–7.
12. See Aristotle, *On Rhetoric: A Theory of Civic Discourse*, trans. George Alexander Kennedy (New York: Oxford University Press, 1991). Aristotle commented on the pedagogical pleasure of metaphors due to their ability to vivify the world and "bring before the eyes."
13. See, for example, "The Egg and the Sperm: How Science Has Constructed a Romance Based on Stereotypical Male-female Roles," *Signs: Journal of Women in Culture and Society* 16, no. 3 (1991): 485–501; Nancy Tuana, *Feminism and Science* (Indiana: Indiana University Press, 1989); Ludmilla J. Jordanova, *Sexual Visions: Images of Gender in Science and Medicine between the Eighteenth and Twentieth Centuries* (Madison: University of Wisconsin Press, 1993); Evelyn Fox Keller, "Gender and science," in *Discovering Reality: Feminist Perspectives on Epistemology, Metaphysics, Methodology, and Philosophy of Science*, ed. Merrill B. Hintikka and Sandra G. Harding, 187–205 (Dordrecht: Springer, 2003).

14. The term "unsee" is inspired by China Miéville, *The City and the City* (London: Pan Books, 2010).

15. Coole, Diana H. and Samantha Frost, eds, *New Materialisms: Ontology, Agency, and Politics* (Durham: Duke University Press, 2010), 2–3; Stacey Alaimo and Susan J. Hekman, eds, *Material Feminisms* (Bloomington: Indiana University Press), 2008.

6. Susan Hekman, "Constructing the Ballast: An Ontology for Feminism," in *Material Feminisms*, ed. Stacey Alaimo and Susan J. Hekman (Bloomington: Indiana University Press, 2008), 85.

16. Barad, *Meeting*, 33.

17. Barad, *Meeting*, 132; emphasis added.

18. Barad, *Meeting*, 24, and xi. Also see, Joseph Rouse, "Barad's Feminist Naturalism," *Hypatia* 19, no. 1 (2004): 142–161.

19. Both from Barad, *Meeting*, 3.

20. Barad, *Meeting*, 72–3.

21. Donna Haraway, *Staying With the Trouble: Making Kin in the Chthulucene* (Durham: Duke University Press, 2016), 5.

22. Richard Feynman, *The Character of Physical Law* (Cambridge: MIT Press, 2017), 129.

23. Ibid.

24. For an array of perspectives on the measurement problem in physics, Tim Maudlin, *Philosophy of Physics: Quantum theory* (Princeton: Princeton University Press, 2019); Cord Friebe, Cord, et al., *The Philosophy of Quantum Physics*, trans. William D. Brewer (Cham: Springer, 2018); Robert Batterman, ed., *The Oxford Handbook of Philosophy of Physics* (Oxford: Oxford University Press, 2013).

25. For more on decoherence and the measurement problem in physics, see Maximilian Schlosshauer, "Decoherence, the Measurement Problem, and Interpretations of Quantum Mechanics," *Reviews of Modern Physics* 76, no. 4 (2005): 1267. And John Archibald Wheeler and Wojciech Hubert Zurek, eds, *Quantum Theory and Measurement*, vol. 49 (Princeton: Princeton University Press, 2014).

26. Stefan Gerlich, et al., "Quantum Interference of Large Organic Molecules," *Nature Communications* 2 (2011): 1–5, https://doi.org/10.1038/ncomms1263.

27. H. Dieter Zeh, "What is Achieved by Decoherence?," in *New Developments on Fundamental Problems in Quantum Physics* (Dordrecht: Springer, 1997), 441.

28. H. Dieter Zeh, "Roots and Fruits of Decoherence," in *Quantum Decoherence* (Basel: Birkhäuser, 2006), 17.

29. Ibid. For a clear discussion of why decoherence was ignored, see the introduction to Maximilian Schlosshauer, *Decoherence and the Quantum-to-Classical Transition* (Berlin: Springer, 2007).

30. Quotations are taken from Barad, *Meeting*, 160, 35, 168, 179, 270, 279. In comparison, Barad uses "indeterminacy" 173 times, "entanglement" 361 times, "diffract" 311 times.

31. See Barad's discussion on how representationalism "magically" presents "the given." *Meeting*, 360.

32. *Meeting*, 350

33. *Meeting*, 348; italics in original.

34. Barad's rejection of the collapse aligns her with the Many Worlds approach, originally formulated by Hugh Everett in 1957 and popularized by Brian Greene.

35. Ibid.

36. I have written in more detail about the interpretations of the measurement problem in quantum physics as related to material feminisms. See Stacey Moran, "Quantum Decoherence," *Philosophy Today* 63, no. 4 (Fall 2019): 1051–1068.

37. Philip C. E. Stamp, "The Decoherence Puzzle," *Studies in History and Philosophy of Science Part B: Studies in History and Philosophy of Modern Physics* 37, no. 3 (2006): 467–497.

38. Diderik Batens and Jean-Paul van Bendegem, eds, *Theory and Experiment: Recent Insights and New Perspectives on their Relation*, vol. 195 (Dordrecht: Springer, 2012).

39. Trevor Pinch, "Review Essay: Karen Barad, Quantum Mechanics, and the Paradox of Mutual Exclusivity," *Social Studies of Science* 41, no. 3 (June 2011): 431–441, https://doi.org/10.1177%2F0306312711400657; Schweber, Silvan S., Review of *Meeting the Universe Halfway: Quantum Physics and the Entanglement of Matter and Meaning*, by Karen Barad, *Isis* 99, no. 4 (2008): 879–882, https://doi.org/10.1086/597741; Dorothea Olkowski, "The Cogito and the Limits of Neo-materialism and Naturalized Objectivity," *Rhizomes: Cultural Studies in Emerging Knowledge*, no. 30 (2016), https://doi.org/10.20415/rhiz/030.e09.

40. Karen Barad, "Erasers and Erasures: Pinch's Unfortunate 'Uncertainty Principle,'" *Social Studies of Science* 41, no. 3 (2011): 443–454, https://doi.org/10.1177%2F0306312711406317.

41. Haraway, *Staying with the Trouble*, 3.

42. Clare Hemmings, *Why Stories Matter: The Political Grammar of Feminist Theory* (Durham: Duke University Press, 2011), 24; Sara Ahmed, "Open Forum Imaginary Prohibitions: Some Preliminary Remarks on the Founding Gestures of the 'New Materialism,'" *European Journal of Women's Studies* 15, no. 1 (2008): 23–39.

43. Hemmings, *Why Stories Matter*, 1 and 16.

44. Barad says that critique is too often a destructive practice, rather than "a deconstructive practice of reading for the constitutive exclusions of those ideas we cannot do without." "'Matter Feels, Converses, Suffers, Desires, Yearns and Remembers': Interview with Karen Barad," in *New Materialism: Interviews & Cartographies*, ed. Rick Dolphijn and Iris van der Tuin (Ann Arbor: Open Humanities Press), 49, http://dx.doi.org/10.3998/ohp.11515701.0001.001.

45. Barad, *Meeting*, 238.

46. Barad, *Meeting*, 128.

47. Maureen McNeil, "Post Millennial Feminist Theory: Encounters with Humanism, Materialism, Critique, Nature, Biology and Darwin," *Journal for Cultural Research* 14, no. 4 (2010): 427-437; Mercedes Bunt calls it "the era of affirmation." Mercedes Bunz, "Facing Our New Monster: on critique in the Era of Affirmation." Position Paper, "Terra Critica: Re-visioning the Critical Task of the Humanities in a Globalized World," December 7/8, 2012, Utrecht University.

48. Karen Barad, "Diffracting Diffraction: Cutting Together-Apart," *Parallax* 20, no. 3 (2014): n63, https://doi.org/10.1080/13534645.2014.927623.

49. McNeil, 433.

50. Bruno Latour, "Why Has Critique Run Out of Steam? From Matters of Facts to Matters of Concern," *Critical Inquiry* 30, no. 2 (2004): 225–248, http://www.jstor.org/stable/10.1086/421123.

51. Ibid.

52. Adam Kleinman, "Intra-actions," *Mousse Magazine* 34, Summer 2012, 76–81.

53. Barad, "Matter feels," 50.

54. Barad, "Erasers and Erasures," 450.

55. Kathrin Thiele, "Ethos of Diffraction: New Paradigms for a (Post)humanist Ethics." *Parallax* 20, no. 3 (2014): 202–216. https://doi.org/10.1080/13534645.2014.927627; emphasis mine.

56. Iris van der Tuin, "'A Different Starting Point, a Different Metaphysics': Reading Bergson and Barad Diffractively," *Hypatia* 26, no. 1 (2011): 22–42; see also Rosi Braidotti's ethics of care in *Transpositions on Nomadic Ethics* (Cambridge: Polity, 2012).

57. Ibid. See Rebecca Hill, "Phallocentrism in Bergson: Life and Matter," in *Deleuze and Gender*, ed. Claire Colebrook and Jami Weinstein (Edinburgh: Edinburgh University Press, 2011), 123–136.

58. Elizabeth Grosz, *Time Travels: Feminism, Nature, Power* (Durham: Duke University, 2005), 3, quoted in, Iris van der Tuin, "A Different Starting Point," 23.

59. Ibid. 27.

60. Karen Barad, "Posthumanist Performativity: Toward an Understanding of How Matter Comes to Matter," *Signs: Journal of Women in Culture and Society* 28, no. 3 (2003): 812n14, quoted in Iris van der Tuin, "A Different Starting Point," 27.

61. Note that Van der Tuin's use of the word "complement" differs from Bohr's concept of complementarity. Usage here relies on the colloquial term derived from the Latin *complere*, "to fill up or complete." It is worth noting that both complement and compliment derive from the same verb. *Complement* (from 1610) means "to exchange courtesies." *Compliment* (seventeenth-century French) emerges from "to complete the obligations of politeness." The exchange between the Bergson and Barad is conceived implicitly as a "polite" one. This demand for propriety saturates the discourse of new material feminism, at the expense of engaging with Bohr's theory of language for quantum "objects."

62. van der Tuin, "A Different Starting Point," 34.

63. Barad, *Meeting*, 90.

64. Iris Van der Tuin, "Deflationary Logic: Response to Sara Ahmed," *European Journal of Women's Studies* 15, no. 4 (2008): 412.

65. Taylor, Carol A. "Close Encounters of a Critical Kind: A Diffractive Musing In/Between New Material Feminism and Object-Oriented Ontology." *Cultural Studies? Critical Methodologies* 16, no. 2 (2016): 201–212.

66. Thiele, "Ethos of Diffraction," 203.

67. Melanie Sehgal, "Diffractive Propositions: Reading Alfred North Whitehead with Donna Haraway and Karen Barad," *Parallax* 20, no. 3 (2014): 188–201. https://doi.org/10.1080/13534645.2014.927625.

68. McNeil uses the monikers "post-gender" and "post-millennial." Cf. McNeil, "Post-Millennial Feminist Theory."

69. Ahmed, "Open Forum," 23–39. See also, Stacey Gillis, et al., *Third Wave Feminism: A Critical Exploration* (Basingstoke: Palgrave Macmillan, 2004); Stacy Gillis and Rebecca Munford, "Genealogies and Generations: The Politics and Praxis of Third Wave Feminism," *Women's History Review* 13, no. 2 (2004): 165–182; Jo Reger, *Different Wavelengths Studies of the Contemporary Women's Movement* (London: Routledge, 2014).

70. Zoe Todd, "An Indigenous Feminist's Take on the Ontological Turn: 'Ontology' is just another Word for Colonialism," *Journal of Historical Sociology* 29, no. 1 (2016): 4–22; see response, Peta Hinton and Xin Liu. Hinton, Peta, and Xin Liu. "The Im/Possibility of Abandonment in New Materialist Ontologies," *Australian Feminist Studies* 30, no. 84 (2015): 128–145. Also see Sari Irni, "The Politics of Materiality: Affective Encounters in a Transdisciplinary Debate," *European Journal of Women's Studies* 20, no. 4 (2013): 347–360.

71. Peta Hinton and Iris van der Tuin Hinton, Peta and Iris van der Tuin. "Preface," Special issue, *Women: A Cultural Review* 25, no. 1 (2014): 1–8.

72. Mary Hawkesworth, "The Semiotics of Premature Burial: Feminism in a Postfeminist Age," *Signs: Journal of Women in Culture and Society* 29, no. 4 (2004): 961–985, quoted in Clare Hemmings, *Why Stories Matter*, 72–3.

73. Clare Hemmings, "Invoking Affect: Cultural Theory and the Ontological Turn." *Cultural Studies* 19, no. 5 (2005): 548–567, https://doi.org/10.1080/09502380500365473; van der Tuin, "A Different Starting Point." See also Grosz, *Time Travels*, and Braidotti, *Transpositions*. Regarding the question of how feminist is new material feminism, see Peta Hinton and Iris van der Tuin, eds, "Feminist Matters: The Politics of New Materialism," Special issue, *Women: A Cultural Review* 25, no. 1 (2014): 1–122. For critique of abstract versus concrete, see McNeil, "Post-Millennial Feminist Theory," 431. On feminisms that ignore corporeal life, see Nikki Sullivan, "The Somatechnics of Perception and the Matter of the Non/Human: A Critical response to the New Materialism," *European Journal of Women's Studies* 19, no. 3 (2012): 299–313.

74. Horst W. Rittel and Melvin M. Webber, "2.3 planning problems are wicked," *Polity* 4, no. 155 (1973): e169.

75. Donna Haraway, "Reading Buchi Emecheta: Contests for Women's Experience in Women's Studies," *Women: A Cultural Review* 1, no. 3 (1990): 15, https://doi.org/10.1080/09574049008578043.

76. Barad describes the difference between critique and affirmative "engagement." "Diffracting Diffraction," n63.

77. Karin Sellberg and Peta Hinton, "Introduction: The Possibilities of Feminist Quantum Thinking," *Rhizomes: Cultural Studies in Emerging Knowledge*, no. 30 (2016), https://doi.org/10.20415/rhiz/030.i01.

78. Rosi Braidotti notes that ethics is the new politics. "Affirmation versus Vulnerability: On Contemporary Ethical Debates," in *Ethics After Poststructuralism: A Critical Reader*, ed. Lee Olsen, Brendan Johnston, and Ann Keniston (Jefferson: McFarland, 2020), 248.

79. Todd, 17. See also Dianna E. Anderson, *Problematic: How Toxic Callout Culture is Destroying Feminism* (Lincoln: University of Nebraska Press, 2018).

80. Braidotti, "Affirmation," 251.

81. Haraway, "Reading Buchi Emecheta," 192.

Chapter 5

Reading Speculative Horror Readings Diffractively

Peter Schuck

1. WELCOME

Speculative thought and horror fiction have made a couple since the discourse of speculation surfaced the Humanities.[1] The horror speculation embraces is a horror of the "radical Outside,"[2] most prominently to be found in Lovecraft, who is honored by speculative critics as a literary predecessor of their theoretical work.[3]

My approach to the relation of horror and speculation, however, is slightly different. What I'm about to conduct in the following is an experiment in what Karen Barad refers to as "diffractive reading."[4] Barad borrows "diffraction" from optics and quantum physics, where it denotes "the way waves combine when they overlap and the apparent bending and spreading of waves that occurs when waves encounter an obstruction."[5] Diffraction in this sense includes "intra-actions," "agential cuts," and "entanglements": "[I]ntra-actions enact agential cuts, which" neither "produce absolute separations" nor "unities" but "[e]ntanglements" that "entail differentiatings" just as "differentiatings entail entanglings. One move—*cutting together-apart*."[6] As Thiele and Kaiser emphasize, Barad understands diffraction in terms of an ontological relationality where "[e]ntities and phenomena do not pre-exist their relations, but are constituted by them."[7] Drawing on Donna Haraway's previous appropriation of diffraction and exploring the concept's potential to investigate cultural formations, "diffraction" to Barad is "an apt metaphor for describing the methodological approach . . . of reading insights through one another in attending to and responding to the details and specificities of relations of difference and how they matter."[8]

That said, I will concentrate my diffractive interest on three interrelated texts of the speculative sort. The first one is Reza Negarestani's

Cyclonopedia, which is attributed as theory fiction.[9] The other two are essays by Eugene Thacker. "Black Infinity; or, Oil discovers Humans"[10] is a reading of Fritz Leiber's story "Black Gondolier" Thacker contributed to a conference volume on *Cyclonopedia*. "*Caltiki the Immortal Monster X: the Unknown Leiber's* 'Black Gondolier,'" dealing with ooze in pulp horror films and Leiber's story, is paragraph 6 of the "Six *lectio* on Occult Philosophy" chapter from *In the Dust of this Planet*, the first volume of his *Horror of Philosophy* series.[11]

One of my claims is that these texts bring about insights resonating with the concept of diffraction and/or perform diffractive gestures. Hence, the two diffractive gestures I'm going to perform here. The first one is reading *speculative horror* readings *diffractively*, implying that I interlace Baradian New Materialism itself with the "outside-oriented" speculations of Negarestani and the like.[12] As Austin Lillywhite notes, both directions are concerned with "inhuman matter before it is taken up in human conscious activity."[13] But while, as Kameron Sanzo summarizes, New Materialism "works against inert, extra-discursive, and non-generative conceptions of matter,"[14] "speculative realism," as Lillywhite points out, discards "any approach that substitutes relations . . . for real objects in themselves, independent of human consciousness." Thus, when reading *speculative horror* readings *diffractively*, I diffract New Materialism and speculative realism as such. In doing so, and since I also make use of poststructuralist thought, I share an intuition with Lillywhite who investigates the interrelation between materialist ontologies in general and poststructuralism and sees a materialism emerge in the writings of Jean-Luc Nancy and prefigured in Merleau-Ponty's "guiding metaphors of chiastic intertwining and reversibility" that invites us to "think . . . about being in a way that is *both realist and relationally constructed*."[15] As Barad already has it, "diffraction is not only a lively affair, but one that troubles dichotomies . . . such as organic/inorganic and animate/inanimate."[16] Thus, neither does diffraction reject the radical outside (which is also metaphorically apt since even the densest pattern features holes and thus figures as what *Cyclonopedia* terms "( )hole complex"[17]) nor is that outside only a matter of speculative *contemplation*. Therefore, the second gesture I'm going to perform along the first one is reading speculative horror *readings* diffractively, that is, investigating a rather theoretical body of work *on* horror: Thacker's essays philosophically read horror fictions, and *Cyclonopedia* is a *theory* fiction involving readings of other horror fictions.

Inspired by Nils Plath's constellational readings of Derrida, Kafka, and others[18] and *Cyclonopedia*'s concept of "Hidden Writing,"[19] I also follow Armen Avanessian's and Björn Quiring's remark about the very literaricity of speculative thought[20] and am indebted to Melanie Sehgal's suggestion that diffraction always already speculates[21] when I claim that the texts of my choice diffractively *partake in* the horror they speculate on to diffract into a furiously self-multiplying "love letter to the outside."[22]

2. HIDDEN WRITING/DIFFRACTIVE READING

That *Cyclonopedia* entangles theory and fiction already becomes clear on the first pages. A frame narrative stages Kristen Alvanson, "[a]n American artist" who "travels to Istanbul to meet a mysterious online contact" that "never shows up."[23] Instead, she finds and subsequently *edits* "[a] thick piece of writing titled *Cyclonopedia* with the name Reza Negarestani handwritten on it."[24] As Pamela Rosenkranz points out, "Kristen, in addition to being a character, is the creator of the book's magnificent cover; she is credited on the title page beneath Reza Negarestani, who is book's author—and also the author of the manuscript Kristen finds." It is thus an instance of "metafiction,"[25] yet also of diffraction that one cannot tell the pages of the book at hand from the manuscript Kristen is editing. We're reading "a process and the result of a process at the same time"[26] that for Kristen "is like suddenly falling into the holes of a smoothly narrated story [she has] been reading for years – suddenly page numbers warp and things go missing." The manuscript contains fragments and paraphrases of writings by the Iranian "archeologist . . . Dr. Hamid Parsani."[27] Scouring the web for more information, Kristen discovers *Hyperstition*, an online forum where users discuss Parsani's work. As Kate Marshall summarizes:

> [T]he manuscript *Cyclonopedia* is a posthumous collaboration between Parsani and the distributed anonymous author-collective *Hyperstition*, is narrated by or addressed to the fictional quantity Reza Negarestani, and is edited, introduced, annotated and ruthlessly deformed by Kristen Alvanson.[28]

Parsani delivers interpretations of ancient Middle Eastern apocalyptic mythologies and their artifacts returning in the War on Terror at the beginning of the twenty-first century. For Parsani, the ancient material medium upon and through which this war is carried out and for the inhuman agency of which "Bush and Bin Laden are obviously petropolitical puppets" is oil. As a "singular anorganic body with its own agendas," it operates among and against these "war machines" through "blobjectivity": "According to a blobjective point of view, petropolitical undercurrents function as narrative lubes: they interconnect inconsistencies, anomalies or what we might simply call the 'plot holes' in narratives of planetary formations and activities." Bringing 'plot holes' into play, 'blobjectivity' is a main characteristic of what Parsani terms "*Kareez'gar*" which, "with considerable mutilation," translates as "'( )

hole complex', since Parsani's original term implies both a destitute Whole ... and a holey-ness." Employing the onto-epistemology of holes "oscillating between surface and depth" ( )hole complex is a formation of drastically perforated matter where "void" and "solid" violently deconstruct each other in the "process" of "ungrounding." Undoing "unitary or binary logics" such as those "of inner and outer" or "inclusion and exclusion," it evolves into what is called "Tiamaterialistic differentiation" when oil is part of the game. A paradoxical procedure in which ( )hole complex and ungrounding presuppose, enable and entail the flow of oil to generate "nemat-space," the "Lovecraftian worm-ridden space" where "the flow of the fluid and the deformation of the solid matrix" entangle into "foundations of radical participation." Such "worm-entities"[29] are not foreign to Barad. She describes diffraction as "re-turning" in the sense of "processes" conducted by "earthworms" like "turning the soil over and over—ingesting and excreting it, tunneling through it, burrowing."[30] Diffracting Barad's with *Cyclonopedia*'s worm-conducted ungroundings, one can say for the moment that each concept "re-turns" the implications of the other. Accordingly, *Cyclonopedia*'s literary theory for ( )hole complex strongly resonates with the concept of diffractive reading. "Hidden Writing" entangles reading and writing in a way that on the one hand analyzes plot holes, the perforations of a textual formation, and on the other hand itself continues to further perforate and thereby generate (write) the text. Exaggerating the concept of intertextuality, it undermines the single author position with—note the double genitive—the reading/writing of "anonymous collectives (the crowd)"[31] that compromisingly constitute the text by constitutively compromising it. *Cyclonopedia* is itself an instance of Hidden Writing[32]—and diffractive reading. Accepting the pointlessness of making sense or a whole of the manuscript, Kristen concludes: "If I can't pass through these plot holes then it is the best to leave my own holes."[33] In other words, she teams up with the crowd and becomes a diffractive reader who intra-actively reads, alters, and thus *constitutes* the manuscript in the editing process.

Submitting to *Cyclonopedia*'s "demand for complicity,"[34] on March 11, 2011—"the same date as the first page of the *Cyclonopedia* manuscript itself!"[35]—the *Cyclonopedia* symposium "Leper Creativity" was conducted. The contributions were published in a volume of the same title in 2012. In her contribution, Melanie Doherty—in a fashion mimicking Kristen's—documents her *Cyclonopedia* research as a Kafkaesque journey of "burrowing through ... *Hyperstition*, every blog post and journal article, every conference announcement and facebook page." Observing how it "had spilled beyond" its own "covers," *Cyclonopedia* to her is not a novel for "[i]t doesn't work on the level of representation." Alluding to its heretic appropriation of Deleuzo-Guattarian vocabulary, she perceives *Cyclonopedia* as "a textual machine designed to produce other machines."[36] As the back cover comment informs, the *Leper Creativity* volume is itself designed to operate as this kind of machine that "both faithfully interprets the text and realizes it as a loving, perforated host of fresh heresies."[37] Thus, what Doherty attributes to *Cyclonopedia* also matters for its readings in and beyond *Leper Creativity*. They partake in its peculiar "textuality" and "produc[e] effects by simultaneously scrambling existing codes, disrupting expectations, casting the reader outside the covers of the book" and generating "new forms of practice and critique." When Doherty suggests "[w]hat *mattered*" were "the circulation and the effects of the text in the world,"[38] she basically describes intra-activity since in "practices of intra-active encounters (of readers with texts with texts with readers)," as Kaiser argues, "not only texts are made to matter, but 'world' is also in the making."[39]

3. THACKER READING LEIBER

As one of *Leper Creativity*'s editors, Thacker contributed "Black Infinity; or, Oil discovers Humans." It kicks off as a reading of Leiber's "Black Gondolier," a story set in Southern California about "the mysterious disappearance of [the narrator's] friend Daloway" who had cultivated a "fascination . . . with oil . . . as an ancient and enigmatic manifestation of the hidden world." In the story, "oil is described as an animate creeping ooze that . . . courses through all the channels of modern industrial civilization."[40] The narrator's conclusion "man hadn't discovered oil, but . . . oil had found man"[41] is essential for Thacker's developing of a four-stage model to flesh out the ways in which one "encounters" the "the *unhuman*"—"something that one is always arriving at, but which is never circumscribed within the ambit of human thought." Of the four stages—"*anthropic subversion*," "*anthropic inversion*," "*ontogenic inversion*," and "*misanthropic subtraction*"—the last one is particularly interesting. While Thacker traces the first three in Leiber's story, "*misanthropic subtraction*" is to be witnessed in those passages of "supernatural horror and weird fiction" *in general* where language borders its representational capacity. This is indicated by "minimalism"—like "'nameless', 'formless', 'lifeless'"—or "hyperbole." For Thacker, especially Lovecraft makes use of these two "strategies" that eventually "dovetail into a singular epiphany concerning the faltering not just of language but of thought as well." "Taken together," Thacker writes, the "four stages of the unhuman result in a paradoxical revelation, in which one thinks the thought of the limit of all thought." Calling "that moment when philosophy and horror negate themselves, and in the process become one and the same" a "*black illumination*,"[42] he contemplates the *entanglement* of horror and philosophy.

Prior to "Black Infinity" though, Thacker already plotted some holes particularly in his *"Caltiki"* essay where he traces the motif of ooze along a similar trajectory of stages, yet not in one text but from several oozy pulp horror films to "Black Gondolier." He concludes with Leiber's story and the notion of an ooze that "take[s] on the qualities of thought itself."[43] Since I will elaborate on *"Caltiki"* and "Black Infinity" further below, for the moment we can note that each of Thacker's pieces features at least one of two different reading modes. I'm referring to Plath's deconstructive take on these modes when I classify Thacker's readings by the names these modes carry in German literary studies. Whereas "Black Infinity" figures as "statarische Lektüre" (of which the English equivalent is "close reading") as Thacker mostly focuses on Leiber's story, *"Caltiki"* puts several texts on the map and thus conducts a "'kursorische' [Lektüre]"[44] (translating as "cursory reading").[45] As Plath argues, close and cursory reading are neither pure when exercised nor synthesizable.[46] Therefore, Thacker's readings deserve to be read in terms of Hidden Writing that itself rejects the "hermeneutic rigor" of "deep reading" and "operates on the plane of textual perforation."[47]

4. GALLOWAY/THACKER

Before getting to Thacker's texts in more detail, let's have a look at Alexander Galloway's *Leper Creativity* contribution in which he suggests a "crypto-ontology for oil" and to grasp it "not simply as dark but as infinite blackness ... absolutely foreclosed to us, but also to Being itself." Galloway arrives at this idea from a contemplation of light in philosophy, theology, and a matter of interest for Barad: optical physics. Drawing on François D'Aguilon's "early-seventeenth-century opus on optics," he distinguishes two sorts of light. While *"lumen"* denotes the "illumination" of "refraction" and as a light having "passe[d] through transparent materials" is associated with "transparency," "lux" is the "light" of "reflection," indicating the "opacity" of the "objects" from which it "bounces off." To Galloway, darkness and blackness complement *lumen* and *lux*. Whereas darkness complements *lumen* in terms of refractive darkening, blackness complements *lux* as the "shadows of black Being." *Cyclonopedia*'s oil is both. "[A]s transubstantiated sunlight" it is "some product" of *lumen* but also black as its "tellurian core wells up" from the inaccessible crypt to "annihilate ... societies."[48]

Of course, diffraction is already at play. Although Galloway doesn't touch diffractions at all—which, as Kaiser and Thiele explain, in contrast to refraction and reflection "are the patterns effected in-and-by encounters of differences"—he still gives us a diffractive idea of oil when he concludes that it is dark *yet also* black. The way in which Galloway's and Thacker's contributions interfere appears as a version of the "'two-slit experiment',":

> A thought-experiment to determine if light was particle (as classically held by Newton) or wave (as experimentally shown by Young in 1803). The outcome predicted by Bohr was that under certain conditions (namely if it remains unclear through which of the two slits the photon passes) the results are a wave pattern, while under other conditions (namely if we determine the path the photons take by equipping the two-slit interference device with a "which-path detector") light behaves like a particle.[49]

When Barad states that "the apparatus is an inseparable part of the observed phenomenon," this also applies to the interference of Galloway's and Thacker's texts when using the "apparatus" of Baradian thought. Barad refers to Francesco Grimaldi who conducted a two-slit experiment *avant la lettre* in mid-seventeenth century, showing how "[b]ands of light appear inside the shadow region . . . and bands of darkness appear outside the shadow region." She describes how "Grimaldi studies what happens when sunlight passes through two adjacent pinholes" the result of which is "that darkness is not a lack" but "can be produced by 'adding new light' to existing light."[50] To Barad, this has ethical implications as it questions the racial coding of the light/darkness binary. She quotes Gloria Anzaldùa on how "primordial darkness had been split into light and dark," a distinction in which the latter is "identified with the negative, base and evil forces" which "are identified with dark skinned people."[51] Diffracting Grimaldi with Anzaldùa, Barad observes how Anzaldùa "pokes a hole in the colonizer's story of how darkness is the other of light"[52] when she describes "mak[ing] 'sense' of something" as "kicking a hole out of the old boundaries of the self."[53] Barad concludes: "The two-slit diffraction experiment queers the binary light/darkness story" as "darkness is not light's expelled other" but "haunts its own interior."[54]

With this in mind, we can return to Galloway and Thacker. Galloway refers to Thacker's "world-without-us" and "cosmic pessimism" when it comes to the blackness of oil.[55] And Thacker's contribution directly follows up to Galloway's in *Leper Creativity*. Furthermore, Galloway's darkness/blackness distinction returns twice in "Black Infinity" when Thacker (1.) describes how in Leiber's story "Daloway is weirdly carried off into the viscous night where *oil and nocturnal darkness merge into one*"[56] and (2.) when Thacker arrives at his term "*black illumination*." If illumination is *lumen* (i.e., its equivalent, darkness) and blackness is the "contradistinction to *lux*,"[57] the term "*black illumination*" oxymoronically queers both lights/darknesses. When to Nicola Masciandaro—whose *Leper Creativity* contribution follows up to Thacker's—it is the "twist of the image" that "shadows forth precisely by distortion the unimaginable shape of the real,"[58] the term "*black illumination*" twistingly diffracts *lux*/blackness and *lumen*/darkness, thus signifies *and* performs its speculative implications.

In the upcoming paragraphs, I want to flesh out how "*black illumination*" emerges in/through "*Caltiki*," "Black Infinity," and their interference.

5. PARENTHESIS AS PLOT HOLE

Since Barad's emphasis on pinholes in the two-slit experiment and Anzaldùas discourse evokes a ( )hole complex, I begin with "*Caltiki*" as a visible instance of the latter.

At a first glance, in the essay ooze appears as a mere motif with its variations from several films to Leiber's story. At a second glance, however, it works as a diffractor of these fictions. The essay's heading is noteworthy in this respect: "*Caltiki the Immortal Monster X: the Unknown Leiber's* 'Black Gondolier'," applying what the Microsoft Word catalog of symbols terms as "swung dash." Regardless of its being a detail in layout in other headings of Thacker's book, in "*Caltiki*" it becomes an icon for the movement of a wave and an allegory for the flow of ooze from story to story. Thacker's cursory reading participates in the story's oozy flow as the texts he reads are made to matter in terms of matter: ooze. Thus, the swung dash evolves into an allegory for "the way waves" of ooze "combine when they overlap" as well as for their "apparent bending and spreading . . . when they encounter an obstruction,"[59] for instance, a formation perforated with plot holes. This is what happens when Thacker literally plots a hole and figuratively has more oil spatter his writing. The hole reads as follows: "(I write this during the tragic saga of the Gulf oil spill, the scale of which eerily evokes Leiber's story, as well as Reza Negarestani's inimitable *Cyclonopedia*.)"[60] Here, the parenthesis is what *matters*. As critics such as Holt Meyer and Uwe Wirth have persuasively argued, interrupting syntactical and narrative orders, thus implementing potentially uncontrollable digressions, parentheses have inclusion and exclusion overlap and deconstruct the inside/outside boundary constitutive for the textual integrity by way of allowing for other voices to enter.[61] Since the undoing of inclusion/exclusion and inside/outside is a crucial feature of ( )hole complex, it is obvious that the (non-)word "( )hole complex" stages what it denotes by virtue of what Lennard refers to as "lunulae,"[62] that is, the marks composing a parenthesis—( )—that slash a hole in the written text.[63] In cyclonopedian vocabulary, parentheses perforate the text into a ( ) hole complex, entangling inside and outside into the "*intricate meshwork* of nemat-space."[64] Thacker's parenthesis not only invites *Cyclonopedia* in by direct reference but paves the way for its structural apparition. Indicating what Rüdiger Campe with Rodolphe Gasché calls "The Scene of Writing,"[65] "(I write this . . .)" parenthetically stages a writer writing and renders undecidable whether this process of writing points toward an actual writer outside or a fictional writer inside the text.[66] Since this recalls that writers appearing as "I"s in their writings reveal as *personae* rhetorically *feigning* authenticity,[67] Thacker joins the collective of Hidden Writing and practices "[i]nauthenticity" as "complicity with anonymous materials."[68] When the scene of writing establishes a "bracketing of interrupting and articulating,"[69] this process is parenthetical and can be reformulated with Barad as a "cutting together-apart" with diffractively blackening ramifications in Thacker's text. The parenthetical gash constitutes a scene of writing in the double sense of the terms *writing* and *écriture* signifying that which is written and/as the process of writing.[70] This leads us back to the swung dash. If the "lunulae" of a parenthesis may iconically articulate to a "full moon,"[71] they may also constitute a "vertical swung dash" when shifted vertically. *Cyclonopedia* itself contains a vertical swung dash and theorizes its implications. Kristen's absent online contact "goes by [a] serpent-like initial" that is obviously an instance of what later on is theorized as "Hydraglyph" and "'snake writing'." According to Parsani, the latter is "associated with the excessive curvature of letters, as in Arabic and Pahlavi languages" and performs "a worshipping of the ancient serpents." As "disentanglements . . . of dynamic complexities," these twisted letters "are written" "in flowing manners" "and characterized by gates and thresholds." The swung dash can be seen as a "Hydraglyph" returning in/as Thacker's parenthetical scene of writing, a ( )hole complex spilling the oil/ink of at least two other plots—*Cyclonopedia* and the 2011 Gulf oil catastrophe—out of and into the text via the plot hole agentially marked by the ( ). Thacker reconfigures the flow-allegorizing swung dash into a parenthesis to provoke further entanglements and become a "hidden snake writer" in the wake of Hamid Parsani who states that "'the bottom line of my texts is written in oil'."[72]

6. THE BLACK INFINITY OF ( )HOLE COMPLEX

This is continued in "Black Infinity." As Thacker makes clear, the connection between "Black Gondolier" and *Cyclonopedia* is oily: Middle Eastern oil leaks from every plot hole in *Cyclonopedia*, Californian oil blackens "Black Gondolier." "Middle Eastern" and "Californian" oil, however, are "blobjectively" inappropriate terms. As an "autonomous terrestrial conspirator," oil doesn't belong to either of these regions but rather encourages their "helical entanglement," that is, that of "Islam and Capitalism"[73]; or in the present case: *Cyclonopedia* and Thacker's text. The "snake writing" continues as the texts partake in the same holey oily story.[74] From a blobjective viewpoint,[75] oil is the "lube for" *this* story's "divergent lines of terrestrial narration," of its "plot holes."[76]

Like "*Caltiki*," "Black Infinity" reveals as a textual accomplice in the story's spill, too. At the point where Thacker identifies the collapse of language and thought in the "minimalist" and/or hyperbolic language of supernatural horror, he points his attention to some Lovecraft passages, including a larger one from "The Unnamable."[77] This is peculiar for a reason. "Why Lovecraft?" one might ask, when in "*Caltiki*" Thacker already emphasized "*Leiber*'s hyperbolic prose."[78] Chances are that he performs an agential cut since he states that "*[t]aken together*," the "four stages of the unhuman result in" the "paradoxical revelation" of "*black illumination*."[79] Bringing the Lovecraft passages into play, he opens his close Leiber reading and allows for Lovecraft to enter his text. This results in a diffraction of Leiber with Lovecraft—and *Cyclonopedia*: Thacker arrives at "*black illumination*" through a plot hole, that is, a passage between texts marked by the name of Lovecraft. The latter for his part is a major accomplice in *Cyclonopedia*'s conceptualization of ( )hole complex. It includes a *reading* of a passage from Lovecraft's "The Festival" of which I reproduce the line that *matters* for *Cyclonopedia*: "Great holes secretly are digged [*sic*] where earth's pores ought to suffice, and things have learnt to walk that ought to crawl."[80] "In this alarming but neglected passage," the cyclonopedian comment reads, "Lovecraft addresses . . . ( )hole complex . . . as the zone through which the Outside gradually but persistently creeps in (or out) from the Inside."[81] In this passage, Lovecraft is made to matter for *Cyclonopedia et vice versa*.[82] Both bodies of work entangle into a ( )hole complex where "[t]hings leak into each other according to a logic that does not belong to us" and "invite (seduce) the outside in order to be cracked open from the other side"[83]: *Cyclonopedia* becomes a passage for a "neglected" H.P. Lovecraft passage that itself deals with passages (holes)[84] (thus Hamid Parsani is "*Cyclonopedia*'s crafty H.P."[85]) just as "Black Infinity" becomes a passage for the unhuman of "*black illumination*" by way of Thacker cutting his Leiber reading into a passage for "The Unnamable" and thereby allowing for *Cyclonopedia* and "The Festival" to articulate with this passage by virtue of *their* passages—a ( )hole complex with(in) a ( )hole complex.

7. FLOWING HOLES

The cyclonopedian "outside is deeply swamped in oil," which accounts for the circumstance that oil is at once an instance of the outside *and* its medium that is *itself* mediated through the ( )hole complex it *fabricates* in

"Tiamaterialistic differentiation": "Agitated by the flow of fluids (which themselves have been anomalized in the nematical machine or vermicular space), elastic waves dissipate through solid matrices and radically displace the grains of the solid skeleton throughout ( )hole complex."[86] As such, oil also appears to *mediate and be* that very outside the implications of which are concentrated in Thacker's *"black illumination."* Therefore, the intra-activity of his readings deserves further analysis. Although Thacker sees Leiber's (and *Cyclonopedia*'s) oil as "fully continuous,"[87] he intra-actively *(re-)implements* its continuity because "[c]ontinuity is . . . *made*, instance for instance."[88]

Given that ( )hole complex is at play in each of Thacker's texts, it is not so farfetched to perceive the two texts as a pattern that constitutes a ( )hole complex itself. The specific shape of this pattern emerges in a manner investigated by Allen McLaurin. In the last chapter of his study on Virginia Woolf, McLaurin analyzes Woolf's *To the Lighthouse* with respect to the connection between the "typographical device" of "square and round brackets" in the text and the text itself "the whole form" of which "can be seen as a parenthesis":

> The first and last sections, being parallel, form brackets around the central section "Time Passes." Throughout the novel smaller parentheses mirror this overall pattern; the book is made up of "curves and arabesques flourishing around a centre of complete emptiness."[89]

Thacker's two texts can be seen as such a parenthesis as well—with each text being one "lunula" of the ( ). However, whereas in Woolf typographical parentheses in and the parenthetical structure of the text reflectively "mirror" each other in their circling of the empty center, Thacker's pattern—to put it with Masciandaro—is more of a "centerless center"[90] spreading (its emptiness). As seen in the readings above, each of Thacker's texts is a ( )hole complex welcoming other plots and their holes. This spreading of agentially cut plot holes, of parentheses within/out of parentheses, is extended when the two texts constitute a parenthetical pattern that spreads the "small" parentheses from within its components. Thus, the parenthesis in "( )hole complex" iconizes the parenthetical structure of Thacker's pattern that in turn becomes an instance of *and thereby spreads* the ( )hole complex(es) already perforating its "lunulae." In this respect, Thacker's pattern involves *Cyclonopedia* not only through reference but, being parenthetical, enacts the cyclonopedian assumption that "[i]n any composition (as in ( )hole complex) the solid is the possessed narrator of the void."[91]

In turn, the holey "solid" of Thacker's pattern also operates as the narrative spreader of the oily outside and thus evokes the image of the cyclonopedian "feedback spiral" that "is a cyclone and an oil drill"[92] at once. When according to the logics of "Tiamaterialistic differentiation" the outside is an attribute of *and* mediated by oil that is itself mediated by the ( )hole complex it fabricates, Thacker's parenthetical pattern begins to engender what Sehgal describes as a diffractive pattern in Whitehead's metaphor of the "ripples" caused by "the plunge of the stone thrown into the water. The ripples release the thought, and the thought augments and distorts the ripples."[93] Diffracted with Thacker's oily parenthetical pattern and *Cyclonopedia*, Whitehead's ripples on water spread and thicken into ripples on oil.[94]

This diffraction follows "the logics of petropolitical undercurrents" onomatopoetically (as one can hear a plunging sound in the word "blobjectivity") and (according to the logics of "Tiamaterialistic differentiation"[95]) structurally: The diffractively thickened metaphor of the ripples can be made to signify the spreading of holes (void)—parentheses parenthesizing parentheses and so on[96]—and the flow of the fluid at once. It is a paradox in which *holes flow* and thereby (agentially) *cut and constitute* the texture they're passing through. The parenthetical pattern of flowing holes[97] in/of Thacker's texts features and spreads the "squishy materiality"[98] of perforated solids doused in the oil of the outside.

8. NEGARESTANI/BARAD

In this respect, Thacker's parenthetical pattern also enacts the question whether light is "wave or particle." From a diffractive viewpoint, light is both since "wave and particle, position and momentum do not exist outside of specific intra-actions that enact cuts that make separations . . . *within* phenomena."[99] When the flow of oil and the holey solid are "tiamaterialistically" entangled, this reads as a version of the wave-particle-entanglement that allows to associate the flow of oil with wave and momentum, and the hole with particle and position. However, although both Barad and Negarestani have metaphorical worms do some ungrounding, they partially disagree on the role of holes. Whereas *Cyclonopedia*'s "[n]emat-space is infected with gate hysteria" since it "creates more passages than are needed,"[100] for Barad "quantum tunneling" doesn't necessitate holes at all:

> (An irresolvable internal contradiction, a logical disjunction, an im-passe (from the Latin *a-poria*), but one that can't contain that which it would hold back. Porosity is not necessary for quantum tunneling—a specifically quantum event, a means of getting through. Tunneling makes mincemeat of closure, no w/holes are needed.)[101]

Barad's aforementioned emphasis on the pinholes in the two-slit experiment suggests to read this passage against the grain, and according to its performativity. Typographically embedding the description of quantum tunneling in a parenthetical ( )hole complex, it literally double-parenthesizes an "*a-poria*." Consequently, the explication of the latter as "an im-passe" "that can't contain that which it would hold back" happens *outside* of the parenthesis parenthesizing "*a-poria*" yet *within* the parenthesis parenthesizing the *parenthesis* "(from the Latin *a-poria*)." Pursuing what this "*a-poria*" structurally (parenthetically) entails, Barad's double parenthesis entangles quantum tunneling and ( )hole complex.

Accordingly, Barad's and Negarestani's concepts entangle regarding the dissolution of wholeness, unity, closure. Both concepts figuratively give voice to the undoing paradox they share by playing on the assonance of "hole" and "whole." Furthermore, the processes described by these concepts not only have worms but also butchers do the job of (agential) cutting when it comes to closure. Whereas Barad's quantum tunneling *expressis verbis* "makes mincemeat of closure," "Tiamaterialistic differentiation" appears as an occasion of the "irreversible process of opening" in which the outside acts in a way that "is so radical and tenacious in its intention to cut through any instance of closure that it can only be addressed in terms of butchery and its related nomenclature: blade, butchershop and cuts."[102] Thus, when both concepts butcher closure, this also applies to their "relation" which can be seen as a (meta-)aporetic (non-)simultaneity of "gate hysteria" (pores/passages) and "*a-poria*" (no pores/passages at all), or as mincemeat moved by flowing holes.

9. (NON-)SIMULTANEITY AS *BLACK ILLUMINATION*

This (meta-)aporetic pattern allows us to continue to associate the hole with particle and position, and flow with wave and momentum by adding Thacker's close and cursory readings to the equation. To recall, whereas "Black infinity" approaches Leiber's story in a (rather defaced) close reading, "*Caltiki*" orchestrates a (rather uncontrollable) cursory reading. While of close reading it can be said that it focuses the single entity, the position, the particle, or the hole, cursory reading is rather affiliated with flow, momentum, the wave, the fluid. However, when holes flow, the fluid is not completely fluid just as the hole is not completely singular, not a full circle. As I tried to show in my readings of Thacker's essays, close and cursory reading tends to sacrifice their distinctiveness, too. Accordingly, one can argue that both reading modes constitute a textual "two-slit apparatus" that also is the parenthetical pattern produced by it. In a resonating way, Plath has elaborated on the paradoxical interrelation of close and cursory reading. Reading scenes of reading in Kafka read by Adorno and Walter Benjamin, Plath shows how Benjamin's and Adorno's Kafka readings themselves are scenes of reading that continue what is at issue in Kafka's scenes. Interrupting his

Kafka reading to gather Benjamin and Adorno for his constellation, Plath *performs* his conjecture that any synthesis of close and cursory reading to a unitary interpretation is doomed to fail since both modes are irreducible to each other; one can only read in and about one mode at a time. Eventually, instead of synthesis or unity, spatial and temporal gaps occur between the two, carrying out their *aporetic* (non-)simultaneity.[103] While this is to some extent already happening in each of Thacker's texts, the parenthetical pattern they constitute *performs* this (non-)simultaneity constellationally. As "lunulae," "Black Infinity" (close reading) and "*Caltiki*" (cursory reading) expose that the figure of the parenthesis is itself an open constellation the components of which do not unite to a full circle but leave gaps on the upper and the lower sides of the pattern—a two-slit apparatus and/as a ( )hole complex. When close and cursory reading never synthesize to a whole, their entanglement agentually cuts closure into a ( )hole complex. It evokes the (non-)simultaneity of close and cursory reading *neither* close *nor* cursory reading—*nor* their (impossible) combination—are capable of engulfing since one can never close the spatiotemporal gap between them but only continue its spreading by—endlessly—switching back and forth between the essays and the reading modes they represent.[104] It is a "spacetimemattering"[105] caused by and retroactively signifying an agential cut, a "chasm *being* the interior gnawing *and* the yawning exterior."[106]

As such, this holey pattern entangles "gate hysteria" and "*a-poria*" into a diffractive *performance* of "*black illumination*" as it—in Thacker's words— "not just" indicates the "relative horizon of the thinkable, but" unfolds an "enigmatic revelation of the unthinkable."[107] To put it with Peter Gratton who sees "a speculative move to a 'real' time" in Derrida's "rethinking of writing," it brings about a temporality of paradox that "would not be correlationist"[108] as it is never encompassed by human rationality.[109] Here, thought not only augments and distorts the pattern as in Whitehead but is itself distorted into what can be described with Woodward as "Negarestani's decayed becoming" that implements "a spatiotemporality undermined by thought yet not exteriorized and thrown far beyond it in such a way that thought cuts it without cutting thought in total ruin."[110] Spatiotemporally (dis-)articulating its already agentially mutilated "lunulae," Thacker's parenthetical "*black illumination*" manifests their spatiotemporal (non-)simultaneity to speculate on "what *could* be but not yet *is*."[111]

10. OPEN FRAMES, OPEN READINGS

Cyclonopedia has a formula for this: "*Incognitum Hactenus*—not known yet or nameless without origin until now" serves as "the model of time in ( )

hole complex" and "Nemat-space" as it denotes "a double-dealing mode of time connecting abyssal time scales to our chronological time, thus exposing us to the horror of times beyond."[112] What, then, are parentheses other than "double-dealing" inasmuch as they—with Plath and Barad—diffract "here" and "elsewhere," "now" and "then?"[113] Obviously, this leads us back to Kristen, the fictional editor of *Cyclonopedia*, since *Incognitum Hactenus* is also the title of her frame narrative.[114] Clarifying the accuracy of this title, Masciandaro states that *Incognitum Hactenus*—a "time that never was ours"—is "the time of *Cyclonopedic* writing" itself, an "evental logic" which "deals with local and cosmic time as it does with fiction and theory." Sharing Plath's, Barad's, and Negarestani's skepticism toward synthesis, he explains that cyclonopedian "theory-fiction is . . . not about unifying and resolving their double truth" but "a trisonic betrayal that is treacherously against both via treason of each to the other."[115]

The most treacherous figure in this respect is Kristen, to Doherty "[t]he female cutting edge of the Outside ripping open phallic closure" and "*invaginating* the space around the boys-club bloggers!"[116] Doherty's attribution remarkably outlines the parentheticality of Kristen's frame narrative. That a frame narrative itself functions as a parenthesis is noted by Mary Anne Caws in her study of narrative frames with a reference to McLaurin's reading of Woolf's typographical and textual parentheses.[117] But also the following description applies to the parentheticality of Kristen's frame narrative that—like the parenthesis in Thacker's "*Caltiki*"—is a "hydraglyphical" scene of writing and makes itself readable via thoroughgoing annotation.[118] To Caws, frame "passages" appear as "*agents de change*, since they alter the preceding sight and psychological mind set, but also as culminations in themselves of the intensive mode characteristic of genre crossing."[119] Bearing Masciandaro's and Doherty's conjectures in mind, in calling such passages "*agents de change*," Caws' choice of vocabulary allows for a reading of Kristen's frame narrative as an *agential cut* that implements the "genre crossing" of theory and fiction, in a way that can be put with Barad as "[a] cut that is itself cross-cut."[120] When (with Barad) "[t]o witness the dispersion of a wavepacket, is to see the force of indeterminacy in action"[121] (with *Cyclonopedia*) "[i]n *Incognitum Hactenus*, you never know the pattern of emergence." In this sense, Kristen's frame narrative appears as a theory fictional two-slit-experiment, parenthetically partaking in what it produces. And it is diffractively continued in Thacker's texts that fabricate a ( )-shaped pattern of readings only loosely tied with *Cyclonopedia* to diffractively expand and exacerbate its ( )hole complex into "[an] *entangled* mess of vortical and corkscrewing motions" that is "the rotating debacle of the cyclone."[122]

This appears as a twisted example of what Andrzej Warminski's points out in his reading of Heidegger's parenthetical Hegel reading: to parenthesize

"Being" and thereby revealing it to be only an "example," thus only another "being" (as Heidegger does with Hegel), necessarily results in becoming part of the parenthesis.[123] But while in Warminski's deconstructive approach the parenthesis (also, as he is aware, *his* parenthesizing of Heidegger) indicates how "Being" is always already dissolved in parentheses, the resonating texts I focused on in this paper speculate on the outside exactly by parenthesizing. Each reading of *Cyclonopedia* and ( )hole complex becomes "a schizostrategic two-edged blade"[124] *and* a two-slit—( )—agentially plotting more holes, adding more parentheses, layers, and ripples, thus writing the outside in parenthetical curves.

NOTES

1. For an overview, see Armen Avanessian and Björn Quiring, eds, *Abyssus Intellectualis: Spekulativer Horror* (Berlin: Merve 2013), a volume gathering some of the most influential essays on the topic from last decade and a half by speculative critics.

2. Reza Negarestani, *Cyclonopedia: Complicity with Anonymous Materials* (Melbourne: re.press, 2008), 50, 213–215. See also Quentin Meillassoux' "great outdoors" in *After Finitude: An Essay on the Necessity of Contingency*, trans. Ray Brassier (London: Continuum, 2008), 7, and the comparison of Negarestani's and Meillassoux' notions of contingency in Ben Woodward, "Untimely (and Unshapely) Decomposition of Onto-Epistemological Solidity: Negarestani's *Cyclonopedia* as Metaphysics," in *Leper Creativity:* Cyclonopedia *Symposium*, edited by Nicola Keller, Nicola Masciandaro, and Eugene Thacker (New York: punctum books 2012), 219–221.

3. See Armen Avanessian and Björn Quiring, "Zur Einführung" in Avanessian and Quiering, *Abyssus Intellectualis*, 11–14, or Austin Lillywhite, "Relational Matters: A Critique of Speculative Realism and a Defence of Non-Reductive Materialism." In *Chiasma* 4, no. 4 (2017), 19. For speculative readings of Lovecraft, see Graham Harman: *Weird Realism: Lovecraft and Philosophy* (Winchester: zero books, 2012) or Anthony Sciscione, "Symptomatic Horror: Lovecraft's 'The Colour Out of Space'," in Keller, Masciandaro, and Thacker, *Leper Creativity*. But the list of speculative Lovecraft readings is much longer.

4. Karen Barad, *Meeting the Universe Halfway: Quantum Physics and the Entanglement of Matter and Meaning* (Durham: Duke University Press, 2007), 71–94. See also, Birgit Mara Kaiser and Kathrin Thiele, eds, *Diffracted Worlds— Diffractive Readings: Onto-Epistemologies and the Critical Humanities* (London: Routledge, 2018), previously published in *Parallax* 20, no. 3 (2014).

5. Barad, *Meeting*, 74.

6. Karen Barad, "Diffracting Diffraction: Cutting Together-Apart," in Kaiser and Thiele, *Diffracted Worlds*, 4, 12.

7. Birgit Mara Kaiser and Kathrin Thiele, "Preface" in Kaiser and Thiele, *Diffracted Worlds*, xi–xii.

8. Barad, *Meeting*, 71.

9. See, for instance, Kate Marshall, "*Cyclonopedia* as Novel (a Meditation on Complicity as Inauthenticity)," in Keller, Masciandaro, and Thacker, *Leper Creativity*, 151.

10. Eugene Thacker, "Black Infinity; or, Oil discovers Humans," in Keller, Masciandaro, and Thacker, *Leper Creativity*, 173–180.

11. Eugene Thacker, *In the Dust of this Planet*, vol. 1, *Horror of Philosophy* (Winchester: zero books, 2011), 88–97.

12. See Negarestani, *Cyclonopedia*, 212–213, for "Outside-oriented experiments." Yet, as Lillywhite summarizes, "speculative realism" refuses to assemble a movement since even the thinkers aligned with it are either criticizing the term and its usage or each other. See Lillywhite, "Relational Matters," 15–24, for the critique of "speculative realism" from without and within its discourse.

13. Lillywhite, "Relational Matters," 13.

14. Sanzo, Kameron. "New Materialism(s)," *Critical Posthumanism: Genealogy of the Posthuman*, April 25, 2018. http://criticalposthumanism.net/new-materialisms/.

15. Lillywhite, "Relational Matters," 14, 30, my emphasis.

16. Barad, "Diffracting Diffraction," 4.

17. Negarestani, *Cyclonopedia*, 42.

18. See Nils Plath, *Hier und Anderswo. Zum Stellenlesen bei Franz Kafka, Samuel Beckett, Theodor W. Adorno und Jacques Derrida* (Berlin: Kadmos, 2017).

19. Negarestani, *Cyclonopedia*, 60.

20. See Avanessian and Quiring, "Zur Einführung," 12–13.

21. See Melanie Sehgal "Diffractive Propositions: Reading Alfred North Whitehead with Donna Haraway and Karen Barad," in Kaiser and Thiele, *Diffracted Worlds*, 26, 30, 33.

22. This is how Zach Blas describes *Cyclonopedia* in "Queerness, Openness," in Keller, Masciandaro, and Thacker, *Leper Creativity*, 111.

23. Pamela Rosenkranz, "Cyclonopedia—Artforum International: Best of 2009," https://re-press.org/cyclonopedia-artforum-international-best-of-2009/, previously published in *Artforum International* 48, no. 4 (December 2009).

24. Negarestani, *Cyclonopedia*, xii.

25. Rosenkranz, "Cyclonopedia."

26. Sehgal, "Diffractive Propositions," 25.

27. Negarestani, *Cyclonopedia*, xii, 9.

28. Marshall, "*Cyclonopedia* as Novel," 147.

29. Negarestani, *Cyclonopedia*, 20, 16, 42, 43, 45, 43, 54, 58, 48, 49. For an elaboration on cyclonopedian and other worms, see Nicola Masciandaro "WormSign," in Nicola Masciandaro and Edia Connole, *Floating Tomb: Black Metal Theory* (Milan: Mimesis International 2015).

30. Barad, "Diffracting Diffraction," 4.

31. Negarestani, *Cyclonopedia*, 60. See Kiene Brillenburg Wurth, "Diffraction, Handwriting and Intra-Mediality in Louise Paille's *Livres-livres*," in Kaiser and Thiele, *Diffracted Worlds*, 94 for a comparison of diffractive reading and intertextuality.

32. See, for example, Marshall, "*Cyclonopedia* as Novel," 148.

33. Negarestani, *Cyclonopedia*, xviii.

34. Marshall, "*Cyclonopedia* as Novel," 148.

35. See Melanie Doherty, "Non-Oedipal Networks and the Inorganic Unconcious," in Keller, Masciandaro, and Thacker, *Leper Creativity*, 117 for the quote and the back cover of *Leper Creativity* for the date, as well as footnote 4 in Nicola Masciandaro, "Gourmandized in the Abattoir of Openness," in Keller, Masciandaro, and Thacker, *Leper Creativity*, 182, where he elaborates on the significance of the conference taking place at the "seventh anniversary of the text's opening." For a reading of dates as singular and repetitive at once see Plath, *Hier und Anderswo*, 90–110.

36. Doherty, "Non-Oedipal Networks," 116, 122, my emphasis, 129.

37. See the backcover of *Leper Creativity*.

38. Doherty, "Non-Oedipal Networks," 122, my emphasis.

39. Birgit Mara Kaiser, "Worlding CompLit: Diffractive Reading with Barad, Glissant and Nancy," in Kaiser and Thiele, *Diffracted Worlds*, 120, 112.

40. Thacker, "Black Infinity," 173–174.

41. Fritz Leiber, "Black Gondolier," in *Night Monsters*, Ace (New York, 1969), 14, quoted in Thacker, "Black Infinity," 175.

42. Thacker, "Black Infinity," 177–180.

43. Thacker, *In the Dust*, 88, 91.

44. See Plath, *Hier und Anderswo*, 57.

45. I'm avoiding the term "distant reading" here for it evokes the concept of the same name coined in Franco Moretti, "Conjectures on World Literature," *New Left Review* 1 (January/February 2000), which—although opposed to close reading, too—entails quantifying a large number of texts with respect to questions of canon and literary history.

46. See Plath, *Hier und Anderswo*, 56–66.

47. Negarestani, *Cyclonopedia*, 62–63.

48. Alexander R. Galloway, "What is Hermeneutic Light?," in Keller, Masciandaro, Thacker, *Leper Creativity*, 172, 168, 163–164, 171–172.

49. Kaiser and Thiele, "Preface," xii–xiii.

50. Barad, "Diffracting Diffraction," 16, 6–7.

51. Gloria Anzaldùa, *Borderlands/La Frontera: The New Mestiza*, San Francisco: Spinsters/Aunt Lute, 1987, 49, quoted in Barad, "Diffracting Diffraction," 7.

52. Barad, "Diffracting Diffraction," 7.

53. Anzaldùa, *Borderlands*, 49, quoted in Barad, "Diffracting Diffraction," 7.

54. Barad, "Diffracting Diffraction," 7.

55. See Galloway, "What is Hermeneutic Light?" 171. While I'm finishing this essay a couple weeks after George Floyd was brutally killed by a police officer, Anzaldùa's and Barad's suggestion to queer the racial coding of the light/darkness binary calls for an even stronger emphasis. Thus, although this is not the point of my approach, it should be stressed that critics have discussed the racialization of matter, also with respect to cyclonopedian oil. For instance, Oxana Timofeeva makes the connection between the blackness of oil and black bodies when she identifies both in terms of "that which is exploited, consumed, and burned up in the production of surplus." Thus, "oil," she concludes, "is not a master, but a kind of ultimately inhuman

black slave, one that literally occupies the lowest—and the biggest—strata of the pyramid of exploitation, and creates the core of our capitalist unconscious." Oxana Timofeeva, "Ultra-Black: Towards a Materialist Theory of Oil," *E-Flux Journal* 84 (September 2017), https://www.e-flux.com/journal/84/149335/ultra-black-towards-a-materialist-theory-of-oil/.

56. Thacker, "Black Infinity," 177, my emphasis.
57. Galloway, "What is Hermeneutic Light?," 172.
58. Masciandaro, "Gourmandized," 186.
59. Barad, *Meeting*, 74.
60. Thacker, *In the Dust*, 93.
61. See Holt Meyer, "Durch den Regenbogen," in *Den Rahmen sprengen: Anmerkungspraktiken in Literatur, Kunst und Film*, ed. Bernhard Metz and Sabine Zubarik (Berlin: Kadmos, 2012), 82, 87. (Meyer's reading of rainbows, the phenomenon of which evokes reflection, refraction, and diffraction, appears itself diffractive as it makes the entanglement of literal and figurative rainbows-as-parentheses intelligible); Uwe Wirth, "(In Klammern)," in *Satzzeichen: Szenen der Schrift*, ed. Helga Lutz, Nils Plath, Dietmar Schmidt (Berlin: Kadmos, 2017), 32; Renate Lachmann, "Die Parenthese und ihre Umklammerung," in Lutz, Plath, and Schmidt, *Satzzeichen*, 38. See also John Lennard, *But I Digress: The Exploitation of Parentheses in English Printed Verse* (Oxford, Oxford University Press, 1992).
62. Lennard, *But I Digress*, 5.
63. See also the elaboration on Merleau-Ponty's "*thisness* of a given object" implemented by "a punctuation or node in a 'fabric', 'weave', 'field', or 'constellation'" in Lillywhite, "Relational Matters," 30.
64. Negarestani, *Cyclonopedia*, 51, 48, my emphasis.
65. See Rüdiger Campe, "Die Schreibszene: Schreiben," in *Paradoxien, Dissonanzen, Zusammenbrüche: Situationen offener Epistemologie*, ed. Hans Ulrich Gumbrecht and Karl Ludwig Pfeiffer (Frankfurt am Main: Suhrkamp, 1991), 759–772. For the English term "The Scene of Writing" Rodolphe Gasché is credited with a reference to his essay of the same title published in *Glyph* 1, no. 1 (March 1, 1977): 150–171.
66. See Campe, "Die Schreibszene," 767.
67. See Paul de Man, "Autobiography as De-facement," *The Rhetoric of Romanticism* (New York: Columbia University Press, 1984).
68. Negarestani, *Cyclonopedia*, 62.
69. Campe, "Die Schreibszene," 770, my translation.
70. See Campe, "Die Schreibszene," 759 and Sehgal, "Diffractive Propositions," 25.
71. See Lachmann, "Die Parenthese und ihre Umklammerung," 38.
72. Negarestani, *Cyclonopedia*, x, 164–165, 41.
73. Negarestani, *Cyclonopedia*, 27, 177.
74. In the sense Haraway's "histories of western science" too "are necessarily and explicitly stories." Sehgal, "Diffractive Propositions," 27.
75. "Petroleum … narrates … from a 'nethermost' point of view. And this too is unstable, because petroleum is the point of view itself." Marshall, "*Cyclonopedia* as Novel," 154–155.

76. Negarestani, *Cyclonopedia*, 19, 13.
77. See Thacker, "Black Infinity," 178.
78. Thacker, *In the Dust*, 92, my emphasis.
79. Thacker, "Black Infinity," 178–179.
80. H.P. Lovecraft, "The Festival," *Weird Tales* (1925), quoted in Negarestani, *Cyclonopedia*, 43–44.
81. Negarestani, *Cyclonopedia*, 43.
82. Accordingly, Masciandaro uses a passage from "The Unnamable" as "a theory of reception [for *Cyclonopedia*] as *real theory* or vision of the incommunicable real." Masciandaro, "Gourmandized," 184. For a cyclonopedian Lovecraft reading, see Scizione, "Symptomatic Horror."
83. Negarestani, *Cyclonopedia*, 49, 214.
84. This is what Plath in *Hier und Anderswo* refers to with the German word "Stelle," which—to borrow from *Cyclonopedia*, 42—"with considerable mutilation" translates as *passage*, denoting textual phenomena such as quotes and dates oscillating between—as an English translation of the book's title may describe—"Here and Elsewhere." Referencing Plath's book here, I continue its performativity, diffract it with this context and exercise a different reading of the—thereby altered—book, which *deals with* passages but also *performs as* passage open to other contingent readings.
85. Dan Mellamphy and Nandita Biswas Mellamphy, "Phileas Fogg, or the Cyclonic Passepartout: On the Alchemical Elements of War," in Keller, Masciandaro, and Thacker, *Leper Creativity*, 194.
86. Negarestani, *Cyclonopedia*, 24, 48.
87. Thacker, *In the Dust*, 93.
88. Sehgal, "Diffractive Propositions," 32.
89. Allen McLaurin, *Virgina Woolf: The Echoes Enslaved* (New York: Cambridge University Press, 1973), 198.
90. Masciandaro, "Gourmandized," 187.
91. Negarestani, *Cyclonopedia*, 45.
92. Negarestani, *Cyclonopedia*, 36.
93. Alfred North Whitehead, *Modes of Thought* (Cambridge: Cambridge University Press, 1938), 36, quoted in Sehgal, "Diffractive Propositions," 33.
94. For "napalm" that equally "flows more smoothly" when "facilitated by the flow of water," see Negarestani, *Cyclonopedia*, 38–39.
95. Negarestani, *Cyclonopedia*, 36, 16, 48.
96. See Lachmann, "Die Parenthese und ihre Umklammerung."
97. The term "flowing holes" rhymes and shares some speculative implications with what Nicola Masciandaro and Edia Connole with the black metal band Inquisition call "floating tomb." For this figure "keep[s] up with the ancient view of cosmos as a cavern or crypt" and is "both womb and grave," defining black metal's "counter gravity that draws one, inwardly and outwardly, into the living presence of unlimited reality." Nicola Masciandaro and Edia Connole, "Introduction," in Masciandaro and Connole, *Floating Tomb*, 10–12. Accordingly, Masciandaro draws on "nemat-space" and ( )hole complex in "WormSign," 93–94.
98. Woodward, "Untimely (and Unshapely) Decomposition," 214.

99. Barad, "Diffracting Diffraction,"17, 11.
100. Negarestani, *Cyclonopedia*, 66.
101. Karen Barad, "Quantum Entanglements and Hauntological Relations of Inheritance: Dis/Continuities, SpaceTime Enfoldings, and Justice-to-Come," *Derrida Today* 3, no. 2 (2010), 240–268, quoted in Barad, "Diffracting Diffraction," 16.
102. Negarestani, *Cyclonopedia*, 214. Negarestani opposes this "radical Outside" "by" which one is "opened" to a rather vitalist outside-as-environment for the living "to" which one supposes to be "open" and that for that reason invites the "radical Outside" to butcher it. See Negarestani, *Cyclonopedia*, 210–215. For an investigation drawing on this distinction, favoring the radical over the vitalist outside, and identifying the latter with Derrida's notion of the other and as survivalist, see Rick Dolphijn, "Undercurrents and the Desert(ed): Negarestani, Tournier and Deleuze Map the Polytics of a 'New Earth'," in *Postcolonial Literatures and Deleuze: Colonial Pasts, Differential Futures*, edited by Lorna Burns and Birgit M. Kaiser (London: Palgrave MacMillan, 2012), 212.
103. See Plath, *Hier und Anderswo*, 56–66.
104. See Plath, *Hier und Anderswo*, 66.
105. Barad, "Diffracting Diffraction," 4.
106. Woodward, "Untimely (and Unshapely) Decomposition," 223, my emphasis.
107. Thacker, "Black Infinity," 179.
108. Peter Gratton, *Speculative Realism: Problems and Prospects* (London: Bloomsbury, 2014), 215–216.
109. See Negarestani, *Cyclonopedia*, 68, for the similar structure of memory holes as gateways for the outside.
110. Woodward, "Untimely (and Unshapely) Decomposition," 219.
111. Sehgal, "Diffractive Propositions," 32.
112. Negarestani, *Cyclonopedia*, 49.
113. See Barad, "Diffracting Diffraction," 4.
114. See Negarestani, *Cyclonopedia*, ix.
115. Masciandaro, "Gourmandized," 183, 182.
116. Doherty, "Non-Oedipal Networks," 125, my emphasis.
117. See Mary Anne Caws, *Reading Frames in Modern Fiction* (Princeton: Princeton University Press, 1985), 293–294.
118. For the theoretical implications of the practice of annotation see the contributions in *Anmerkungspraktiken in Literatur, Kunst und Film*, eds Bernhard Metz and Sabine Zubarik.
119. Caws, *Reading Frames*, 7.
120. Barad, "Quantum Entanglements," 240, quoted in Barad, "Diffracting Diffraction," 16.
121. Barad, "Diffracting Diffraction," 14.
122. Negarestani, *Cyclonopedia*, 49, 36, 35.
123. See Andrzej Warminski, "Parenthesis. Hegel by Heidegger," in *Readings in Interpretation: Hölderlin, Hegel, Heidegger*, Introduction by Rodolphe Gasché (Minneapolis: University of Minnesota Press, 1987), 152. I'm indebted to Holt Meyer, who pointed my attention to Warminski's essay.
124. Negarestani, *Cyclonopedia*, 215.

Part II

DIFFRACTING LITERATURE

DIFFRACTIONS OF THE WORLD-TEXT-READER ENTANGLEMENT

Chapter 6

Diffractive Poetics in William Carlos Williams's *Paterson*

Brendan Johnston

INTRODUCTION

William Carlos Williams's long poem *Paterson* is a local, material reaction to the cosmopolitan modernist epics of Eliot, Joyce, and Pound. As he announces in the poem's invocation, it is a "reply to Greek and Latin with the bare hands" in favor of "a local pride," a "gathering up" of one very particular place and culture.[1] He describes the impetus of this local epic project in his autobiography: "the first idea centering around the poem, *Paterson*, came alive early: to find an image large enough to embody the whole knowable world around me. . . . [I]t would be as itself, locally, and so like every other place in the world. For it is in that, that it be particular to its own idiom, that it lives."[2] Here, Williams appeals to the local, the idiomatic, and the particular as a means to ground his poem in the material-cultural soil of Paterson, New Jersey.[3] As he describes in the same section, "[t]hat's the poet's business. Not to talk in vague categories but to write particularly, as a physician works upon a patient, upon the thing before him, in the particular to discover the universal."[4] This wariness of "vague categories" or abstraction in favor of concrete, worldly particulars is a departure from the poetics of an erstwhile Romanticism; but it is even more directly a reaction to the polyglot erudition and cultural amalgamations of the looming epics of modernism. Yet, as I will argue, Williams's material focus in his local poetics also resonates with the new materialist theories of Donna Haraway and Karen Barad, particularly their concern with articulating the porous boundaries between the natural and the cultural.

Donna Haraway, like Williams, also professes what she describes as an "allergy to abstraction," favoring interpretive tools and conceptual frameworks that arise out of concrete, "worldly examples."[5] One enduring theoretical apparatus she has developed out of these worldly examples is her scientific metaphor of diffraction, which she proposes as a useful counter to the reflection and mirroring of traditional critique. But it is Karen Barad who theorizes, beyond Haraway's metaphorical analogy, that diffractive reading is a method that can be generously applied in mapping the interference between all manifestations of matter: waves, particles, cultures, and even conceptual and discursive practices.[6] As a scholar of literary studies, I am not prepared to endorse the complete scientific veracity of Barad's radical quantum application of the phenomenon of diffraction.[7] However, I believe that her extension of Haraway's scientific and worldly metaphor envisions a productive new way of tracing the underexamined interaction between physical and cultural materiality. This is why I find the direct comparison of *diffraction* and *diffractive reading* to Williams's material poetics in *Paterson* to be particularly productive. While not seeking to overspeculate on Williams's engagement with diffraction in the new materialist sense, I do wish to highlight Williams's sustained focus on dissonance and improvisation as a means to discover the entanglement or, as Williams describes, "interpenetration, both ways"[8] of material place and culture. Rather than seeking a final epic unity, Williams expresses a world already entangled, too capacious to be finally integrated, but yet capable of moments of tangible material disclosure.[9]

Diffraction in New Materialism and *Paterson*

Paterson is Williams's largest demonstration of a lifelong concern with the material, consequential relationship of poetry to the physical world. In the long poem, he draws from the particulars of the town of Paterson (the history, the people, the physical features) to generate a heterogeneous, unfiltered expression of modern life. The creation of *Paterson* was an ongoing process, spanning over four decades from 1927 to 1961, meant to render an organic, empirical description of a particular locale. As he opens "Book I," "[t]o make a start,/ out of particulars/ and make them general, rolling/ up the sum, by defective means—."[10] The poem is not meant to be a merely reflective representation but, rather, an extension, an elaboration, and a direct expression of reality. As Williams declares in his early prose-poem, *Spring and All* in 1923, "the word must be put down for itself, not as a symbol of nature but as a part, cognizant of the whole—aware—civilized,"[11] or even more mythically, "the work of the imagination is not 'like' anything, but transfused with the same forces which transfuse the earth—at least one small part of them."[12] This deliberate refusal to distinguish the reality of the discursive from the physically tangible has continued to influence contemporary eco-poetics. Even recent poets such as Eleni Sikelianos and Brian Teare have reiterated this entangled state of the textual within the worldly—often directly invoking Williams's early call.[13]

Williams's *Paterson* is a poem that not only encourages diffractive reading but is itself a product of a diffractive composition process. Throughout the long poem, Williams uses linguistic and conceptual enjambement to provoke or help disclose moments of discursive, cultural, and material entanglement. Many of the cascading lines of the poem are formally enjambed, the final word ending one line but beginning a new phrase or idea. But this enjambment also occurs on a macro-scale with the overlapping rhetorical and material constructions that he attempts to assemble in unusual ways. I argue that *Paterson*'s failing attempts or experiments at unity deploy a capacious (and somewhat capricious) methodology that refuses to look at cultural-social and material-natural expressions as separate phenomena, but rather as endlessly overlapping, entangled *relata* that enact differences upon one another. Furthermore, this diffractive writing, which I find prevalent throughout *Paterson*, anticipates new materialist and posthumanist methods for approaching and articulating the embedded relationship between nature and culture. Williams's *Paterson* highlights and indeed turns on the interpretive discovery that often arises out of dissonance. In much the same way, Haraway and Barad encourage reading methods more attuned to interference and inter-field entanglement, which, they argue, offers productive alternatives to the reflexive mirroring that often occurs in purely social and cultural paradigms of critique. Here, I offer a brief overview of my own understanding of Barad's use of the term of diffraction from its emergence in theoretical physics to its potential application in cultural and literary studies.

Barad asserts, reiterating Haraway, that "diffraction can serve as a useful counterpoint to reflection: both are optical phenomena, but whereas the metaphor of reflection reflects the themes of mirroring and sameness, diffraction is marked by patterns of difference."[14] Diffraction is a phenomenon that occurs on the atomic level, but it is also something that can be observed by the naked eye—like the overlapping ripples caused by two stones dropped on a placid body of water. The diffraction *pattern* is where the two waves overlap, which can cause either a cessation or an amplification of the force of the other. As Barad explains, "[d]iffraction can occur with any kind of wave: for example water waves, sound waves, and light waves all exhibit diffraction under the right conditions."[15] According to classical physics, the *medium* for the waves might be physical—like the water in the pound—but the waves themselves are considered as non-physical disturbances or interference patterns. Barad goes on to clarify:

> It is important to keep in mind that waves are very different phenomena from particles. Classically speaking, particles are material entities, and each particle

occupies a point in space at a given moment of time. Waves, on the other hand, are not things per se; rather, they are disturbances (which cannot be localized to a point) that propagate in a medium (like water) or as oscillating fields (like electromagnetic waves, the most familiar example being light). Unlike particles, waves can overlap at the same point in space.[16]

These patterns come together in what is referred to as a *superposition*, which is a moment of direct overlap or interference; and they either amplify or diminish the intensity of the alternate wave. But as Barad suggests, diffraction poses a structural challenge to Newtonian physics because, at the quantum level, the phenomenon of diffraction has been observed occurring in particles as well as waves. This superposition or entanglement of matter is considered impossible by Newtonian standards. And it is this quantum entanglement of various states of matter that Barad uses to assert her application of diffractive interference to interdisciplinary contexts. Both Barad and Haraway pay particular attention to the imprint left by diffraction that can be observed in both physical and non-physical entities; and both theorists have continued to argue for the benefits of tracing this material impression of inter-field activity.

I will leave it to scholars more adept at the nuances of contemporary theoretical physics to ascertain whether Barad has solved the two-system dilemma (between the internal functionality of both classical and quantum physics and their remaining incompatibility or decoherence with one another) by her strong appeal to (literally) universal diffraction.[17] But what both Haraway and Barad suggest, and what I find incredibly useful from my literary studies perspective, is that these optical and textural phenomena may also occur in conceptual and discursive realms. For immanent materialists, these supposedly non-material realms are actually expressions and extensions of the physical rather than pure abstractions that replace or supersede physical reality.[18] As Barad argues, "[t]o theorize is not to leave the material world behind and enter the domain of pure ideas where the lofty space of the mind makes objective reflection possible. *Theorizing, like experimenting, is a material practice.*"[19] Williams makes much the same claim in his recurring mantra in *Paterson*, "no ideas but in things," and at the end of "Book III," when he declares that "this rhetoric/ is real!"[20] What I am arguing here is that *Paterson*, as a poem, is consumed with this idea of overlap and categorical transgression; and that Williams intentionally attempts to create or recreate interactions between these physical, cultural, and discursive fields to demonstrate their interpenetration as well as to come upon haphazard, inventive moments of material disclosure and expression.

Perhaps one of the best examples of Williams's diffractive poetics appears in the opening book of *Paterson*, where he describes the endlessly complex entanglements that make up his project—at once centered on a city, a man, and a natural-cultural ecology:

> [T]he city
> the man, an identity—it can't be
> otherwise—an
> interpenetration, both ways. Rolling
> up! obverse, reverse;
> the drunk the sober; the illustrious
> the gross; one. In ignorance
> a certain knowledge and knowledge,
> undispersed, its own undoing.
>
>   (The multiple seed,
> packed tight with detail, soured,
> is lost in the flux and the mind,
> distracted, floats off in the same
> scum).[21]

Here, Williams gives us a template for the imperfect formulas of his entangled world-construction in *Paterson*. Notice his focus on imbrication and entanglement: "it can't be/ otherwise—an/interpenetration, both ways." This positional posture is very much akin to Haraway's own firmly materialist template for approaching her non-dualistic theorization of nature and culture, or as she terms it, "'naturecultures'—as one word—implosions of the discursive realms of nature and culture."[22] Here, Williams attempts to articulate a poetics that recognizes both the "multiple seed" construction of an individual's cultural identity and the construction of an ecology of place that is in part derived from the human and nonhuman entities that populate it: "shells and animalcules/ generally and so to man, /to Paterson."[23]

Williams attempts to create a verse that is a more organic, capacious expression (rather than being just a correspondence or representation) of the urban ecology around him. Again, referring to his early argument in *Spring and All* for the material extensions of discursive practice, he argues that "the work of the imagination is not 'like' anything, but transfused of the same forces which transfuse the earth—at least one small part of them."[24] This does not suggest that his poetics in *Paterson* is perfectly contiguous with the diffractive theories of Barad and Haraway, but that his willingness to explore the interpenetration of physical place and cultural identity and, to some extent, ignore or intentionally problematize the natural/cultural dichotomies of our modern and contemporary conceptual frameworks, leaves the poem open to the transdisciplinary overlap of contemporary diffractive reading methods. As John Beck describes the empiricism of Williams's poetic process: "The poet, like the scientist, discovers connection through the observation of individual, specific occurrences—the local—and compiles these specifics, relates each to the other, to extrapolate meaning. The observer is the organizing force, located within the field, and therefore all observations are relative, related, to him or herself."[25] This sense of poet as material observer or scientist highlights the diffractive interference entailed in empirical observation as well as its positional limitations. Barad credits Niels Bohr's early notion of complementarity, as opposed to Heisenberg's uncertainty principle, as being vital to her own arguments about the co-relational entanglements of scientific observation. She reiterates that it is impossible to divorce the role of the observer and the apparatus in the construction of the thing being observed; there is a diffractive relationship between the two, not because they are separate entities, but because they are always already entangled with one another.[26] Though, for Barad, as for Bohr, this does not take away from the veracity of the observation, nor does it imply that, since observation is always mediated by a cultural subject, that the material is therefore subordinated to mere cultural observation. For her, it only demonstrates the imbrication of cultural expression within the non-anthropocentric universe and vice versa. For both Bohr and Barad, a certain measure of objectivity is possible, but their sense of objectivity does not imply a separation between the observer and the observed or a Cartesian sense of independence or observational austerity. As Barad argues, rejecting Protagoras's famous dictum that "man is the measure of all things":

> Posthumanism, as I intend it here, is not calibrated to the human; on the contrary, it is about taking issues with human exceptionalism while being accountable for the role we play in the differential constitution and differential positioning of the human among other creatures (both living and nonliving). Posthumanism does not attribute the source of all change to culture, denying nature any sense of agency or historicity. In fact, it refuses the idea of a natural (or for that matter, a purely cultural) division between nature and culture, calling for an accounting of how this boundary is actively configured and reconfigured.[27]

Here, Barad confirms, with much more philosophic and scientific acumen than Williams, his own articulation of the "interpenetration" of the natural and the cultural, the observer and his/her/their physical location. Furthermore, her notion of natural/cultural imbrication also pushes against any sort of homogenized merging of the natural-material and the cultural-transcendent. She consistently counters the subsuming narratives envisioned by the strong theories of scientific realism and cultural constructivism. For

Williams, there is a constant move in *Paterson* toward a gathering up and rolling up of the sum; but the result is always a heterogeneous, messy, local totality that does not and perhaps should not formally cohere into a final articulation. As Barad suggests, the boundary or point of interference must be "actively configured and reconfigured." Or as Kai Merten argues in the introduction to this volume, citing the work of Hans Blumenberg, "with the advent of modern science, a new notion of reading (nature) emerged that conceived of reading not as the reception of a coherent text, a unified whole, anymore, but rather as the deciphering of discrete units, whose totality is not (yet) known to the reader and can therefore not provide the horizon for the reading process."[28] *Paterson*, as a late modern epic, certainly sustains this peripheral or localized approach to the conception of totality, "rolling/ up the sum by defective means," "a mass of detail/to interrelate on a new ground."[29]

Early eco-criticism has already drawn attention to Williams's anticipation of some of the ecological thinking that often attends new materialist theory. In Michael Long's essay, "William Carlos Williams, Ecocriticism, and Contemporary American Poetry," he argues that some of the natural-cultural entanglements in *Paterson* presage the now more rigorously theorized foundations of eco-poetics.[30] Rather than nature being merely a place of wonder, escape, and renewal or, conversely, an opaque backdrop to the primacy of cultural reality, Long argues that Williams presents an ecology where man, nature, and the modern city are intricately and inseparably enmeshed:

> Theories of writing and reading poetry that underscore language as a function of *poesis* suggest the inadequacy of the view that language separates us from the world—the idea that all human patterns of thought, schemas, and generalizations are impositions on a preexisting state we call nature . . . The crucial point is that Williams's poetics looks back not at reestablishing a lost connection with the world because, as I have said, we are always already in that world. Rather the problem the poet faces is looking forward to the ways that we are able to become present to the possibilities of the phenomenal world where we have been living all along.[31]

Here, Long highlights the ontological rapprochement between nature and culture in literary studies and earlier eco-criticism that philosophers of science and culture like Haraway, Barad, and Latour have been simultaneously theorizing for nearly just as long. Rather than continuing the conceit perpetuated by *both* scientific realism and cultural constructivism, that the human observer is somehow apart or outside the natural constitution of the world, Williams's poetics assumes that we are always already deeply embedded within it. As Williams opens "Book II" of *Paterson*:

>   Outside
>
> >   outside myself
> >
> > >   there is a world,
>
> he rumbled, subject to my incursions
> —a world
> >   (to me) at rest,
> > >   which I approach
>
> concretely—³²

In this declaration, Williams reiterates his materialist commitments to concrete embeddedness rather than poetic or cultural abstractions. Yet, even here, Williams dithers on the relational status of this entanglement of the human and nonhuman world. He defines the world as "outside," "at rest" but yet "subject" to his incursions. But, notice the parenthesis around the words "to me" that break up this static image of the human observer in a world which is tangible but without apparent motion. Williams/the speaker suggests that there is a world outside himself, beyond himself, a world responsive to his interaction and incursions, but the subjectivity introduced by the "(to me) at rest" suggests that great portions of the world are active in ways beyond the limited capabilities of his concrete, yet subjective incursions.³³ The world is "at rest," or must appear to be, for the purposes of both the organization of the poem and for the functionality of being in the world. Yet, on the molecular and cosmic level, even early modern physics and astronomy suggest rapid movement, constant flux and reformation within the actual constitution of our physical reality. And twentieth- and twenty-first-century physics have further borne out the parallax and quantum states of being that, while sometimes determined to be in one position, are in fact constantly in motion. In measuring the positions of external objects, so much depends upon the observer's own relationship to those objects. Bohr defined this as complementarity; Barad extends this idea to material-cultural diffraction. In these lines, Williams intimates the capriciousness of the outside world while also recognizing that this capriciousness is often un-regarded by the limited position of the observer.

While moving away from an anthropocentric point of view is an important gesture, it is also an impossible one as well. Many of the understandings we have of the natural world extend only to our interaction, inference, and physical superposition with it. Here, Williams's lines expressing the slippery relationship between human entanglement and interaction with the outside world coalesce with Barad's notion of a diffractively mediated relationship. She argues that the incursions of material reality and discursive practices are far more interrelated and influential than they are often conceptualized or articulated either in scientific or cultural theory. As she asserts in the introduction to *Meeting the Universe Halfway*:

Performative accounts that social and political theorists have offered focus on the productive nature of social practices and human bodies. By contrast agential realism takes account of the fact that forces at work in the materialization of bodies are not only social, and the bodies produced are not only human. Crucially, I argue that agential realism clarifies the causal relationship between discursive practices and material phenomena. That is, I propose a new understanding of how discursive practices are related to the material world.[34]

While Williams is, of course, neither a theoretical physicist nor a new materialist philosopher, *Paterson,* as a whole, is concerned with finding a more concrete approach to accessing the "outside" world. This desire to articulate the connection between the physical material and the discursive is palpable throughout the poem. And many of the (sometimes jarring) linguistic assemblages that make up the scattered roots of the poem serve to instigate the intentional trespassing of discursive and material boundaries. They attempt to chart and register these moments of discursive connection to the material. Barad and Haraway describe this as the mapping of diffractive patterns of interference; Susan Heckman refers to this as material disclosure; Williams, in "Book IV" of *Paterson*, describes it as the dissonance that leads to discovery, which I will discuss in the final section of the chapter.[35]

Dissonance, Discovery, Diffractive Poetics

From his early prose improvisations in *Kora in Hell*, Williams consistently maintains a method of carelessness and haphazard linguistic invention encouraged by his commitment to conceptual errantry and disjunction. The poetry becomes a process of continuously failing experiments that may lead to discovery, often by very productive mistakes or new, field-generated, hypotheses. As he argues with deliberate incongruity at the beginning of the third section of "Book III": "It is dangerous to leave written that which is badly written. . . . Only one answer: write carelessly so that nothing that is not green will survive."[36] Rather than taking the premise that bad writing is dangerous and should be avoided, Williams counterintuitively argues that this should inspire carelessness rather than refinement, that affected or cautious writing can actually lead to the "recurring deadliness" of the tired, well-worn paths of the earlier poetic traditions. He insists instead that poetic carelessness can actually generate new discovery and uncanny connections that might not arise from deliberate, linear contemplation. As he asserts in another section, perhaps deriving his argument from similar lines in the lyrics of Emily Dickinson, "Let the words/fall any way at all—that they may/hit love aslant. It will be a rare/visitation."[37] This intentional errantry in poetic composition was actually taken up by later movements in the New American poetry such as the Beatniks, the Black Mountain School, and, to some extent, the Language School. This rough-hewn, inspired poetics is often described using Allen Ginsberg's mantra: "First thought, best thought."[38] But here, Williams invokes the idea as a method, not only of avoiding tired, Euro-inflected frameworks for American poetry, but also as a means of establishing a more tangible connection to reality—even if the bulk of this careless production leads to dead ends. Williams takes up this notion again in "Book IV," using the chemist Marie Curie's accidental discovery of the radioactive properties inherent in different variations of uranium as an example of what he refers to throughout this passage as "the radiant gist" of haphazard discovery:

A dissonance
in the valence of Uranium
led to the discovery

Dissonance
(if you are interested)
leads to discovery

—to dissect away
the block and leave
a separate metal.[39]

While Curie did not discover uranium, in her experiments she came across some of its radioactive iterations such as radium and thorium; and she found that their powerful properties, though caused by particular catalytic interactions between elements, actually emerge from within the subatomic particles themselves. Though Williams's scientific analogy is a good deal more simplified than the emergent process of radioactivity itself, this late modernist, post-nuclear description of the radioactive potential of poetic discovery also overlaps with Barad's argument for diffractive interpretation, finding productive interference between areas that are traditionally theorized as separate or unrelated.

Paterson, as both poem and material object, is a form of diffractive writing, blending the genres of poetry and prose, integrating historical and contemporary examples, overlapping and conflating scientific discoveries with those of poetics. Using dissonance as the catalytic method here, Williams's purpose is not to generate a syncretic, fully integrated totality or some sort of elegant remainder, but rather to generate productive moments of interstitial superposition. As Haraway explains, "[a] diffraction pattern does not map where differences appear, but rather maps where the effects of difference appear."[40] For both Barad and Haraway, mapping patterns of diffraction entails looking for these traces of material, cultural, and linguistic interference. For Williams, his structural apparatus in *Paterson* entails finding moments of interpenetration or productive interference, where the effects of the natural, the cultural, and the personal are momentarily disclosed.

For Williams, the most important physical feature and metonymic image that serves to sustain the energy of the poem is the Passaic Falls. In each of the five books of *Paterson*, he returns to the Falls as a source of both poetic and material inspiration, recognizing it as the kinetic life-force to the town of Paterson. It is also the physical feature that most clearly exemplifies Williams's own conception of diffractive poetics. As Williams describes in a statement preceding the poem, "[t]he noise of the Falls seemed to me to be a language which we were and are seeking and my search, as I looked about, became to struggle to interpret and use this language. This is the substance of the poem."[41] Throughout *Paterson*, Williams offers up the geographic feature as both a generative and destructive force. It powers the great engines of industry to the benefit of urban growth and to the detriment of the local ecology.[42] But it also consumes two of its historic citizens, the daredevil, Sam Patch, and the ambiguous suicide, Mrs. Cummings. Williams brings their respective falls into recursive contemplation throughout the first three books.[43] But at the end of "Book III," Williams returns to the waterfall in a moment of creative crisis. And in this extended passage, he articulates the volatile energy of the waters, relating it to his own—at times unwieldy—foray into the creative process of composing the lengthy poem. In this turbulent section of emotionally agitated, almost destabilized writing, Williams attempts to end the third book. In the diffractive, dissonant *metonymic metaphor* of the falls, Williams reveals his own internal conflict and misgivings, and he reexposes the precarity of the loose structural grounding of the long poem itself:

> The past above, the future below
> and the present pouring down: the roar,
> the roar of the present, a speech—
> is, of necessity, my sole concern   .
>
> They plunged, they fell in a swoon   .
> or by intention, to make an end—the
> roar, unrelenting, witnessing   .
> Neither past nor the future
>
> Neither to stare amnesic—forgetting.
> The language cascades into the
> invisible, beyond and above: the falls
> of which it is the visible part—

>   [. . .] I must
> find my meaning and lay it, white,
> beside the sliding water: myself—
> comb out the language—or succumb
>
> —whatever the complexion. Let
> me out! (Well, go!) this rhetoric
> Is real!⁴⁴

Here, many of the themes of *Paterson*, its embedded history, its physical expression, its conceptual-discursive iteration of an individual and cultural identity, all converge in an image of heterogeneous confusion and existential crisis. "Book III" ends with a wish to escape and with the plea being granted. This is more than a bit ironic since both the luckless Sam Patch and the "swooning" suicide of Mrs. Cummings are mentioned at the top of this section: "they plunged, they fell into a swoon . / or by intention to make an end." While in "Book I," Williams takes time to explore the possible reason for their leaps, here the speaker seems to be contemplating his own creative leap with the poem, tying in the physical leap with his rhetorical, discursive leap: " [a] speech—/ is, of necessity my sole concern." But clearly this leap at this first attempted ending to *Paterson* is intended to be more than merely rhetorical.⁴⁵ And Williams intentionally combines the physical and discursive aspects of this scene, "[t]he language cascades into the/ Invisible, beyond and above: the falls/ Of which it is the visible part—." Here, Williams is excessively vehement in merging the expressions of both the natural and the discursive, the visible and the invisible. And he adds to this the anxiety of historical influence, which converges both at the top of the falls (the past) and the bottom (the future). While denying neither the past nor the future, the speaker makes a final decision to seek for meaning in the turbulent confusion of the physical and discursive present—though this decision will not necessarily generate a successful synthetic outcome: "I must/find my meaning and lay it, white,/beside the sliding water: myself—/Comb out the language—or succumb." Here, in this very diffractive analogy, Williams argues that this dance of meaning or determination seems to be at the center of a number of different referential frameworks: the historical, the natural, and the present, provisionally discursive; to "comb out the language" and "find the meaning" between these overlapping words and waters.

The scene at the Falls serves as both a metaphor and a physical example of his notion of dissonance as a form of discovery, but also of its precarity and potential failure. He articulates the natural, violent, creative powers of the plunging water, while suggesting that they overlap with—rather than merely abstractly resemble—his own linguistic forays into world and culture creation. The Falls serve as a metonymic extension *of* rather than a purely metaphorical substitute *for* his own process of aesthetic creation—though the image is strained enough to exhibit aspects of both metaphor and metonymy. His own discursive assemblages and conceptual enjambments throughout *Paterson* are meant to be linguistic, but nevertheless material, examples of nature rather than detached representations of it. It is also important to note the looming importance but also the un-sublimated role of history in this passage. He ends this third book with both a concession to the inability to evade historical influence—its presence within the present—but he also argues that an overreliance on historical determinacy can become a pitfall that can paralyze or occlude the possibility of discovery in the present moment.

CONCLUSION

Moving from this tumultuous and unresolved moment at the center of *Paterson*, I would like to return to my larger argument that diffractive reading can be a productive method to examine our own natural, cultural, and historical critical moment, though not without its limitations. In Moran's essay, "Decoherent Reading," she notes that Barad's expansive use of diffraction neglects to account for the remaining problem of quantum decoherence—that the existence of the quantum states of matter does not necessarily explain why matter most often still follows the rule of classical physics. However, Moran argues that this "decoherence" problem might productively disturb and refine the application of diffraction as a reading methodology. "Holding onto this tension, or 'staying with the trouble', as Haraway puts it, could stave off the desire to make hierarchizing moves that privilege the quantum over the classical, matter over meaning, science over storytelling (or their opposites)."[46] Here, I find myself in strong agreement with Moran's argument. From my own literary studies perspective, Barad's diffractive reading is indeed a useful tool for finding some of the occlusions and gaps created by bounded commitments to cultural constructivism and dialectical materialism. But replacing one strong theory of materialism with another more "faithful" to reality ends up neglecting and flattening the ontologies it purports to be recovering.

Sociohistorical methods of critique still remain prescient. At the beginning of the twenty-first century, we are still affected by the same issues as those at the start of twentieth century. We are still ruled by the same stars of a long modernity shaped in many ways by the uneven distribution of material and ecological resources. But, perhaps some of these critical reading methods remain overly dependent on the dialectical revolutions of Hegelian thought, restricted in their adherence to continual synthesis and reflective mirroring, performing complex demonstrations that only seem to recapitulate the same diagnoses.[47] And, as Barad and Haraway argue, there is perhaps much potential in using diffraction as a critical interpretive practice, not as a replacement to historical critique but as a productive and timely supplement: one that explores patterns of interference that exist beyond purely anthropo-dialectical thought, moving beyond the overdeterminations in criticism that are at times too reliant on methods of endless reflection and mirroring. As Donna Haraway argues in her book *Modest Witness*, "[r]eflexivity has become much recommended as a critical practice, but my suspicion is that reflexivity, like reflection only displaces the same elsewhere."[48] Or as she argues in "The Promises of Monsters," the social and linguistic turns in cultural studies, while a very necessary response to modernist and scientific essentialism, have only managed to reflect an inverse mirroring of the Enlightenment mind/body dualism, trading one transcendental signified for another: "[I]t will not do to approach science as cultural or social construction, as if culture and society are transcendent categories, any more than nature or the object is."[49] Likewise, I am arguing that while we should never deny or ignore the centrality of history in our understanding of materiality, it is perhaps both useful and timely to refresh the lenses in our understanding of our relationship to the physical world, to each other, and to ourselves—that the choice between scientific materialism/realism on the one hand and social constructivism on the other is perhaps another false binary left over from the hangover of transcendent notions of the powers of interpretation—the desire to still think in terms of totality. In modernist literary studies, Paul Saint-Amour has recently argued for a move toward what he terms a weakening of theory, arguing that the "political formalism" in cultural theory may in fact be producing the same mirrored negatives of the capitalist logics that it means to counter:

> I might begin by saying that capitalism, not least in its neoliberal morphology, is the ultimate strong theory without a theorist, the ultimate sovereign field without a sovereign. When we oppose it with an equally totalizing theory of anti-capitalism, we often mass-produce the same findings and refusals we've been cranking out for decades, multiplying these across the landscape in a strange parody of the thing we wish to challenge. Yes, these are oppositions that bear repeating and disseminating. But when what you oppose has a death-grip on repetition and dissemination, you may need to shift registers: you may need not only different ways of speaking your opposition, but different scales and intensities at which to speak it.[50]

Here, Saint-Amour, in a different academic context, recaptures the tenor of Haraway's critique of dialectical reflection which "only displaces the same elsewhere." Rather than reading science through the critical lens of social constructivism or subjecting the complexities of culture to the cold gaze of scientific realism, there are perhaps other useful paths of critique that refuse or at least attempt to avoid the endless mirroring of these subsuming frameworks. One way is through diffractive reading, which focuses on the moments of interference between fields that are too often constituted as disciplinarily distinct or, alternately, subordinated to the service of the other's singular vantage point. Williams's *Paterson* is a poem that willingly exhibits this notion of diffractive interference, and, in fact, uses a diffractive poetics at the center of its generative process.

NOTES

1. William Carlos Williams, *Paterson,* ed. Christopher MacGowan (New York: New Directions, 1992), 2.

2. William Carlos Williams, *The Autobiography of William Carlos Williams* (New York: New Directions, 1967), 391 and 392.

3. In "Book III," Williams goes as far as to include an historical chart outlining the specific mineral composition of the different layers of substrata at the artesian well at the Passaic Rolling Mill. Williams, *Paterson*, 139.

4. Williams, *Autobiography*, 391.

5. Donna Haraway, *How Like a Leaf: An Interview with Thryza Nicholas Goodeve* (New York: Routledge, 1998), 106–108. As she argues: "It's almost like my examples are the theories. Again, it's that my sense of metaphor is drawn from the literal biological examples and my theories are not abstractions. If anything, they are redescriptions. So if one were going to characterize my way of theorizing, it would be to redescribe, to rescribe something so that it becomes thicker than it first seems."

6. Karen Barad, *Meeting the Universe Halfway: Quantum Physics and the Entanglement of Matter and Meaning* (Durham: Duke University Press, 2007), 88–91.

7. See Stacey Moran's essay in this collection, "Decoherent Reading: On the Constitutive Exclusions of Diffractive Reading." Here, Moran argues that Barad's strong claim concerning diffraction is an *artifactual* rather than a purely *scientific* theory. Yet, it is precisely the artifactual nature of diffraction which is a useful challenge to reigning scientific and cultural paradigms which contain their own underlying narratives and descriptive statements. Moran argues that Barad's notion of diffraction would benefit from a complementary engagement with the ongoing problem in physics of the *decoherence* between classical and quantum states of matter.

8. Williams, *Paterson*, 4.

9. This sense of the word *disclosure* is inspired by Susan Hekman's argument in *The Material of Knowledge: Feminist Disclosures* (Bloomington: Indiana University Press, 2010), 93. Drawing from both Barad and Latour, Hekman suggests that working within different epistemes entails different levels of material disclosure, where different knowledge are revealed through different paths of disciplinary

investigation: "Disclosure is not a refutation of relativism or skepticism but a new way of approaching the issues of knowledge and reality . . . Disclosures have real material consequences . . . We still cannot argue for absolute truth. But we can make arguments grounded in the material consequences of the disclosure that we practice."

10. Williams, *Paterson*, 3.

11. William Carlos Williams, *Imaginations* (New York: New Directions, 1971), 102.

12. Williams, *Imaginations*, 121.

13. As Teare argues in the opening of his chapbook: "I want to get/closer to where material/touches language." *Companion Grasses* (Richmond, CA: Omnidawn Publishing, 2013), 19; spaces in the original. Or, as Eleni Sikelianos suggests in an essay on her material poetics, "I write to find that place where language wakes us up, with a smack or gently, rather than putting us to sleep. That means rummaging around in the gap between language and body/consciousness to make the real *real*. In that sense, it is a devotional act whose mission is to attend to the particulars of self and other (and others are also animals, rocks, trees, and dirt), to particularize the world (in contrast to the generalizing forces of power)." "Refuse/Refuge: Be Longing," *Poetry Foundation*, February 12, 2018, https://www.poetryfoundation.org/harriet/2018/02/refuse-refuge-be-longing. Her last sentence in particular directly invokes the opening of *Paterson*: "To make a start,/ out of particulars/ and make them general."

14. Barad, *Meeting*, 71.

15. Ibid., 74.

16. Ibid., 76.

17. For example, early in her chapter on diffraction, Barad makes the claim: "there is a deep sense in which we can understand diffraction patterns—as patterns of difference that make a difference—to be the fundamental constituents that make up the world." *Meeting*, 72. This attempt to turn diffraction into a singular material substrate is a bit too ambitious and speculative an assertion for me to maintain—at least without further reinforcement from other scientific thinkers.

18. In fact, much of new materialist theory returns to the monism espoused in Spinoza's work in his *Ethics*, often subtitled "God and/or Nature." This immanent materialist philosophy asserts that any sense of the transcendent, conceptual, or universal ultimately has its origin in the physical foundation of matter. While considered blasphemous in its own time and still controversial today, Spinoza's thought is echoed in the works of materialist thinkers as various as Karl Marx, Bruno Latour, Alfred North Whitehead, Gilles Deleuze, Jane Bennett, Karen Barad, and Donna Haraway.

19. Barad, *Meeting*, 55. Italics in original.

20. Williams, *Paterson*, 6, 9, 145.

21. Williams, *Paterson*, 4.

22. Haraway, *How Like a Leaf*, 105.

23. Williams, *Paterson*, 5.

24. Williams, *Imaginations*, 121.

25. John Beck, *Writing the Radical Center: William Carlos Williams, John Dewey, and American Cultural Politics* (Albany: State University of New York P, 2001), 139.

26. Barad terms this relationship *intra-action* rather than inter-action, since the latter implies a sense of autonomy that violates her notion of an already entangled universe. She defines and distinguishes both terms in *Meeting the Universe Halfway*, "I introduce the neologism 'intra-action' to signify the mutual constitution of objects and agencies of observation within phenomena (in contrast to 'interaction', which assumes the prior existence of distinct entities)" (197).

27. Barad, *Meeting*, 136.

28. See Merten, Introduction, 9.

29. Williams, *Paterson*, 3, 19.

30. For examples of the engagement of recent eco-criticism with new materialist and posthumanist theory, see *Material Ecocriticism*, ed. Serenella Iovino and Serpil Oppermann (Bloomington: Indiana University Press, 2014), *Ecopoetics: Essays in the Field*, ed. Angela Hume and Gillian Osborne (Iowa City: University of Iowa Press, 2018), and *Posthuman Ecologies: Complexity and Process after Deleuze*, ed. Rosi Braidotti and Simone Bingall (London: Rowman and Littlefield International, 2019).

31. Mark Long, "William Carlos Williams, Ecocriticism, and Contemporary American Poetry," in *Ecopoetry: An Introduction*, ed. J. Scott Bryson (Salt Lake City: University of Utah Press, 2002), 59, 65.

32. Williams, *Paterson*, 43.

33. Barad argues throughout *Meeting the Universe Halfway* for the activity and liveliness of supposedly inanimate matter; this *liveliness* is the specific focus of Jane Bennett's political approach to new materialism. See Jane Bennett, *Vibrant Matter: A Political Ecology of Things* (Durham: Duke University Press, 2010).

34. Barad, *Meeting*, 33–4.

35. Williams, *Paterson*, 175.

36. Williams, *Paterson*, 129.

37. Williams, *Paterson*, 142.

38. Williams actually includes correspondence between himself and Ginsberg, a Paterson native and, at the time, a fledgling poet, in "Book IV" and "Book V" of *Paterson*. See *Paterson*, 172–4, 193, 210–11.

39. Williams, *Paterson*, 175.

40. Donna Haraway, "The Promises of Monsters: A Regenerative Politics for Inappropriate/d Others," in *Cyber Sexualities: A Reader on Feminist Theory, Cyborgs and Cyberspace*, ed. with intro. Jenny Wolmark (Edinburgh: Edinburgh University Press, 1999), 320.

41. Williams, *Paterson*, xiv.

42. Williams, *Paterson*, 69–74.

43. Williams, *Paterson*, 14–16, 83–85, 145.

44. Williams, *Paterson*, 144–45.

45. The epic version of *Paterson* was originally intended to be three books, then it became four, and eventually five. There is even a sixth book that Williams was working on at his death. See *Paterson*, 237–40.

46. From Moran, "Decoherent Reading," 79..

47. As Latour argues: "The question was never to get *away* from the facts but to get *closer* to them, not fighting empiricism but, on the contrary, renewing empiricism." "Why Has Critique Run Out of Steam? From Matters of Facts to Matters of Concern," *Critical Inquiry* 30, no. 2 (2004): 231; emphasis in original, http://www.jstor.org/stable/10.1086/421123. And as feminist materialists like Karen Barad, Donna Haraway, and Susan Hekman have reiterated (often citing Latour's specific argument here), this idea of renewed empiricism is not a return to the false sense of objectivity in scientific realism, but a new settlement that refuses to allow either scientism or cultural constructivism to transcend the other. As Barad argues in a 2012 interview drawing from the Latour's essay directly: "Epistemology, ontology, and ethics are inseparable. Matters of fact, matters of concern, and matters of care are shot through with one another. Or to put it yet another way: matter and meaning cannot be severed." "'Matter Feels, Converses, Suffers, Desires, Yearns and Remembers': Interview with Karen Barad," in *New Materialism: Interviews & Cartographies*, ed. Rick Dolphijn and Iris van der Tuin (Ann Arbor: Open Humanities Press, 2012), 69, http://dx.doi.org/10.3998/ohp.11515701.0001.001.

48. Donna Haraway, *Modest_Witness@SEcond_Millennium.FemaleMan©_Meets_OncoMouse*™ (New York: Routledge, 1997), 16.

49. Haraway, "The Promises of Monsters," 358.

50. Paul K. Saint-Amour, "Weak Theory, Weak Modernism," *Modernism/Modernity* 27, no. 3 (September 2018): 455, https://doi.org/10.1353/mod.2018.0035.

Chapter 7

Sauron's Sliding Door

The Diffraction of Mythological and Intimate "Evil" in Tolkien

Bo Kampmann Walther

I

A landscape of degradation forms the backdrop of the final resolution of the story of the One Ring and the overthrow of Sauron, and thus ends J. R. R. Tolkien's great epic *The Lord of the Rings*. Shortly after he began what he thought should be a sequel entitled *The New Shadow*. Tolkien only completed a few pages and then abandoned the project entirely. Perhaps he arrived at the conclusion that the opposition of good and evil had already been resolved, and that the sequel would be a one-dimensional replay of the events. Sauron was a thing of the past. The elves had left the stage, shipped to the shores of Aman, and natural history, the history of men, had begun.

This chapter sees it otherwise. Through a diffractive reading technique inspired by Karen Barad, Georges Bataille, and Gilles Deleuze, I shall oppose the above view, that there is nothing more to be said after the extinction of the last nonhuman personalization of evil. Indeed, there is. Not only in the sense that *The New Shadow* would have been a magnificent "thriller" and insight into the psychological and political structures that drive mankind, but also because the text is a great lens with which to magnify a much wider context (which can only be hinted at here), and at the same time a much more meticulous microcosm of Tolkien's fiction. The result of such a reading is the disclosure of a counter-story that allows for a more intimate documentation of the terror that lurks underneath a culture that moves away from the Evil of myth to the malevolence of Men.

In a way, "the Fall" depicted in Tolkien's fiction is not only comprised in the narrative of history's hubris and nemesis, the tale of how the original light blackened and splintered.[1] It is also the downfall of Sauron, of Evil, in person or character, upholding some sort of representational recognizability. Suddenly, cruelty as a fantastic presence stands in opposition to the tamed but effectively much more sinister and "modern" evil entering our intimate ménage yet, at the same time, dimly resonating with the power of good old Evil. However, this dichotomy must not be treated as a cut separating an authorial inclusion, which iconized itself in *The Lord of the Rings* and *The Silmarillion*, from a geeky add-on. Rather, it poses as ever-present modifications exploding with validity. Inspired by Karen Barad and her *Meeting the Universe Halfway* and the notion of what Gilles Deleuze calls "the virtual," there is a possibility that the "intra-actions" of such a reading catalyze these separations and their diffusing temporalities so one can examine them long enough to gain knowledge about them. I see diffractive reading here as a kind of close reading, a mode of highlighting strange causalities and temporal loops. The upshot of this is the suggestion of new reading policies to act against the hegemony of Tolkien exegesis. Or, even better, to *superimpose* the kind of reading that is suggested here, a diffracted reading, onto the landscape of Tolkien's tropes, motives, and themes. We shall try to read anti-authorially yet affectionately materialistically in favor of what the texts themselves illuminate. This, in turn, as we shall see, will require some bizarre, causal twists as well as treating some of Tolkien's lesser text fragments as major contributions and procedural guidelines.

The first part focuses on the concept of diffraction as it has been coined and developed by Donna Haraway and Karen Barad. This leads to a discussion of the notion of the material imaginary by Georges Bataille and the insistence upon a "base materialism," as he calls it, dwelling in an obscure vicinity of the duality of signifier and signified. The next section deals explicitly with *The New Shadow*, set in The Fourth Age in the aftermath of the great downfall of Sauron, in which the refrains of self-corruption and dominance form a potent backdrop. Also, the ever-present motives of shadows, spite, and fear of the unknown reside here. Third, I turn to an equally small text that Tolkien abandoned, included in *The Peoples of Middle-Earth*, the short tale of "Tal-Elmar." Through Tolkien's imagery, we learn of a taxonomy of, on the one hand, closeness and familiarity, and hazard and transgression, on the other. The aim is to unwrap difference, unceasingly cross-cut and cross-cutting,[2] in its uncanny, repressed form, and to show that a watchfulness toward intra-relations not just as representations (signs) but as *real objects in their own right* may uncover this very difference. Essentially, this is what Tolkien calls "fantasy" (and *phantazein*, "to make visible"), and what Deleuze names "the virtual," which will be examined in the final part. Tolkien's evils exemplify a kind of *phantazein*, which also acts as a "new" material between signifier and signified, graspable in/as Deleuze's virtual.

The following reading openly claims that *The New Shadow* and "Tal-Elmar" are the results of a fiction leading from the mythologization of evil to the normalization of it; but also that the texts contain *the source* (an awkward, backward kind of source) of images from the chronologically preceding texts. Working with diffractive methodology means to enter a zone of "entangled relationalities to make connections between entities that do not appear to be proximate in space and time."[3]

II

Both Haraway and Barad see diffraction as a unique way of performing science that embraces difference rather than reiterate the "sameness" of reflexive interpretation. As Haraway notes:

> Reflexivity has been much recommended as a critical practice, but my suspicion is that reflexivity, life reflection, only displaces the same elsewhere, setting up worries about copy and original and the search for the authentic and really real.[4]

Diffraction becomes a tactic for producing differences instead of copiously reproducing textual identity in the shape of male dominance, the relation between autonomous humans and nonhuman entities, or in the more abstract sense of overtaking a Cartesian epistemology. The latter is the belief that we have direct access to representations that correlate with the impartiality of our individual self and the outside material world.[5] Barad claims, in an implicit homage to the tradition of Adorno's "non-identity" and the difference thinking of French poststructuralism, that diffraction unshackles our responsiveness toward material engagement and "the relations of difference and how they matter."[6]

While for Haraway diffraction is treated as a kind of figuration pointing toward knowledge production and reception, Barad extends the tropical notion and proposes a much more physical approach focusing on the entanglement of matter and meaning and using key ideas from Niels Bohr's quantum physics (the so-called Copenhagen Interpretation) as well as Werner Heisenberg's uncertainty principle. One of many obscure features of quantum physics is the superposition of waves and particles and the impossibility of an observer establishing the exact position and velocity (momentum) of a photon. This leads to the theory of superposition, the fact that photons can be two places at once in the universe, not to mention the infamous wave-particle duality and Heisenberg's claim that while there may be a fundamental ambiguity at play at the smallest scale of our universe there is nevertheless a physical model (derived from classical, linear physics) which provides a statistical *probability* based on said uncertainty.⁷ Although quantum physics may not be fathomable it is still accountable. In Heisenberg's view, epistemological undecidability and ontological methodology coexist. Barad also insists on the indeterminacy principle, implying that light is *ontologically* undefined before it hits the observation screen or diffraction grating. In view of this, she sees Heisenberg's uncertainty principle as falling too short because it is mainly about an epistemological uncertainty and not an ontological one.

Barad is furthermore concerned about the intra-actions that exist between humans, texts, and nonhumans. These intra-actions are grounded—although they also "float"—in agential, performative events. Rather than being the effect of an analytical framework that dictates the representational ontology of differences, that is, what these differences "are"; diffraction tries to shed light on how differences *emerge*.⁸ As Barad puts it in *Meeting the Universe Halfway*:

> Unlike methods of reading one text or set of ideas against another where one set serves as a fixed frame of reference, diffraction involves reading insights through another in ways that help illuminate differences as they emerge: how different differences get made, what gets excluded, and how these exclusions matter.⁹

Such relational ontology where the reading of a text promotes a liberation from the usual tyranny of source-copy, world-mind correlations, is echoed by various New Materialism theorists and thinkers of Ecocriticism, who all wish to escape the representational trap of figuring out what a subject—or an ecological catastrophe—is and stands for. As noted by Lenz Tagushi, classical interpretation has a very specific agenda:

> As an act of thinking, interpretation in reflexive analysis is about reflecting sameness (as in mirroring), or identifying differences from something previously identified and acknowledged; a thing, an identity, a category, a discursive theme or a subject position.¹⁰

Diffraction is not only a mental activity separated by a correlation of Cartesian res cogitans and res extensa. To join in diffractive analysis means to scan the faculties of knowing as an enactment *in* the materiality of a world however momentarily it may seem through the superimposition of "mind" and "matter." Thus, a diffractive methodology de-centers the onto-epistemological thinking and in turn defies the ruling interpretivism of splits like subject-object, human-nonhuman, and so on. What Barad's methodology has in common with Graham Harman's Object-Oriented Ontology is the belief that relational ontology exactly collapses the material *and* the discursive into one and the same exercise of difference.[11] What this means is that the connections within and between different bodies, and between body/mind and text/discursive structures, are themselves comprehended as material objects and not just representational projections.

Clearly, then, a diffractive reading practice wishes to peep into the dark, suppressed, nonidentical constituent of signs and texts and other discursive structures and reclaim their material base potential and being.[12] In his text "Deconstruction and/as Ecology," Timothy Morton writes of the "dark dimension of things" explored by phenomenological philosophers, such as Edmund Husserl, Maurice Merleau-Ponty, and Martin Heidegger, and later in David Abram's *The Spell of the Sensuous*, and their affection with the mundane features of human experience.[13] Writers, Morton states, engage with reading the world so as to articulate the ghostly properties of the thing. Reading is "formally ecological"[14] since it considers the dusky sides of things, masked as linguistic representations of unreachable presence. Morton speculates that there is a stance toward this opaque phenomenology of signs and objects within the deconstruction of Jacques Derrida and his talk of a text's fundamental undecidability.[15] It is this undecidability, this resistance to, and at the same time desire for, unveiling—even freeing—the ecological materiality of a text, that lies at the heart of what has been coined the "material turn."[16] Not in any strict ontological sense obeying the law of non-contradiction; and neither as a direct claim for confronting the transcendental signifier, which would simultaneously count as godly viewpoint and rock solid foundation. Narratives can never, in a Kantian reasoning, be things *an sich*. Yet, these things, especially their dark parts, may be heard *für uns* as the distant, beating drum of a text's ontic epistemology, echoes below a simulation of a world and its conversion from knowledge to signs and symbols. In other words, being on the lookout for this underlying quality of a text, the dark side of the sign-matter, means to search for a material imaginary.

In a reading of Jacques Lacan's notion of "the imaginary" and George Bataille's concept of "nonlogical difference," F. Scott Scribner offers an account of "the material imaginary" as a moment of collapse between signified and signifier.[17] Bataille's return to what he calls a "base materialism" implies a conflation of these two orders, thing and sign, because the disobedience of the symbolic and the real precisely means overthrowing the symbolic order—and hence distance—that abides in the chasm between the object-thing and the signifier, its arbitrary pointer.[18] Base materialism is a way of reclaiming the true ontological yet impossible superiority of materiality. Bataille's conviction is that "dead matter" may be dead in a Kantian science of Being and that the debate of whose primacy is to be trusted, Idea or Matter, is a moot point. "Base matter is external and foreign to ideal human aspirations, and it refuses to allow itself to be reduced to the great ontological machines resulting from these aspirations," Bataille writes in his essay "Base Materialism and Gnosticism."[19]

This doggedness toward the thing itself and its spectral side is a shared feature of Barad and Bataille. Something which is both "real," in a materialistic sense, and at the same time the product of fairy imagination may coexist as an object of onto-relational activity. This cohabitation of idea and matter has a counterpart in Tolkien's notion of *sub-creation*. The term "sub-creation," first developed in the essay "On Fairy-Stories" from 1939, was used by Tolkien to refer to the process of world-building and reassembling bits of known myths.[20] A human author is a "little maker" creating his own world within God's primary creation. Like the beings of Middle-Earth Tolkien believed that his work emulated the true creation performed by a deity. In his own words:

> What really happens is that the story-maker proves a successful "sub-creator." He makes a Secondary World which your mind can enter. Inside it, what he relates is "true": it accords with the laws of that world. You therefore believe it, while you are, as it were, inside. The moment disbelief arises, the spell is broken; the magic, or rather art, has failed. You are then out in the Primary World again, looking at the little abortive Secondary World from outside.[21]

Note the importance of *consistency*. The internal structure of the secondary world must be designed according to the laws of said world. Elves, dwarfs, dragons, magic may reside in such a world; but there cannot be both dragons and not dragons, at the same time. The truthfulness of a second world relies on the consistency and the structural strictness of its idioms, habitats, and populaces, in short: its *legendarium*, which springs from the imagination of the author and his ability to transform the mythopoetic sources into a coherent work of fiction.[22] Should this consistency be broken, it violently affects the cogency of the sub-creation and the delicate fabric of the fiction. The outer shell that protects the "true inside" of the creation is destroyed, and the spell is broken indicating the failure of art. If the sub-creator breaks the laws—or if the reader does not trust the validity of the world—the trickery that suspends the reader is traumatized and the force of the secondary world will be lost. Tolkien's passages of long description with minute details of setting demonstrate his theory: because Tolkien is the literal creator of the world of Middle-Earth, he must clearly and thoroughly express the properties of that world.[23]

III

Not long after completing *The Lord of the Rings*, Tolkien began work on what was supposed to be a sequel called *The New Shadow*. The action is set

100–150 years later during the reign of Aragon's son Eldarion. What links the two stories is the minor character Beregond, a disgraced soldier of Faramir's Gondor army whose son Borlas is the main protagonist of *The New Shadow*.

The context very much hinges on geopolitical trouble. Not only does Tolkien place us in a time in which the last reign of Evil is forever gone, destroyed by the Ringbearer and the prominence of Gandalf who managed to form one last alliance between the peoples of Middle-Earth. *The New Shadow* also, almost casually, informs us that the culmination of the king's return was short-lived. The elves and the wizards have gone from Middle-Earth. The dwarfs have moved to their rocky facilities underground, and the hobbits are now geographically as well as politically isolated if not forgotten in an enclave of the land of Eriador, the Shire.

Overlooking the great city of Minas Tirith, two men have a conversation in a garden. Borlas, an old man, speaks of the constant presence of evil in the hearts of Men and likens it to a dark tree that cannot be felled forever, while Saelon, the young man and a friend of Borlas' son, is doubtful. The pride in remembrance that Borlas uses against the rancorous revolt of Saelon is dependent on the loss of a world where elves executed their magic as both source and demise of myth and creation. Stories of the Ring and the Great War are now dissipated from living memory, and Borlas seems to live in an age where people have become trapped in self-representation and a thirst for supremacy. Children, we are told, play Orcs for fun and cut down trees, perhaps the most sacred of Tolkien's all-natural phenomena.[24] The death of Elessar threw Gondor into political striving and reactionary plots, one of them being a secret death cult of devil worshipping spreading through the military elite of Gondor.

Of this plot we do not hear much. Borlas' son, Berelach, may have been killed by the cult, and Saelon, the antagonist of the story, a childhood friend of Berelach, may or may not be a member of it. After a heated debate between Borlas and Saelon, mostly consisting of arguments pro et contra tree cutting and "orcish" behavior among youngsters, Borlas, an aging man outside his time, resolves to join Saelon in the tryst, unaware of his true motives and whether it is an ambush. Of course, the reader does not know either.

In May 1964, Tolkien wrote about *The New Shadow*:

> I did begin a story placed about 100 years after the Downfall, but it proved both sinister and depressing. Since we are dealing with Men, it is inevitable that we should be concerned with the most regrettable feature of their nature: their quick satiety with good. So that the people of Gondor in times of peace, justice and prosperity, would become discontented and restless—while the dynasts descended from Aragorn would become just kings and governors—like Denethor or worse. I found that even so early there was an outcrop of

revolutionary plots, about a centre of secret Satanistic religion; while Gondorian boys were playing at being Orcs and going around doing damage. I could have written a "thriller" about the plot and its discovery and overthrow—but it would have been just that. Not worth doing.[25]

In Tolkien's commentary, the text is "not worth doing" and quickly becomes a temporary respite from a nightmare history in which things always turn out wrong.[26] An era of peace is not "worth recounting," he writes, and even though world-weariness could make up for a neat spectacle there is almost an air of self-fulfilled prophecy about the "inevitable boredom of Men with the good."[27] Maybe the true purpose of Borlas is to set up the drama, in thriller fashion, before Borlas is slain by a villain. Or maybe not. But all the while Tolkien did try to ignore the fate of the Fourth Age and the landmass of Middle-Earth as a cursed and fallen place, he nonetheless did *not* forget (our perhaps he *could* not forget) the techniques of language powerfully combining that which is gone with that which can (only) be sensed. This is how *The New Shadow* ends:

> The door under the porch was open; but the house behind was darkling. There seemed none of the accustomed sounds of evening, only a soft silence, a dead silence. He entered, wondering a little. He called, but there was no answer. He halted in the narrow passage that ran through the house, and it seemed that he was wrapped in a blackness: not a glimmer of twilight of the world outside remained there. Suddenly he smelled it, or so it seemed, though it came as it were from within outwards to the sense: he smelt the old Evil and knew it for what it was.[28]

The phrase concerning "the old Evil" is a remarkable one in the sense of both direction and agency. Evil "came as it were from within outwards to the sense," and in this way it can be perceived, not entirely as an external power but as a darkness within the protagonist. Playing with the double nature of the concept of evilness is usually put into a moral-religious framework by Tolkien. In many instances throughout his body of work he portrays internal battles such as the case of Frodo, in *The Return of the King*, who gets defeated by Gollum and his own inner desires to claim the Ring himself and deploy it to his own interest. However, he emerges victorious in the end by an act of destiny and, as it were, a kind of exorcism. Yet, the vision contained in *The New Shadow* could also be that of a Jungian archetype advancing a psychological process of overthrowing otherness in the shape of "blackness" from a fairy-tale mythological realm—Sauron as personalized nonhuman Evil—and thus accepting the otherness *within*.[29] Rather than a localizable foul lodging in a real spot in "the world outside," darkness sneaks through narrow passages and "wraps" itself completely into Borlas. For Jung, this is a process of healing or individuation; acknowledging the Shadow (the archetype) within.[30] Paradoxically, the collective unconsciousness, or Shadow, which is the agency forming subjectivity is also that which shatters the subject's control of perception: Borlas can no longer trust "[any] of the accustomed sounds of evening." But if we read it this way it also means that we will have to abort the religious category of "evil" since it cannot be incorporated but must be vanquished or ultimately destroyed. While this destruction is indeed the context of the "plot" in *The New Shadow*—men have forgotten the epic battle against Evil and is now on the verge of producing a second malice out of boredom and "for fun"—it is rather the suppressed image of an intra-psychic knowledge, both potentially therapeutic and crippling, that springs to mind here. Evil is "old" and knowable for "what it is"—not because of its place in the hierarchy of moral-religious myth, and thus in fiction, but because it is grounded, and has been for a long time, in the individual itself.

IV

"Tal-Elmar" is the title of an incomplete narrative written during the 1950s in two manuscripts separated by several years, in which the character Tal-Elmar is the main protagonist. The story offers a glimpse of the Númenórean colonization of Middle-Earth from the perspective of its indigenous inhabitants and was, like *The New Shadow*, published in the volume *The Peoples of Middle-Earth*.

The story centers on Tal-Elmar and his father, Hazad Longbeard. Tal-Elmar's land was a region of green hills situated "three leagues away" from the shores of the Great Sea. From the top of a hill, in one Spring morning, Tal-Elmar and Hazad spotted four Númenórean ships, of which one had black sails, heading toward their lands. The two rushed toward their town to alert the people. In the time of the tale the "Go-hilleg" or "High Men of the Sea," as Númenóreans were called, were greatly feared, because they attacked and plundered those who dwelt on the shores of the sea. Furthermore, it was told among the people of Agar that they brought the captives onto the ship with the black sails, where they were kept until either slaughtered and eaten or sacrificed to the Dark.

Before the typescript text breaks off to be followed by a manuscript entitled "Continuation of Tal-Elmar," the story comes to a halt:

> [Tal-Elmar] ran to the hill's foot, and out over the long grass-meads, and so came to the first thin straggle of the woods. Dark they lay before him in the valley between Agar and the downs by the shore.

> It was still morning, and more than an hour ere the noon, but when he came under the trees he halted and took thought, and knew he was shaken with fear. Seldom had he wandered far from the hills of his home, and never alone, nor deep into the wood. For all his folk dreaded the forest.[31]

The threat of a distressing destiny anthropomorphizes nature. Tal-Elmar's fear is a fear on behalf of his people, who are used to being subjugated to higher powers, and who are now under pressure from both sides, the king of Middle-Earth (Sauron), and the equally terrifying rally of Númenor. It is also a fear of a potential savagery against the pastoral landscape itself; the distress that history, shaped through geography, and instilled in its topography, is under siege. Even to the point where Tal-Elmar is more frightened of life "under the trees," away from the "long grass-meads," than of the impending Númenóreans. In *The New Shadow*, the plot is the consequence of a process of de-mythologization, which was also a journey from an archetype of Evil to the modern household of individuation. It is a tale of the workings of reduction; neither Evil nor evilness can take on material form. Although, of course, the first kind of Evil is a mythical personalization, and the second kind, evilness, is the symbol of individuation, both emblematic portrayals, in *The New Shadow* and in "Tal-Elmar," concern blackness *as such* as well as fear *itself*.

One way of showing this pictorial reduction is to experiment figuratively with the elements of Evil. In "Myths Transformed," section (iii), of the volume *Morgoth's Ring*, Tolkien takes an interest in reflecting how Evil was initially deprived of form. At the end of the War of Wrath, during The First Age, the original Evil, Sauron's predecessor, Morgoth (sometimes referred to as Melkor) was judged, and eventually taken out of the Blessed Realm. He was, Tolkien writes, "*executed*: that is *killed* like one of the Incarnates."[32] The italicized words are Tolkien's own as if to mark the grim fate of a fallen angel second only to Eru (Ilúvatar), the One God. And further:

> Though he [Morgoth] had "disseminated" his power (his evil and possessive and rebellious will) far and wide into the matter of Arda, he had lost direct control of this, and all that "he," as a surviving remnant of integral being, retained as "himself" and under control was the terribly shrunken and reduced spirit that inhabited his self-imposed (but now beloved) body. When that body was destroyed he was weak and utterly "houseless," and for that time at a loss and "unanchored" as it were.[33]

Tolkien also toyed with the idea that Morgoth was "put outside Time and Space," that is, outside of the world or universe itself. The depiction of Morgoth's physical murder highlights all the omens of men's fate, almost like a wayward story of the Fall. As a roaming spirit Morgoth is "houseless," robbed of both a "self-imposed" body that he loves now that he has lost it and a kingdom.

At the end of The Second Age, where "Tal-Elmar" plays out, Sauron's ring is cut from his finger by Isildur, the eldest son of the elf king Elendil, in an act of de-personalization. He still, however, has a face, so he is not utterly defaced. Rather, this is an inevitable process of reduction right up to the point where Sauron, the second evil guy, loses not only his factual form entirely but is dispossessed of any potency and recognizable props—only darkness, blackness, and fear. The relentless course of modernization further resonates in the fact that Sauron at the time of the war of the ring is reduced to a quasi-omnipresent "Eye"[34] held upright only by a "fake" icon of individual achievement—the tower of Barad-dûr.

Overall Sauron was a "problem that Men had to deal with finally," Tolkien remarks.[35] He was a definite power-point, a fuse of Evil, combat-ready, and the last of those in mythological personalized (but nonhuman) form.

By deploying the motif of Tal-Elmar's folk and the undisclosed geography of southwest Middle-Earth, Tolkien also records the inexorable rush of civilization. Clearly, this is incarnated stuff, messy, and man-made. Some of the Númenóreans fled to the shores of Middle-Earth to the east prior to the Fall and left a trail of blood and gore that is heartbreaking for both Tal-Elmar and Longbeard. Yet, others chose to repel the wrath of Ilúvatar who eventually ended up flooding the island of Númenor. Apparently the Númenóreans serve the greater good in slaying an even more sinister Evil ("the Kings," meaning Sauron residing in Mordor), but through their mayhem, told by Tolkien in an abandoned appendix to the authorial package of *The Silmarillion*, they continue to do injustice to Tal-Elmar and his fellow men. These men insist on neither having any relation to nor serving Sauron's violent regime.[36] Told backward from a point outside the chronology of Tolkien's body of art, "Tal-Elmar" is a fiction within the fiction that underwent authorial eradication as it needed to be killed in the service of a greater good: the telling of the story of the war of the rings and the much, much more detailed events of the Third Age. We can only wonder about the lot of Tal-Elmar the same way we are only given hints about the "thriller" in *The New Shadow*. Both fragments, however, are clearly up to something; and yet they were entombed in retroactive *eucatastrophe* that left them diminished and unfulfilled.

V

Gilles Deleuze elaborates on the philosophical term "the virtual," to which we shall now turn since it holds a striking resemblance to the notion of "fantasy." The virtual is a concept—or perhaps even a "thing"—that equally hovers between two borders, the Aristotelian "Potential" and "Real." While the potential only subsists as the undeveloped occurrence of a fulfilled event, the real has been actualized and therefore allowed into being. Deleuze scrutinizes these matters particularly in his books *Bergsonism*, *Difference and Repetition* and *The Logic of Sense*, all three of which try to tackle the Bergsonian claim that "the virtual" not yet sprung into pragmatic existence must be viewed in its active sense thereby implying some sort of ontological status.

Interestingly, when compared to Tolkien's idea of *phantazein* as imagination's way of not only imitating an appearance but actually *making it appear* through the act of sub-creation, Deleuze arrives at a classification of the virtual, not because of the concept in itself but rather as a response to a problem with ontological implications posed by structuralism. How can the underlying structures exist if they do not belong to either the mind of a subject or the material world of objects? Deleuze's answer is that these structures, which act as conditional guidelines for present actualizations, represent something that "is," ontologically speaking, "in-between" subject and object, and this is exactly virtuality.

How is it possible, Deleuze asks, for something to be a condition of being, to catalyze actualized presence, while not being discernible or measurable, or being located in one particular person's mind, or otherwise embedded in a material world? The difficulty is to insist that this ontology is in fact *the* most comprehensive form of reality and, at the same time, a detached and left behind reality. (Much the same way a photon can be said to exist in a given position while at the same time, in the very moment of observation, bounces off to a completely different location). Tolkien would perhaps tell us that we would only have to "remember" such a reality to create it once again.[37] But he would also say that this reality with its aging myths and fading mirages is kept away from our known world. In *The New Shadow* Borlas moans the fact that the peoples of Middle-Earth have forgotten the heroes and gods of the old ages. Part of the answer lies in Deleuze's deliberate Kantian design. Similar to Kant's notion of space and time as unifying forms imposed by the subject that do not, in themselves, exist *in* space and time, Deleuze holds that pure difference is non-spatiotemporal. It is a reality without actualization, ideality without abstraction.

The reason why "the virtual" appears obsessively contrary to reality, Deleuze says, is because we fail to acknowledge virtuality as the "real" condition of actuality, and also because we one sidedly prioritize the actual as the being-present over the virtual as pure Being. The virtual is *not* nonexistence. Rather, it is real, and it creates genuine spaces, times, and sensations. The virtual is an object and is not an object, paradoxically at one and the same time; not because of its noncontradictory identity to itself but because it is the very real possibility of the actualization of this identity. Deleuze writes in *Bergsonism*:

> We have . . . confused Being with being-present. Nevertheless, the present is not; rather, it is pure becoming, always outside itself. It is not; but it acts. Its proper element is not being but the active or useful. The past, on the other hand, has ceased to act or be useful. But it has not ceased to be. Useless and inactive, impassive, it IS, in the full sense of the word: it is identical with being in itself.[38]

The word "fantasy" that figures so largely in Tolkien's discussion of fairy stories—including his own—is etymologically tied to the word *phenomena*. Tolkien's reason is such that phenomena is the word for the appearances of our Primary World, the world we live in revealed and fixed as concepts by words, while fantasy is involved in or rather directly the cause of the making of a Secondary World:

> Both terms—*phenomenon* and *fantasy*—derive from Greek, *phenomenon* from *phainesthai*, "to appear," and *fantasy* from *phantazein*, "to make visible." The difference is that one, *phainestahi*, is an intransitive verb having no object, and the other, *phantazein*, is transitive, that is, it affects an object external to and other than itself.[39]

Tolkien's collaborator and former student Simone D'Ardenne recalls an encounter with the author about the true nature of the Faërian drama. In the essay, "The Man and the Scholar" she writes:

> I said to him once: "You broke the veil, didn't you, and passed through?" which in fact he did and which he readily admitted. No wonder, therefore that he could recapture the language of the fairies. . . . Tolkien belonged to that very class of linguists, now becoming extinct, who like the Grimm brothers could understand and recapture the glamour of "the Word."[40]

Verlyn Flieger notes that the term "glamour" means the power to alter perception and penetrate the veil separating realities and reveal the connection between them.[41] We could also say that this play with perception and reality is a kind of Deleuzian virtual that, in a very sentimental fashion, accentuates the mind's transitive attribute. Our Primary World corresponds to Bergson's "useless and inactive, impassive" being, a thing of the past, something passed by, contrary to which the Secondary World "is not; but it acts." Fantasy in its purest form seems to contain both meanings: an imagination inferring a separation of concept and reality, word and thing, *and* a unifying imagination that actively makes things appear.

VI

Throughout his work, Tolkien chronicles a de-personalization, de-materialization and interiorization of evil which at the same time seems to imply a new, interior, abstract, "virtual" materiality. Fantasy, Tolkien writes in "On Fairy-Stories," is the ability to make things appear and *make* things that appear.[42] This appearance comes in the shape of *aletheia*, the Greek word for disclosure or truth. Tolkien had a remarkable affection for *eponyms*, persons, places, or things after whom or after which something is named, since he believed such names to be closer to an original translucence of words and things. But apart from being "glamorous," his images and sceneries are (also) depictions of the shadowy and violently unknown; in *The New Shadow* we hear of a both acquainted and alien darkness ready to enter household and soul; in "Tal-Elmar" we learn of black ships that will brutalize a people and poison its deep-rooted pastures. Tolkien's "virtual" emerges as a dual phenomenon. On the one hand, the virtual hovers between signifier and the signified stripped of any ontic realization yet residing in what Deleuze would call the true ontological realm. It is an idea that springs forward in Tolkien's philosophical belief in an eponymous language and the idea that imagination can quite literally form a story as well as the fantastic objects in it. The upshot of this belief, which also leads to his meticulous sense of detail and narratological consistency, resembles Bataille's insistence upon a material imaginary, which is non-reducible to ontology's dominion, and thus equally close to Barad's conception of that which emerges as an event—rather than being shaped through representational affinity. On the other hand, and through the diffractive existence of the "apocryphal," alternate universe-like texts *The New Shadow* and "Tal-Elmar," Tolkien fleshes out not only the simultaneity of two kinds of evilness; he also hints at a superimposed landscape of signs and texts in which it would be possible to treat the chronologically subsequent mode of Evil as the offspring of a peculiar backward causality loop. Evil in its individualized (Jungian) shape would then actually—or, rather, virtually—*make* the imaginative mythologization of evil materialize. Sadly, Tolkien put that aside because he was not interested in writing a "thriller" of the horrors of individualism and the rise of modernity.

Such playful interference with the disciplined linearity commonly found in the exegetic Tolkien tradition makes it possible to conjecture that Tolkien is indeed a precursor to New Materialism and the art (and acts) of diffractive reading. Not only does he tell the story of how an archaic power to make visible—the act of *phantazein*—has been splintered, from Gods to elves to men, from age to age. He also brewed his fiction from a recipe of otherness and sameness, diffraction and reflection, as we saw in the tiny afterthoughts of *The New Shadow* and "Tal-Elmar" and their tapestry of Evil. Reading

Tolkien is to follow an undeviating path of fairy story logic. And yet, it is also a look into a sprawling artwork where "photons" of symbolic significance bounce off to a strange place. One such place is the seaboard of South Gondor. Another is Borlas's encounter with Evil minus the safety net of good old mythopoetics.

NOTES

1. See Paul E. Kerry, ed., *The Ring and the Cross: Christianity and the Lord of the Rings* (Lanham: Fairleigh Dickinson University Press, 2011).
2. Cf. Karin Sellberg and Peta Hinton, "Introduction: The Possibilities of Feminist Quantum Thinking," *Rhizomes: Cultural Studies in Emerging Knowledge* 30 (2016), https://doi.org/10.20415/rhiz/030.i01.
3. Karen Barad, *Meeting the Universe Halfway: Quantum Physics and the Entanglement of Matter and Meaning* (Durham: Duke University Press, 2007), 74.
4. Donna Haraway, Modest_Witness@Second_Millenium.FemaleMan©_Meets_OncoMouse™: Feminism and Technoscience (New York: Routledge, 1997), 16.
5. Cf. Bo Kampmann Walther, "Big Theory—Strong Theory: The Ontological Ghost of Post-Ontological Epistemology," *Cybernetics and Human Knowing* 11, no. 3 (2004): 30–55.
6. Barad, 71.
7. Cf. Werner Heisenberg, *Physics and Beyond: Encounters and Conversations* (New South Wales: Allen and Unwin, 1971), 1049–1070, which provides a model for incorporating information about a particular wave function to predict quantum mechanical outcomes based on probability estimations. Cf. Franz Klaus Jansen, "Revisiting Quantum Mechanical Weirdness From a Bio-Psychological Perspective," *Philosophy Study* 8, no. 8 (August 2018): 343–354.
8. Cf. Vivienne Bozalek and Michalinos, "Diffraction or Reflection: Sketching the Contours of Two Methodologies in Educational Research," *International Journal of Qualitative Studies in Education* 30, no. 2 (2017): 111–127.
9. Barad, *Meeting*, 30.
10. Lenz Tagushi, "A Diffractive and Deleuzian Approach to Analyzing Interview Data," *Feminist Theory* 13 (2012): 269.
11. See Graham Harman, *The Quadruple Object* (Winchester: zero books, 2011).
12. See also the relation between sign and being in biosemiotics and the close connection to diffractive reading in the introduction to this volume.
13. Timothy Morton, "Deconstruction and/as Ecology," in *The Oxford Handbook of Ecocriticism*, ed. Greg Garrard (Oxford: Oxford University Press, 2014), 291–304.
14. See also Benjamin Maxwell Garner, "Far over the Misty Mountains Cold: An Ecocritical Reading of J. R. R. Tolkien's *The Hobbit*" (Honor Theses, Bucknell University, 2015), https://digitalcommons.bucknell.edu/honors_theses/291.
15. See especially Jacques Derrida's *Dissemination*, trans. Barbara Johnson (London: Athlone, 1981).

16. Cf. Sten Pulz Moslund, *Literature's Sensuous Geographies: Postcolonial Matters of Place* (New York: Palgrave Macmillan, 2015).

17. Cf. F. Scott Scribner, "Towards a Material Imaginary: Bataille, Nonlogical Difference, and the Language of Base Materialism," *Pli*, no. 13 (2002): 209–220.

18. See Scribner, "Towards a Material Imaginary," 211.

19. George Bataille, "Base Materialism and Gnosticism," in *Visions of Excess: Selected Writings, 1927–1939* (Minneapolis: University of Minnesota Press, 1985), 45. See also Benjamin Noys, "Georges Bataille's Base Materialism," *Cultural Values* 4, no. 2 (1998): 499–517, https://doi.org/10.1080/14797589809359312.

20. "Sub-creation," as a noun, refers to both process and product and indicates their interwoven nature, the same way Tolkien believed language and idea were inseparable. See also Randel Helms, *Tolkien's World* (London: Thames and Hudson, 1974).

21. J. R. R. Tolkien, "On Fairy-Stories," in *Tree and Leaf* (Boston: Houghton Mifflin, 1965), 37.

22. Cf. the section on biosemiotics and modeling in the introduction to this volume.

23. Cf. Mark Rowell Wallin, "Myth, Monsters and Markets: Ethos, Identification, and the Video Game Adaptations of *The Lord of the Rings*," *Game Studies* 7, no. 1 (August 2007), http://gamestudies.org/0701/articles/wallin. See also Catherine Butler, "Tolkien and Worldbuilding," in *J. R. R. Tolkien: "The Hobbit and* The Lord of the Rings." New Casebooks, ed. Peter Hunt (New York: Palgrave 2013), 106–120.

24. See Patrick Curry, *Defending Middle-Earth: Tolkien, Myth and Modernity* (Edinburgh: Floris Books, 1997).

25. Humphrey Carpenter and Christopher Tolkien, eds, *The Letters of J. R. R. Tolkien* (Boston: Houghton Mifflin, 2000; London: Allen and Unwin, 1981). See especially no. 256.

26. Gerry Canavan, "From 'A New Hope' to no hope at all: 'Star Wars', Tolkien and the Sinister and Depressing Reality of Expanded Universes," *Salon*, December 24, 2015.

27. Humphrey Carpenter and Christopher Tolkien, eds, *The Letters of J. R. R. Tolkien* (Boston: Houghton Mifflin, 2000; London: Allen and Unwin, 1981). See especially no. 338.

28. J. R. R. Tolkien, "The New Shadow," in *The Peoples of Middle-Earth*, ed. Christopher Tolkien, vol. 12 of *The History of Middle-Earth* (London: Harper Collins, 1996), 418.

29. See Thomas Honegger, "More Light than Shadow? Jungian Approaches to Tolkien and the Archetypical Image of the Shadow." *Tolkiendil* (fansite), last modified April 6, 2020, 16:47, http://www.tolkiendil.com/essais/tolkien_1892-2012/thomas_honegger.

30. Cf. Carl Gustav Jung, *Archetypen*, ed. Lorenz Jung (Munich: Deutscher Taschenburg Verlag, 2001), 255ff.

31. J. R. R. Tolkien, "The New Shadow," 432.

32. *Morgoth's Ring*. Vol. 10 of *The History of Middle-Earth*, ed. Christopher Tolkien (London: Harper Collins, 1993), 403.

33. Ibid.

34. Robert T. Tally Jr. notes that Sauron, in *The Lord of the Rings*, serves as the figural embodiment of surveillance itself. He represents the supremely terrifying force that instills fear. Cf. "Tolkien's Geopolitical Fantasy: *Spatial Narrative in* Lord of the Rings *in Popular Fiction and Spatiality*," in *Popular Fiction and Spatiality: Reading Genre Settings*, ed. Lisa Fletcher (New York: Palgrave, 2016), 125–140.

35. Ibid., 404.

36. See "Middle-Earth," in *J. R. R. Tolkien Encyclopedia: Scholarship and Critical Assessment*, ed. Michael D.C. Drout (New York: Routledge, 2007). Also Deborah Sabo, "Archeology and the Sense of History in J. R. R. Tolkien's Middle-Earth," *Mythlore* 26, no. 1/2 (Fall/Winter 2007): 91–112.

37. Indeed, Tolkien asserted that all his stories about Middle-Earth, and especially those from The First Age, were "mythical" in the sense that they were (oral) narratives handed down from generation to generation in an attempt to explain how things came to be. See Humphrey Carpenter, *J. R. R. Tolkien: The Authorized Biography* (Boston: Houghton Mifflin Company, 1977), 144.

38. Gilles Deleuze, *Bergsonism*, trans. Hugh Tomlinson and Barbara Habberjam (New York: Zone Books, 1988), 55.

39. Verlyn Flieger, *Splintered Light: Logos and Language in Tolkien's World*, rev. ed. (London: Kent State University Press, 2002), 45. The subtle aspect of the Greek term *phantazein* (cf. the Greek loanword in Latin: *phantasma*) is furthermore that the exact meaning differs slightly when considered A) to *make* visible, B) to *cause* to be seen, or C) to have (or invoke) the *power* to be seen/make visible. As such, the term is rather like a spectrum ranging from a creation of the imagination or fancy and all the way to possessing the means to produce "things" in themselves. In any case, each meaning centers on the significance of a *maker*.

40. Simone D'Ardenne, "The Man and the Scholar," in *J. R. R. Tolkien, Scholar and Storyteller: Essays in Memorian*, ed. Mary Salu and Robert T. Farrell (Ithaca: Cornell University Press, 1979), 33–37, quoted in Verlyn Flieger, "But What Did He Really Mean?" *Tolkien Studies* 11 (2014): 149–166.

41. Ibid.

42. Cf. Tolkien, "On Fairy-Stories."

Chapter 8

Sensing I and Eyes in Ali Smith's *How to Be Both*[*]

Daniela Keller

Ali Smith declares in *Artful* that "[y]ou can't step into the same story twice,"[1] which is a circumstance that the reading of Smith's novel *How to Be Both*[2] performs in a most conspicuous manner. Because the novel exists in two versions that begin with either the part called "Eyes" or the other one referred to as "Camera," there are at least two different reading experiences; the order determines, for example, whether one is aware of Francescho spying on George from the beginning or only halfway through the book. Francescho is a fresco painter of the fifteenth century who comes to life in "Eyes" and finds himself observing George in a twenty-first-century setting. George, who is unaware of this presence, is introduced in "Camera," which describes how her recently deceased mother took her and her brother to Ferrara to see Francescho's frescoes. Once these two parts are read in a particular order ("Camera," "Eyes" or "Eyes," "Camera"), it is impossible for the same reader to experience the other version with an equally fresh mind; a second reading may enrich one's knowledge of the plot, but it will not be the same as encountering the two protagonists for the first time.[3] It is therefore not only possible to determine a minimum of two different, but also two mutually exclusive, reading experiences based on the mere condition that there are two versions.[4] The fact that the publishers agreed to bind the two parts in two distinct orders, draws attention to the novel's material composition and its relationship to

---

[*] Acknowledgements: A diffractive analysis of Ali Smith's <i>How to Be Both</i> was first presented at the international conference "Shifting Grounds" in Zürich in 2016. I wish to thank Melanie Küng and Maryanne Keller for their critical comments on an earlier version of this essay, as well as the students of my seminar on Ali Smith for their lively discussions in autumn 2015 and their recent help in collecting publication details of Smith's book. I am also grateful to Mario Piscazzi, Noah Regenass, Bettina Roncelli, and the Musei di Arte Antica in Ferrara for their assistance in acquiring images and texts.

the readers' mental engagement with the text. This is the first reason why I consider *How to Be Both* an exemplary piece of diffractive literature as it entangles matter with meaning, and thus epitomizes a "material-discursive phenomenon"[5] that is "iteratively reconfigure[d]"[6] with every new instance of reading.

Secondly, this novel is recognized as diffractive because it emphasizes difference rather than similarity or sameness. As Donna J. Haraway suggests, a diffractive way of thinking pays attention to difference rather than sameness because "reflexivity, like reflection, only displaces the same elsewhere."[7] Diffraction thus constitutes "a metaphor for another kind of critical consciousness"[8] that allows one to undermine fixed binary relationships, not by erasing the distinctive qualities, but by zooming in on them and redefining them as continuous, multitudinous and "agential intra-activity,"[9] as well as by acknowledging their convoluted complexity. This means that a diffractive analysis of *How to Be Both* pays attention to the small but significant differences in the novel that are otherwise in danger of being overlooked.

Several critics focus on a simultaneity between Smith's two parts, for example, and stress that the material condition serves to overcome the inherent sequentiality of narration, namely that it is impossible to narrate two events at the same time[10]; a diffractive analysis of the two parts, on the other hand, which is attentive towards difference, offers complementary readings of Smith's experimental fiction. Diffracting the descriptions of George's bedroom in both parts, for instance, enables one to identify her bedroom as a significant spatial marker of a difference in time: in "Camera," George's friend Helena Fisker marvels at the posters and photographs on the four walls in George's bedroom and notices that George is trying to cover a damp patch on one wall with "pictures of kittens." Francescho describes the same bedroom but recognizes that a previously damp "north wall" has had "some dampwork done and plastering which has an air of recency." Furthermore, the kitten pictures decorating the north wall in "Camera" have been replaced in "Eyes" by pictures of a house.[11] The diffraction therefore shows that the two parts do not happen simultaneously and instead determines a chronological order of the present-day events in both sections, confirming that "Eyes" necessarily follows after "Camera."

Time and context make a difference and Cara L. Lewis similarly registers this crucial mindset in Smith's novel when she states:

> [W]e find numerous consonances between Francescho's and George's halves of the novel, including their ambiguous gendering, their acute grief at the death of their mothers, and their close friendships that depend on a forestalled attraction. These are commonalities, but not necessarily interactions. . . . [T]hey serve primarily to underscore the differences between George's world

and Francescho's world, and between both of these worlds and our own, even though there are moments in which it seems like this boundary will be breached.[12]

Both Lewis's and Elizabeth S. Anker's postcritical readings of *How to Be Both* excavate many significant foci that are also relevant to a diffractive reading.[13] Their concrete analyses of the same novel have helped me sharpen the value and idiosyncrasies of diffraction, which, as the following discussion aims to show, offers a slightly more radical reconceptualization of literary analysis, especially in relation to (extra-textual) materiality. As Anker rightly asserts, the novel undermines and redefines common categories, such as gender or habitual ways of interpreting literature, yet a focus on extra-textual materiality, as I argue, exposes most strikingly that this initial destabilization demonstrates that some decision (or state) is nevertheless *always* manifested, that this happens continuously, and that this carries significant consequences.[14]

As Lewis's statement above reveals, a major concern of Smith's narrative is the ways in which the fictional as well as the actual worlds meet. *How to Be Both* is a diffractive text, and a text that seeks to be read diffractively—a method and way of thinking that "read[s] insights through one another in ways that help illuminate differences as they emerge: how different differences get made, what gets excluded, and how those exclusions matter."[15] As I elucidate elsewhere, it purposely "distinguishes itself from merely engaging with literature as representation and instead focuses on how meaning comes into being performatively by emphasising its material components (actual space, the physical book or the reader's corporeality)."[16] Most importantly, *How to Be Both* is not a text that simply alludes to other texts, but it is a material-discursive book that finds innovative ways to intra-act with materiality and actual space, and thereby captures in a nutshell the creative possibilities of literature's entanglements with materiality in a material, and not only figurative, sense.

Significantly, diffractive foci such as materiality, can be addressed in fiction as themes within a story or can be dealt with extra-textually by embracing "our own"[17] world, as is the case with *How to Be Both*. Thus, the subsequent literary analysis expands from the world *within* the text to the world *of* and *outside* the text. It is divided into two main sections: the first elucidates the diffractive structure and plot of the two chapters "Eyes" and "Camera" ("Diffractive Structure") to establish, in the second section ("Extra-Textual Entanglements"), why and how Smith's novel is considered an exemplary piece of diffractive literature that reaches beyond the limits of its text.

However, before I delve into more detail, there remains one more, somewhat unconventional (and therefore all the more diffractive), aspect to address: Sonya Andermahr notes in a comparison of Smith's novel with Brigid Brophy's *In Transit* that the novels prominently "hand . . . over responsibility to the reader,"[18] as the readers are asked to "cocreate [the characters'] gender identity."[19] *How to Be Both* suggests that the narrator of "Eyes," Francescho, who is based on the actual fresco painter Francesco del Cossa, was in fact a woman and had to dress as a man to learn his craft. Because Smith exercises great care in upholding Francescho's gender ambiguity by turning him into a first-person narrator and a ghost (who could therefore be referred to as "it"), the reader is confronted with the choice of a pronoun. I refer to Francescho as "him" because it allows me to distinguish more easily between him and his female counterpart George. Nevertheless, as this example shows, my decision intra-acts with the meaning of the story and destroys the ambiguity by brutally determining Francescho's gender as male.

In the same manner, the following diffractive reading of *How to Be Both* will manifest an ingenious twist in the novel which is difficult to ignore once it becomes known. This formidably illustrates why it is impossible to "step into the same story twice" and, because this twist functions according to an epiphany, why reading this essay deprives the novel of the revelatory effect and surprise for future readers. To share this diffractive analysis, therefore, carries consequences because it does not simply add to the interpretation of the novel but also steals some of its magic and mystery—mystery "originally mean[ing]," as the novel declares, "an agreement or an understanding that something would not be disclosed." The novel hints regularly at this "twist in the tale,"[20] which it simultaneously seeks to keep secret. It aims to trigger the discovery by each reader but to ensure individually experienced revelations among its readers, it has to prevent this knowledge from spreading, from losing its epiphanic effect and becoming less-spectacular information.[21]

This concern is voiced through Francescho who explains how he added details to his paintings that "you'd only see if you really looked" but served his "pleasure alone cause no one else'd notice."[22] *How to Be Both* makes me, as a reader and literary critic, particularly aware of my responsibility and wish to share an exciting aspect about Smith's piece of fiction that the artist (and implied author), however, implicitly asks readers to keep to themselves; because the artist enjoys the pleasure of the paradox—of making something visible without it being seen—and because the "twist in the tale" is in danger of losing its vibrant quality of "only just" being missed or discovered if the twist becomes common knowledge.[23]

Both features, namely the novel's existence in two editions and the reader's momentous interference, illustrate that "you cannot step into the same story twice" and that you cannot step back in time either. *How to Be Both* is about seeing things and not being able to "unsee" them afterwards. It is a demonstratively diffractive novel precisely because it affects its readership to such an explicit extent but, more importantly, as it points a finger at their influence as readers and critics. I hope to have partially solved and shown the "moral conundrum" of "saying out loud" what is meant to be left "unsaid"[24] by highlighting the consequences of reading the following diffractive analysis, before the essay turns to a discussion of the novel's diffractive structure and then to its extra-textual entanglements.[25]

DIFFRACTIVE STRUCTURE

My edition of *How to Be Both* begins with "Camera" and a third-person narrator who conveys that the protagonist, sixteen-year-old George (actually Georgia), is mourning her mother's death.[26] The narrative is set in the twenty-first century, a couple of months after George's tragic loss, and begins at a few minutes past New Year's Eve.[27] We accompany George through different strategies of overcoming her grief, such as her visits to the school counsellor Mrs. Rock, or witness her taking on her mother's daily ritual of dancing to "Let's Twist Again." A major part of this chapter, however, covers George's memories of her mother and, in particular, their trip to the Palazzo Schifanoia in Ferrara to see the frescoes painted by the Renaissance artist Francesco del Cossa.

The novel takes inspiration from the actual Palazzo Schifanoia, which was built in 1385, and the frescoes in its *Salone dei Mesi* (hall of the months) that were commissioned by the Duke of Ferrara, Borso d'Este, in 1466 (see figure 8.1).[28] As the novel points out, and as art historians explain, the fifteenth-century frescoes in the *Salone dei Mesi* were uncovered in the earlier nineteenth century,[29] and it was not until the late nineteenth century that Adolfo Venturi found a letter written by Francesco del Cossa on March 25, 1470, demanding more money for his work, which enabled the identification of del Cossa as the definitive artist of the months March, April, and May.[30] These coincidental, yet highly influential, circumstances, as well as the frescoes' continuous enigmatic nature,[31] set the frame for Smith's imagination. The novel adheres to the generally accepted historical facts but takes the freedom to fill remaining gaps with an interpretation of the frescoes through the eyes of George and her mother in "Camera," and especially with the creation of events told by Francesco del Cossa's ghost in the second part "Eyes."

The "Eyes" section begins with the first-person narrator, "Francescho," who squeezes through the earth "upwards past maggots and worms."[32] The first thing he sees is George's back in the National Gallery in London. Francescho hovers in a parallel space to George's world from which he can see and hear George, but cannot be heard or seen himself.[33] He realizes that George is looking at one of his paintings, namely "Saint Vincent Ferrer,"

Figure 8.1 Francesco del Cossa's "March" in the Palazzo Schifanoia in Ferrara. *Source*: By permission of Musei di Arte Antica di Ferrara, photo: Ghiraldini-Panini.

and when George leaves the gallery to follow Lisa Goliard—a friend of her mother who seemed to spy on her mother while she was still alive—Francescho is forced to follow George as if his "foot's caught in the stirrup of a saddle on a horse."[34] Francescho witnesses how, from then on, George spends hours outside Lisa Goliard's home, taking pictures of the house and, by doing so, looking back at her mother's spy "[i]n honour of her mother's eyes."[35] Like in George's part, these observations take place in the twenty-first century but are regularly interspersed by Francescho remembering events of his previous life that lie several hundred years in the past.

As mentioned above, there are many "consonances"[36] between George and Francescho's worlds, and both parts contain a scene that evokes the idea of waves running through each other beyond the borders of their immediately visible worlds. In "Camera," George realizes that with every visit to the National Gallery, St. Vincent Ferrer appeared "less severe," as if "he's not bothered by anything—the other paintings in the room, the stuff happening in them, the people passing back and fore in front of him . . ., the whole rest of the gallery, the square, the roads, the traffic, the city, the country, the sea, the countries radiating out beyond the gallery and away." While Ferrer seems unconcerned about his surroundings, he is nevertheless "looking past and above you, or into the far distance, like there's something happening beyond you and he can see what it is."[37] If one considers the other half, Ferrer's gaze is hinting at the space behind his spectators and therefore the space from which Francesco del Cossa's ghost is staring back at his own painting. Hence, although Ferrer appears ignorant, the readers should be all the more attentive toward the various spaces that are described in such a way as if circles, like waves, were expanding from the painting that lies at their centre.[38]

These metaphorical waves seek to intra-act with the waves coming from Francescho's part: he remembers being highly disappointed as a child when a seed "twisting itself down through the air" fell into a "pool of horse piss" and the expanding circles of the rippling surface "got to the edges and vanished."[39] Both scenes invite readers to diffract the two halves, that is, to pay attention to where and how these two worlds meet, to continuously change perspective and look from the inside-out as much as from the outside-in to scrutinize the boundaries. The diffracting waves indirectly encourage readers to open their eyes (and minds) to the spaces that lie beyond the immediately visible, because the circles and rings nevertheless continue beyond the horizons of their (fictional) worlds, cutting agentially between textual and extra-textual realities.

The resonances—to use another wave metaphor—that occur between the two parts create a complex pattern[40]; in particular, those related to the concept of a "twist," which surface in various shapes in the novel and are key to its diffractive pattern. The word "twist" occurs prominently when George sends Helena a message, stating *"Let's helix again, like we did last summer"* and adds: *"(Helix : Greek for twist.)."*[41] The song line explicitly connects the instances that mention "helix" with the passages that include "twist," such as "Oliver Twist" or *"Helix the Cat"* but, most importantly, it draws attention to "the twist in the plot" or the "twist in the tale" and its relationship to the helix structure(s).[42]

The spiral figure appears in diverse ways and contexts but is explicitly introduced in relation to actual X-ray *"diffraction (!)."*[43] *How to Be Both* explains that the methodology was applied to discover DNA's double helix structure. Writing to her friend, Helena, George asks her: *"And did you know (you probably did) that Rosalind Franklin nearly didn't get credited for the double helix discovery?"*[44] Like Francesco del Cossa, whose contribution to the frescoes came to light thanks to the discovery of his letter in which he, ironically, asked to receive the (monetary) acknowledgement he thought he deserved, Rosalind Franklin "only just" made it into the history books of DNA. According to Franklin's biographer, Brenda Maddox, the so-called dark lady of DNA "remained virtually unknown outside her immediate circles until 1968 when Watson published *The Double Helix*, his brilliant, tactless and exciting personal account of the discovery"[45]—the irony being, in Franklin's case, that although James D. Watson mentions her, he focuses on her appearance rather than her genius.[46] George concludes that the nearly forgotten scientist *"is the kind of historic fact that opposes the making of true history."*[47] Like several instances in the novel, this comment obtains a metafictional quality because it questions historical facts but moreover provokes the idea that the fictional elements in *How to Be Both* could contain "true" history: what if, as Francescho suggests,[48] Francesco del Cossa really was female and had to cross-dress to become a fresco painter?[49] The novel, therefore, establishes an intriguing parallel between X-ray diffraction, that is, an interference of waves that produces an image from which it is possible to deduce the helix structure of DNA, and a diffraction of historical events that sets history straight by acknowledging its neglected participants.

There is another resonant parallel between two types of twists: a DNA cycle path in Cambridge (mentioned in "Camera") and the sections of concrete poetry at the beginning and end of chapter "Eyes." Their diffraction directs the readers' attention towards the difference between the act of seeing and the act of reading. Smith, figuratively and literally, activates this kind of awareness by constantly shifting between imagined and actual senses, as well as imagined and actual worlds. Towards the end of "Camera," George engages with the DNA cycle path which actually exists in Cambridge and along which you can *"cycle the length of one thirty-thousandth of the human genome."*[50] A "double helix sculpture" stands at the beginning and the end of the cycle route and one of them "resembled a joyful bedspring or a bespoke ladder. It was like a kind of shout, if a shout to the sky could be said to look like something." Like the exclamation marks used shortly before and right after the word diffraction,[51] the image represents a literal announcement of the helix structure's significant role.[52] The sculptures that mark both ends of the path allude to the poetic beginning and end of chapter "Eyes" that visually resemble the intertwined strands of DNA (see quotation below).[53]

Smith entangles "opposites," such as space and text, or sculpture and poetry, to highlight their relevance and create new and surprising connections.[54] In opposition to the helix sculptures, the poetic elements are actually, and not just imaginatively, visible to the readers. The concrete poetry "merge[s] from verbal into visual art,"[55] inviting the readers to adjust their eyes and *look at* the text rather than *read it*, and thus to step out of imagination and become more aware of the book as an object they are physically holding in their hands.

At the same time, their diffraction shifts awareness to the beginning and end of both parts and thus also the transitions or agential cuts between them. I mentioned above that, chronologically, "Camera" takes place before "Eyes," which is additionally confirmed by a sudden use of the future tense at the end of "Camera": the narrator prophesies that Lisa Goliard "will . . . stand in front of George between her and the painting of St Vincent Ferrer"[56] (this happens at the beginning of "Eyes"[57]), and the chapter ends with the words: "Not yet, anyway. For now, in the present tense, George sits in the gallery and looks at one of the old paintings on the wall. It's definitely something to do. For the foreseeable."[58] Typical of *How to Be Both*, the novel intra-acts with the readers, tempting them to complete the last sentence with the missing word "future" and making it impossible to overlook the significance of time between the two parts, as well as the manifested sequential order.[59]

In contrast to the ending of "Camera," chapter "Eyes" ends with Francescho gradually losing his memory and receding to the place he emerged from, which is metaphorically accompanied by the reversed production process of an arrow:

   the treebranch thick with
     all its leaves before even the
        thought of the arrow
how
        the root in the dark makes its
           way under the ground
             before there's
                any sign of the tree
            the seed still unbroken
        the star still unburnt

```
              the curve of the eyebone
                         of the not yet born
                       hello all the new bones
                     hello all the old
                   hello all the everything
             to be
                   made and
                         unmade
                              both[60]
```

Once the arrow disintegrates into its original form, namely the seed of a tree, the poetic ending appears to switch direction (like an arrow), facing and greeting ("hello") the things to come that are "not yet born."[61] The ending of the chapter thus, in line with the novel's pervasive theme of "being both," turns backwards in time as well as forwards into a new beginning: it either constitutes the ending of the first half, moving back in time to begin with George's story in the second half; or the ending of the novel, inviting readers to return to George's story and reread it with the fresh knowledge that Francescho's ghost is watching her. Hence, the timeline of the twenty-first-century events follows a quasi-circular route that simultaneously moves forwards in time, insisting that "[y]ou can't step into the same story twice"[62] and resembling a spiral rather than a circle (see figure 8.2).[63] The spiral structure is thus not only embodied by the secret codes of life but also by the novel's material-discursive arrangement of plot—and both of these are constituted through a methodology of diffraction.[64]

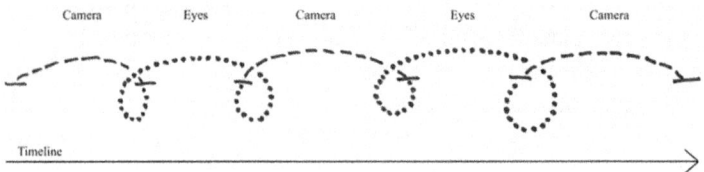

Figure 8.2 The Spiral Structure of Reading Ali Smith's *How to Be Both*, Illustrated by Keller. As this visualization shows, the "temporal loop[s]"[65] are primarily part of "Eyes" and not "Camera," which is confirmed by the fact that "Eyes" ends and begins with spiraling concrete poetry.

The lively back-and-forth between text and space, as well as between reading and seeing, serves to evoke an awareness of their differences and mutual enrichment. This is, of course, most obviously achieved by Smith's dialogue between the frescoes in the *Salone dei Mesi* and the novel, which several critics explore.[66] Anker, as well as Lewis, take the issue of seeing and reading a step further and recognize the novel's request not only to compare text and painting, but also to engage with different methods of seeing and reading. They separately claim that *How to Be Both* functions like "a kind of manual"[67] or "playbook in postcritical reading" and highlights the novel's metalevels that by way of "metafictional and auto-critical" statements tend to "interpellat[e] the academic reader."[68] Having looked inwards to the smallest scales of the book's DNA, the next section turns the gaze outwards to sharpen the contours of the novel's material effects and elucidate how these interpellations become defined in a diffractive manner.

EXTRA-TEXTUAL ENTANGLEMENTS

Diffraction insists on being a *material*-discursive methodology and thus challenges a diffractive reader of literature to determine the material potential; not only how materiality is dealt with thematically in the story, but also where "fiction meets the natural world."[69] The novel and the reader co-constitute a boundary between themselves that is seldom assigned exact spatial-temporal coordinates; instead, one merely acknowledges that there is a distinction between the narrator and the narratee. But how and where precisely do they meet? A diffractive reading of *How to Be Both* zooms in on the dividing line between the fictional and the actual world and shows how it is brought into being as an agential cut—a boundary that simultaneously separates as it connects.

To accurately capture such borders, the fictional and actual worlds are best diffracted by reading the novel's most obvious actual element, Francesco del Cossa's frescoes, through the imaginative and aesthetic world of *How to Be Both*. A diffractive approach aims to unearth how differences between these worlds matter materially and discursively. It therefore requires one to *actually look* at the *Salone dei Mesi* and Smith's book in their entirety (content, form, paper and ink, the reader, etc.) and asks for the activities of looking and reading to be diffracted as well.

Taking an *actual* closer look at the frescoes themselves, in particular the month of March, co-creates further resonances between these images and the novel (see figure 8.1). A long passage in "Camera" delivers a detailed description of the frescoes in the hall of months, where the narrator turns to the month of March in particular, stating: "Down here there are eyes looking out of a black archway while people talk and do business and don't notice the looking."[70] This detail gains relevance because of the proximity of the spectator (George) to the image, looking very closely and from "down here," as well as by the circumstance that Francescho recalls how he spent his last night in Ferrara working on the same area, below "the word JUSTICE" and "h[olding] the mirror up to [his] own eyes." Francescho indirectly admits that he painted his own reprimanding eyes above the "kindly generous charismatic Borse d'Est [*sic*],"⁷¹ who ironically refused to pay him more money and was therefore anything but just.

"Eyes" recounts that Francescho was successful with his "secret" revenge: his assistant Ercole reported to the dying Francescho that many people pretended to pay their respects to Borse d'Est when in fact they wanted "to see the face you painted in the blackness, the face there's only half of, whose eyes—your eyes, Master Francescho—look straight out at them, as if the eyes can actually see them over the top of Borse's head." In accordance with the novel's paradoxical tendency to remain "both blatant and invisible," or outspoken and silent, Francescho denies that they are his eyes, while confessing that he "was frightened that something [he]'d done or made might have such wild effect."⁷²

The "wild effect" grows wilder when the act of reading these passages is diffracted with the act of actually looking at those same eyes in the fresco (see figure 8.3). The readers are asked to invert these acts by "reading" the fresco and instead "looking at" the text. This leads me to the "twist in the tale" that I announced at the beginning of this essay and for which the narrator prepares its readers at the end of "Camera" with an unusually explicit metanarrational comment: "This is the point in this story at which, according to its structure so far, a friend enters or a door opens or some kind of plot surfaces." A couple of pages later, and in the other half, Francescho "twist[s]" as if through a "6 foot thick wall made of bricks" and various layers of blue in a painting⁷³ to the tip of a stem (in allusion to Francesco del Cossa's painting of Saint Lucy and the icon adorning the first page of "Eyes"):

   and up at the ends of the stalks
   there are flowers that open for
   all the world like
       eyes :
         hello :
           what's this?
             A boy in front of a painting.⁷⁴

Looking at these lines, rather than reading them, it should dawn on the observer that the colon signifies more than just Francesco del Cossa's writing style (inspired by his seminal letter), because these two dots turn into Francescho's eyes.⁷⁵ This revelation fundamentally shifts the whole construction of the novel as the two parallel worlds expand into the extratextual world because Francescho stares back at his readers.⁷⁶ The "no-eyed painter"⁷⁷ is suddenly "all eyes" and makes the readers realize that they were

Figure 8.3 Detail of Francesco del Cossa's "March" in the Palazzo Schifanoia in Ferrara.
Source: By permission of Musei di Arte Antica di Ferrara, photo: Ghiraldini-Panini.

watched throughout, what they believed to be, their private and anonymous enjoyment of George's and Francescho's lives.

Regardless of whether the reader is receptive to a (potentially) shuddering and "physically sensed"[78] epiphany, the metaleptic twist, if it is recognized by the reader, cuts agentially between the fictional and actual world. Although

Francescho's metalepsis creatively invites readers to imagine him transgressing the threshold between story and reality, he still remains a fictional character.[79] Nevertheless, the metalepsis manages to locate the point where the reader is most immediately and intimately confronted with the limits of the fictional space. As Lewis highlights, this "highly complex event of 'seeing and being seen'[[80]], or what I [Lewis] will call 'beholding'" prevents the "beholder . . . [from] retreat[ing] to a safe critical distance."[81] The proximity between the reader and Francescho is further underscored by the fact that the reader is not addressed by the second-person pronoun but looked at instead. Brian McHale elucidates that "every reader is potentially *you*" and the pronoun thus "an 'empty' linguistic sign."[82] Francescho's eyes, however, are far more powerful because they theoretically see *each* individual reader and invade the readers' personal space by stealing their anonymity. Consequently, *How to Be Both*'s epiphanic energy tears the readers out of their imaginative engagement with the novel and makes them self-consciously aware of their observed corporal "I" that is entangled with the narrator's eyes. Even if, or precisely because, this sensation is only felt for a very brief moment, it demonstrates how delicate and individual the act of reading is.

How to Be Both epitomizes the literary possibilities of material-discursive entanglements and finds further ways to bring its material edges into sharper focus. As already mentioned, the two versions create a minimum of two mutually exclusive reading experiences based on materiality alone, irrespective of the multiplicity of readers and the exponential amount of reading experiences. Furthermore, the fact that both editions carry the same ISBN and that nothing on their covers reveals whether "Eyes" or "Camera" comes first,[83] forces readers who intend to buy a specific edition to visit a bookstore.

Other instances in the novel invite readers to "leave the armchair," especially to study the artworks that are mentioned in the book with the help of other resources. Even though George's mother explicitly says, after failing to remember Francesco del Cossa's name, "[l]et's not look anything up. . . . It's so nice. Not to have to know,"[84] the readers are nevertheless inclined to do the opposite. When George and her mother debate about a word in a song line by the Pet Shop Boys, the novel again explores the ways of finding out about art: George offers to "look up the lyrics online right now" but her mother insists that they "use [their] human ears and listen together to the original when [they] get home." Who actually wins the bet of "fifty pounds"[85] is never disclosed, but the readers can hear for themselves to determine who was right.[86]

Crucially and finally, Smith's novel encourages its readers not only to hear but also to see for themselves. Animated by St. Vincent Ferrer's gaze that focuses on the space behind George in the National Gallery, "like there's something happening beyond you and he can see what it is"; by the knowledge that Francescho appears to surface through a painting on the opposite wall; and by the recognition that diffractive readings of the fictional and actual worlds co-create small but significant details, the reader's curiosity is aroused: one wonders whether a diffraction of "Room 55" in the National Gallery and Francescho's concrete poetry would disclose further exciting connections, such as the actual location of Francescho's "eyes: ."[87] However, because the exhibition in the National Gallery has changed since the novel's publication, and St. Vincent Ferrer is now displayed in room 54 instead of 55, a diffractive reading requires more effort than simply browsing through the gallery.[88]

The passing of time has involved a shift in the spatial constellations of the actual object world with which the novel explicitly intra-acts. This development demonstrates very vividly that "you cannot step into the same story twice," not only because a story unfolds but also because time passes in actual space. In contradistinction to the National Gallery, Bell compares the medium of a book to the Hall of Months and remarks that, unlike a book, the four walls are more successful in depicting "the course of one year as a closed circle."[89] This may be the case if time is understood as repetition (and therefore as a "closed circle") and not as change. The latter, however, is a far more accurate description of time and is ingeniously performed by the novel's spiraling intra-actions with its readers and with its two editions. Hence, "reading" the book "through" its actual spaces, namely the National Gallery and the *Salone dei Mesi*, points at *How to Be Both*'s fundamental achievement in enacting how time and materiality—that is actual space, the physical book and the reader's corporeality—matter to its meaning.

NOTES

1. Ali Smith, *Artful* (2012; London: Penguin, 2013), 31. All subsequent citations refer to the 2013 Penguin edition.
2. Ali Smith, *How to Be Both* (2014; repr. London: Penguin, 2015). Page references are to the 2015 Penguin edition.
3. See also Eva von Contzen who observes that "we cannot undo our first reading experience and start afresh." "'Both close and distant': Experiments of Form and the Medieval in Contemporary Literature," Special issue, *Frontiers of Narrative Studies* 3, no. 2 (2017): 290, https://doi.org/10.1515/fns-2017-0019.
4. Emily Hyde points out that the two versions "posed a problem for the e-book, and the publishers had to include a special note." "Eyes, Camera. Camera, Eyes," *Post45*, October 10, 2015, http://post45.research.yale.edu/2015/11/eyes-camera-camera-eyes/.
5. Karen Barad, *Meeting the Universe Halfway: Quantum Physics and the Entanglement of Matter and Meaning* (Durham: Duke University Press, 2007), 381.
6. Ibid. 142.

7. Donna J. Haraway, *Modest_Witness@Second_Millenium.FemaleMan©_Meets_OncoMouse™: Feminism and Technoscience* (New York: Routledge, 1997), 16.

8. Ibid. 273.

9. Barad, *Meeting*, 141.

10. For a focus on simultaneity, see, for example, Tory Young, "Invisibility and Power in the Digital Age: Issues for Feminist and Queer Narratology," *Textual Practice* 32, no. 6 (2018): 996–97, https://doi.org/10.1080/0950236X.2018.1486546; or Hyde, "Eyes, Camera."

11. Smith, *How to Be Both*, 144, 289, and 325.

12. Cara L. Lewis, "Beholding: Visuality and Postcritical Reading in Ali Smith's *How to Be Both*," *Journal of Modern Literature* 42, no. 3 (Spring 2019): 143, Project MUSE.

13. In their collection *Critique and Postcritique*, Anker and Rita Felski argue that "[t]he current moment in literary and cultural studies . . . involves a broad interest in exploring new models and practices of reading that are less beholden to suspicion and skepticism, [and] more willing to avow the creative, innovative, world-making aspects of literature and criticism." Introduction to *Critique and Postcritique*, ed. Elizabeth S. Anker and Rita Felski (Durham: Duke University Press, 2017), 20. Diffractive reading joins these calls for a change in criticism but to what extent their interests coincide remains to be clarified. While Lewis's analysis of *How to Be Both* addresses difference, Anker's foregrounds other diffractive concerns, namely materiality and embodied experience. "Postcritical Reading, the Lyric, and Ali Smith's *How to Be Both*," *Diacritics* 45, no. 4 (2017): 28-35, https://doi.org/10.1353/dia.2017.0018.

14. Diffractive thinking and reading can be thought of as a cluster of characteristics: an "attenti[on] to[wards] fine details," as well as towards difference (agential cuts) as opposed to sameness or reflexivity; towards multiplicity, performativity (agency) and, of course, materiality. Barad, *Meeting*, 93. A diffractive literary analysis (or a diffractive text) is therefore only fully diffractive (in a Baradian sense) if it adheres to all of these criteria at the same time. Because a diffractive reading pays attention to small details it always involves close reading but with a particular emphasis on difference and materiality, as well as an acceptance that the reading and its elements are "iteratively reconfigured" and multiple. Diffractive reading is a method that chooses proximity over critical distance (see note 80) and an attitude or rather a certain understanding of how worlds come into being. For insightful diffractive readings in literary studies that influenced my own approach, see Birgit Mara Kaiser, "A New German, Singularly Turkish: Reading Emine Sevgi Özdamar with Derrida's *Monolingualism of the Other*," *Textual Practice* 28, no. 6 (2014): 969–987, https://doi.org/10.1080/0950236X.2014.925492; "Worlding CompLit: Diffractive Reading with Barad, Glissant and Nancy," *Parallax* 20, no. 3 (2014): 274–287, https://doi.org/10.1080/13534645.2014.927634.

15. Barad, *Meeting*, 30.

16. Daniela Keller, "Germany and Physics in English Fiction after 1960: A Diffractive Reading of Anglo-German Entanglements," (PhD diss., University of Basel, 2019), 4–5.

17. Lewis, "Beholding," 143.

18. Sonya Andermahr, "Both /And Aesthetics: Gender, Art, and Language in Brigid Brophy's *In Transit* and Ali Smith's *How to Be Both*," *Contemporary Women's Writing* 12, no. 2 (July 2018): 260, https://doi.org/10.1093/cww/vpy001.

19. Ibid. 261.

20. Smith, *How to Be Both*, 72 and 182.

21. This information has begun to spread: in the process of writing this essay, Lewis published her article which partially hints at this particular twist in its last endnote. "Beholding," 147n21.

22. Smith, *How to Be Both*, 193 and 201.

23. On the responsibility of the reader and how a diffractive reading embraces the diffractive readers themselves, see also Kaiser, "Worlding CompLit," 277 and 285; and Iris van der Tuin, "Diffraction as a Methodology for Feminist Onto-Epistemology: On Encountering Chantal Chawaf and Posthuman Interpellation," *Parallax* 20, no. 3 (2014): 231, https://doi.org/10.1080/13534645.2014.927631, as well as Kai Merten's introduction and Agnieszka Kotwasińska's contribution in this volume.

24. All preceding three citations are from Smith, *How to Be Both*, 3, 279, and 122.

25. The "moral conundrum" actually refers to a question that George's mother Carol poses: she asks George to imagine herself "an artist" (namely Francesco del Cossa) who is asking for more money because he believes to be better than the other painters working on the same project. Many statements in *How to Be Both* are not only directed at the characters but seem to address the readers too. Hence, Carol's request to imagine "[y]ou're an artist" is also an appeal to the readers to put themselves in the author's position. Smith, *How to Be Both*, 3, 6–7, and 3.

26. Both parts are 186 pages long ("Camera" 1-186; "Eyes" 187–372) and are entitled "one."

27. Smith, *How to Be Both*, 4. The reference to time serves to highlight the parallels between George's part that starts at the beginning of the year and ends sometime after the beginning of March, and Francesco del Cossa's frescoes that depict the months March, April and May. Smith, *How to Be Both*, 134. Because March was considered the first month of the year (Aby Warburg, "Italienische Kunst und internationale Astrologie im Palazzo Schifanoja zu Ferrara," 1912, in *Die Erneuerung der heidnischen Antike: Kulturwissenschaftliche Beiträge zur Geschichte der europäischen Renaissance*, ed. Horst Bredekamp and Michael Diers, vol. 1.2 of *Aby Warburg: Gesammelte Schriften; Studienausgabe* [Berlin: Akademie Verlag, 1998], 464; Peter Bell, "Regent unter dem Himmel: Die Sala dei Mesi des Palazzo Schifanoia in Ferrara als Modell eines astrologischen Weltbildes," in *Weltbilder im Mittelalter: Perceptions of the World in the Middle Ages*, ed. Philipp Billion et al. [Bonn: Bernstein, 2009], 13, https://doi.org/10.11588/artdok.00002074), there is an interesting resonance between "Camera" that accompanies George during the first three months of a year in the twenty-first century and del Cossa's frescoes that spatially represent the first three months of a year in Renaissance Italy.

28. Bell, "Regent," 2. According to Bell, the frescoes originally represented the twelve months of the year and decorated all four walls but only seven of the twelve months still exist. "Regent," 2.

29. Robert Kusek and Wojciech Szymański, "Ali Smith's *How to Be Both* and the *Nachleben* of Aby Warburg: 'Neither here nor there'," *Hungarian Journal of English and American Studies* 23, no. 2 (2017): 265, ProQuest.

30. Warburg, "Italienische Kunst," 469; Smith, *How to Be Both*, 56–57.

31. Bell, "Regent," 7.

32. Smith, *How to Be Both*, 189. This part "Eyes" is told in Francescho's words and the stylistic features that can be found in his famous letter are reapplied in the narrative: in the letter he referred to himself as "Francescho" with an additional "h" or wrote "Ferara" with only one "r." Smith, *How to Be Both*, 221 and 196. He also made extensive use of colons which the narrative imitates and which will be discussed in more detail below (see a transcription of the letter in Eberhard Ruhmer, *Francesco del Cossa* [Munich: F. Bruckmann, 1959, 48).

33. Although Francescho can hear George, he does not understand her, as he does not speak English. Smith, *How to Be Both*, 288.

34. Smith, *How to Be Both*, 224.

35. Smith, *How to Be Both*, 185. It is never resolved whether Lisa Goliard actually spied on George's mother or whether she was simply in love with her. However, Young spotted that "the word 'liar' is embedded in her name, nested graphically in the word 'God', the symbol of ultimate surveillance," which may justify George's suspicion. "Invisibility and Power," 999.

36. Lewis, "Beholding," 143.

37. Smith, *How to Be Both*, 156, 156–157, and 155.

38. By contrast, von Contzen, in "Both Close and Distant," discovers in her fascinating comparison of *How to Be Both* and medieval plot structure that Smith's novel is driven by a "centripetal" (as opposed to "centrifugal") dynamic, in which "separate items are being drawn towards the centre"—the centre being Francesco del Cossa's frescoes. Anthony Davenport, *Medieval Narrative: An Introduction* (Oxford: Oxford University Press, 2004), 269, quoted in von Contzen, "Both Close and Distant," 295.

39. Smith, *How to Be Both*, 202, 202, and 203.

40. Resonance describes the physical phenomenon of waves enhancing each other. As Ann Breslin and Alex Montwill explain, "suspension bridges, guitar strings or the air in an organ pipe . . . have natural frequencies at which they will vibrate if prompted by an impulse of the right frequency" *Let There Be Light: The Story of Light from Atoms to Galaxies*, 2nd ed. (London: Imperial College Press, 2013), 165. See also sociologist Hartmut Rosa's *Resonance: A Sociology of Our Relationship to the World*, trans. James C. Wagner (Cambridge: Polity Press, 2019), which uses the concept of resonance to describe a subject's relationship to the world. Barad applies the phenomenon (in a figurative sense but by no means without material consequences) to the institutional isolation of disciplines, for example, and states that "the division of labor is such that the natural sciences are assigned matters of fact and the humanities matters of concern, for example. It is difficult to see the diffraction patterns—the patterns of difference that make a difference—when the cordoning off of concerns into separate domains elides the resonances and dissonances that make up diffraction patterns that make the entanglements visible." "'Matter Feels, Converses, Suffers, Desires, Yearns and Remembers': Interview with Karen Barad," in *New Materialism:*

Interviews & Cartographies, ed. Rick Dolphijn and Iris van der Tuin, 48–70. (Ann Arbor: Open Humanities Press, 2012), 50, http://dx.doi.org/10.3998/ohp.11515701.0 001.001.

41. Smith, *How to Be Both*, 170; italics in original.

42. Smith, *How to Be Both*, 59, 167, 178, and 182; italics in original. Another example visualizes the twist: George remembers how her mother used to collect "pencil shavings," and the narrator recounts how George noticed "the tiny zigzags of colour made into the shapes like the edges of those scallop shells by the twist of the pencil in the sharpener." Smith, *How to Be Both*, 29.

43. Smith, *How to Be Both*, 173; italics and exclamation mark in original.

44. Smith, *How to Be Both*, 173; italics in original.

45. Brenda Maddox, *Rosalind Franklin: The Dark Lady of DNA* (London: Harper Collins, 2002), xviii.

46. The novel hints at Watson's disrespectful treatment of Franklin (Smith, *How to Be Both*, 173–74; see also Maddox, *Rosalind Franklin*, xviii). In his monograph, Watson also criticizes, for example, that she "might have been quite stunning had she taken even a mild interest in clothes [etc.]." *The Double Helix: A Personal Account of the Discovery of the Structure of DNA* (London: Weidenfeld and Nicolson, 1968), 17.

47. Smith, *How to Be Both*, 174; italics in original.

48. Smith, *How to Be Both*, 215–22.

49. Anker also points out that "by reinventing the life of del Cossa, *How to Be Both* conducts its own act of historical recovery." "Postcritical Reading," 21.

50. Smith, *How to Be Both*, 173; italics in original.

51. Smith, *How to Be Both*, 172 and 173.

52. Lewis reads the shout as George's "feminist uprising," as "an upward-springing history that excites joy." "Beholding," 138.

53. For a discussion of "editing" DNA in genetics as a special kind of diffractive reading, see Merten's introduction to this volume.

54. Smith admits elsewhere to being "a fan of the unexpected connection[s] . . . between the art forms." "Brighton Festival 2015 Trailer," YouTube Video, 1:40–1:45, April 15, 2015, https://youtu.be/7CW3CsVNcyQ).

55. Stephen J. Adams, *Poetic Designs: An Introduction to Meters, Verse Forms and Figures of Speech* (1997; repr. Peterborough: Broadview Press, 2003), 188. See also Andermahr, "Both/And," 260; Young, "Invisibility and Power," 996.

56. Smith, *How to Be Both*, 173, 182, and 183.

57. Smith, *How to Be Both*, 222–24.

58. Smith, *How to Be Both*, 186.

59. Note also Smith's play with words that refer to the act of seeing or looking throughout the novel (fore*see*able). Lewis offers a detailed discussion of the "different kinds of sight [that] stimulate different modes and degrees of knowledge." She unveils that "variations on the word 'look' appear about 400 times over the course of the novel, which is more than once a page." "Beholding," 136 and 134.

60. Smith, *How to Be Both*, 371–72.

61. As mentioned, these lines resemble a double helix structure; see also Lewis, "Beholding," 139. Maria Micaela Coppola observes that the change of direction is

visualized by the position of lines gradually shifting from left to right or vice versa. "'A whole spectrum of colours new to the eye': Gender Metamorphoses and Identity Frescoes in *Girl Meets Boy* and *How to Be Both* by Ali Smith," *Textus: English Studies in Italy* 28, no. 1 (January–April 2015): 183.

62. Smith, *Artful*, 31.

63. Coppola discusses the novel's circular features, claiming that George's ending and "Smith's novel as a whole . . . spin a sort of 'temporal loop'." "Spectrum of Colours," 182. Furthermore, Smith's experimentation with narrative circularity is prominently explored in Seasonal Quartet (*Autumn* [2016], *Winter* [2017], *Spring* [2019] and *Summer* [2020]).

64. The spiral structure of the book gains further complexity if one considers that both halves constantly return to memories of past events. These analepses create more spirals on a smaller scale, or rather turn the spiral structure into a spiraled spiral (like the DNA helix).

65. Mark Currie, *About Time: Narrative, Fiction and the Philosophy of Time* (2007; repr. Edinburgh: Edinburgh University Press, 2012), 29, quoted in Coppola, "Spectrum of Colours," 182.

66. Renate Brosch, for instance, focuses on the novel's ekphrastic passages that serve to "stimulate the reader's imagination and creative participation in the construction of new meanings" and to undermine "the binary relationship of viewing subject and perceived object." "Ekphrasis in Recent Popular Novels: Reaffirming the Power of Art Images," *Poetics Today* 39, no. 2 (June 2018): 421 and 419, ProQuest. Similarly, Milly Weaver remarks that "Francescho's painterly way of seeing and articulating urges Smith's reader to give thought to the visual" and suggests analyzing the novel "through the lens of visual portraiture." "Reading Words Alongside Images: Ali Smith and Visual Portraiture," *Interdisciplinary Literary Studies* 20, no. 4 (2018): 537 and 532, Project MUSE. See also Coppola, "Spectrum of Colours," 180.

67. Lewis, "Beholding," 133.

68. Anker, "Postcritical Reading," 19 and 26.

69. Smith, "Brighton Festival 2015 Trailer," 0:39–0:43.

70. Smith, *How to Be Both*, 50. There are descriptions of a very similar constellation, such as Helena "ca[tching] George's eye over the tops of [other girls'] heads," and George doing the same in return. See Smith, *How to Be Both*, 75, 78, and 320.

71. Smith, *How to Be Both*, 322 and 258.

72. Smith, *How to Be Both*, 354, 142, 354, and 356–57.

73. Smith, *How to Be Both*, 182, 189, and 190.

74. Smith, *How to Be Both*, 191.

75. The two dots can be read as a literal representation of Wordsworth's description of epiphany as "spots in time." William Wordsworth, *The Prelude XII* [1805], quoted in Robert Langbaum, "The Epiphanic Mode in Wordsworth and Modern Literature," *New Literary History* 14, no. 2 (Winter 1983): 336, https://www.jstor.org/stable/468689.

76. It encompasses both parts because the colon is used in "Eyes" and in "Camera" (see for example Smith, *How to Be Both*, 13, 19, 22, 43, etc.).

77. Smith, *How to Be Both*, 223.

78. Langbaum, "Epiphanic Mode," 341.

79. See Lewis's discussion of Francescho's painterly techniques, such as the *trompe l'oeil* which is very similar to his metalepsis. "Beholding," 143–44.

80. Smith, *How to Be Both*, 106.

81. Lewis, "Beholding," 134 and 142. Both diffraction and postcritique seek to minimize the critical distance. Barad argues that "[r]eflexivity, like reflection, still holds the world at a distance. It cannot provide a way across the social constructivist's allegedly unbridgeable epistemological gap between knower and known, for reflexivity is nothing more than iterative mimesis: even in its attempts to put the investigative subject back into the picture, reflexivity does nothing more than mirror mirroring." *Meeting*, 87–88. Anker says in direct relation to *How to Be Both*: "postcritique [must] necessarily . . . begin and end with sheer entanglement with literature. Throughout, the novel effectuates a materialist, sensory, and embodied immersion in the experience of reading that short-circuits whatever negative distantiation Warner and others attribute to critique." "Postcritical Reading," 20.

82. Brian McHale, *Postmodernist Fiction* (1987; repr., London: Routledge, 2001), 223; italics in original.

83. I am very grateful to Smith's German publishers for confirming this.

84. Smith, *How to Be Both*, 60.

85. Smith, *How to Be Both*, 149–150.

86. Hence, in intra-action with the readers, the actual world contributes to the meaning-making process of the fictional world. It is only by hearing for oneself that one can decide whether George or her mother is wrong, and yet readers may still disagree because hearing is a highly individual activity. My ears, for example, tell me that George was right.

87. Smith, *How to Be Both*, 155, 153, and 191.

88. The National Gallery confirmed that del Cossa's painting was on display in room 55 from August 23, 2013 until February 9, 2018. Unfortunately, they were not able to provide the exact locations of the other paintings in the same room.

89. This is my translation; the original sentence in the German version reads: "Deutlicher als es im Medium Buch möglich wäre, bildet der Raum das kosmische Phänomen des Jahreslaufes als geschlossenen Kreis ab." Bell, "Regent," 9.

Chapter 9

Practices of Entanglement
Unreading the Genre in China Miéville's **The Scar**

Agnieszka Kotwasińska

"I always preferred them stories without the morals"

—Miéville 2002, 33

To say that I was surprised by my intense relationship with China Miéville's *The Scar*[1] is a vast understatement. Never much for pirate stories, Sea Gothic, let alone ships, sea voyages, and open waters, I was nonetheless immediately drawn to *The Scar*'s two protagonists: a floating pirate city of Armada and Bellis Coldwine, an émigré linguist and unwilling participant in Armada's greatest almost adventure. One could suggest, and rightly so, that *The Scar* is simply a superb example of primary and secondary world-building, and thus my love for the book stems from its ability to transform into a fantastically wrought escape machine.[2] Still, looking at *The Scar* only through the lens of escapism, whether politicized or not, does not satisfy my own curiosity, personal, and critical alike. A simple explanation would chart a commonality between Bellis and myself: we are, after all, both trained linguists and translators. More importantly, however, we are both cultural émigrés working in alien and alienating circumstances: Bellis, an academic press-ganged into a pirate city workforce, uses her unique skill set to manipulate her way out of Armada; I, a Polish academic, use my English-language skills to maneuver my way into the mythic West, a post-Soviet interloper seeping in through the academic cracks.

Whereas Miéville jokingly calls Bellis "a gothy Jane [Eyre],"[3] I see myself as a Gothicist: the indefinite article "a" masking the cultural, national, and linguistic specificity of the Gothic, thus allowing me a momentary pretense of boundless universality. But when I speak of Gothic things, I do not mean the few scattered Polish texts, but a multitude of English and American ones which, for better or worse, have defined Gothic production for more than three centuries. I stand on shaky ground, my Gothic credentials wobbly, as my research practices did not develop in a comparative literature program, let alone Gothic Studies. Polish universities, based to a large extent on a nineteenth-century German model, offer a chance to study non-Polish literatures principally in philology departments (and, to a lesser degree, in cultural studies programs), which are structured around either particular languages (or language groups) or geographic regions. If, at least nominally, Western comparative literature programs revolve around the comparison of world literatures, Polish departments of English studies or American studies set up clear hierarchies of knowledge production and dissemination, in which literary boundaries are erected and maintained through a postcolonial directionality, not least because of the singular value accorded to English language and Anglo-American cultural production in post-1989 Eastern Europe.

As a Gothicist (a Polish Gothicist? an Anglo-American Gothicist from Warsaw?), I cannot but search for traces of the Gothic in *The Scar*. While looking for a "gothy" Bellis and, crucially, for a Gothic medley of popular genres and a Gothic *enstrangement*, I stumble upon signs that I too have been Gothicized, my research practices made spectral and uncanny. I turn to diffraction as a reading practice, because reading *The Scar* diffractively means giving "the fullest possible account of [my] praxis" and I do believe that a diffractive reading needs to "be aware of itself as an effect of *this* specific apparatus (this reader with proficiencies and limits, embedded in these historical, linguistic, political struggles) and of the diffraction patterns that result from the productive passing through one another of two or more elements (the texts, the readers, their linguistic sensitivities, their cultural repertoires)."[4] Simply acknowledging my position, my politically uncomfortable Eastern European situatedness, is never enough.

1. ENTANGLED AND DIFFRACTED: A NOTE ON THEORY

Diffraction, understood here "as an ongoing movement of entanglement,"[5] is not part of a revelatory paradigm of criticism, in which the critic-cum-archaeologist moves through an ominous castle to reveal its mysteries, no matter how tempting such a Gothic analogy might be for me. If anything, a diffractive reading strikes me as a different type of knowledge production, one that does not necessarily build upon what has already been written to add one more layer of meaning or to deconstruct someone else's interpretation.

Rather, diffractive methodology, as formulated by Karen Barad in her germinal *Meeting the Universe Halfway*, is a critical practice committed "to understanding which differences matter, how they matter, and for whom,"[6] one that speaks to a deep ethical engagement with the differences that are produced in each and every reading. Thus, for Barad, diffraction emerges as "a method of diffractively reading insights through one another, building new insights, and attentively and carefully reading for differences that matter in their fine details, together with the recognition that there intrinsic to this analysis is an ethics that is not predicated on externality but rather entanglement."[7]

Heeding Serenella Iovino and Serpil Oppermann's call "to conceive textual interpretation as a 'practice of entanglement',"[8] I want to see if a diffractive reading might foster a better understanding of *The Scar*'s Gothic becomings. Diffraction is employed here as a certain model of research practice, a kind of a critical tesseract that allows the researcher (me), research equipment (literary theory) and the object of research (*The Scar*) to intra-act more freely than a purely epistemological model would have it. Moving into the territory of onto-epistemology means that the classic triad (the researcher-the equipment-the object of study) is no longer a fixed starting point but rather a contingent end result and an ever-surprising consequence of enacting "agential cuts."[9] Because diffractive research practice is conceived as an experiment in intra-acting it ceases to be a pseudo-objective act of studying and disassembling a pliant and immobile object carried out by an equally unmovable distant agent. In Barad's own words, "[e]ntanglements are relations of obligation—being bound to the other—enfolded traces of othering."[10]

Rather than trying to prove why *The Scar* does (not) belong to a specific genre, I would like to point to the abundance of generic markers that cohabit the same narrative: this splendid, uneasy, startling cohabitation resists the conventional poststructuralist critique, understood as a form of subtraction[11] and classification. In a novel so openly fascinated with quantum potentialities, Gothicized practices of reiteration and accretion, and material and discursive uncanniness, the narrative comes to matter through generic openness rather than closure and through multitude rather than finitude. One could argue that genre fiction is not, by its own nature, a very diffractive sort of literature in that it relies on sameness and recognition of familiar tropes rather than production of differences and uncertainties. Which is why I remain suspicious of a wholesale rejection of "the entrapping binary of sameness and difference,"[12] a well-worn binary often deployed in literary criticism but one that lies at the core of genre formation and accentuates the generic pleasures of encountering both the boringly familiar and the imaginatively unexpected. Short of dismantling genres altogether, I see no way of avoiding the interplay of similarities and differences in genre fiction, even if such reading practices might be considered static or too conventional. What is possible, however, is attending to how this binary is not a given but rather a singular phenomenon taking place anew with each reading, each text, and each reader. Thus, reading genre fiction diffractively means paying close attention to how and what kinds of generic entanglements emerge out of such readings. Kaiser's evocative reading of how "world" in "world literatures" does not preexist the literature in question might be of value here, especially when one replaces "world" with "genre": "The entanglement of matter and meaning, or the fact that 'things' in their being are entangled with the measurements they participate in, means that the world [the genre] is not 'out there' to be grasped by a subject separated from it, but that the world [the genre] in each 'phenomenon' is a congealing or a continuous *spacemattering*."[13]

I respond to the generic openness of *The Scar* and its sticky embrace of the past, the former, and the abandoned by re-turning to Viktor Shklovsky's classic 1919 text, "Art, as a Device," newly translated from Russian into English by Alexandra Berlina.[14] The decision to diffract *The Scar* through Shklovsky's *ostranenie* (in itself diffracted through a brilliantly enstranged new translation) stems from my desire for a different cartography of the weird; one that is not reliant on a linear passage of time or highly stratified concepts of literary progress and one that moves the discussion from under the shadow of the Freudian uncanny. But choosing *ostranenie* as a literary tool is for me also a strategic decision—a way to signal that diffractive reading does not necessarily have to rely exclusively on Baradian (or Harawayan) terminology and conceptual tools. Reading fiction diffractively, to my mind, also means working with whatever toolkit a researcher finds useful, be it a schizoanalysis or psychoanalysis, eco-criticism or reader-oriented theory, agential realism or postcolonial theory. My understanding of diffraction is driven by the awareness of how these tools are in themselves subject to the experiment, how the researcher herself is reconstituted by the experiment and the tools she is using, how the object of study is never a static given but a rather a restless pulsing mass of potentialities never fully graspable before the analytical experiment begins. I am paying close attention to the interpretative differences that emerge out of this experiment, slight variations in my understanding of *The Scar* triggered by *ostranenie*, and theoretical divergences facilitated by what ultimately is simultaneously a deeply personal and political choice. At the same time, I am mindful of how deploying particular conceptual and formal tools, in this case *ostranenie*, reintegrates me in the virtual fold, in which material-discursive choices (reading, making notes, re-reading, re-arranging thoughts, applying concepts, thinking theory) create a kind of research potentiality, an alternative academic present, if you will.

2. ENSTRANGING THE WEIRD IN *THE SCAR*

Working with Shklovsky's text, fifteen years after having read it in literary theory classes, is both an exercise in critical enstrangement and a constant struggle against research anxiety that urges me to go with the latest, most advanced, most theoretically challenging texts rather than with a Russian Formalist's short article published a hundred years ago and long relegated to the margins of hegemonic literary theory. Were I to choose a genealogical approach to the weird rather than a cartographic one, I suspect I would simply end up reiterating critical steps that somehow always begin and end in Anglo-American research and theory. Choosing to follow an Eastern European theory, canonized by Western literary schools, but only barely, questions my never-still politics of belonging (rather than the static politics of location): a baffling tangle of feminist criticism(s), French poststructuralist thought learned through its Anglo-American propagators and critics, Western-based and Western-oriented gender studies and cultural studies programs—all streaked with an acute sense of post-communist Otherness and weighed down by a double-split of postcolonial history: belonging to a country that has been colonized and that has colonized repeatedly.

My pleasures, for there are many, involved in reading and re-reading *The Scar*, follow its genre formation. Intuitively, the novel's dark incandescence springs from the way it manages to contain within its 800 pages a multitude of genres, never submitting to any of them but rather allowing them to coexist uncomfortably, to form unholy alliances and to wage wars for readers' attention. The popular genres of the fantastic that Miéville weaves together—fantasy, weird fiction, science fiction, steampunk (of sorts), horror—are all brought to the surface, only to be ironically dismantled and imaginatively rewritten and remade into new constellations of generic markers. *The Scar* is not, however, a literary orphan waiting to be rescued from the pit of genre-less despair. Rather, Miéville's Bas-Lag trilogy (*Perdido Street Station, The Scar, Iron Council*)[15] is held as a prime example of the New Weird, a new-old genre that has grown so many strange appendages, viscous bulbs and ponderous tentacles that it now stands for a vague gesture and a rather flat description. Put differently, the New Weird "does" rather than "is"; it gathers, distributes, reacts to and with, magnifies, expands and restricts themes and formulas swarming within the fantastic. The New Weird simply diffracts the fantastic, with each New Weird text forming its own little experiment in recreating and reframing the tropes of the fantastic genres. The indelible satisfaction I find in reading *The Scar* is partly based on the recognition of familiar tropes and the acknowledgment of moments when these tired tropes are questioned and reversed—two rather typical pleasures of genre-reading. Nevertheless, my principal pleasure lies in rearranging the generic pieces with each subsequent re-reading and, simultaneously, resisting the temptation to settle on one final interpretation.

The adjective "new" in the "New Weird" gestures not only to the future (new directions, fresh perspectives) but also to the past (challenging what has already been written, reacting to the old). Thus, a certain linear temporality seems to have taken shape in most critical ruminations on the New Weird: the latest incarnation of the genre is said to be more progressive and more transgressive (albeit in a good anti-establishment way) than its grandiose, fusty, and somewhat socially awkward grandfather—the (original) weird fiction penned by the likes of H.P. Lovecraft, Arthur Machen, and Robert W. Chambers.[16] Where the original weird tales accentuated their authors' fear of modernity and the inevitable march of social and cultural progress in the early twentieth century, the New Weird giddily embraces the incongruities of postmodernity and the beauty of its postanthropocentric monsters.[17] And yet, thinking about the New Weird as an update on the old weird strikes me as insufficient to account for either literary manifestation. In my own working definition of the New Weird (which echoes Miéville's musings on the topic as well as Weinstock's, Noys and Murphy's, and Luckhurst's formulations),[18] the weird is located in the everyday rather than in the cosmic, as was the case with its initial version. Granted, "the everyday" that is en-weirded may be wholly quotidian and well known to its readers, but it may just as well be rooted in a fantastic world carefully constructed by the author, as in Miéville's Bas-Lag, in which the weirdness lies in is very ordinariness.

Before distancing himself and his fiction from the weird in the late 2000s, Miéville argued that since the weird does not concern itself with the return of the repressed, the notion of the "abcanny" is actually more accurate of a descriptor of the weird.[19] Put differently, the weird resides alongside the known and the canny, and erupts on the pages not via hauntologically inflected revenants of genre fiction, but via tropes that generate new forms of generic un/familiarity. For Miéville, fantastic horror vacillates between these two poles (the uncanny and the abcanny).[20] And whereas the (original) weird fiction supposedly rejected Gothic imagery and plot devices, the New Weird, perhaps because of its shaky status as (someone's) successor and descendant, is already embroiled in a (Gothicized) literary family drama. The tension between abcanny enstrangement and Gothic iteration is what draws me to *The Scar* and what drowns me in it every time I read it. Here, the Gothic stands not so much for particular images and tropes one might readily link with Gothic romances or neo-Gothic narratives, but rather for a series of movements and intensities associated with notions of falsity, indeterminacy, and monstrosity as well as returning (and re-turning) of the previous and the forgotten. While *The Scar* is not a Gothic narrative, it is marked by a typically Gothic fascination with repetition and renovation of the old (genres, concepts, tropes)—processes that are successfully captured and further en-weirded by Miéville.

3. THE RE-MADE: MONSTERS, HYBRIDS, AND GENRES

Take monsters, a standard feature of all the genres of the fantastic. While *The Scar* is richly populated by monsters of all shades and shapes (quite familiar, though not quite, vampires, or an essentially unknowable gargantuan sea monster—the avanc), the Remade are a particularly vivid example of how *The Scar* enstranges monstrosity. In fact, Miéville himself admits that through the Remade he was attempting "to interrogate notions of the monstrous and teratological as they have been used in Gothic and postgothic texts, but also to indulge them."[21] Thus, the Gothic fascination with the monstrous, the grotesque, and the villainous is tempered by a much more mundane approach to the Remade, one that defamiliarizes their monstrosity by, somewhat paradoxically, naturalizing it.

Criminals found guilty by the New Crobuzon judicials are bio-thaumaturgically altered in "punishment factories": "Some were shaped for industry, while others seemed formed for no purpose other than grotesquerie, with misshapen mouths and eyes and gods knew what."[22] Tanner Sack, an engineer punished for an unspecified crime with two lifeless tentacles attached to his torso, accompanies Bellis to the colonies as part of "the ship's sentient cargo."[23] Upon their arrival, Bellis would probably scrape a living as a translator in an involuntary exile, while he would be swallowed up by the colonial slave force. Their journey is, however, interrupted: first by the machinations of a New Crobuzon spy, Silas Fennec, and then by pirates, who commandeer the ship and pressgang its reluctant crew into their own ranks, while freeing the "sentient cargo"—the Remade slaves—and offering them Armadian citizenship. Their roles somewhat reversed, Bellis witnesses how the Remade are unconditionally accepted as fellow Armadians and gratefully transform from prisoners into free agents; she, on the other hand, never ceases to feel as a prisoner, even though she too is given ample opportunity to make Armada her home.

Back in New Crobuzon, the Remade are truly made monstrous in the sense that they are forced to carry their perceived moral inadequacy (that is, socially constructed criminality) as signs on their bodies, there for everyone to read. They are thus forced to *demonstrate* and perform their *monstrosity*—a gesture that excavates the original etymology of the word "monster"—the Latin *monstrare* ("to show" and "to indicate"). Tanner, after being accepted as an Armadian, uses his remade body to his advantage by accepting the position of an expert diver and underwater engineer, with his tentacles finally becoming an integral part of him rather than a mere vexing appendage. More than that, he decides to pay for an additional round of remaking to become an even better diver, an even more useful Armadian. In a fragment heavily redolent of Victor Frankenstein's work, he undergoes a surgery that tips the scale from human to amphibian (gills, webbed hands and feet, an additional pair of transparent eyelids etc.).

Superficially, Tanner is asking to be made even more monstrous and less human than he already was. In this sense, the "Remade" suggests a certain dehumanization, a reification of sorts. Yet, it is also clear that the earlier connotations of shame, public humiliation, physical impairment, and performance of monstrosity are effectively erased through Tanner's exercising his agency by first choosing and then paying for the new procedure. He is r/Remade according to his own specifications and needs, which gives him more freedom, but also ultimately ties him to the ocean even more, a decision not without its own hefty price.

> [The chirurgeon] scored deep gashes in the sides of Tanner's neck, then lifted off the skin and outer tissue, gently wiping away the blood that coursed from the raw flesh. With the exposed flaps oozing, the chirurgeon turned his attention to Tanner's mouth. He reached inside with a kind of iron chisel and slid it into the pulp of the throat, twisting as he pushed, carving tunnels in the flesh.
>
> He stoked the fire that drove his bulky analytical engine, and fed it program cards, gathering data. Finally, he wheeled into place alongside the gurney a tank containing a sedated cod, and linked the motionless fish to Tanner's body by a cryptic and unwieldy construction of valves, gutta-percha tubes, and wires.
>
> Homeomorphic chymicals sluiced dilute in brine across the cod's gills, and then through the ragged wounds that would be Tanner's. Wires linked the two of them. The chirurgeon muttered hexes as he operated the juddering apparatus—he was rusty with bio-thaumaturgy, but methodical and careful—and kneaded Tanner's bleeding neck. Water began to drool through the holes and over the opened-up skin.[24]

The strength of this particular scene lies in its successful appropriation of several generic tropes of transformation, which, when put together, convey the overall banality and stark hideosity of the procedure. At the same time, the rapid cascade of visual registers—the gore of body horror, the computer programming of cyberpunk, the magic spells of fantasy—successfully preempts a calcification of the entire process and interrupts narratological habituation. This also marks a diffractive moment for the reader, as she is invited to follow a multiplicity of generic waves rippling through the narrative and engage with those that hold her attention most fully, ones that her imagination and readerly experience are drawn to the most. If, as Shklovsky suggests, "[t]he goal of art is to create the sensation of seeing, and not merely recognizing, things,"[25] then Miéville manages precisely that by showing each step in vivid detail, with enough generic cues to prompt the readers' recognition, yet without enough background information to fully understand what is happening. For Shklovsky, "the process of perception" is the ultimate goal of arts, increased and supported by "'enstrangement' of things and the complication of the form."[26] Arguably, the remaking, which seems to rely on a simple framework of sympathetic magic and alchemical correspondences, is enstranged not by the suppression of information but rather through a profusion of visual cues and generic references and a cornucopia of abcanny details that are not all recognizable to readers.

"The goal of an image is not to bring its meaning nearer to our understanding but to create a special way of experiencing an object, to make one not 'recognize' but 'see' it."[27] Recognizing and seeing can be folded back onto the uncanny-abcanny spectrum: that which was already known but was then imperfectly repressed will be warily recognized once it resurfaces; that which was never known can only be seen rather than recognized once it appears. In the same way, I do not *recognize* the Remade, or the Anophelii or the Cacti, or other fantastic Bas-Lag races, but rather *see* them as beings *other* than humans yet not necessarily *Othered*. Othering only works if there exist an easily recognizable center (us) and its margins (not-us), and *The Scar* successfully resists such center-margin structuring of social relations. At a glance, the Remade could be read simply as a potent metaphor for the socially disenfranchised, their enstrangement a sign of social or political alienation, but in the world of *The Scar* they function primarily as vehicles of difference or, more precisely, as crisis engines, to borrow a concept from the first Bas-Lag novel, *Perdido Street Station*. According to Bellis's ex-lover, Isaac, "it's in the *nature of things* to enter crisis," to "turn themselves inside out by virtue of being things," which is how he was trying to tap into the excess energy released in crisis situations.[28] While the Remade are in a state of perpetual crisis by the very nature of their thaumaturgic modifications, Armada thankfully lacks a "mad scientist" who would tap their crisis energy; instead, it is the narrative itself that utilizes their power to throw generic markers off balance. The Remade's hybrid bodies do not reflect the generic hybridity of *The Scar*, they produce it.

4. BELLIS: LOST AND FOUND IN TRANSLATION

While Bellis, as readers' human stand-in and our reluctant guide to Armada, may be at times disgusted, frightened, or perplexed by certain Bas-Lag races or the Remade, their customs or embodiments, she never stoops to exoticize or explicate them. Haughty and emotionally distant, Bellis's sense of superiority stems from her *misrecognizing* herself rather than from having any anthropocentric (or misanthropic) bias. The novel suggests, but never explores, the underlying reason for Bellis's cold demeanor (reflected not only in her surname "Coldwine," but also unkind nicknames given to her by others: Coldarse, ice-woman, Miss Cold). A woman competing in male-dominated academia and, more generally, living in a deeply patriarchal society of New Crobuzon, Bellis arms herself with stark makeup, austere clothing, chilly manner, and a talent for extricating herself quickly from any relationship or situation that might render her vulnerable. I would like to say that this is where I part my ways with Bellis, that I do not *recognize*, let alone *see* myself in her, but that would not be true. I know her tactics all too well and understand her decision to use a gender-neutral appellation (with just a hint of the masculine), "B. Coldwine," as her authorial presence in the books she has published; although, truth to be told, I would prefer to simply anglicize my name and finally stop seeing it misspelled and hearing it mispronounced. But just as Bellis's icy tactics do not shield her from harm, my half-hearted attempts at Western-passing are fleeting, at best. Still, affinity does not equal identification, and while we may be both strangers in strange lands, and I feel Bellis's fear of exposure and her righteous fury, reading myself through her fills me with sorrow rather than pleasure, shame rather than pride. Her hubris reminds me of mine.

While admittedly a shrewd and discerning observer, Bellis puts too much faith in her knowledge and linguistic skills. Granted, language is a skeleton key that helps her open a great many locked doors first in New Crobuzon and later on Armada, and her being an expert on the ancient language of High Kettai makes Bellis indispensable to her Armadian rulers—the Lovers—and to their enigmatic quest. While Shklovsky does not mention translation as a potentially enstranging process, a series of interlocking translations, including standard translation between languages but also linguistic manipulations and corrupt storytelling, form the very cornerstone of *The Scar*'s abcanny architecture.[29] This translatory enstrangement brings into focus the diffractive nature of all translation, understood as a practice of reading the world through details and differences, correspondences, and correlations. *The Scar*'s plot reads like a series of manipulations and misdirections with Bellis trying to use others only to end up being manipulated into doing or triggering certain events for Silas Fennec, a New Crobuzon spy, and Uther Doul, the Lovers' right-hand man. Even though Bellis scoffs at being treated as a voiceless conduit when she is acting in her official capacity as a translator, she is reduced to precisely that—a mere vessel that has facilitated the flow of information but has been never actively involved in shaping the knowledge passing through her. In an ironic twist of fate, she becomes the actual material that is being mediated by other actors, molded to their needs and translated anew. Bellis (and the reader) belatedly realizes she has been diffracted through narrative conventions she misunderstood and misapplied entirely; she has mistaken herself for a savvy heroine when in reality (or perhaps in several coexisting generic realities), she has been switching back and forth between different roles: a hapless victim, a fool, an anti-heroine, perhaps a villainess too.

Melancholy creeps on this page as I reflect on my own role as a translator and researcher decoding Western cultural production at a post-1989 Polish university. If I am aware of, and even welcome, the West-East intra-actions through which I am constituted as a Gothicist, a feminist critic and cultural studies researcher, am I diffracted by and through my research, the patterns of reading I generate, the texts I choose to follow, the unpopular popular genres I stubbornly cling to? Should diffraction be this miserable? Working in English 90 percent of the time, on English and American cultural texts, leaning on either English translations of Western theory or simply Anglo-American criticism, struggling to catch up to my Western colleagues (wearily a Sisyphean effort), I am no longer sure how to read Polish texts outside Western paradigms I have so thoroughly imbibed. Am I "broken" as an Eastern European researcher the same way Bellis is "ruined" as a translator? Have we both been translated into someone else by the very languages/ fictions we have been studying for so long, by the very tools we have armed ourselves with? If Bellis's hubris results from her overestimating her prowess, mine lies in misrecognizing my research practice as universal and transnational and naively imagining myself unaffected by it.

Nevertheless, I am acutely aware that the melancholic loss of linguistic and/or cultural innocence I am experiencing is a postcolonial fantasy, a convenient political arrangement, which establishes the East and the West as stable and definable constructs that enter predetermined archetypal relations—the petitioner and the benefactor, the poor cousin and the rich aunt, the backward and the sophisticated, the premodern and the postmodern, the post-Soviet and the neoliberal, and so on. Thinking the East and the West diffractively as "relata" rather than preexisting historical sociopolitical agents substitutes vacuous nostalgia with generative curiosity. Each instance of inter(intra)cultural translation, each application of literary tools and critique, each encounter generates transient linguistic borders and delineates new nomadic cultures. On the one hand, by choosing Shklovsky and *ostranenie* rather than the Freudian uncanny, I catch a glimpse of a could-have-been in which Freud's theory of repression does not get to define the twentieth-century scholarship of the fantastic, and a formalist emphasis on textuality trumps sexual psychopathology as a reigning critical paradigm in Gothic Studies—for once, the East triumphs. On the other hand, I *am* working with a contemporary English translation of Shklovsky's essay, published in a leading American journal of literary studies, which means I am following an already existing line of flight, a could-have-been reconfiguring the East and the West binary into a new assemblage and translating my anxiety into a cautious sense of wonder.

Translation-as-reconfiguration hints at a highly subjective, idiosyncratic, perhaps even serendipitous nature of translation, which I understand here not just as linguistic conversion but also as a reading practice. In turn, such perception of translation links it with possibility mining, an ancient (and possibly alien) Bas-Lag technology that bypasses the theory of probability to secure successful results every single time. Rather than deploy it for sly time travel shenanigans, Miéville uses possibility mining to comment on the nature of story-telling and the deceptive allure of finitude in fiction.

5. TOWARD A POTENTIAL UN-ENDING

In the novel, Bellis slowly discovers that the Lovers' plan is based on their desire to harness possibility mining at its very source—the titular Scar, a rift in reality caused by the Ghosthead race crashing into Bas-Lag thousands of years ago. When the Ghosthead came to Bas-Lag (in all probability from a different planet or, perhaps, even plane of existence), the force of their arrival fractured not just the material world but its ontology and the rules governing reality as well. Throughout the three novels, it is suggested that it was "the chaos of the [ensuing] Torque" that shaped Bas-Lag and its peoples, their technologies and embodiments. Uther Doul, a scholar of the Ghosthead, explains to Bellis that "[a] cataclysm like that, shattering a world, the rupture left behind: it opens up a rich seam of potentialities," which the Ghosthead mined by failing and succeeding at the same time. The technology is best explained with Uther Doul's own Possible Sword, a Ghosthead artifact capable of tapping into a myriad of potentialities and mining them for successes: when Uther Doul is fighting, "[h]is sword blossoms. It is fecund, it is brimming, it sheds echoes. Doul has a thousand right arms, slicing in a thousand directions. His body moves, and like a stunningly complex tree, his sword-arms spread through the air, solid and ghostly." The wounds inflicted by his sword seem unnatural as they "shiver between states, deep rents that were suddenly insubstantial and dreamlike." And yet, the Scar offers so much more than a mere object as it is "teeming with the ways things weren't and aren't but could be." The deeper Armada travels into the pernicious Hidden Ocean, the more the Scar bleeds with potentialities: gambling becomes even more randomized with cards changing colors after they have been dealt, spirits and strange creatures slither in out of nowhere, and finally an unexpected guest arrives with a story that changes everything. It is a tale that ultimately buries the Lovers' plan. Hedrigall, a beloved crewmember and a trusty Cacti lookout, who has mysteriously abandoned Armada in the middle of the Hidden Ocean, suddenly reappears while they are closing in on the Scar. According to his chaotic tale, he is in fact a Hedrigall from an alternative reality, one in which the avanc pulled Armada over the edge thus destroying the whole floating city, with only Hedrigall miraculously escaping certain death. Of course, there is no way of telling if he truly is a different-reality Hedrigall or if perhaps the original Hedrigall simply hid for a couple of weeks and then performed this horrifying story for the Armadians. Was he coached by Uther Doul? Or was it Doul who actually orchestrated this game of potentialities by playing a Ghosthead instrument, a perhapsadian, and "making a concerto of likelihood and unlikelihood?"[30]

The big climax—the moment Armada finally reaches the Scar—never quite materializes and instead turns out to be an intricately woven gambit with Bellis right at the dead center of it. She becomes instrumental in relaying to the Armadian masses Hedrigall's story and the Lovers' attempt to suppress it, which sparks a bloodless coup d'état and a retreat from the Hidden Ocean. Depending on one's reading, Hedrigall's story is either an apt ending or a fitting un-ending, or perhaps, as an instance of possibility mining, both and neither. If, re-turning to Shklovsky, "deautomatizing perception" is the paramount goal of all poetic language, then, somewhat paradoxically, Hedrigall's chilling story defamiliarizes the very concept of narrative closure.[31] Stark images of Armada's inevitable demise, of a frantic avanc falling through the crack in reality, and of the Lovers' towering hubris can be seen as an ironic substitute of the "real" ending. But they are the *real* ending after all, one that has already taken place, is taking place right now and will take place somewhere in the future. It is the sheer immensity of this discomfiting un-ending that forecloses even a thought of a different ending and a happier outcome, which is what makes the Armadans fall back. Hedrigall's story, whether made-up or real, relates *The Scar*'s un-ending to the virtual plane, where it remains locked in a continual process of becoming-ending.[32] This is also the point at which diffraction ceases to inform Miéville's story and a vast ocean of potentialities turns into a mere puddle, where only one outcome is imaginable, and no real difference is discernible. And the experimenters—the Armadans—are no longer interested in carrying out the grand finale, and as they simply walk away from their project, they leave the readers stranded amid generic markers leading nowhere in particular.

It seems clear to me now that by writing about the grand un-ending and Hedrigall's story, I too play possibilities the way Uther Doul played/might have played/did not play the perhapsadian. Where my reading practice overlaps with possibility mining, my objective, as in *The Scar*, is to sift the potentiality stream for successful outcomes, in this case, a sense of a true ending regardless of the novel's refusal to provide one. But while the grand Armadian adventure might be happening else*where* and else*when*, a smaller and perhaps more fitting "ending" returns me to Bellis, who muses whether she still is the real Bellis ("fact-Bellis") or maybe she is now a different iteration of herself ("a nigh-Bellis"), plucked from an alternative timeline by Uther Doul, a substitute "pulled through into existence to replace a dead woman." Now subdued and humiliated, yet somehow also tougher and wiser, she finally finishes a letter she has been writing ever since her flight from New Crobuzon. A letter to no-one in particular and to everyone, to her "dear friend" and maybe just to herself teaches me that this was, primarily, Bellis's tale and that conclusion to her story is still pending, despite my protestations and critical interventions. As Bellis sourly reflects, "[t]here is nothing to be learnt here. No ecstatic forgetting. There is no redemption in the sea."[33] My perhapsadian is broken; closure is the Scar that has never healed properly.

And yet, tenacious being that I am, I play the (broken?) perhapsadian over and over again. Reading *The Scar*, I am ceaselessly mining for Gothic possibilities, moments where the dominant fantasy framework is enstranged and en-weirded, fragments in which the accumulation of generic markers makes for an ironic commentary on the plasticity of the fantastic genres and their inherent disloyalty. At the same time, I do not see *The Scar* as a Gothic novel. It is quite clearly and quite ambiguously a New Weird magnum opus, both a pinnacle of contemporary weird fiction and an unsuccessful (though accidental) attempt at canonizing the New Weird. The Gothic intensity, however, is what aids the narrative in its becoming-New-Weird by continually delaying satisfactory endings or explanations and by simultaneously embracing and defamiliarizing generic markers. Of course, it is entirely possible that the Gothic is in the eye of the beholder and it is my own (heavily Gothicized) theory apparatus that imbues *The Scar* with the Gothic. And maybe, just maybe, I am playing my own "concerto of likelihood and unlikelihood" with the Gothic as my unique goal and purpose.[34]

Still, diffraction is not about exchanging one toolkit for another, and I have not shed my Western practices in lieu of Eastern ones, or poststructuralist critique in lieu of literary formalism. Rather, diffraction allows for a sort of indeterminacy that supports interpretative experiments and critical openness; openness not merely to particular texts or concepts but to one's own critical leanings, research practices, and personal histories. Thus, I arrive at a series of interlocking entanglements: entangling my (mostly) Western-centric critical apparatus with Shklovsky, the weird with *ostranenie*, *The Scar* with the Gothic, my usual critical practices with diffraction, and, finally, entangling myself with *The Scar* even more.

NOTES

1. China Miéville, *The Scar* (2002; London: Pan Books, 2011). All subsequent citations refer to the 2011 Pan Books edition.
2. Found both in the Frankfurt School's critique of mass culture and contemporary laments over the disappearing gap between literary fiction and genre fiction, a routine criticism leveled at genre fiction argues that popular genres entrap readers in escapist fantasies thus limiting the readers' political and/or critical engagement. Still, the distinction between popular genres and literary fiction has always been based, to a large degree, on social and class conventions, critical reading practices, and marketing rather than on any intrinsic differences between the two. For more on this debate, see, for instance, Berenice M. Murphy, *Key Concepts in Contemporary Popular Fiction* (Edinburgh: Edinburgh University Press, 2017) and Ken Gelder's edited volume *New Directions in Popular Fiction: Genre, Distribution, Reproduction* (London: Palgrave Macmillan, 2016). The debate is not limited to academics though, and is also carried out by critics, journalists, and authors themselves (see, for instance, Lev Grossman, "Literary Revolution in the Supermarket Aisle: Genre Fiction Is Disruptive Technology' *TIME*, May 23, 2012," http://entertainment.time.com/2012/05/23/genre-fiction-is-disruptive-technology/; and Joshua Rothman, "A Better Way to Think about the Genre Debate," *The New Yorker*, November 6, 2014, https://www.newyorker.com/books/joshua-rothman/better-way-think-genre-debate.)
3. Miéville, quoted in Kirsten Tranter, "An Interview with China Miéville," *Contemporary Literature* 53, no. 3 (September 2012): 431.
4. Birgit Mara Kaiser, "Worlding CompLit: Diffractive Reading with Barad, Glissant and Nancy," in *Diffracted Worlds—Diffractive Readings: Onto-Epistemologies and the Critical Humanities*, ed. Birgit Mara Kaiser and Kathrin Thiele (London: Routledge, 2018), 121; emphasis in original.
5. Kiene Brillenburg Wurth, "Diffraction, Handwriting and Intra-Mediality in Louise Paille's Livres-livres,'" in Kaiser and Thiele, *Diffracted Worlds*, 100.
6. Karen Barad, *Meeting the Universe Halfway: Quantum Physics and the Entanglement of Matter and Meaning* (Durham: Duke University Press, 2007), 90.
7. Karen Barad, "'Matter Feels, Converses, Suffers, Desires, Yearns and Remembers': Interview with Karen Barad." In *New Materialism: Interviews & Cartographies*, edited by Rick Dolphijn and Iris van der Tuin, 48–70. (Ann Arbor: Open Humanities Press, 2012), 50, http://dx.doi.org/10.3998/ohp.11515701.0001.001.
8. Serenella Iovino and Serpil Oppermann, "Introduction: Stories Come to Matter," in *Material Ecocriticism*, ed. Serenella Iovino and Serpil Oppermann (Bloomington: Indiana University Press, 2014), 9.
9. Karen Barad, "Diffracting Diffraction: Cutting Together-Apart," *Parallax* 20, no. 3 (2014): 168, https://doi.org/10.1080/13534645.2014.927623.
10. Karen Barad, "Quantum Entanglements and Hauntological Relations of Inheritance: Dis/continuities, SpaceTime Enfoldings, and Justice-to-Come," *Derrida Today* 3, no. 2 (2010): 265.

11. Karen Barad, "'Matter Feels, Converses, Suffers, Desires, Yearns and Remembers': Interview with Karen Barad." In *New Materialism: Interviews & Cartographies*, edited by Rick Dolphijn and Iris van der Tuin, 48–70. (Ann Arbor: Open Humanities Press, 2012), 49–50, http://dx.doi.org/10.3998/ohp.11515701.0001.001.

12. Jacob Edmond, "Diffracted Waves and World Literature," in Kaiser and Thiele, *Diffracted Worlds*, 82.

13. Barad, "Diffracting Diffraction," 114; emphasis in original.

14. For more on "re-turning as a mode of intra-acting with diffraction," see also Barad, "Diffracting Diffraction," 168–187.

15. The trilogy includes *Perdido Street Station*, *The Scar*, and *Iron Council* which was published in 2004.

16. The past decade saw an unprecedented proliferation of critical takes on the old and the New Weird (for instance, Benjamin Noys and Timothy S. Murphy, "Introduction: Old and New Weird," *Genre* 49, no. 2 [July 2016], 117–134; Roger Luckhurst "American Weird," in *The Cambridge Companion to American Science Fiction*, ed. Gerry Canavan and Eric Carl Link [New York: Cambridge University Press, 2015] 194–205; Roger Luckhurst "The Weird: A Dis/orientation," *Textual Practice* 31, no. 6 [2017], 1041–1061; Timothy Jarvis, "The Weird, the Posthuman, and the Abjected World-in-itself: Fidelity to the 'Lovecraft Event' in the Work of Caitlín R. Kiernan and Laird Barron," *Textual Practice* 31, no. 6 [2017]: 1133–1148; two anthologies ed. Ann VanderMeer and Jeff VanderMeer, *The New Weird* [San Francisco: Tachyon Publications, 2008] and *The Weird: A Compendium of Strange and Dark Stories* [New York: Tor, 2011]; and China Miéville's essays "Long Live the New Weird," *The 3rd Alternative* 35 [2003]: 3, "M.R. James and the Quantum Vampire Weird; Hauntological: Versus and/or and and/or or?" *Collapse* 4 [2008b]: 105–128 and "Weird Fiction," in *The Routledge Companion to Science Fiction*, ed. Mark Bould, et al. [London: Routledge, 2009]: 510–516), the old weird and H.P. Lovecraft's oeuvre (for example, Kate Marshall, The Old Weird," "*Modernism/ Modernity* 23, no. 3 [2016]: 631–649; Michel Houllebecq, *H.P. Lovecraft: Against the World, Against Life*, trans. Dorna Khazeni [n.p.: Believer Magazine, 2005]; Graham Harman, *Weird Realism: Lovecraft and Philosophy* [Winchester: Zero Books: 2012], Carl H. Sederholm and Jeffrey Andrew Weinstock's edited volume, *The Age of Lovecraft* [Minnesota University Press, 2016]), and the intimate ties between the weird and other genres of the fantastic (for instance, Sara Wasson, "China Miéville's *Perdido Street Station* [2000] – Gothic Literary Science Fiction," in *The Gothic*, ed. Simon Bacon [Oxford: Peter Lang, 2018], 203–210; Jeffrey Andrew Weinstock, "Jeff VanderMeer's *Annihilation* [2014] – Gothic and the New Weird," in *The Gothic*, ed. Simon Bacon [Oxford: Peter Lang, 2018], 211–216; Isabella van Elferen, "Techno-Gothics of the Early-Twenty-First Century," in *The Cambridge Companion to the Modern Gothic*, ed. Jerrold E. Hogle [Cambridge: Cambridge University Press, 2014], 138–154). Two book-length publications were devoted to Miéville's fiction, Carl Freedman's *Art and Idea in the Novels of China Miéville* (Canterbury: Gylphi, 2015) and Caroline Edwards and Tony Venezia's edited volume *China Miéville: Critical Essays* (Canterbury: Gylphi, 2015), followed closely by a number of articles,

symposia, panels, and conferences dedicated to his work and its influence on the fantastic.

17. Sandy Rankin, "AGASH AGASP AGAPE: The Weaver as Immanent Utopian Impulse in China Miéville's *Perdido Street Station* and *Iron Council*," *Extrapolation* 50, no. 2 (June 2009): 239–257; Noys and Murphy.

18. See China Miéville, "Weird Fiction," in *The Routledge Companion to Science Fiction*, ed. Mark Bould, et al. (London: Routledge, 2009), 510-516; Weinstock, "The New Weird,"; Noys and Murphy, and also Luckhurst, "American Weird."

19. China Miéville, "M.R. James and the Quantum Vampire Weird; Hauntological: Versus and/or and and/or or?" *Collapse* 4 (2008): 105–128.

20. Tranter, "An Interview," 424.

21. China Miéville, "Gothic Politics: A Discussion with China Miéville," *Gothic Studies* 10, no. 1 (2008): 68.

22. Miéville, *The Scar*, 35.

23. Miéville, *The Scar*, 30.

24. Miéville, *The Scar*, 212–213.

25. Viktor Shklovsky, "Art, as Device," trans. with intro. Alexandra Berlina, *Poetics Today* 36, no. 3 (September 2015): 162.

26. Shklovsky, "Art, as Device," 162.

27. Shklovsky, "Art, as Device," 167.

28. China Miéville, *Perdido Street Station* (2000; London: Pan Books, 2011), 207; emphasis in original. Page references are to the 2011 Pan Books edition.

29. Even Tanner's transformation into a fully amphibian Remade reads like a translation procedure: a great analytical engine, program cards, hexes, chymicals, electricity, and biothaumaturgy all conspire to translate fish-like appendages and capacities onto a human body through a set of correspondences. And yet, just as Tanner's remaking (translation) into an amphibian is a manipulation of sorts, Bellis's use of her language skills relies on crafty misdirection too.

30. All quotations are from Miéville, *The Scar*, 543, 580, 78, 748, 789.

31. Shklovsky, "Art, as Device," 171.

32. The unending also functions as Miéville's critique of storytelling formulas prevalent in the fantasy genre, specifically a desire for a big and rewarding finale. The highly anticipated grand adventure is forfeited for purely pragmatic reasons—the Armadians are tired of the Lovers' nebulous plans and grandiose posturing; they want to continue their slow but steady pirating and boring yet dependable trading. The fantasy quest's resolution is denied and revealed as, at best, a potential sham or, at worst, a lethal delusion.

33. Both quotations are from Miéville, *The Scar*, 789, 791.

34. Miéville, *The Scar*, 789.

Chapter 10

The Entanglements of Harry Burden
A Diffractive Reading of Siri Hustvedt
Matthias Stephan

Siri Hustvedt's sixth novel, *The Blazing World*, is an ambitious text predicated on the compilation of a series of documents related to the life and career of the artist Harriet Burden. The novel can be read as an intervention into feminist debates in the art world (the world of Harry Burden), the act of writing and literature (the world of Siri Hustvedt), and even the concept of mind (an academic interest of Siri Hustvedt, which Harry seems intimately familiar with). Siri Hustvedt is not only a novelist, but also an essayist, a writer of memoirs, an academic writer publishing on neuroscience and psychology, and is often self-reflective about her own work. In 2010, she published a memoir, *The Shaking Woman or a History of My Nerves*, in which she attempts to come to terms with the phenomenon of her involuntary physical shaking, while maintaining control over her mind and thoughts.

> The search for the shaking woman takes me round and round because in the end it is also a search for perspectives that may illuminate who and what she is. My only certainty is that I cannot be satisfied with looking at her through a single window. I have to see her from every angle.[1]

The memoir presents numerous attempts to address the phenomenon, but only represents one such output in Hustvedt's works which deal with the phenomenon.

In 2017, in conjunction with a visit promoting a translation of *A Woman Looking At Men Looking At Women* into Danish, Hustvedt gave a lecture and workshop at Aarhus University.[2] At that time, Hustvedt suggested that her 2014 novel, *The Blazing World*, the memoir *The Shaking Woman*, and the essay collection *A Woman Looking At Men Looking At Women*, each relate, in their own ways, to her coming to terms with that physically manifesting condition, which the doctors described variously as *vascular migraine syndrome*, *hysteria*, and *dissociative (conversion) disorder*.[3] Essentially, each of these texts offers the reader a different window, to use Hustvedt's analogy, into her coming to terms with her entangled experience. Taking that as a starting point, I propose a diffractive reading of *The Blazing World* and its associated texts, as a way to seek insight into the works of Siri Hustvedt on the whole, and the entanglements embedded in each of the manifestations of her ideas.

In this model, not only would the protagonist's theorizing of her own artistic project, *Maskings*, be considered as an onto-epistemological entanglement,[4] one which is complicated by the inclusion of other artists in the production of the artworks, but furthermore Hustvedt's own creative enterprise can also be read diffractively. The reading, following Barad's model,[5] does not consider the novel a discrete entity of analysis, but, as Kaiser and Thiele aptly describe it, as "processually, relationally and asymmetrically produced"[6] with the larger body of her works, her own subjective construction and its phenomenological embodiment, and an insight into the process itself. The reading of that text is paired with both her nonfictional, personal reflections in *The Shaking Woman* and the essays in her most recent collection—all of which she described as different "ins" to the same phenomenon she is seeking to understand.

READING DIFFRACTIVELY

A diffractive reading allows one to seek knowledge beyond the construction of objectivity, and absent ties to a reflective ideology. Haraway's definition of diffraction is "a mapping of interference, not of replication, reflection, or reproduction"[7] with the interference leading to specific patterns through which one can achieve insight into a phenomenon. Building upon Haraway's theories, Karen Barad considers implications of knowledge from outside the humanities, drawing on research in quantum physics to challenge existing metaphors operating in the humanities. In a reading of Bohr's two-slit experiment, Barad notes that the apparatus allows not only an understanding of the epistemological status of the phenomenon but that its ontological status is also tied up in the means by which we understand things. This "onto-epistemological thinking"[8] destabilizes a number of traditional concepts, and opens our readings to look beyond traditional binaries, whether they are nature/culture, subject/object, or those related to gender.

Birgit Kaiser argues that "the notion of diffraction . . . pertains not only to a certain behavior of matter, but also to a method of reading."[9] Rather than suggesting a single entity, such as Siri's novel, with her essays, secondary sources, and the reader's position shedding light upon it, this essay will use the successive windows of each text to shed light on the overall phenomena. This builds upon the notion that "entities do not have an inherent fixed nature,"[10] but rather are a product of *intra-acting* with the particular apparatus of insight. As Siri suggested in her interview, each of the texts shed light on a phenomenon that doesn't have a fixed definition, nor even distinct contours, which the author (Siri Hustvedt) or the reader(s) can point to "without" the intra-action between them. These readings are entangled, inevitably, in an "always-already" fashion, by the very notion of its construction as literature, as writing, and as philosophy. Using Barad's model, this essay will focus on close readings of the texts chosen, reading each through the other, in an effort to explore the insights provided through such an analysis. Barad specifically invokes the ethical, and elsewhere refers to this method not just as an entanglement of the ontological and epistemological, but also the ethical, an "*ethico-onto-epistemological* approach,"[11] which is also particularly salient in Hustvedt's body of work.

Thus, in the following, I will suggest different patterns of reading texts through one another, using embedded frames to consider what Barad calls *inventive provocations*. This will be done first through the story of Harry Burden herself, and the development of her *Maskings* project, found within the novel *The Blazing World*. The second section will pertain to the larger construction of the novel, which is created through a series of texts not only those by Harriet Burden (her series of notebooks), but interviews with family, friends, and associates, newspaper clippings, and published articles. This compilation will be considered as entangled with the inner construction in various ways, and will be considered in its approach to the presentation of Harry Burden, and its insight into her artistic projects. The final section will again zoom out to consider the novel as a whole as embedded within Siri Hustvedt's larger literary project, her implication within the novel as well as its author, and the insights provided through her memoir and essays, and the entangled understanding of both the nonfictional and fictional texts when read through one another. It is this final level that demonstrates the onto-epistemological entanglement of her work, but by unpacking these Chinese boxes systematically, the intention is to show how Hustvedt includes representations of her entanglement within her fictional works, just as she does in her memoir and essays. Each subsequent level of insight represents an agential cut, a momentary snapshot that is always already entangled. As Barad notes, "agential cuts never sit still; they are iteratively reworked. Inside/outside is undone."[12] The novel, through its structure and various windows into the characters, teaches us how to read the larger intertextual body of her work.

THE ENTANGLEMENTS OF HARRY BURDEN

The main conceit of Hustvedt's novel revolves around the *Maskings* project. Harriet Burden, the wealthy, highly intelligent, middle-aged, overweight widow of a prominent art collector, feels herself sidelined as an artist by virtue of the various components of her identity—as a woman, by virtue of her age, by her appearance, by her first husband's prominence in the art world as a collector, by her intellect. In essence, for Harriet, her life has become a burden, and she needs to shed herself to achieve her own potential, as she sees it. To that end, she devises a complex art project which requires the inclusion, and intervention, of several masks, which take the form of stand-ins for her artwork. As the presumed editor, I.V. Hess, in his introduction claims: "She titled the whole project *Maskings*, and declared that it was meant not only to expose the antifemale bias of the art world, but to uncover the complex workings of human perception and how unconscious ideas about gender, race, and celebrity influence a viewer's understanding of a given work of art."[13] The pieces are thus aesthetic as well as intellectual exercises, as much about audience reaction as their own intrinsic artistic merits.

To that end, she develops, as we read in the course of the novel, three distinct masks—which are performed by the artists Anton Tish, Phineas Q. Eldridge, and Rune in successive phases. The structure of *Maskings* is a combined piece of artwork, ostensibly created in coordination between the two artists in question, Harry and her accomplice. As Tougaw explains, "Harriet Burden, a giant, loquacious autodidact of an artist, hires successively three men to exhibit her works as their own."[14] Each piece is then presented to the art world as by the *mask*, and reviewed accordingly, as if the proxy is the sole creator of the artwork. From Harry's perspective, each piece represents her idea with a false front, the mask, representing a separation of a private and public persona, of mind (Harry) and body (the mask). Yet, each of these pieces also functions as an exploration of the onto-epistemological entanglement of the two artists in question. As becomes increasingly apparent, both to the reader as the novel progresses, and to the protagonist in her own development and self-reflection, neither the PR presentation of the artworks, nor Harry's supposition of independent authorship can account for the entangled nature of the artistic endeavor. It is not a matter of simply *knowing* who created the artwork, or an ontological status of the work itself, but those categories are always already complicated by the very notion of the experiment.

The first piece is *The History of Western Art*, in coordination with a young, relatively unknown artist who champions Andy Warhol and produces a series of screen art in his style. Tish[15] is seemingly selected for his look.

Anton Tisch looked right. He was tall, almost my height, a skinny kid in loose jeans with a significant nose and searching eyes that seemed unable to fix on anything for long, which gave him a distracted air that could be interpreted as restless intelligence under the right circumstances. And he was an artist.[16]

The work in question is a complex piece, which provides intertextual reference to a great deal of art and theory, much of which seems far beyond Tish, thus suggesting to the reader that Burden is the author, especially as we assign authorship with the intellectual property associated with a work of art—the romantic privileging of idea over craft. Rohr notes that "Harry's first surrogate, the young and inexperienced Anton Tish, is indeed hailed as a rising star in the art scene for the exhibition *The History of Western Art*, but he is deeply disturbed by his sudden fame and, after making a melodramatic scene at Red Hook, retreats into remote corners of the world to recover."[17] Tish's removal from the scene, so to speak, leaves a vacuum in which to interpret Tish's involvement. This allows Burden's own interpretations to become the driving force in this relationship—focused through Burden's self-perception, and developed in her private notebooks. Even at this stage, there is a clear combination of interests in the interpretation. The art world gives Tish credit by virtue of just those categories that Burden used in selecting him for her partner—his youth, good looks, ontological status as "an artist" and the surface impression of a deeper intellectual curiosity. At the same time, Burden's assertions to the reader retain main credit for her contributions—the intellectual heft of the artwork, and the originating idea. He, in Burden's presentation, is her mask; she is the force behind the mask. Yet, credit for the project is a matter of perspective.

This same pattern is perpetuated in the second *Maskings* project. "Her second substitute, Phineas Q. Eldridge, a performance artist and one of her lodgers, is a more mature personality and is able to professionally handle the attention that he receives due to the exhibition, but the show *The Suffocations Rooms* is only a moderate success."[18] For the second show, Burden chooses an older artist, and this forms a pattern in her project, in which her masks can be seen to also represent three successive stages of life, as well as the development in the artist's work. Tish is hailed as much for youthful achievement as he is for the work itself. Eldridge is a performance artist, whose identity is always at play—by virtue not only of the medium chosen, but also of the representation of his identity—homosexual, mixed-race, male. Thus, the interpretation of this piece hinges on using the mask to deflect a reading based on Harry's identity. In Notebook B, dated January 18, 2000, Burden questions the viability of her project to achieve her own stated ends, even as it begins to have commercial success. "As for the plot, it seems to be working. Phineas has been offered a show of *The Suffocation*

Rooms at Begley in the spring of next year"[19] and yet in nearly the same breath, she also questions whether she "could show work by Anonymous" suggesting a lack of confidence about the underlying project. However, her partner disagrees with her assessment, drawing her attention back to the necessity of the masks to demonstrate the gender bias, and the consequent prejudices that this enables.

> He has seen that it matters little what I say; my intelligence is discounted. Piffle and twaddle. Were I to come out with *The Suffocation Rooms*, the powers-that-be would instantly back away.
>
> The work would look different.
> Would it look old-womanish all of a sudden?
> I insist that this is a question with urgency.

Just as with the Tish collaboration, the intellectual aspects of the piece are overlooked in favor of a superficial presentation. The immediate interpretations of the pieces are seen through the lens of the artist, and the artist's performed identity, rather than a close reading of the piece itself. This provides, if exposed, a commentary on not only the art world, but our social structure as a whole. While we seemingly privilege intellectual achievement, and invest a lot of resources in producing educated citizens, that preference is only sufficient up unto the point of expectation—actual intellectual ability is devalued if it doesn't align with other important aspects of identity—notably gender and age. These factors are entangled, both ontological and epistemologically—and that critique comes not only from the outside but also from Harry's anxieties.

Eldridge, in his own account in the novel, states:

> When *The Suffocation Rooms* were shown, they were read through me—P.Q. Eldridge was exploring his identity in his art. White boys, the Anton Tishes of the world, have no need to explore their identities, of course. What is there to explore? They are the neutral universal entity, the unhyphenated humans.

While an outside perspective assumes a single artist (unaware of the involvement of Burden), for both Harry and Eldridge this is an entangled collaboration. When Harry put on the *mask* of Eldridge, it wasn't simply her presentation with his external form, but she is also fundamentally different by virtue of the mask. "She put on her own mask, and once it was on, she got better at the role, more confident. It suited her. In fact, she was more truthful." While this seems to highlight a separation, Harry is as invested in the role as Eldridge.

The third mask is the most complicated in its construction, and in the perception and relationship to Burden's work. The entanglement with Rune is presented, by Burden in her notebooks, as constructed from the base through the operation of masks. In a performative game, Rune and Harry don masks which are very similar but include faint traces of stereotypically opposite gender markers. Then, without fixed characters to play, they act out their own masks in dialogue and interplay with each other. Harriet Burden occupies the role of Richard Brickman, a male persona, while Rune uses the character of Ruina, a submissive, groveling, female persona, who Brickman can then dominate. This exchange formed the basis of their partnership, through which the creation of the art piece *Beneath* became possible. Rune is himself already a highly successful artist, which allowed for suppositions that he would not need to rely on a collaboration, as would Tish and Eldridge, to produce such a work intellectually. Furthermore, considerations of the form of the artwork, a solid, angular installation, was deemed far different from Burden's known artworks, which were often soft doll-like structures, more similar to the giant female form which forms the background of *The History of Western Art* presented by Tish.

As with the first two parts of the *Maskings* project, Harry Burden does not publicly assert that she is the author of *Beneath* initially. However, it is clear through her own notebooks that she perceived Rune as functioning as her proxy, which develops out of their collaboration and at her instigation. She notes that "[t]he subterfuge was right up Rune's alley, a ploy that wowed him because, if it all went as planned, he could become the biggest art world kidder of them all. He would expose the critics (some of whom he hoped to draw and quarter) as clowns." She also describes how the lines between her and Rune would need to be disguised, "the project would have to disguise the line of suture, the incision between his art and mine." This description parallels a diffractive reading, in which the cut represents not only a separation, but always also a recognition of their interaction and interdependency. "Interlacing the nature/s of matter/s with knowledge/s of/in it, diffraction highlights the systemic intra-actions and unavoidable 'agential cuts' that co-constitute subjects, objects and the ongoing pattern-formations in which they/we participate."[20]

In Harry's mind, and her descriptions as detailed in her own notebooks, she created an artwork that went beyond the individual three pieces that form *Maskings*, and constituted a larger work of artistic commentary. However, as we can see when considering the other contributions compiled by I.V. Hess into the collection that forms *The Blazing World*, how others perceived the *Maskings* project, Burden's contribution, and the author-ity behind its construction, has multiple perspectives. How one views this project seems to stem from the *window* through which one undertakes the viewing, which includes not only the critics, but also the collaborators, and Harry's closest friends and relations.

"THE PROLIFERATIONS": PERSPECTIVES ON HARRY

While the initial project is presented, by the editor, as Harriet Burden's, we come to realize that not only is *Maskings* always already onto-epistemologically entangled, but that this is part of the project, entered into by each set of artists. Hess states that "[a]lthough there is a consensus that Burden made Tish's *The History of Western Art* as well as Eldridge's *Suffocation Rooms*, there is little agreement about what actually happened between her and Rune." This is presented to the reader through the views of sceptics of the project, in the shape of art critics or biographers of Rune. Hess presents Rune's inclusion in the project, and the interpretation of his involvement, as controversial, or at least not straightforward. "There are those who believe Burden is not responsible for *Beneath* or contributed very little to the installation, and others who are convinced that Burden created it without Rune. Still others argue that *Beneath* was a collaborative effort."[21] To further complicate these matters, some of the additional sources provide insight seemingly from Tish, Eldridge, and Rune, perspectives that challenge the notions assigned to Harry Burden. Combining these perspectives with (re)readings of aspects of the notebooks presents a much more entangled conception of *Maskings*. While Burden asserts her role, and thus ownership, of the artworks, the picture painted through the multiple perspectives challenges the very nature of that ownership.

We will first consider Hess's assertion that Burden was responsible for the first two masks. In discussing the collaboration with Tish, Harry asserts that "Big Venus belongs to Anton Tish" as a work that came into being between him and me because it was made by a boy, an *enfant terrible*, not by me, old lady artist Harry Burden with two adult children and a grandchild and a bank account." This reinforces the entangled nature of the project, as the reception of the audience, the fame that Tish acquired and the positive reactions to the piece, were a product of the fusion of Burden and Tish— without Tish as a mask, the piece would not only have been received differently, but it would *be* different. We also, through the perspective of Sweet Autumn Pinkney, the new age thinker who meets Tish, have some insight into Tish's thinking. She reported that "everything had gone wrong with her. He felt like a reflection in one of those fun-house mirrors. 'You don't get it,' he said. 'She's me. I'm her'." While Tish asserts a co-creation, a hybrid collaboration, in which each loses a part of themselves into a common project, this also becomes a matter of perspective, and interest. Rachel Briefman presents both Harry and Tish as asserting that they deserve more credit for *The History of Western Art*, and for different reasons—demonstrating both the entangled nature of artistic creation, and how diffracted through different apertures, different truths becomes apparent. In recounting Tish's confrontation with Harry, Briefman quotes Tish taking credit. "'The whole thing. They wanted me. Do you think they would have wanted you? Isn't this what it's all about? Without me, none of this would have happened'." In this, Tish asserts that his role was most important, and that the audience placed no value in Harry's intellectual contribution. "All your learning, all your esoteric crap; it's worth nothing out there, less than nothing." Thus he deserves the credit. Harry, on the other hand, claims that "he seemed to have forgotten that she had made the artworks, that the boxes had come out of her body, out of years of work and thought." Yet, upon reflection, Harry comes to understand the Tish experiment as a failure specifically because the level of contribution was unclear, and that "she wasn't sure what had happened."[22]

Part of the structure of the novel is the interweaving of the different sources into a coherent narrative. The supposed work of the editor, I.V. Hess, this presents for the reader the sense of learning about the story as it happens, even though the contributors are reflecting back upon elements of the narrative. This means that even this novel is co-created through the selections of pieces, the order they are placed in, and the narrative of the editor and not just the author of each piece. Consequently, we learn about these complications with Tish's story before we are introduced to the collaboration with Eldridge, and take that knowledge with us when encountering his story, as well as the story about his encounter. Again, for the reader, the knowledge of the encounter, our epistemological underpinning, is already entangled with what actually happened, the ontological level, and are inseparable.[23]

Like the Tish story, we are initially presented with *The Suffocation Rooms* giving ultimate credit to Harry, through the lens of I.V. Hess. Differently than Tish, Eldridge is presented as both initially aware, and completely satisfied with the collaboration. "I played Harriet Burden's mask briefly, and I do not regret it for a second," he states in his own written statement. While Tish is approached to represent a young, attractive debut artist, Eldridge is used to present a reading based on identity—a reading that Harry is afraid will be done in her case. Projecting such a reading onto Eldridge, which is how the artistic community views *The Suffocation Rooms*, undermines the biographical attachment that many artistic and literary interpretations make, especially in nonacademic circles, as the narrative presents the ideas (Burden's) separate from the mask (Eldridge), a role that Eldridge himself has been working through in his own art and his own public persona.

I am a performer, and I know that my face onstage can often be more intimate and more honest than the one I wear in the wings. But I have two identities offstage. In 1995, I slithered out of my first persona, the one I was born with, to become my second self: Phineas Q. Eldridge. The person who preceded P.Q.E., John Whittier, was a good boy, well behaved.[24]

Susanne Rohr describes Eldridge as "a more mature personality and . . . able to professionally handle the attention that he receives due to the exhibition."[25] Furthermore, the contribution made by Harry is clear in Eldridge's case, which he presents in his own voice. "No one saw it then, but Harry and I recorded our story in full on the wallpaper of *The Suffocation Rooms*. We mixed in the narrative of P.Q. as Harry's mask with automatic writing, scribbles, doodles, and some palimpsest effects—writing over what he had written—but it's all there." Thus, the project succeeded, perhaps not commercially, but in the sense that Eldridge was read as the creator, successfully acting as Harry's mask. At the same time, the palimpsest represents a material manifestation of the entanglements that the artistic project theorizes (of course, only a fictional representation of such). Therefore, this intellectual success is entangled with the simultaneous idea that the *Maskings* project could not have existed without the mask. "It was true they didn't want Harry the artist. I began to see that up close . . . She knew too much, had read too much, was too tall, hated almost everything that was written about art, and she corrected people's errors."[26] Thus, while Eldridge agrees with the assessment of Hess that the second project is Harry's, each project—Tish (diffracted through Pinkney) and Eldridge—is also described as an entangled project, not possible without the mask, and the mask an integral part of the project's success. Both perspectives are true.

This is most clear in the final stage of *Maskings*, with the creation of *Beneath*. This project is born out of a collaboration between Rune and Harry, and we are presented with their own rehearsal of a mask play at the beginning of their introduction. Tougaw presents this as a game. "The climax of Burden's relationship involves a private game in which the two artists don masks and engage in some gender-switching role playing—embodied portraits of characters that represent their commingled fantasy lives. Burden loses."[27] What does come out of this game is the project *Beneath*, and what Harry sees as the culmination of her work. "With your name on my work, I said, it will *be* different. Art lives in its perception only. You are the last of three, and you are the pinnacle."[28] This represents both an assertion of the continuity of her project, her claim that it forms part of "my work," as well as acknowledging the role of the mask in shaping the project, which she didn't fully do with Tish or Eldridge. The main difference is that *Beneath* is claimed by Rune as his own, and due to the privileging that has already been shown, and Rune's existing artistic reputation, the piece is asserted to be by him. This interpretation is reinforced by Oswald Case, who is added to the collection to represent Rune's perspective, despite the seeming conflict of interest in objectivity, as Case is Rune's biographer and stands to gain from his continued reputation. His reasoning is presented within the collection.

> I know that Harriet Burden believes she had found a third cover for her this-woman-can-become-a-celebrity-artist-too campaign. The question is, did she intervene enough to rob Larsen of credit for the works, which would be shown a year and a half later? I think not. I think he knew exactly what he was doing. *Beneath* hit the art world like a tornado.

The presupposition is that it is Larsen's work, and she would need to steal (or prove?) that she had tangible parts of it to claim credit. This was possible with Tish and Eldridge, as the work moved out of their knowledge bases, on logical (masculine coded) grounds—though not true on other grounds such as celebrity, as Tish asserts, and Harry confirms. Here, however, she has no legal or logical grounds, even if the situations are the same. Without clear credentials, an irrefutable argument with evidence, the male author is the default.

The project with Rune is also the most clearly entangled of the projects. Even if it is clear that Rune's ability to take credit for the work is based on patriarchal assumptions of artistic trends, it is not presented as clear that Harriet Burden created, even intellectually, *Beneath* alone, with Rune as "just" a mask. Just as their role play produced a character change for both Rune (into Ruina) and Harry (into Richard Brickman), it seems that the encounter altered both of them as well as contributed to the piece. Rune's final piece, *Houdini Smash*, reflects not only *Beneath* but earlier work by Burden. If tracing Rune's development, as Case does, there are clear arguments that this final artwork, the site of Rune's death, was Rune's own creation. If you see it through Harry's body of work, however, and know her more intimately, as Bruno Kleinfeld and her son Ethan Lord do, one can see it as derived from the work of Harriet Burden. Both are true, from a certain perspective. Furthermore, Harry's description of their involvement seems to reflect a new understanding, for her, of what collaboration implies. She has evolved along with her *Maskings* project in her thinking. For her, "[i]t was a question of becoming;" a "double consciousness."[29]

ARE YOU SIRIUS?: THE ONTO-EPISTEMOLOGICAL ENTANGLEMENTS OF SIRI HUSTVEDT

The introduction of the character of Richard Brickman, who is both the character created in the interplay with Rune, as well as the pseudonym used by Harriet Burden to shape the understanding of her *Maskings* project to the press, also belies another level of entanglement, that of the author. At all levels of the novel, authorship and perspective are entangled. Furthermore, she also uses genre, with each form's set of expectations and conventions, as an entangling category. This is true not only of the various recordings, written statements, and notebooks that form the novel, but the very idea that this is a fictional text which overtly explores its citations, sourcing, and engagement with the difference between idea and practice, between mind and body. The novel itself purports to be initiated by the editor in conversation with Maisie Lord, a documentary filmmaker who also attempts to recreate her mother (Harriet Burden) through that medium. She claims that it was the letter that was identified by Hess, penned by Richard Brickman (later identified as a pen name of Burden herself), which documents the project "Missive from the Realm of a Fictional Being" which is formed by the notebooks (all but one of them, the missing "Notebook I," are used a basis for the novel). Burden's Notebooks, Hess's novel, and Maisie Lord's documentary all provide insight into the same phenomenon. This is a proxy for the work that Hustvedt herself is doing with this novel, which is also one in to her exploration of mind, body, and art. As Tougaw states, "[u]nlike Burden, Siri Hustvedt does not mask herself with pseudonyms when she publishes articles in peer-reviewed science journals . . . Instead she creates new frames for her ideas about relationships between mind, body, self, and art."[30]

Siri Hustvedt's own project has a similar trajectory. The novel *The Blazing World* can be seen as one entry into her consideration of the entanglement of the body and the mind, even as she asserts that both of those words reflect the same corporeal materiality. In her collection *A Woman Looking at Men Looking at Women*, Hustvedt refers to her own character from *The Blazing World*, who states

> Every dying person is a cartoon version of the Cartesian dualist, a person made of two substances, *res cogitans* and *res extensa*. The thinking substance moves along on its own above the insurrectionist body formed of vile, gross matter, a traitor to the spirit, to that airy *cogito* that keeps thinking and talking.[31]

That article, "Philosophy Matters in Brain Matters" goes on to explain that this experience also reflects her own personal encounter with a physical manifestation that highlights the entanglement between a seemingly internal mental process and an external physical body.

> I am one of countless people in the world beset by an undiagnosed and medically unexplained symptom of a neurological character. I wrote a book about it called *The Shaking Woman or A History of My Nerves* that was published

in 2009. The book is an interdisciplinary investigation of my symptom, which draws on insights from philosophy, the history of medicine, psychiatry, psychoanalysis, neurology, and neuroscience research.[32]

That text is a memoir of her experience, in which she thinks through the relationship between her body and the internal narrative which we tend to call our mind. As Barad notes:

> Bohr argues that this materialist understanding of concepts, in combination with the empirical finding that there is a quantum discontinuity, undermines the notion of an inherent fixed (apparatus-independent, Cartesian) subject-object distinction . . . There are no separately determinate individual entities that *interact* with one another; rather, the co-constitution of determinately bounded and propertied entities results from specific *intra-actions*.

With this in mind, one could even argue that Hustvedt's attempts to separate for analysis the disparate apertures through which she considers her own identity and entanglement, her "external" body and her "internal" mental processes, *diminish* consideration of the material intra-actions that make up her own self, and that a diffractive reading, such as this one, highlights this nature of her larger body of work. I argue that, when considered within her body of work, the larger project also draws on creative writing and literary criticism in providing interdisciplinary insights, fields of the humanities that Hustvedt, as an author, either discounts or takes for granted as understood influences on her own production.

Her memoir is both a history of her dealing with the illness and a prescription of how she understands this entanglement. In it, she tries to come to terms with her own entangled existence. Hustvedt's own explanation of the phenomena drifts from the scientific and academic, referring to neuroscience and citing authorities on the subject, to the self-narrative, a form of auto-ethnography or narrative exploration of her process. "The strangeness of a duality in myself remains, a powerful sense of an 'I' and an uncontrollable other. The shaking woman is certainly not anyone with a *name*. She is a speechless alien who appears only during my speeches."[33] In this description, Hustvedt tries to explain the sense of separation between her physical self, over whom she cannot exert her will, and her mental, rational self, who continues to operate. This represents an onto-epistemological entanglement, as the physical manifestation of her conditions is co-constructed with the medical and psychological discourse surrounding it. As Barad notes, "the material-discursive apparatus, in addition to giving meaning to specific concepts to the exclusion of others, also enacts a specific cut between 'observed' and 'agencies of observation'."[34] The bodily and the discursive are thus only two apertures onto the same phenomenon, and it is not only the memoir that is so entangled as part of the discursive.

This is parallel to the condition that she gives to the voice of Harriet Burden, in describing the betrayal she sees as her own body breaks down during her finally fatal battle with cancer—an illness that can be described as separate from oneself ("I have cancer") and is, at the same time, literally one's own body attacking itself (the mutation of the body's own cells). In attempting to come to terms with this, Hustvedt, in *The Shaking Woman*, uses a literary parallel, the famous novel by Robert Louis Stevenson. "I have come to think of the shaking woman as an untamed other self, a Mr. Hyde to my Dr. Jekyll, a kind of double. Doubles in literature almost always torment and sabotage the desires and ambitions of their originals and, often, they take over."[35] What Hustvedt offers first in her memoir, then in her essays and novels, are different means of coming to terms with this entanglement.

The memoir genre seemingly allows her to tell a personal story, but it cannot escape delving into literary narrative and allusion, which also form a part of Hustvedt's means of expression. It also only offers a perspectival approach to the truth—a truth from Hustvedt's current (at the time of writing) understanding and reflection upon her life. She argues in her 2012 essay collection, *Living, Thinking, Looking*, that "[w]riting a memoir is a question of organizing remembrances *I believe to be true and not invented* into a verbal narrative. And that belief is a matter of inner conviction; what feels true now."[36] The contrast implied by her emphasis distances her conception of the memoir not only from fiction, but importantly from documentary or objective facts, and decidedly includes the idea that memory changes. As she discusses in her essays and alludes to in her fiction, our memory is not a photograph or objective recollection of a series of facts, but a revisit of the last time in which we recalled the circumstances. In essence, memory is both a recollection and a creation, a palimpsest of prior and current experiences. This provides her one means of expressing the "truth" of her condition, a truth determined by the form it is considered with. Fictional experiences are recalled in precisely the same way, and our memories of those experiences can be layered with those real experiences inseparably.

In the introduction to the essay collection *A Woman Looking at Men Looking at Women*, Hustvedt represents her working through her allusions and intertexts with other writers. "The truth is I am full to the brim with the not-always-harmonious voices of other writers. This book is to one degree or another an attempt to make some sense of those plural perspectives."[37] This is true not only in the sense that Hustvedt channels the ideas and patterns of other authors, scholars, and characters, but also that her own voice is multiple when she expresses her ideas, and in the form in which she does so. While her essay collection can be seen as her reflective, objective voice, her memoir as a subjective yet personal perspective, and *The Blazing World* as a wholly fictional story about the life and works of Harriet Burden, those lines are not easily disentangled. As she notes in her memoir, "You cannot isolate a person from the world in which he lives, but more than that, notions of outside and inside, subject and object become entwined."[38] Diana Tappen-Scheuermann takes this still further, arguing that "[r]eading *The Shaking Woman* against the background of Hustvedt's fictional works, one finds that fictional and non-fictional texts correspond, dealing with the same discourses in an almost literal manner."[39] What each of the various texts does is frame the position through a different window, demonstrating how Hustvedt's works are all onto-epistemologically entangled with her own material experience. As such, and taking into account the initial anecdote Hustvedt presented in Aarhus, all of the works herein discussed are related to her working through her own material condition, coming to terms with an understanding of the entangled nature of her mind and body, even (and perhaps especially) when they are seemingly at odds.

THE BRIGHTEST STAR IN THE BROOKLYN SKY

Let us return to *The Blazing World*, which ends with the voice of Sweet Autumn Pinkney, who is called back into the story through an unknown voice, articulating the word "Harry," outside of the Siri Pharmacy on Flatbush Ave in Brooklyn (where Siri Hustvedt, the writer, resides). This perhaps represents a joke by the author, but is not the only place in which the author inserts herself into the story (several of the notebooks make allusion to Siri's academic publications, included in what seems like an historical-metafiction mode of including real and fictional footnotes throughout). In this, the pharmacy is both real and fictional—a real Siri Pharmacy does exist in Brooklyn (23 Flatbush Ave.), and yet it features in a fictional story told by Siri Hustvedt, comprising the story of a "Fictional Being." This way, Siri Hustvedt is also entangled into her writing, not just as its creator, but in being fashioned by what she writes. She argues as much in her essays, stating that "[t]he truth about unconscious processes is that the book can know more than the writer knows, a knowing that comes in part from the body, rising up from a preverbal, rhythmic, motor place in the self."[40] Her novel, *The Blazing World,* is part of her own coming to terms with her body, and its ability to speak, from its own perspective, and contribute to the phenomenon that is Siri Hustvedt. Harriet Burden is just another mask that Siri is wearing—a mask that changes the nature of her presentation as each masked persona is onto-epistemelogically entangled. A person is shaped by the mask they wear, and the mask is changed by its bearer. There is no access to a pure perspective.

The novel wraps around to the presence of Siri Pharmacy in Flatbush, from which Siri Hustvedt can prescribe medicine to help us to understand our circumstances, to shed light on our path from the brightest star in the sky, Sirius, who finally sheds her mask of Harriet Burden and presents herself to our blazing world.

NOTES

1. Siri Hustvedt, *The Shaking Woman or A History of My Nerves* (New York: Henry Holt, 2010), 73.
2. Siri Hustvedt in conversation with Andreas Roepstorff, Aula of Aarhus University, August 28, 2017 (Authors in Aarhus Series).
3. Alfred Hornung argues that Hustvedt's 2008 novel *Sorrow of an American* functions as a companion piece to *The Shaking Woman*. "*The Shaking Woman* in the Media: Life Writing and Neuroscience," in *Zones of Focused Ambiguity in Siri Hustvedt's Works: Interdisciplinary Essays,* ed. Johanna Hartmann, Christine Marks, and Hubert Zapf (Berlin: De Gruyter, 2016): 67–82.
4. Although fictional, it serves as a diegetic parallel to the larger body of her work. Thus, the discussions of how this operates within the novel are meant to provide insight into Hustvedt's own understanding of her own entangled intellectual endeavor.
5. Karen Barad, *Meeting the Universe Halfway: Quantum Physics and the Entanglement of Matter and Meaning* (Durham: Duke University Press, 2007), 71–94.
6. Birgit Mara Kaiser and Kathrin Thiele. "Diffraction: Onto-Epistemology, Quantum Physics and the Critical Humanities." *Parallax* 20, no. 3 (2014):166, https://doi.org/10.1080/13534645.2014.927621.
7. Vivienne Bozalek and Michalinos Zembylas, "Diffraction or Reflection? Sketching the Contours of Two Methodologies in Educational Research," *International Journal of Qualitative Studies in Education* 30, no. 2 (2017): 115.
8. Barad, *Meeting*, 185.
9. Birgit Mara Kaiser, "Worlding CompLit: Diffractive Reading with Barad, Glissant and Nancy," *Parallax* 20, no. 3 (2014): 276, https://doi.org/10.1080/13534645.2014.927634.
10. Karen Barad, "Quantum Entanglements and Hauntological Relations of Inheritance: Dis/continuities, Spacetime Enfoldings, and Justice-to-Come." *Derrida Today* 3, no. 2 (2010): 256.
11. Bozalek and Zembylas, "Diffraction or Reflection?," 116.
12. Barad, "Quantum Entanglements," 268n9.
13. Siri Hustvedt, *The Blazing World: A Novel* (New York: Simon and Schuster, 2014): 1–2.
14. Jason Tougaw, "The Self is a Moving Target: The Neuroscience of Siri Hustvedt's Artists," in Hartmann, Marks and Zapf, *Zones of Focused Ambiguity*, 118.
15. Tish's name is spelled differently in Notebook C (Tisch, as in the quote provided) than it is in other portions of Burden's notebooks. Compare pages 37

(Notebook C) and 58 (Notebook A). This remains unexplained in the novel (Hustvedt, *Blazing World*, 37, 58).
  16. Hustvedt, *Blazing World*, 37.
  17. Susanne Rohr, "'The Image Makers': Reality Constitution in the Role of Autism in Siri Hustvedt's *The Blazing World*," in Hartmann, Marks and Zapf, *Zones of Focused Ambiguity*, 251.
  18. Rohr, "Image Makers," 251.
  19. This and the following quotations are all from Hustvedt, *Blazing World*, 148, 128, 127, 164, and 219.
  20. Kaiser and Thiele, "Diffraction," 166.
  21. Both citations Hustvedt, *Blazing World*, 7.
  22. All quotations from Hustvedt, *Blazing World*, 58, 99, 107, 108, and 109.
  23. Due to the narrative strategy that Hustvedt presents, with a series of interwoven narratives, a more complicated analytic structure by which ontological levels within a work can be discerned, as developed by Marie-Laure Ryan in *Possible Worlds, Artificial Intelligence, and Narrative Theory* (Bloomington: Indiana University Press, 1991), and in Brian McHale's *Postmodernist Fiction* (London: Routledge, 1987), and which I use in my own work, *Defining Literary Postmodernism for the Twenty-First Century* (Cham: Palgrave, 2019), can be fruitful. However, with the intervention by Barad, and the concept of agential cuts, our ability to separately consider epistemological and ontological entries, as they are always already entwined, is challenged.
  24. Both from Hustvedt, *Blazing World*, 114.
  25. Rohr, "Image Makers," 251.
  26. Hustvedt, *Blazing World*, 129 and 126.
  27. Tougaw, "The Self is a Moving Target," 123.
  28. Hustvedt, *Blazing World*, 219.
  29. Hustvedt, *Blazing World*, 168 and 219.
  30. Tougaw, "The Self is a Moving Target," 128.
  31. Hustvedt, *Blazing World*, 336.
  32. Siri Hustvedt, "Philosophy Matters in Brain Matters," in *A Woman Looking at Men Looking At Women* (London: Sceptre, 2016), 475.
  33. Hustvedt, *Shaking Woman*, 47.
  34. Barad, "Quantum Entanglements," 253.
  35. Hustvedt, *Shaking Woman*, 47.
  36. Siri Hustvedt, "The Real Story," in *Living, Thinking, Looking* (London: Sceptre, 2012), 105.
  37. Siri Hustvedt, *A Woman Looking at Men Looking at Women* (London: Sceptre, 2016), xii.
  38. Siri Hustvedt, *Shaking Woman*, 92.
  39. Diana Tappen-Scheuermann, "Reality Bites: Fractured Narrative and Author-Reader Interaction," in Hartmann, Marks and Zapf, *Zones of Focused Ambiguity*, 48.
  40. Siri Hustvedt, "Playing, Wild Thoughts, and A Novel's Underground," in *Living, Thinking, Looking* (London: Sceptre, 2012), 39.

Chapter 11

Surfacing

A Diffractive Reading Experiment with Books and Houses in Walter Benjamin's Ich packe meine Bibliothek aus *and Carlos María Domínguez'* Casa de papel

Annina Klappert

I. SURFACING EXPERIMENT

Speaking of diffraction involves considering the notion of surface. Diffractions are often patterns that show themselves *on* surfaces like diffracted shadows or *as* surfaces like diffracted waves. Thus, diffraction is a surface matter, as well as is reading and philosophy in Michel Foucault and Gilles Deleuze. Considering philosophy as an "art of surfaces," Deleuze describes the similarity of his and Foucault's thinking as:

> No taste for abstractions, Unity, Totality, Reason, Subject. . . . We set out to follow and disentangle lines rather than work back to points: a cartography, involving microanalysis. . . . We looked for foci of unification, nodes of totalization, and processes of subjectification in arrangements, and they were always relative, they could always be dismantled in order to follow some restless line still further. We weren't looking for origins, even lost or deleted ones, but setting out to catch things where they were at work.[1]

Thus, the "art of surfaces" consists in cartographic operations. It is not interested in points of origin, but in extrapolating lines that can be followed. Possible foci, nodes, and moments of subjectification remain always preliminary. This is a firmly processual thinking that focuses on things "at work." Deleuze and Guattari are, according to Deleuze, looking "for new things being formed, the emergence of what Foucault calls 'actuality'."[2] The process of forming shows itself only in the actual emergence of forms, and the "art of surfaces" concentrates on this emergence.[3] Following the section above, Deleuze refers to Michel Foucault's approach to reading, which is an important notion for my own conception of diffractive reading as surfacing:

> It's in Foucault himself that surfaces become essentially surfaces on which things are inscribed: this is what utterances being "neither visible nor hidden" is all about. Archaeology amounts to constituting a surface on which things are inscribed. If you don't constitute a surface on which things are inscribed, what's not hidden will remain invisible. Surface isn't opposed to depth (from which one resurfaces) but to interpretation. Foucault's method was always opposed to any interpretative method. Never interpret; experience, experiment.[4]

Thus, reading consists in constituting a "surface on which things are inscribed." This surface is not established by going into an assumed depth and coming up back with a treasure of meaning hidden down there; it's not established by "resurfacing." Foucault's approach to reading is rather pointing to the unhidden *on* the surface, which is nevertheless not yet seen. This unhidden is the "utterance"—which is an entirely new notion in Foucault[5] and that can show itself in its actuality only if a surface is constituted. This methodology is strictly opposed to any kind of interpretation based on the difference of surface and depth. In *Archaeology of Knowledge*, Foucault relates this approach rather to experimental methods, as is also mentioned by Deleuze in the above quote: "Never interpret; experience, experiment."[6] Thus, on the diffracted surface of Foucault's and Deleuze's concepts a reading method becomes visible according to which reading is an experimental way of constituting "surfaces on which things are inscribed," so that we can see what is not hidden.

In the following, I call this kind of reading "surfacing." By "surfacing," I do not mean any ascendance[7] from any kind of depth. Neither do I follow the notion of surface reading as proposed by Stephen Best and Sharon Marcus. Even though they also use the notion of surface in opposition to notions of interpretation that seek the deeper meaning of a text, they remain in a vertical logic, seeing the surface as the "objective," as "what is evident, perceptible, apprehensible in texts."[8] On the contrary, I do not understand the surface as something evident, but as a transient effect of a specific reading process. This processing quality of surface-making I indicate by using "surface" also as a verb—in a specific sense. Surfacing means generating surfaces, which make something perceptible in the first place. It is an operation of the reader/text-apparatus that generates a specific surface for the reading of this text.

Thus, I conceive of surfacing as a reading process of arranging material on the entangled surface of which lines of intra-action can become apparent. These lines can always be seen preliminarily, as they present forms that do not only emerge but do also disappear as soon as new lines are formed and followed on the surface. Thus, surfacing consists in constituting a virtuality, a specific condition of possibility of forming an actuality. It is an experimental process of establishing a surface for a diffractive line-drawing, which implies operations of both mixing and cutting. This is going to become clear in the following.

I start with surfacing Deleuze and Bruno Latour, drawing a first line along diffracted forms of agencement/arrangement/agency. I begin with a further quote from Deleuze: "We set ourselves the task of analysing mixed forms, arrangements, what Foucault called apparatuses."[9] This English translation of the original French notions of *agencement* and *dispositif* is significant in two respects. First, the translation of Deleuze's notion *agencements* into the English word *arrangements* emphasizes the mixed nature of the surface, but rather drops the lexical connection of *agencement* and *agency*. However, this connection is more than a lexical one because it links Deleuze's thought with Latour's philosophy. In Deleuze, *agencement* is a multiplicity of concrete material singularities as the condition of possibility of generating actual forms. It constitutes the surface, "on which things are inscribed." Thus, *agencement* is the material condition of reading inscribed forms on surfaces and stands in correlation with Deleuze's notion of virtuality, which conceives of the virtual not as opposed to the real, but to the actual. My concept of surfacing is based on this notion of virtuality.[10] The condition of possibility of forming an "actuality" corresponds also to a capacity to cause, which is the starting point of Bruno Latour's concept of agency.[11] Thus, agency (and *agencement*) can be considered as a surfacing concept, or, surfacing is always already based on agency, on the capacity to perform.[12]

I constitute the next line by surfacing Foucault and Karen Barad along diffracted forms of dispositif/apparatus. The other translation, of Foucault's notion of *dispositif* into *apparatus*, brings to light an interesting connection between him and Barad: in Barad, the notion of *apparatus* is central to describe the setting of an experiment. In classical physics, for example, a diffraction experiment needs a specific "diffraction apparatus" as an "analytical instrument."[13] This is to be tuned "in a way that is sufficiently attentive to the details of the phenomenon we want to understand. So at times, diffraction phenomena will be an object of investigation and at other times it will serve as an apparatus of investigation."[14] Thus, "a diffractive mode of analysis" is a diffraction apparatus, which one has to "tune" to make something visible. This way, the apparatus constitutes a surface, which is the condition of possibility of generating visibility (of all kind of forms: of knowledge, of an inscription, of a phenomenon). Although Foucault's notion of *dispositif* doesn't refer to any physical experiment, it corresponds to the diffraction apparatus in being both an object of investigation and an analytical instrument. In his widely quoted explanation of the term, Foucault describes the *dispositif* as:

> A thoroughly heterogenous ensemble consisting of discourses, institutions, architectural forms, regulatory decisions, laws, administrative measures, scientific statements, philosophical, moral and philanthropic propositions—in short, the said as much as the unsaid. Such are the elements of the apparatus. The apparatus itself is the system of relations that can be established between these elements.[15]

Especially the last sentence shows that the *dispositif* ("apparatus") is at the same time the investigated system of relations between the heterogenous elements (the investigated object), the nature of which Foucault tries to identify, *and* the analytical instrument, because only in regards to the analytical instrument can the connections of the system's elements be analyzed. Therefore, Foucault's dispositif/apparatus can be regarded as much as a "boundary-drawing practice" as Barad's apparatus,[16] and diffraction as a methodology is "attentive to the material-discursive nature" of it.[17]

In a footnote, the translator of *Negotiations* describes Foucault's and Deleuze's thinking practice in an attempt to explain his translational decisions—which turns out to be an implicit description of a diffractive reading practice very close to Barad's concept of diffraction as a methodology:

> Deleuze and Foucault "begin in the middle" of words and things, in the empirical or experimental interplay of figures or configurations of discourse and other orders of interaction of discursive loci (human bodies, texts . . .) with one another and with nondiscursive loci. The implications of the uses of the words *agencement* and *dispositif* to characterize the primary frame of this empirical interplay . . . cannot be exactly transposed.[18]

The object of reading is conceptualized as an "interplay" and "interaction," which Barad herself calls more specifically "intra-action." With "intra-action," she importantly changes the preposition from "inter" to "intra" to highlight the existence of "entanglements," for which diffraction patterns function as a metaphor: "Like the diffraction patterns illuminating the indefinite nature of boundaries—displaying shadows in 'light' regions and bright spots in 'dark' regions" most realms are entangled in "a relation of 'exteriority within'."[19] Barad focuses not on exclusions, but on linkages, not on "mere homologies between different subject matters of different disciplines, but rather [on] the specific material linkages and how these intra-relations matter."[20] While Barad talks about reading texts "through one another,"[21] Deleuze's translator chooses the modal preposition "with" to describe the interplay of elements "with one another." The spatial prepositions "intra" and "through" are more appropriate to qualify diffractions and specify Barad's concept crucially, but the idea of beginning right "in the middle" of words and things, that engages both Foucault and Deleuze, links to this spatial understanding, too. Furthermore, just as Deleuze's formula of "words and things" implies a broader understanding of the readable,[22] Barad's conception of diffraction as methodology is "attentive to the material-discursive nature of boundary-drawing practices" and examines "important philosophical issues" as well as "the relationship between discursive practices and the material world."[23]

And yet, there has always to be a "frame of this experimental interplay," a specific "arrangement," "apparatus," or other configurational setting. This manifests itself by surfacing Barad, Foucault, and Deleuze and drawing a third line along diffracted forms of dispositif/agencement/apparatus/agential cut. "The apparatus enacts," Barad writes, "an agential cut . . . *within* the phenomenon, and *agential separability—the agentially enacted material condition of exteriority-within-phenomena.*"[24] The terms *agencement* and *dispositif* themselves can be regarded as such frames and cuts, constituting a surface: "The difference between Deleuze's *agencement* and Foucault's *dispositif* might itself be taken as articulating . . . various parallels and differences between the discursive *agencements* / *dispositifs* of the two writers' texts and worlds: each term suggests a reconfiguration of some of the elements in a particular situation, which 'prepares' various new lines of interaction of those elements."[25] Thus, on the one hand, both terms themselves are already arrangements as they suggest reconfigurations and interactions. On the other hand, both terms characterize cutting a "primary frame," and thus not only being surfacings but also characterizing surfacing as a practice. They both define (different) surfaces as they "prepare" new lines of intra-action. Each surface—and each notion as/of surface—is a different material condition of possibility of intra-action, line-making, linkage, making visible inscriptions; it's a specific virtuality, out of which actualities can be formed and made visible. In Barad, too, the *apparatus* can be either a material arrangement that also entails a concept, or a concept which matters due to the material effects it produces. The apparatus has a framing function by enacting an agential cut as "boundary-drawing practice," which she conceives of as relational and preliminary: the diffractive methodology "does not take the boundaries of any of the objects or subjects of these studies for granted but rather investigates the material-discursive boundary-making practices that produce 'objects' and 'subjects' and other differences out of, and in terms of, a changing relationality."[26]

Besides these three lines, a fourth line, the line of "experiment," can be spotted. It traverses the other three lines as it draws together Foucault (do not interpret, but experiment) with Barad (the apparatus as a matter of experiment) and *Niels Bohr* (physical experiments with matter). This fourth line I will follow now. Barad's notion of experiment is informed by a physical perspective, the experiments of Niels Bohr. Bohr discovered that an element reacts as particle *or* wave depending on the way it is measured; therefore, the intra-action of apparatus and object in the laboratory of the physicist becomes visible, because the very nature of the entity changes together with the experimental apparatus used to determine its nature.[27] Given the fact that the experimenter is an intrinsic factor of the experiment, Barad draws two conclusions for her own onto-epistemology: first, neither experiment nor experimenter can be regarded as superior or primary, so that "diffraction does not fix what is the object and what is the subject in advance" and we do not make knowledge from outside but as part of the world.[28] Second, the experiment itself—the respective apparatus—is the concept and reversely "concepts are specific material arrangements." Matter and meaning entail one another, not in the way that knowledge practices have material consequences, but in the way that practices of knowing are specific material engagements that participate in (re)configuring the world.[29]

This self-awareness as a part of the process is commonly described as "self-reflection," as addressing the text's own making as an inherent element of the text. But Barad rejects the idea of reflection as a form of representationalism that implies "reflecting on the world from outside."[30] Instead, she pleads for thinking as a practice of being confronted with the world in which we exist and as a part of this world: "[M]y aim is to disrupt the widespread reliance on an existing optical metaphor—namely, reflection—that is set up to look for homologies and analogies between separate entities. By contrast, diffraction, as I argue, does not concern homologies but attends to specific material entanglements." Following Barad's critique, I too propose to change the concept of "self-reflection" toward a practice of "self-diffraction," which would, then, mean to be aware of one's own material entanglement with the world.

Drawing these lines from Deleuze to Latour and from Foucault to Barad and then again from Deleuze and Foucault to Barad and from Barad to Bohr and Foucault, is what I call surfacing, which means: gathering references, linkages, and intra-acting concepts as a demarcated surface and analyzing the forms that actualize themselves in that surface—to "disentangle lines" (with Deleuze), that show significant "entanglements" (with Barad).

II. BOOKS AND HOUSES: BUILDING SURFACES

To make visible in a self-diffracting manner how surfacing could work in literary texts, I will now describe, how I constitute the surface for my own reading experiment. I chose two texts, which I will "mix" to look for "new things being formed": Walter Benjamin's talk *Ich packe meine Bibliothek aus*[31] and Carlos María Domínguez's novel *Casa de papel*.[32] This surface presents an *agencement*, an arrangement of texts that constitutes a virtuality, out of which forms can emerge as actualities. Concurrently, this choice is an "agential cut," which Barad also calls a "cutting Together-Apart" to express the dis/continuities this cutting arranges at the same time.[33] The specific way of building this surface is my experimental "apparatus," the "primary frame" for my experiment, and therefore a "difference which makes a difference." It *is* a difference, because I will experiment with these texts and not with any other, and it *makes* a difference in regards to the outcome of the insights. As it is me, who chose these texts as the primary frame, I am a part of this experimental setting, and as it is me, who tries to "make visible, what is not hidden," I am responsible for the forms that will actualize on the surface, even if these forms are not "pre-existing"[34]—they are unhidden in their virtuality, but they only begin to be visible in the process of actualizing.[35] As my reading will always be "entangled" with these two texts (beside others I read before as well as beside my experiences and the material conditions in which the idea, the conception and the writing of this actual text in the context of the actual volume have emerged), it becomes undecidable, who is the subject and who is the object of this reading experiment.

I chose these two texts, because I consider their linkage as particularly productive regarding the forms potentially appearing, especially as they both themselves think about building and surfacing. They consider "building" in both grammatical options of the word—building both as operation ("to build") and as effect ("the building")—as they deal with building real houses and real libraries and building houses out of libraries or memories. They think about surfacing inasmuch as they both talk about collections of books, which constitute—in form of a changing and in *this* material sense resurfacing or resurfaced library—the respective surfaces on which the memories and imaginations of the collectors are inscribed. Benjamin's talk *Ich packe meine Bibliothek aus* was published in the volume *Denkbilder*, literally "thought-images." The process of unpacking the library is conceived of as one of these "thought-images," and it is in the same way that I understand the library-house in Domínguez' novel. I will not assume homologies between these texts, but I am going to make visible diffracted forms on the surface that show the entanglement and intra-action of both texts in the following six "lines."

(1) On the Surface: Books/Materiality

While Benjamin's collector-narrator is unpacking the books of his library, he describes their significant materiality right in the first sentences of the talk:

> Ich packe meine Bibliothek aus. Ja. Sie steht also noch nicht auf den Regalen .... Ich muß Sie bitten, mit mir in die Unordnung aufgebrochener Kisten, in die von Holzstaub erfüllte Luft, auf den von zerrissenen Papieren bedeckten Boden, unter die Stapel eben nach zweijähriger Dunkelheit wieder ans Tageslicht beförderter Bände sich zu versetzen.[36]

The books are not yet put on the shelves. Instead, they are located in crates and in piles on the floor. The floor is moreover covered with paper; we do not learn if it's torn pages or packaging material. The dust of wood saturates the air. Altogether, the room in which the library is unpacked is itself a material interplay of books, shelves, wood, air, paper, and cardboard, in the middle of which ("in" the air, "in" the disorder of crates that have been wrenched open, "under" the piles) the speaker moves himself by imagination. The English translation doesn't fully reflect the spatial semantics of Benjamin's original descriptions, which strengthen the material impression of the scene. In the dust that accompanies the unpacking of books materially, Benjamin's texts diffracts with Domínguez's novel. In the latter, the dust comes out of a parcel from Uruguay that contains "a broken-spined old copy of *The Shadow-Line*" by Joseph Conrad with "a filthy crust on its front and back covers. There was a film of cement particles on the page edges that left a fine dust on the surface of the polished desk."[37] The surface of the polished desk is diffracted with the surface in Deleuze's sense of *agencement* insofar as a fine dust comes to a rest on it and poses a reading problem. A reading problem is also posed by the book itself, which is nothing else but a body of matter, "illegible beyond any message she was meant to read in the cement." The dust of wood in Benjamin's text and the fine dust of cement in Domínguez's novel intra-act with the respective books materially. Yet, the dust of wood atomizes into the air, while the dust of cement comes to a rest on the surface of the polished desk. The dust of wood surrounds the many books in an airy movement in the process of unpacking them into daylight, while the cement forms a crusty layer on a single book, which is also unpacked but whose cemented pages will never be in loose contact with air and readable in daylight again. The unpacking of the library out of crates enacts a dissolution of dust from the books "away" into the air, while the unpacking of the book out of the parcel reveals the "binding" of the book with cement, which will now be the material that has to be deciphered.

Casa de papel deals with the materiality of books from the beginning. Books "are dangerous" less because of their content (the typical "books matter"), but rather because of their specific way of being materially entangled with human beings (the book's matter): "An elderly professor . . . was left paralyzed after being struck on the head by five volumes of the *Encyclopaedia Britannica* that fell from a shelf in his library; my friend Richard broke a leg when he tried to reach William Faulkner's *Absalom, Absalom!*, which was so awkwardly placed he fell off his stepladder,"[38] and finally his colleague and friend Bluma, while reading a book on the street, is run over by a car and killed, so that in her case the material practice that books imply (gazing at pages in concentration) claim her life. The death of Bluma actuates the narration, because the first-person narrator as her closest colleague and friend is entrusted with her academic estate, and, in that capacity, opens the parcel that contains the cemented book for her. Even if it is not usable as a book any more, the narrator decides to give it back—as a body that matters whatever—and he identifies as the owner a Carlos Brauer, a bibliophile from Montevideo, who has recently moved to Rocha, a department of Uruguay on the Atlantic Ocean.

This threatening aspect of books' materiality becomes even more obvious in Carlos's house. As Delgado, a former friend of Carlos, tells the narrator, he has an

> allconsuming [*sic*] . . . passion for books, which he kept in vast bookcases that filled the rooms end to end and from floor to ceiling. Not only that, they were piled up in the kitchen, the bathroom, and in his bedroom as well. Not his original bedroom, because he had been forced out of there, but in the attic where he had taken refuge . . . . The stairs leading up to the attic were also full of books, and it was nineteenth-century French literature which watched over his scant hours of sleep.[39]

Carlos's house is filled with books all over. Their massive presence in one room urges him to take refuge in another, and when his ex-wife demands money from him through a lawyer and he has to sell his house,[40] he "felt trapped by his books. How could he move all those shelves?" "His books were already piling up around his bed and along all the corridors: they seemed to be snaking through the house with a life of their own." As soon as books pose problems of storage and moving, their material quality comes to the fore in all its spatio-temporal aspects. In Benjamin, the narrator is unpacking books *from* crates, where they have been stored for two years, and they are *not yet* placed on the shelves. Carlos has to pack his library *into* boxes to move, so the books are, then, *not* standing on their shelves *any more*, but have to leave and to be unpacked on a sandy beach. Thus, in the crates and boxes diffract two forms of transit space, in which the book's situation changes. After unpacking, the books in Benjamin stand in piles on the firm surface of the floor, while Carlos's books are poured on the sand, which is a dissolved surface in itself.[41] The forms of ground, the floor and the sand, specify the way of the book's material "standing." While in Benjamin the books stand stable and the former wooden materiality of their pages seems to expand into the air, the books in Domínguez are located on an instable ground, and their pages will be soon shielded from any air by cement.

(2) On the Surface: Books/Materiality/Imagination

The unpacking of books in Benjamin's talk is a material technique of surfacing as they build—together with the atomized materiality of the wood in the air and the daylight—a surface for the narrator's imagination. They are significant for him not because of their usability, but because of the history of the specific volume, as the collector has a "Verhältnis zu den Dingen, das in ihnen nicht den Funktionswert, also ihren Nutzen, ihre Brauchbarkeit in den Vordergrund rückt, sondern sie als den Schauplatz, das Theater ihres Schicksals studiert und liebt."[42] Things, and books as such, provide a "scene," a "stage" for the imagination. Each particular object constitutes a surface for the collector's imagination as it gathers period, region and craftmanship: "Zeitalter, Landschaft, Handwerk, Besitzer, von denen es stammt—sie alle rücken für den wahren Sammler in jedem einzelnen seiner Besitztümer zu einer magischen Enzyklopädie zusammen."[43] Because of its specific "magic," the collector seems to look through the things in his hands and, inspired by them, far into the distance spatially and historically.[44] In the materiality of books, different times diffract and so do the imaginative practices of the two collectors, as they both use the library as a surface for their imagination. Carlos spends even most of his time with his books, reads them, and arranges them according to his mental concepts and images. Once, Delgado continues, through the open bedroom door, a friend saw "twenty or so books carefully laid out [on Carlos's bed] in such a way that they reproduced the mass an outline of a human body. . . . A woman? A man? His double? . . . No one could be sure, or decide what it meant." As Delgado describes this installation as a "display," the books in Domínguez' and Benjamin's texts diffract in the form of theater. The purpose of Carlos's specific theatrical arrangement remains unclear though: "What was an intelligent man like Brauer doing with his books now? . . . Had he arranged them after thinking long and hard about their meaning?"[45] Carlos can read in the "surface" he has built for himself, but for others it remains as unreadable as the cement, in which he will cover the books later. Yet, the books' theatrical diffraction is different in each case. In Benjamin, the collector's imagination diffracts books in time by looking "through" their actual materiality and regarding them as a stage for his own fate; in Domínguez, the collector's imagination arranges books to actual material forms in the present. Therefore, the books in these two texts diffract in different ways of imaginative stage making: a stage which is dusty, but airy and "permeable" diffracts with a "cemented" and materially dense stage.

The respective surfaces allow to see something that is unhidden, even if this unhidden is only perceptible for a single reader. If the collector in Benjamin's text gazes far into the distance, it's not only a spatial but also a temporal distance insofar as memories come to his mind like a veritable spring tide, a "Springflut von Erinnerungen, die gegen jeden Sammler anrollt, der sich mit dem Seinen befaßt. Jede Leidenschaft grenzt ja ans Chaos, die sammlerische aber an das der Erinnerungen."[46] The past appears in the middle of the chaos the moment the gaze becomes focused, "vor meinem Blick"; the past is there, before his eyes, tinged with contingency and fate, both of which are present in the familiar chaos of books. And their presence is obvious, because the habit of disorder makes its home in the library so much that it appears as order.[47] As different times diffract in the books, the memories become threatening in their chaotic and overwhelming quality, which the apparent order of the library only covers. Even if habit pretends so, memories do not allow themselves to be sorted. Thus, the chaos of memories is ambivalent: on the one hand, the order of books on the shelves exudes a silent boredom,[48] of which the books are redeemed by the collector's unpacking and reassembling that provide a surface that allows the unhidden memories to be seen; on the other hand, the chaos of memories is as threatening as a spring tide, and order is, even if it's only a habit that hides the unhidden, at least reassuring. While in Benjamin the memories gain a material quality like a spring tide on the collector's stage of imagination, in Domínguez it is rather the quantity of bookish material that becomes an act of menace in the scene of the library.

(3) On the Surface: Books/Materiality/ Imagination/Ir/Regularities of Access

Thus, the regularity of access is reassuring in either way, particularly if a library reaches clarity by its arrangement. To deal with his library, a collector needs to find the books he is looking for, and this is guaranteed by a catalogue, which, according to Benjamin's narrator, is the counterpart to the irregularity of the actual books on the shelf: "In der Tat, gibt es ein Gegenstück zur Regellosigkeit einer Bibliothek, so ist es die Regelrechtheit ihres Verzeichnisses."[49] The irregular or chaotic placement of books may be overcome by the order of the catalogue. This is even more important for Carlos, who has a highly idiosyncratic way of organizing his library by an "imaginative system" that takes into account "real affinities" as the most demanding question.[50] This means for example that he has to "avoid putting two authors who had quarrelled on the same shelf" and at the same time to respect relationships between others by placing them together: "*Pedro Paramo* and *Rayuela* are both written by Latin American authors, but one of them leads us back to William Faulkner, the other to Moebius. Or to put it another way: Dostoyevsky ended up closer to Roberto Arlt than he did to Tolstoy." To solve the problem of finding his books Carlos keeps a card index. As he has difficulty to update it, disaster strikes when a fire incinerates his index-file cabinet so that he loses "all possibility of finding most of his books."[51] In addition to that, the connection between the regularity of an index and the chaos of memories is crucial. Carlos tries to arrange his memories in the order of the library, but gives up all hopes in classifying anything after the fire, as his friend Delgado believes to understand:

> Just imagine for a moment that over your lifetime you've stored up memories . . . , the impressions of things that may be unfathomable and chaotic but which when put together constitute the memory of your childhood . . . . After that, you . . . go on accumulating memories of all your experiences right up to the present. Then one day, unexpectedly, you lose the sequence of these memories. They're still there, but you can't find them. You search for the image of your first wife, and you find the shoe a dog was chewing in a distant childhood wasteland. You look for your mother's face, and come up with that of an unpleasant character in some gloomy municipal office. Your personal history is lost.[52]

Thus, in the materiality of the library different concepts of memory diffract as the collector in Benjamin's text despairs of any sequential order in memories. In fact, Carlos does not lose, as Delgado supposes, the sequence of his memories, because there has never been any, but he loses any access to them by means of finding the particular book that would make him remember. And therefore, it is less the personal history that is lost, but indeed the access to the diligent arrangement, the specific surface, that Carlos gave his library to make visible what is actually unhidden: by putting the books in a certain neighbourhood the material location became meaningful. Consequently, Carlos sells his house, gives his ex-wife the money he owes her, packs his library into boxes and travels to "the shore, between the lagoon at Rocha and the ocean . . . , a lost place in the back of beyond."[53] There he unpacks his library like the collector in Benjamin's text. In contrast to this collector, however, he does not use that situation as an opportunity to look through the books into the past, but he converts the books into building stones for a house.

(4) On the Surface: Books/Materiality/ Imagination/Ir/Regularities of Access/Houses

Carlos's way of dealing with the materiality of books consequentially makes him turn them into bricks: "There was a mountain of books the cart had tipped onto the clean white sand," and all the laborer "was worried about was their size, their thickness, how resistant their covers might be to lime, cement and sand. The laborer squared off one of the volumes of an encyclopaedia in the corner angle, then used a string to line the others up to make a straight wall."[54] Delgado imagines how Brauer "handles" this transformation of his books into building stones: he

> must have walked around handing the laborer a Borges to fit in under the windowsill, a Vallejo for the door, with Kafka above it and Kant beside it, plus a hardback edition of Hemingway's A Farewell to Arms; Cortázar and Vargas Llosa, who always writes thick books; . . . Shakespeare fatally bound to Marlowe by the mortar of cement; and all of them destined to raise a wall, to cast a shadow.[55]

He keeps his books as "friends" and builds a "shelter" out of them against sun, rain and wind, but he loses them as an affinity-oriented arrangeable surface: "In a week the laborer raised page by page, volume by volume, edition by edition, the walls of this hut on the sands of Rocha. Carlos Brauer's life's work disappeared under the cement. One work destroyed inside another. Not just sealed up. Demolished in cement."[56] Again, in the materiality of books, different concepts of memory diffract, as Carlos builds his house from the bookish materiality in which his past life disappears. In a similar vein, the collector-speaker in Benjamin's text raises his house out of the memories they assemble: "Alles Erinnerte, Gedachte, Bewußte wird Sockel, Rahmen, Postament, Verschluß seines Besitztums."[57] He imagines a building out of "memories," "thoughts," and "everything conscious," which constitute the "pedestal, frame, base and lock of his property." The books are transformed into building bricks, too, but in a metaphorical way: ghosts have settled inside the collector, and their effect is that he dwells in things, so that one of his dwellings—of his "Gehäuse"[58]—is the actual text, the "building stones" of which are books.[59] Eventually, the first-person narrator (not Carlos!) in Domínguez, too, uses books metaphorically as building bricks for the remembrance of his past: "But how could I throw away *The Call of the Wild* for example, without destroying one of the building bricks of my childhood." Books "stick to us in that pact of need and oblivion we make with them, witnesses to a moment in our lives we will never see again. While they are still there, it is part of us."[60]

(5) On the Surface: Books/Materiality/ Imagination/Ir/Regularities of Access/Houses/History

This presence of and pact with the particular volume refers to the history of the particular copy, to the "journey books themselves make."[61] In Benjamin's talk, the (materially) bound copy with its specific history is focused: Not books in general have their fates as the Latin dictum "Habent sua fata libelli" says, but "copies of books."[62] Particularly, the collector's practice of acquisition renews the book's existence. They become material assets, not in need to be completely (re)read, but rather used as a remembrance of the discovery place[63] and of the act of purchasing. The collector emphasizes *things* as such. Looking for affinities *between* books in the same way as Carlos, Benjamin's collector states that the book has to "belong" to the collector in the first place before he will purchase it. The books gain their genuine freedom only on his shelves, they travel with him and remind him of their former locations, "an die Stuben, wo diese Bücher gestanden haben."[64] Considering this diffraction of the collector's and the book's fates in the materiality of their shelves,[65] it is no surprise that reversely the fate of one single book seals the fate of Carlos at the end of the novel. A fisherman tells the first-person narrator: "The house wasn't bad at all, until he became obsessed with that one book . . . he started to knock holes in it. As I say, for two days he was demolishing the walls."[66] When he finds the sought-after volume, he sends it off by post, tries to rebuild the hut, but fails and destroys it before he disappears: "One afternoon we saw him on the track, carrying a suitcase. He looked back at the demolished hut, waved to us, and walked off in the baking sun. He never came back." The question why Carlos took this one book out of the house of cemented volumes can only be answered by the reconstruction of the specific volume's history. Bluma, his deceased colleague, had met Carlos on a writer's congress, where she had lent him this book. Later, as the narrator learns from a copy of a letter Bluma sent to Carlos, she asked him to send it back, because it was indispensable for her to complete her thesis on Conrad.[67] At that time, the book has long since been cemented: "I imagined Carlos Brauer . . . trying to remember where exactly the book had ended up in the whitewashed wall, blindly running his hand over the rough surface in the hope that a tingling in his fingers might help him to find it, stuck to another book." The journey/fate of this very copy is crucial for the fate of Carlos—and for the fate of the remaining books of his library/house.

(6) On the Surface: Books/Materiality/ Imagination/Ir/Regularities of Access/Houses/History/Processuality

In the materiality of books, different forms of processuality diffract. In *Casa de papel*, the story of Carlos's library is one of living and dying. While the library was his life's work, the end of its organizability and the destruction of the book house make him disappear. The first-person narrator visits the hut after its destruction and further dismantling

> to a sceleton [sic], with the wooden frames still intact but all the rest a pile of rubble. ... And in among the clumps of cement, tiny seashells, and dark lichens, I could make out pages of books baked in the sun then soaked glued together like cuttlefish beaks, the type bleached and illegible; the cover of an encyclopaedia, the swollen white froth of a paperback with its wavy, twisted edges. Half-hidden in the sand around the doors and windows, I found copies of Huidobro, Neruda, and Bartolomé de las Casas; then a solid brick of Lawrence and Marosa di Giorgio, bits of Eliot and Lorca, Burckhardt's Renaissance encrusted with barnacles, an unrecognizable Pallière covered in tar.[68]

The books are in the process of being transformed into another form of materiality by the specific environment, in which they are entangled: sand, seashells, cement, lichens. Printed writing is bleached by the sun, paper is glued together and paperback cover is swollen and deformed by water. The first-person narrator pulls some volumes out of the ground to the surface, where each "volume appeared on the sand like a sinister cadaver. Paper and words, washed out ink, covers drilled by insects that had dug hundreds of small idiosyncratic tunnels between pages and chapter."[69] The materiality of each exemplar is transient, but their leftovers constitute a surface *on* the sand, that can still be read in its own material arrangement. Insects are "reading across" the books, leaving their "reading paths" and dissolve the book like a "cadaver" in the surrounding elements. The process is one of material transformation. It's a resurfacing, but not in the sense of retrieving the significance of a book from a deeper hiding place by bringing it up to the surface, but in the sense of constituting new surfaces by rearranging the former ones. The narrator in *Casa de papel* describes an additional kind of change in the surface's material quality, because the surfacing of the books has passed from the arranging agency of human hands to the arranging agency of sun, wind, lichen, insects, water, and sand.

In Benjamin, the processuality of the books' materiality is not one of dying or dissolving but instead one of *making* live. The books let remembrance happen, they open up a process. The surfacing of the books remains an agency of human hands, yet it takes place in the middle of crates, dust and shelves, and it "takes time" in the middle of temporality. It lasts from noon to midnight and thus in each case the beginning and the end are located "in the middle" of the two periods that structure day and night: "Mittags hatte ich begonnen, und es war Mitternacht, ehe ich an die letzten Kisten mich herangearbeitet hatte."[70] The operationality of the process comes into focus as the text stresses "collecting" over "collection," to grant "einen Einblick ins Sammeln viel mehr als in eine Sammlung."[71] The process of unpacking is at the same time a mining for remembrance and an imagining: "Was drängt nicht alles an Erinnerung herbei, hat man sich einmal in das Kistengebirge begeben, um die Bücher im Tag- oder besser im Nachtbau aus ihm herauszuholen. Nichts könnte die Faszination dieses Auspackens deutlicher machen, als wie schwer es ist, damit aufzuhören."[72] To remember is a temporally bound activity "in the middle of" time and a material bound labour "in the middle of" books, dust, shelves, and crates. This process of remembering persists even after unpacking inasmuch as the narrator proceeds in drifting in images, remembrances, memories of towns and rooms.[73] The oldest memories come from his boyhood room, "aus dem nur noch vier oder fünf der mehreren tausend Bände, die sich um mich zu türmen beginnen, stammen." The collector has access to all of his life's memories through the several thousand volumes of his library. Thus, the opening of crates and unpacking of books brings back the collector's life back in the form of remembrance. This leads to the appearance of ghosts on the surface.

III. GHOSTS ON THE SURFACE

Altogether, my reading experiment consisted in building a surface, following some of the lines that become visible on it as much as the shaping of forms by diffraction. Yet, this always has to remain preliminary, as a host of lines are intra-acting with these. I aimed at what Foucault means by "reading:" To look at the surface and describe the unhidden. The surfaces are in themselves diffracted already, as their elements overlap: Deleuze diffracts Foucault diffracts Barad diffracts Latour diffracts Deleuze diffracts Barad diffracts Bohr. Similarly, the topics of the two literary texts are already diffracted, as they both deal with unpacking books and building houses. My reading has tried to make these linkages visible, which, however, do not express identities, but actualizations of a virtual structure of overlapping topics and entangled lines. So, at first the books diffract the *surfacing practice* of the two collectors. Both characters constitute a surface by handling the books of their library, by layering and arranging them or by changing their order on the shelves or on the floor and by thereby resurfacing them. But then, Carlos continues in a different way. When he loses his index, he boxes his books, but he doesn't, as he could, resurface his library after the relocation and restart his surfacing practice again in the unpacking process like Benjamin's collector. Instead, he actualizes one of the virtually possible arrangements of books by fixing them with cement and thereby stops any further surfacing practice for the time being. Further, the books diffract the *building practice* of the two collectors, which is entangled with their surfacing practices. While Benjamin's collector builds a house out of memories "through the books," to live in these memories, Carlos builds a house "out of books" to literally live in them by using them as bricks against wind, storm, and sun and by destroying the possibility of bringing memories into life through them.

By diffracting the books in the two texts, several forms became visible one after another, which on the surface diffract with(in) each other: forms of materiality, imagination, accessibility, houses, history, and processuality. And at the preliminary end of my diffracting reading activity, some ghosts show up. As ghosts are real, when their past agency is still present, they are unhidden and the practice of surfacing may let them take form. In Benjamin, there are ghosts inside the collector, at least little ghosts, who have settled inside him: "Im Innern [des Sammlers] haben ja Geister, mindestens Geisterchen sich angesiedelt . . . : nicht daß sie in ihm lebendig wären, er selber ist es, der in ihnen wohnt."[74] In these settlements, the collector resides, and in one of them, in the talk about unpacking his library itself, he finally disappears: "So habe ich eines seiner Gehäuse, dessen Bausteine Bücher sind, vor Ihnen aufgeführt und nun verschwindet er drinnen, wie recht und billig."[75] The collector disappears after the speaker has built the ghostly housing metaphorically throughout the speech, so that the written speech can constitute the housing, in which the collector-speaker disappears.

In Domínguez's novel, Carlos himself turns into a kind of ghost by disappearing after the destruction of his book-house. Yet, he became ghostly already by the burning of his card index as he seemed to live only in connection with his imaginations formed with his books. As a ghost, he reappears also inasmuch as the narrator seeks for him as an object of desire throughout the text. Affected by Carlos's story he desires to know its ending, but he can only wonder "where [Carlos] could be, if he was happy without any books, if he had gone into business or if by little, without meaning to, he had set out to build another library."[76] This desire is followed by haunting: when the narrator returns from his journey to the Uruguayan coast he is "[h]aunted by the ghost of Brauer, I made a thorough clear-out and put all the books I judged inessential or not directly useful in big cardboard boxes . . . , glad to have reclaimed places where I could hang a painting or a mirror, a smooth white surface that made no call on my attention." This kind of surface is smooth and white: it's no surface that allows surfacing any more, but a surface for forgetting or at least a surface not calling for attention. However, the most intriguing ghost in *Casa de papel* is the one of Bluma. When the narration begins, she is already dead, but she is still the addressee of the fateful book and she is still the writer of the letter that causes the destruction of Carlos's book-house. Bluma will never be able to look at the volume any more, but her intention is still present. This is all the more ghostly, as she didn't make any notes in that particular volume and could have acquired a new one to finish her thesis, as the first-person narrator states. Thus, after all, it was a pretext that led Carlos to look desperately for the book he thought he had forgotten in the cemented surface of his house. Bluma's desire and Carlos's disappearance are connected even after Bluma's death—a real intra-action of spectres.

Esther Pereen clarifies the notion of the spectre in Jacques Derrida, "that does something to doing by making agency ambiguous and dynamic, causing it to wander in time, in space, and between what or who haunts, and what or whom is haunted."[77] Ghosts are, as Barad formulates, traces of the past in the present,[78] and so in the surfacing of books these ghosts from the past can diffract, as their traces are unhidden, and they can be made visible. The different lines I followed in my surfacing pointed to the relation of books to remembrance and oblivion. This topic diffracts also with Jorge Luis Borges' story "El libro de arena."[79] In Borges' story, the book *of* sand is meant to be forgotten on a moist shelf because of its infinite, dissolving, and therefore dangerous quality, which is taken to be the quality of sand. In Domínguez's novel, Carlos' books are "turning into a nightmare"[80] and have, reversely, to be forgotten by the process of their dissolution *in* the sand. However, the books in Benjamin's talk give lively access to the collector's memories in their liberation into a dusty, but nevertheless airy surrounding.

NOTES

1. Gilles Deleuze, *Negotiations 1972—1990*, trans. Martin Joughin (New York: Columbia University Press, 1995), 86f.
2. Ibid., 86.
3. See more detailed Gilles Deleuze, *Logique du Sense* (Paris: Édicion de Minuit, 2005).
4. Deleuze, *Negotiations*, 87.
5. Ibid., 130.
6. Michel Foucault, *Archaeology of Knowledge*, trans. A. M. Sheridan Smith (London: Routledge, 2004).
7. Nor do I refer to Margaret Atwood's novel *Surfacing* (Toronto: McClelland and Stewart 1972), which also operates with the difference of surface and depth.
8. Stephen Best and Sharon Marcus, "Surface Reading: An Introduction," *Representations* 108, no. 1 (2009): 9. See for further explanation of this approach the contribution of Birgit Mara Kaiser in this volume.
9. Deleuze, *Negotiations*, 86.
10. See Gilles Deleuze, *Différence et Répétition* (Paris: Presses Universitaires de France, 1968). See also for my engagement of Deleuze's concept of virtuality; Annina Klappert, *Sand als metaphorisches Modell für Virtualität* (Berlin: de Gruyter 2020), see especially chapter 2.1.

11. See, e. g., Bruno Latour, *Reassembling the Social: An Introduction to Actor-Network-Theory* (Oxford: Oxford University Press, 2005).

12. See Karen Barad, "Posthumanist Performativity: Toward an Understanding of How Matter Comes to Meeting Matter." *Signs: Journal of Women in Culture and Society* 28, no. 3 (2003): 801–831.

13. Karen Barad, *Meeting the Universe Halfway: Quantum Physics and the Entanglement of Matter and Meaning* (Durham: Duke University Press, 2007), 72f.

14. Barad, *Meeting*, 73.

15. Michel Foucault, "The Confession of the Flesh," a Conversation with Alain Grosrichard, et al., in *Power/Knowledge: Selected Interviews and Other Writings 1972-1977*, ed. and trans. Colin Gordon, et al. (New York: Pantheon Books 1980), 194.

16. Barad is aware of this link to Foucault and also mentions the translation of "dispositive" as "apparatus": "However, Foucault is not clear about the material nature of discursive practices. . . . The closest that Foucault comes to explicating this crucial relationship between discursive and nondiscursive practices is through his notion of *dispositif*, usually translated as *apparatus*." Barad, *Meeting*, 63.

17. Ibid., 93.

18. Deleuze, *Negotiations*, 196n9.

19. Barad, *Meeting*, 93.

20. Ibid., 94.

21. "A diffractive methodology provides a way of attending to entanglements in reading important insights and approaches through one another." Barad, *Meeting*, 30.

22. Deleuze and Stéphane Czerkinsky perform a diffraction of words and things in their dialogical preface to *Mélanges: Pouvoir et surface*. The painter and the philosopher mix ("mélange") their cultural techniques and reveil them as materially entangled. Czerkinsky does the "writing" and Deleuze does "the drawings," letting their positions "slip-sliding" in doing "some surfaces." Gilles Deleuze, "Faces and surfaces," in *Desert Islands and other Texts 1953–1974*, ed. David Lapoujade, trans. Mike Taormina (Los Angeles: Semiotext, 2004), 281.

23. Both quotations are from Barad, *Meeting*, 93 and 94.

24. Barad, *Meeting*, 175.

25. Deleuze, *Negotiations*, 196n9.

26. Barad, *Meeting*, 93.

27. See Barad, *Meeting*.

28. Ibid., 30 and 91.

29. Ibid., 196 and 91.

30. This and the following quote both from ibid., 88.

31. Walter Benjamin, "Ich packe meine Bibliothek aus," in *Denkbilder* (Frankfurt am Main: Suhrkamp, 1974), 88–96. In the following cited with the abbreviation B. English translations are cited with the abbreviation B/E from: Walter Benjamin, "Unpacking My Library: A Talk about Book Collecting," in *Illuminations: Essays and Reflections*, ed. Hannah Arendt, trans. Harry Zohn (New York: Schocken Books, 1968), 59–67.

32. Carlos María Domínguez, *Casa de Papel* (Montevideo : Ediciones de la Banda Oriental, 2002). In the following cited with the abbreviation D.

33. Karen Barad, "Diffracting Diffraction: Cutting Together-Apart," *Parallax* 20, no. 3 (2014): 168–187, https://doi.org/10.1080/13534645.2014.927623.

34. Birgit Mara Kaiser, "Worlding CompLit: Diffractive Reading with Barad, Glissant and Nancy," *Parallax* 20, no. 3 (2014): 276, https://doi.org/10.1080/135346 45.2014.927634.

35. See Deleuze, *Différence et Répétition*.

36. B 88; "I am unpacking my library. Yes, I am. The books are not yet on the shelves ... I must ask you to join me in the disorder of crates that have been wrenched open, the air saturated with the dust of wood, the floor covered with torn paper, to join me among piles of volumes that are seeing daylight again after two years of darkness" B/E 59.

37. D 6, and 9.

38. D 2.

39. D 39.

40. D 45; following citations are from D 46, and 48.

41. See Klappert, *Sand*.

42. B 89; He has "a relationship to objects which does not emphasize their functional, utilitarian value—that is, their usefulness—but studies and loves them as the scene, the stage, of their fate." B/E 60.

43. B 89; "The period, the region, the craftsmanship, the former ownership—for a true collector the whole background of an item adds up to a magic encyclopedia whose quintessence is the fate of his object" B/E 60.

44. B 89.

45. D 54f.

46. B 88; A "spring tide of memories which surges toward any collector as he contemplates his possessions. Every passion borders on the chaotic, but the collector's passion borders on the chaos of memories" B/E 60.

47. B 88 and B 88.

48. B 88.

49. B 89; "And indeed, if there is a counterpart to the confusion of a library, it is the order of its catalogue" B/E 60.

50. D 51, 51, and 49.

51. D 50, 51, and 60.

52. D 66-68.

53. D 65f.

54. D 70-72; A reproduction of Carlos' book/house was exhibited in the Architekturmuseum of the TU München in 2006. A figure of the model is published in *Architektur wie sie im Buche steht: Fiktive Bauten und Städte in der Literatur*, ed. Winfried Nerdinger (Salzburg: Anton Pustet 2006), 264f.

55. D 72.

56. D 73.

57. B 89; "Everything remembered and thought, everything conscious, becomes the pedestal, the frame, the base, the lock of his property" B/E 60.

58. B 96.
59. B/E 67.
60. D 12, and 14.
61. D 89.
62. B/E 61.
63. B 96.
64. B 92
65. B 93 and B96; "[M]emories of the rooms where these books had been housed" B/E 67.
66. This and next quotation from D 98, and 99.
67. This and next quotation from D 101, and 102.
68. D 82f.
69. D 83.
70. B 95; "I had started at noon, and it was midnight before I had worked my way to the last cases." B/E 66.
71. B 88.
72. B 94f; "Once you have approached the mountains of cases in order to mine the books from them and bring them to the light of day—or, rather, of night—what memories crowd in upon you! Nothing highlights the fascination of unpacking more clearly than the difficulty of stopping this activity" B/E 66.
73.
74. B 96; "For inside him [of the collector] there are spirits, or at least little genii, . . . Not that the come alive in him; it is he who lives in them" B/E 67.
75. B 96; "So I have erected one of his dwellings, with books as the building stones, before you, and now he is going to disappear inside, as is only fitting" B/E 67.
76. This and the next quotation from D 88, and 87f.
77. Esther Peeren, "Specters," in *Symptoms of the Planetary Condition*, ed. Mercedes Bunz, Birgit Mara Kaiser, and Kathrin Thiele (Lüneburg: meson press 2017), 168.
78. See Karen Barad, "Quantum Entanglements and Hauntological Relations of Inheritance: Dis/continuities, Spacetime Enfoldings, and Justice-to-Come" *Derrida Today* 3, no. 2 (2010): 264–266.
79. Jorge Luis Borges, "El libro de arena," in *Obras Completas*, ed. Carlos V. Frías, vol. 3, *1975–1985* (Barcelona: Emecé, 2011), 68–71.
80. D 47.

PART III

DIFFRACTING (IN) MUSIC, VISUAL, AND DIGITAL MEDIA

Chapter 12

Diffractive Aesthetics and Holographic Literacies

Transcoding the Gigaton Volume Detector [A Diffracted Photo-Essay]

Jol Thoms

This contribution investigates the processes of a lake becoming a telescope. While a Fellow of Akademie Schloss Solitude, an artist's residency in Stuttgart, I received an invitation from the Irkutsk State University's physics department to join and document the winter assembly of the *Gigaton Volume Detector* (GVD) in southern Siberia. The GVD was being assembled in the deepest regions of the planet's largest freshwater reservoir Lake Baikal 1.4 kms beneath the surface while the lake is frozen over. Baikal's waters matrixially hold thousands of optical modules networked across a cubic kilometre of its deepest region, becoming a "neutrino-telescope." There the lake and the apparatus become intimately entangled establishing the site as a *landscape laboratory* developed to operate beyond human perception—to detect otherwise imperceptible subatomic neutrino particles. The cubic kilometre scale of the GVD is necessary due to the extremely rare interactions of the neutral neutrino particles with our regularly charged, *baryonic*, luminous, optical matter.

This new genre of experimental physical observatory, explicitly employing and embedded with/in vast elemental bodies, operates far outside of traditional limits and ideas of technology, scale or "nature," and this is what specifically interests me about them: their *reach*, only possible through an explicit radical relationality. In my practice, *landscape laboratories* like the GVD are read and (re)written—or *transcoded*—as "enunciative assemblages,"[1] announcing a new order of sense that I aim to expose through a diffractive aesthetic found in my audio-visual and installation work.[2] With some critical attention, these landscape laboratories can refresh our understandings of *what* can be in relation—as Whitehead lucidly noted, "If anything out of

Figure 12.1 *A Borderline Conception Lying at the Extreme Edge of the World of Appearances* (Still) Jol Thoms, 2019. 3 channel a/v composition. *Source*: Courtesy of the artist.

relationship, then complete ignorance as to it."[3] The landscape laboratory's intra-active operations occurring across and beyond traditional borders and limits offer the possibility to critically challenge the project of separation and fragmentation implicit in Modernity, including its assumptions of value and relevance premised on the processes and outcomes of the mathematization[4] and "bifurcation" of nature.[5] "Modernity," writes Denise Ferreira da Silva in Fred Moten and Wu Tsang's *Who Touched Me*, "does not have a monopoly on thinking. Its view and practice of thinking is very limited."[6]

Since diffraction, as elucidated by Karen Barad, "attends to specific material entanglements," as "a way of understanding the world from within and as a part of it,"[7] it is a valuable artistic-research method for engaging and attending to the multiple "characters" (mineral species, elemental bodies, flora, and fauna) of landscape laboratories, their histories, and to read them through the forms of scientific investigation and experimentation that take place there. Diffractively reading and (re)writing the complex multidimensionality of landscape laboratories is a practice I call *transcoding:* that is "a forming process and a process of being informed,"[8] by the site, its histories, materials, and elements; a reading and writing that goes both ways. Transcoding emerges through interferometry, *a measuring of interferences*, capturing and analyzing their emergent patterns, a practice that is inherent to both conceptual and material diffraction. The (re)writing within the practice of transcoding is the gesture of "bringing-to" a physics site its *more-than*: the art of abstracting the overlapping fields, disciplines, concerns, and perspectives that the site, in its

Figure 12.2 4kms from the Shore, a Section of the GVD being Assembled over Baikal's Greatest Depths. *A Borderline Conception Lying at the Extreme Edge of the World of Appearances* (Still) Jol Thoms, 2019. Source: Courtesy of the artist.

human and more-than-nonhuman modes, offers, projects, and performs. By situating physicists' apparatuses in the otherwise overlooked contexts that generally lie outside the scope of a physicist's descriptions or disciplinary concerns, my work operates tangentially to conventional expectations of "science communication," and addresses what is meaningful about physicists' practices from *outside of physics*. My approach, rooted in environmental humanities, decolonial critique, and meta/physics, is deeply indebted to the thought and writing of Karen Barad that "enables a critical rethinking of science and the social in their relationality."[9] With a diffractive aesthetics' critical interferometry, landscape laboratories are transcoded and can contribute to the *Quantum Reformulation of Ontology* that Kathrin Thiele[10] highlights in the work of Barad.

It is due to "nature" or "reality" being truly and essentially entangled, that Baikal can become a sensor of the otherwise imperceptible neutrino particles from cosmically remote, unknown origins. However, the planetary bodies—the lakes, deserts, mountains, and ice shelves of landscape laboratories—are not merely infrastructural supports for the vast optical arrays that compose the technical milieu of the observatories and detectors, but crucially, it is their specific elemental makeup that is the very condition for the detectors themselves to function, technically and optically. It is the *water* of Lake Baikal that holds the detector's most vital capacity to meet or collide with the imperceptible neutrino particles it was built to detect. "Weakly interacting" neutrino particles from unknown regions of spacetime meet atmosphere, meet ice, meet lake, meet hydrogen, and upon an ever so rare

Figure 12.3 *A Borderline Conception Lying at the Extreme Edge of the World of Appearances* (Still) Jol Thoms, 2019. *Source*: Courtesy of the artist.

collision, *cascade* into networks of epistemic practice. These "secondary particle cascades," fluorescing through translucent waters, are what is actually detected by the optical instrumentation of the detector, *not* the neutrino itself. Only the water experiences these ghostly particles directly, always having had encountered what the scientists, optical modules and algorithms can only infer. "In a certain sense," writes Whitehead in *Science and the Modern World*, "everything is everywhere at all times. For every location involves an aspect of itself in every other location."[11] These detectors that enlist planetary bodies as astronomical strategies reinforce the radical relationality of Whitehead's statement. Events from all regions of spacetime are made legible in Lake Baikal, and are related to it; it is both the form of *and* the information generated by landscape laboratories that help to make these entanglements more explicit.

Neutrinos are rebellious little ghosts, imperceptible particles indicating faults in the otherwise rock-solid "Standard Model of Particle Physics," one of the crowning achievement of quantum physics and indeed modern science itself.[12] The Standard Model (SM) is a system that accurately describes three of the four known fundamental forces of nature, and classifies all of the known elementary particles. The neutrino, the smallest and most abundant particle in the universe, spooks the physicists' greatest model because it doesn't follow their formulas, predictions, or generalities.[13] To this degree, neutrinos and their detectors are excellent collaborators for, "thinking [physics-] philosophy as the 'material for an art'"[14]: they're anarchic in ways that upset long held beliefs and expectations. As "epistemic things,"[15] objects

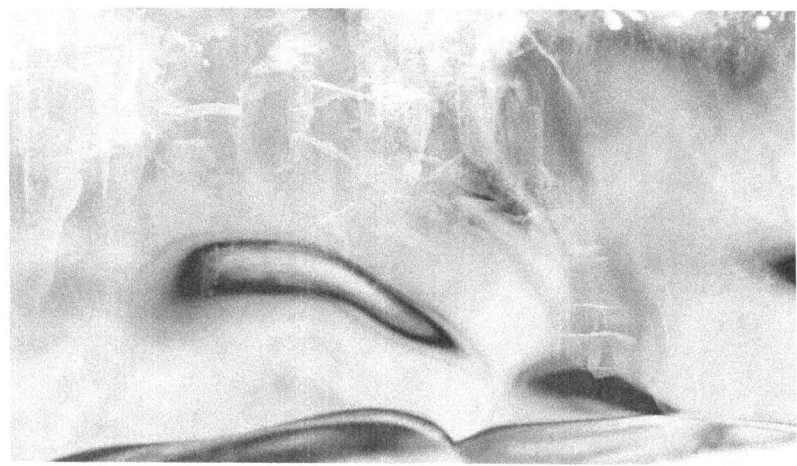

Figure 12.4 A Borderline Conception Lying at the Extreme Edge of the World of Appearances (Still) Jol Thoms, 2019. *Source*: Courtesy of the artist.

of and for thought, they and their detectors are also, in a certain art historical sense, *non-retinal*.[16] Since these particles have theoretical access to the "dark sector" of the cosmos (about 95% of the cosmos' mass and energy that is imperceptible) they're a "non-optical" matter of concern for many physicists who believe that greater understanding of them will eventually lead to another type of physics altogether: physics *Beyond the Standard Model* (BSM). As Barad notes of infinitesimal entities, they "may be small, but [their] consequences may be quite profound."[17]

Lake Baikal has been populated by people and cultures dating back at least 4,000 years, and the majority of these people have had very strong ties to the "sacred waters" of Baikal, their origin stories being located in these waters, their modes of existence being reliant upon them, their gods inhabiting and/or being this majestic lake. The capacity for waters to traverse the knowable and perceivable reaches far outside the mathematization and categorizing practices of a hegemonic master-discipline like physics. "[A]cross human history," writes historian of Russian environmentalism Nicolas Breyfogle, "water represents both the origin of reality and the transformer of realities."[18] In 1958, when the waters of Baikal were to be drastically, if not arrogantly lowered by 5 metres for a brief hydroelectric power surge, causing unheard of devastation to the ecozone, the flora, fauna, and future of the region—Breyfogle writes how biologist M. M. Kozhov's public resistance to the plan initiated a movement that would develop into a profound environmental awakening across all of Russia.[19] Breyfogle elaborates, "It was in the context of the rapidly growing consciousness of the effects of industrial development on Baikal that the 1958 conference (that proposed Baikal as a site of

Figure 12.5 *A Borderline Conception Lying at the Extreme Edge of the World of Appearances* (Still) Jol Thoms, 2019. *Source*: Courtesy of the artist.

extraction and industrial development) took place and that a public defense of the lake came alive."[20] Today, Baikal is a UNESCO World Heritage site, which is crucial to understanding an essential element of a landscape laboratory: their relationships to environmental stewardship.

"We are created in water, we gestate in water, we are born into an atmosphere of diffuse water, we drink water, we harbour it, it sustains and protects us, it leaves us—we are always, to some extent, in it. The passage from body of water to body of water is never merely metaphoric, but rather radically material. The watery condition of being literally flows into, out of and from beings themselves in a multiplicitous hydrological cycle of becoming –evolutions of gestation, repetition, differentiation and interpermeation."[21] This understanding of water contributes to Astrida Neimanis' notion of the *amniotic onto-logic*, a concept that she activates toward thinking of water *bodies* as "hydro*commons*."[22] In my audio-visual work, the waters of Baikal are foregrounded, evidenced in each of the still images included in this diffracted photo-essay. Here, gesturing to a complex watery relationality, linking beings and distant events of spacetimematter, I hope to reveal some of the complex overlapping waves inherent to the site of the GVD. In these interferometric practices of transcoding a site's multidimensionality, the term "holographic" seems apt. Technically a holo*gram* is the appearance of a physical structure that emerges through "interference patterns of diffracted light."[23] A holo*graphic,* as I am introducing it here, is not a mere image or physical 3D structure but a multiple, dynamic, entangled *extradimensional object* of and for thought, sense/experience, poetics, and aesthetics—it is the phase space of

Figure 12.6 *A Borderline Conception Lying at the Extreme Edge of the World of Appearances* (Still) Jol Thoms, 2019. *Source*: Courtesy of the artist.

entangled spacetimematter and meaning that cannot remain flat, because, "[t]he total range of issues involved in meaning cannot be resolved at one "level" or locus, or within one dialectic."[24]

In my practice, as I get closer to the agential capacities of materials, waters, minerals, species, a figure-ground reversal emerges, and through this I also become more aware of and sensitive to what might be termed the *ineffable* or the *intangible*. "Intangibility," writes Macarena Gómez-Barris, drawing from an indigenous Andean phenomenology, "names . . . the capacity of life otherwise to reroute itself around commodification and scientific classification."[25] The domains of the intangible are connective realms without bifurcation; they do not carve up, but radically, agentially link and intra-weave. The *ineffable*, "which cannot be captured by language in any form," according to Federico Campagna, and "that, as life, traverses uninterrupted through all that exists," challenges, "the very metaphysical foundations on which our world currently rests."[26] These "reroutings" and traversals that bypass the logics inherent to what Whitehead called the *bifurcations of nature*[27] offer to the holographic that which is beyond a limited Western cosmology. The ineffable enlarges the possibility for legitimate non-linguistic communication between humans and the world, an iterative bio/geosemiosis. The many layers and dimensions of resistance to typical forms and nomenclatures inherent to the diffractive aesthetic and its holographic objects of research challenge our own mis/understandings of meta/physical categories premised on separation and division and could help us look to the interstitial and overlooked regions that are filled with irresolvable, vibrant messages. A diffractive aesthetics is a process of mapping and/or inheriting from those unspeakable resonances through

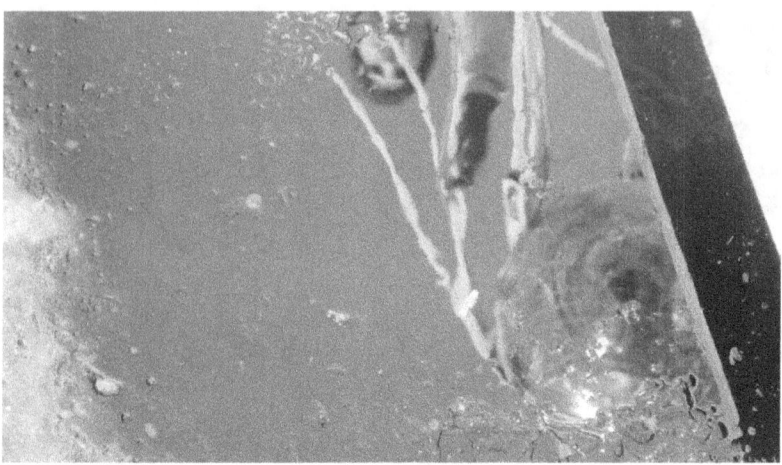

Figure 12.7 *A Borderline Conception Lying at the Extreme Edge of the World of Appearances* (Still) Jol Thoms, 2019. *Source*: Courtesy of the artist.

transcoding and *isomorphic* practices that expand and condense geometries of difference in spacetimematter.

Taking the elemental materialities of landscape laboratories into account is a process of "isomorphic projection" that reveals dimensionality, depth, and form, causing generative interference patterns along the way. A diffractive aesthetic renders the flattened spaces of a discipline's plains and boundaries into $n+$ volumes by transcoding the landscape laboratory's extra- and non-disciplinarity, accounting for it geographically, archeologically, geopolitically, historically; as a resource, a technology, and as a living, perhaps *supercelestial* creature (as in the ocean being of Tarkovsky and Lem's *Solaris*). At borderspaces of elemental dynamism and hydrologic cycles—where water becomes solid, liquid or vaporous—in those transitory spaces that seem unintelligible or illegible, the holographic is making itself apparent through diffraction patterning. Non-retinal, non-optical, non-linguistic relations and information are available there. Images of these surfaces and depths may seem abstract because they condense too much information and too much dimensionality into a single plain, or, they may seem abstract in that something unrecognizable is operating somewhere beyond our standard perception, cognition, or literacy—becoming *fuzzy*. At the GVD, built to operate beyond scales of human perception, it comes as no surprise that the environment itself re-enacts and reinforces these themes. What I found in that body of water—in Baikal—in its hydrological cycles, its ices and their crystallizations, in its various forms, dynamisms and states, and its cultural histories, was an entangled multidimensionality appearing as abstraction: the actual imaging of nature *by* nature. The critical value of the diffractive aesthetic is

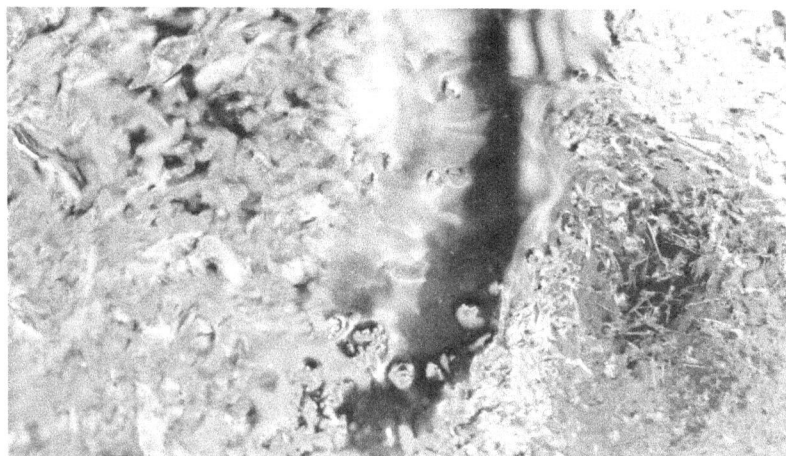

Figure 12.8 *A Borderline Conception Lying at the Extreme Edge of the World of Appearances* (Still) Jol Thoms, 2019. *Source*: Courtesy of the artist.

a result of its capacity to engage these extensive excesses of performativity occurring outside the human experience; excesses inherent to a holographic literacy and to my practice, to the "ecology of practices"[28] intermingling in the diffractive transcoding of the landscape laboratory.

The holographic is both what the landscape of spacetimematter offers and what is beyond its scientific reach: a phase space of possibility and meaning that does not collapse simply by being observed or described; the plural; the plural aggregate modes of possible encounter, description, experience, communication—without disciplinary, bodily, linguistic, regional or historical bias. What is important in distinguishing the holographic from *the virtual* is that it does not only refer to potentiality, but to actually operating agencies that are overlooked and undermined by "Western hegemonic practices."[29] Critical interferometry is the transcoding of interference patterns emerging from the holographic, a communing that is made explicit by the landscape laboratory's serendipitous, entangled and resolute modes of intensive scrutiny of what is perceivable about reality and/or the cosmos. This results in audio/visual compositions such as *A Borderline Conception Lying at The Extreme Edge of the World of Appearances* that bring in and out of focus what is un/knowable, non/local, and un/separable about the cosmo-logics of a landscape laboratory. The geometries of thought that reorganize meta/physics at these sites are entangled with/in the materiality of the local elements, and nature itself reflects, responds to, and performs this without our having to intervene. I understand these performances by nature as proof of the intangible and ineffable operating behind and beyond scientific perception and measurement. Something important is being expressed there about the

Figure 12.9 *A Borderline Conception Lying at the Extreme Edge of the World of Appearances* (Still) Jol Thoms, 2019. Source: Courtesy of the artist.

radical relationality inherent to being and inherent to our regular immersion within an agential, non-linear holographic. In an extractivist age that demands climate and social justice, finding tools and concepts for eliciting, maintaining, and attending to existing and hidden relations is essential. The GVD however, is developed as a radically, inhumanly sensitive device, capable of peering into regions of the insensible/imperceptible, beyond thresholds of perceptuality itself *only* by transgressing and mutating onto-epistemic boundaries: only by *becoming-lake*, only by collaborating with the specificity of the site—its depths and waters—is new knowledge of physical reality and the cosmos formed and produced. Here, with the waters, neutrinos, hidden dimensions, and the landscape-laboratory of Lake Baikal's GVD, I have attempted to extend the depths of concern of physics into other dimensions beyond those of spacetimematter as it is classically conceived. In getting a closer reading of the many characters and elements that make up a complex assemblage like the GVD, the important journey of *situating* current scientific experimental practice outside the measure and restriction of the scientific paradigm is an important step in addressing what cannot be spoken of or mathematized, allowing for a reconnection with the ineffable intangibility of the living landscape itself. In attending to the *matters that matter* in these *eco-techno-cosmo-logical* assemblages, in the age of the Capitalocene, something urgently echoes and enunciates.[30] An essential part of my practice as an artist is the precarious attempt, however belated, failed, in/accurate, or otherwise, of opening and inviting space for these reverberations to accrue, spread, proliferate, while paying homage to the lively abundant Earth and all the plural possibilities of responsibly intra-acting with them.

Figure 12.10 *A Borderline Conception Lying at the Extreme Edge of the World of Appearances* (Still) Jol Thoms, 2019. Source: Courtesy of the artist.

NOTES

1. Félix Guattari, "The Three Ecologies," trans. Chris Turner, *New Formations*, no. 8 (1989): 131–147.

2. Diffraction is a set of *phenomena*, the result of interfering waves, particles, desires, disciplines, objects, languages, or ideas. The phenomena of diffraction often leave a signature pattern, and these patterns reveal crucial information about the interfering, conjoining objects that would otherwise remain imperceptible, illegible, or unknowable. Diffraction has been closely attended to in physics for more than a century because of its ability *to reveal*, leading to unprecedented discoveries in the realm of matter, energy, nature, and the cosmos rewriting our very understandings of reality. In 2017, diffraction patterns of gravity waves were used to discover and sonify perturbations in the very geometry of spacetime from colliding neutron stars with a set of 2 kilometre laser "interferometers."

3. Alfred North Whitehead, *Science and the Modern World* (New York: Macmillan, 1954), 26.

4. Quentin Meillassoux, *After Finitude: An Essay on the Necessity of Contingency*, trans. Ray Brassier (London: Continuum, 2008).

5. Alfred North Whitehead, *The Concept of Nature: The Tarner Lectures Delivered in Trinity College November 1919* (Ann Arbor: University of Michigan Press, 1957).

6. Da Silva quoted in Fred Moten and Wu Tsang. "'Who Touched Me'? If I Can't Dance, I Don't Want To Be Part Of Your Revolution," ed. Frédérique Bergholtz and Susan Gibb (Amsterdam: If I Can't Dance, I Don't Want To Be Part Of Your Revolution, 2016), 50.

7. Karen Barad, *Meeting the Universe Halfway: Quantum Physics and the Entanglement of Matter and Meaning* (Durham: Duke University Press, 2007), 88.

8. Hans-Jörg Rheinberger, "Forming and Being Informed: Hans-Jörg Rheinberger in Conversation with Michael Schwab," in *Experimental Systems: Future Knowledge in Artistic Research*, ed. Michael Schwab (Leuven: Leuven University Press, 2013), 198.

9. Barad, *Meeting the Universe Halfway*, 93.

10. Kathrin Thiele, "Ethos of Diffraction: New Paradigms for a (Post)humanist Ethics," *Parallax* 20, no. 3 (2014): 202–216, https://doi.org/10.1080/13534645.2014.927627.

11. Whitehead, *Science and the Modern World*, 93.

12. For a recent discussion on the neutrino and their telescopy's philosophically troubling qualities, please see: Jol Thomson and Sasha Engelmann, "Intra-acting with the IceCube Neutrino Observatory, or; how the technosphere may come to matter," *The Anthropocene Review* 4, no. 2 (2017): 81–91.

13. The neutrino, unlike any other known particle, *oscillates*, which is a way of saying that, while the wave function does collapse when it is observed, the neutrino still remains in a state of superposition—a possible "flavour" spectrum of shifting weights termed *muon*, *tau*, or *electron*. The neutrino's oscillations therefore trouble fundamentally what physicists think they know about matter and energy. For a brief discussion, please see Wikipedia, s.v. "Beyond the Standard Model," last modified May 3, 2020, 07:24, https://en.wikipedia.org/wiki/Physics_beyond_the_Standard_Model.

14. François Laruelle quoted in Robin Mackay, "Introduction: Laruelle Undivided," in *From Decision to Heresy: Experiments in Non-Standard Thought*, ed. Robin Mackay (Falmouth: Urbanomic/Sequence Press, 2012), 29.

15. Rheinberger, "Forming and Being Informed."

16. "Non-retinal" was a term used by proto-conceptual artists to describe an expansion of arts concerns and practices away from the merely visual. Marcel Duchamp famously used this term to discuss his "readymades," which radically challenged and rethought twentieth-century art form and practice.

17. Barad, *Meeting the Universe Halfway*, 110.

18. Nicholas B. Breyfogle, "Sacred Waters: The Spiritual World of Lake Baikal," in *Meanings and Values of Water in Russian Culture* (Abingdon, Oxon: Routledge, 2016), 34.

19. This event is analogous and coeval with Rachel Carson's pivotal work in the West, *Silent Spring*, considered to have, "altered the balance of power in the world, . . . [and] partly responsible for the deep ecology movement and the strength of the grassroots environmental movement since the 1960's." Cf. Patricia H. Hynes, *The Recurring Silent Spring* (New York: Pergamon Press, 1989). For an excellent review of Baikal's coming into being as a protected national symbol of Russian environmentalism, please see Nicholas B. Breyfogle, "At the Watershed: 1958 and the Beginnings of Lake Baikal Environmentalism," *Slavonic & East European Review* 93, no. 1 (2015): 147–180.

20. Breyfogle, "At the Watershed," 166.

21. Both quotations are from Astrida Neimanis, "Bodies of Water, Human Rights and the Hydrocommons," *TOPIA: Canadian Journal of Cultural Studies* 21 (2009): 164.

22. "An onto-logic is a common way of being expressed across a difference of beings. As opposed to the way in which ontology is traditionally understood, an onto-logic does not propose to solve the question of Being, nor does it purport to reveal or describe all of being's facets or potential expressions. Like a template, an onto-logic can highlight something that helps us understand a common how, where, when and thanks to whom that seemingly disparate beings share." Neimanis, "Bodies of Water," 161–182.

23. Cf. Wikipedia, s.v. "Holograpghy," last modified May 27, 2020, 07:55, https://en.wikipedia.org/wiki/Holography.

24. Roy Wagner, *An Anthropology of the Subject: Holographic Worldview in New Guinea and its Meaning and Significance for the World of Anthropology* (Berkeley: University of California Press, 2001), 127.

25. Macarena Gómez-Barris, *The Extractive Zone: Social Ecologies and Decolonial Perspectives* (Durham: Duke University Press, 2017), 18.

26. Frederico Campagna, *Technic and Magic: The Reconstruction of Reality* (London: Bloomsbury Academic, 2018), 121, 216, 89.

27. Whitehead, *The Concept of Nature*.

28. Isabelle Stengers, "Introductory notes on an Ecology of Practices," *Cultural Studies Review* 11, no. 1 (2005): 183–196.

29. Here, I also refer to artist and filmmaker Francois Boucher's forthcoming "On the Use of the Word 'Code' by a Kogi Translator (an eccentric account)," who writes about the holo*gram* of La Sierra Nevada de Santa Marta, Mexico, and its intricate maintenance by Kogi shaman.

30. #eco_techno_cosmo_logic is the name of a series of transdisciplinary workshops and critical excursions that I run with the support of art and physics institutions in Europe and Canada.

Chapter 13

Diffracting Maternal and Female Midlife Sexual Assemblages in Postfeminist Popular Culture

Susan Yi Sencindiver

"I'm not a woman anymore, I'm a mom."

—Saturday Night Live, "Mom Jeans"

Conventional images of motherhood dictate a new mother's overnight metamorphosis whereby she awakens to garbs that have grown turtlenecks, "mom jeans," frumpy hairdos, and the miraculous birth of her paradoxical sexual purity; as encapsulated by Saturday Night live's skit on mom jeans: "I'm not a woman anymore, I'm a mom."[1] Analogously, the cultural myths surrounding the aging process incorporate a curious double standard in which female sexuality to a far greater extent than its male counterpart is labeled with an expiry date. However, hot mom and hot older woman images now widely circulate in mainstream media under the colloquial terms "milf" and "cougar" respectively, as evident by their leading role in a rapidly growing number of films, television shows, hen and mom lit reads, and by the influx of cougar-cub dating websites along with the media frenzy spotlighting the rapidity by which a post-pregnant celeb can squeeze back into her pre-pregnant "skinny jeans." This shift in sexual norms raises interesting questions as to the socio-historical conditions enabling the emergence of these sexual identities at this precise juncture, the discursive and material means by which this coupling of sexiness, motherhood, and female senescence is no longer construed as intolerable or incongruous, and which ideological, biopolitical, and commercial interests are invested in such a cultural sanction.

On the one hand, we could perhaps read these women in relation to what Anthony Giddens and Ulrich Beck see as the destabilization of a traditional social order, whereby their sexualization is part of wider opportunities for personal freedom, choice, and agency, especially in the wake of women's professional and economic success. On the other hand, the emergence of milfs and cougars could be diagnosed as a thickening instance of the expanding "sexualization of culture,"[2] ensnaring and commodifying formerly excluded demographic segments, which, as Foucault cautioned, may function to extend the surveillance and regulation of bodies. This sexualization may assume the form of a postmodern power that, as Slavoj Žižek maintains, compels us to "enjoy" our repression, which echoes Foucaultian-inspired scholars' warnings against postfeminism's pleasurable yet self-disciplining gender regimes. To end the analysis according to this binary emancipation/oppression model—whether the sexualization of mothers and older women is conceived as having an inclusive effect in terms of the "democratisation of desire"[3] or women's self-imposed sexual objectification in "raunch culture"[4]—would be to overlook how the privileges, policing, and parameters of sexualization unevenly emerge, diffractively operate and fluctuate, as well as how new diffractive realignments introduce other differential axes of sexual norms. By analyzing the formation of sexualities and mores as dynamic kaleidoscopic assemblages that are diffractively modulated around particular combinations of socio-material configurations, we can move beyond simple binaries of normative and nonnormative sexualities. As Karen Barad observes, "[d]iffraction queers binaries."[5] Accordingly, this chapter observes a diffractive method of reading, "of reading insights through one another,"[6] and maps the diffractive intra-active relations shaping sexual norms and realities, illustrated by a case study on the assemblage formations of contemporary maternal and midlife female sexualities in postfeminist media. The corpus of materials that are diffractively read with and against each other include popular cultural texts ranging from rom coms with mature leads and milf music videos to milf handbooks and cougar guides.

In theorizing how to figure the intra-actions among the component parts of a sexual assemblage, it is well to keep in mind Candace West and Sarah Fenstermaker's apprehension about the unsaid implications of the mathematical metaphors used to figure the relationships among differences prevalent in feminist scholarly literature. There are, for example, additive or multiplicative models, and geometric patterns implied in the study of intersectional and interlocking forms of discrimination, whereby the effects of the whole are calculated from the combinatory equations of its different parts. These mathematical metaphors, they argue, fail to account for lived experience, varied social situations, simultaneity, dynamic processes, as well as link institutional with interactional practices,[7] which a coalition of diffraction and assemblage theory could remedy. With the concept of assemblage, I refer to Manuel DeLanda's appropriation of Deleuzian assemblages as complex wholes irreducible to their constituents, yet whose emergent qualities arise from the interactions between these components. His understanding of assemblages resonates with Barad's agential realist thought to the extent that they both endorse a processual and relational ontology, which departs from essentialist forms of realism that presume a universe composed by autonomous "organic totalities."[8] In contrast to "the Cartesian cut," which assumes inherent properties and demarcations, Barad stresses "the ontological inseparability of agentially intra-acting 'components'," which is, however, not tantamount to the erasure of differences; rather, diffractive entanglements "cut-together apart" in one single move.[9] An intra-action, she explains, as opposed to interaction, "recognizes that distinct agencies do not precede, but rather emerge through their intra-action," enacting an agential cut, which designates "a local resolution," whereby provisional differential bounds become determinate.[10] Just as Barad eschews the idea of "non-relational properties,"[11] DeLanda similarly highlights a component's *capacities*, which are not fixed (as in constitutive properties), but are activated and realized by their intra-active relations with other entities: these capacities "form a potentially open list, since there is no way to tell in advance in what way a given entity may affect or be affected by innumerable other entities," and "they may go unexercised if no entity suitable for interaction is around."[12] The emergent effects of the intra-actions between assemblage components may also be understood through the diffraction analogy of the composite effect of coinciding or overlapping waves (see also Merten's "Introduction"); in other words, the superimposition or interference of the relative differences in amplitudes and phase variations of component waves, which may enhance, abate, or cancel each other out. Their emergent effect, therefore, ensues from the varied impact of joint relational differences.[13] Correspondingly, a diffractive notion of sexualities heeds to the ways in which the different enactments of, for instance, gender, motherhood, age, and sexuality, understood as products of intra-acting socio-material relations, may disturb, reinforce, or annul each other. Sexual formations are thus not static, uniform unities but momentary, diverse tangles of diffracting networks that cut across multiple forms of narratives, changing corporealities, and everyday interactions that entwine somatic and sociopolitical realms.

Avoiding the false alternatives of conceiving sexual realities in either purely physiological or discursive terms, the figure of diffraction furthermore provides a conceptual groundwork capable of rearticulating sexualities in terms of somatic textures in knotty intra-actions with their cultural intelligibility. A diffractive methodology, as Barad argues, is particularly attuned to "think the social and the natural together" and does so without "holding either nature or culture as the fixed referent for understanding the other."[14] Correspondingly, despite the political focus of this project, it does not confine agency to a discursive political dimension nor chart how socially constructed power exerts control over biology. Redressing poststructuralist models that overstate the power of discourse and construe matter as inert, passively shaped, and more tractable and uniform than is the actually the case, this study expands the notion of politics to include a web of competing and entangled forces that encompass the agentic thrust of matter, which features its own self-organizing capacities and impetus in reconfiguring the social expression and experience of particular sexualities. The flesh is, as Annemarie Mol says, "stubborn," and matter, in Baradian idiom, "kicks back."[15] Attending to the overlooked yet consequential factor of material agency in analyses of power may deepen, dilate, and refine ideological critique. The comedian Jim Gaffigan humorously highlights this point of fleshly agency and embodied specificities. "Women are amazing," he claims, because

> a woman can grow a baby inside their body. Then somehow a woman can deliver the baby through her body. Then, by some miracle, a woman can feed a baby with their body. When you compare that to a male's contribution to life, it's kind of embarrassing, really. The guy's always like, "You know, I helped, too. For like five seconds. Doing the one thing I think about twenty-four hours a day."[16]

Significantly, Gaffigan's account details how it is not only a woman but also a woman's *body* that, evincing a self-emanating directedness, can grow, deliver, and feed a baby, and how materially distinctive bodies possess discrepant (and sometimes flagrantly lopsided) functions. Deeply shaping an individual's experience of sexuality, a particular body's configurations, activities, and conditions form part of the infrastructure from which varieties of sexual and gendered social realities emerge. Insofar as corpomaterial complexions differentially modulate discursive inscription processes, we need to account for enfleshed variance to address why specific semiotic-somatic configurations become sticky with certain symbolic meanings and why particular sexual norms cluster around certain bodily features.

Drew Leder's elucidative concept of the body's "phenomenological vectors," for example, emphasizes how bodily praxis ensues not from essence but corporeal structures exhibiting certain proclivities, that is, "vectors," enabling and encouraging implied modes of usage and ways of interpreting bodily expression, which are, however, neither compulsory nor invariable since uses of the body and culture are mutually shaping. For example, the mouth's function "as an agent of primary communication is vectorial, not invariant . . . in sign language it is substituted for by the hands."[17] We can endorse the notion of gender as performative and affirm that body parts and physiologies alone are insufficient in establishing gender while simultaneously recognizing how they nevertheless play a role. According to Mol, "[p]erforming identities is not a question of ideas and imaginations devoid of materiality either": among the "stage props" of a gender performance are corporeal styles based on materially specific bodies, which "do not oppose social performances, but are a part of them."[18] Bodily aging, health, fitness, menopause, sex, and gestation eminently figure among such corporeal stage props when observing maternal and female midlife bodies in contemporary media; and these active corporeal processes are arguably co-productive in the sociocultural organizations of sexual norms.

Texts also function as a crucial agentic component embedded in, affecting, and affected by a given assemblage. A diffractive understanding of the ontology of texts, however, postulates not a correspondence of words-to-things (a representational notion of texts as reflecting reality) or words-to-words (the idealist notion of texts as constituting reality), but an intricate entanglement of words-to-things and words-to-words, as well as things-to-words (accounting for the agentic impact of matter on systems of meaning) and mutual intra-actions between words and things, in which local agential cuts enact their provisional "cutting together-apart."[19] Since cultural texts are not only symptoms of but also partake in reshaping realities, we should be wary, in a Baradian vein, of overlooking their intra-active mutual imbrications, whereby they also contribute in promoting certain agential cuts as well as normative sexual formations over others. The text's entanglement with the world means that, to borrow a Latourian term, the text is an actor, a mediator rather than an intermediary, a reality rather than a reflection. A given cultural text plays a role in the very formation of its context, but it does not, to paraphrase Barad, intervene from the outside but intra-acts from within, "as part of, the phenomena produced."[20] In other words, the text is not to be understood as a discrete object of analysis, but as an *action* diffractively enmeshed with, emerging from, and participating in everyday realities. Yet, the agency of the text is not isolated; the performative capacity of texts, for example, would remain unactualized without its readers, which thus necessitates their co-creative alliance. Highlighting the text as an actor, moreover, does not mean that texts carry equal stakes since their intra-active relations within a given assemblage, which includes a multitude of other actors, materialize in numerous ways, in which some of its capacities may, for example, cooperate, enhance, or clash with the varying capacities of a reader.

The intra-active entanglements between text and reader often involve readers' use of texts as creative resources meaningfully integrated into their everyday lives. In this respect, the cross-media portraits of maternal and midlife femininities, which depict or question how women perceive and negotiate their sexualities, may be mined for the reflexive practices of self-interpretation in relation to the norms as well as affective and bodily experiences of aging and motherhood. While the bodies depicted in media texts are invariably shaped by and present social meanings, these bodies—which grow, gestate, lactate, age, and sicken—bear traces of their debt to a material nature that is not elusive. The act of reading these bodies often subsumes an immersive, refractive technique for making sense of lived sexual realities, for revising and grappling with one's somatic sexual self-understanding. In this way, reading may be considered as a "material [practice] of intra-acting within and as part of the world," producing "specific worldly configurations."[21] Therefore, texts, readers, and readings function as vital actors in the assemblage constellation, and thus, I think, as privileged sites in terms of analytical access to a study of sexual assemblages. Yet, insofar as reality is "multiple," in the sense that it is "*done* and *enacted* rather than observed,"[22] we should heed to Mol's entreaty that we consider "a politics that includes ontology rather than presuming it,"[23] since these actors, including a critic's and my own reading, partake in the enactment of certain agential cuts, pushing and pulling realities into one shape or another while overlooking alternative "worldly configurations."

A transversal-sensitive analysis tracing the diffraction patterns between media texts portraying women's social dimensions and agentic living matter as a co-creator of sexualities lends theoretical dynamism to the static homogeneity and discrete analytics of the social categories "women," "mothers," and "older people." It enables, I argue, an identification of the contingent terms and new realignments of their normative and taboo sexualization. Examining the uneven diffracting nature of their sexual contours, we may uncover which tentative diffracting attributes elicit cooing, shaming, or ageist trolling; and in this respect, how they revise while at the same time subtly reinforce the inveterate Madonna-whore dichotomy. These new diffracting sets of sexual licenses and constraints on doing maternal and midlife gender alongside the twenty-first-century emergence of new maternal and mature female sexual identities in the mediascape may be read as overdetermined by the convergence of shifting, kaleidoscopic socio-material components characterizing the present. Here, we can point to demographic shifts, the aging of Western populations, increased life expectancy, rising divorce rates, new family configurations, anti-aging lifestyle services, sophisticated biotechnologies that pertain to health, aging, fertility, and sexual function, and, in relation to popular media, postfeminism is of particular interest.

Mingling feminist and anti-feminist ideas, postfeminism's smooth adulterating incorporation of feminist rhetoric co-opts and commodifies "the cultural power of feminism, while often emptying it of its radical critique."[24] As a result, women are "disempowered through the very discourses of empowerment they are being offered as substitutes for feminism."[25] Second, the sexualization of these female figures invites an inquiry into the current redefinitions of maturity, life course, and the blurring of age-differentiated sexualities, in which cultural markers of age become reworked into markers of youth by the cultural and medical expansion of middle age into later life. This reconceptualization—buoyed by the youth-based standards of "successful aging" or "new agelessness" hyped by health benefits campaigns, policymakers, and lifestyle industries—also reverberates with a postfeminist tenor: the buoyant idiom of positive aging likewise promotes a (lifelong) process of self-improvement and (later life) sexual empowerment through bodily health management mediated by the consumption of appropriate products promising the transcendence of age as well as expertise on prudential risk-aversive measures, whereby, like postfeminist body regimes, corporeality is construed as unruly risky equity in need of self-vigilance.

It is by no means coincidental that the new sexy Madonna ideal emerges across mainstream media at this sociohistorical moment in which mothers are pursuing a career. In certain respects, the context from which these sexualized mother images emerge resembles the circumstantial narrative of the birth of postfeminism. Angela McRobbie maintains that it is precisely on account of the growing socioeconomic gender equality, with increasing gains in women's power acquired by education and employment opportunities, that postfeminist discourses emerged to tame and leverage the risk of a destabilized gender hierarchy.[26] Gender disparity is resecured, for example, by the persuasion that a sexy body is a woman's key asset, her source of identity and empowerment, and by the "post-feminist masquerade," exemplified by the "fashionista" and other variants of normative hyper-femininities that are adopted in the name of free (and thus "feminist") personal choices, but, McRobbie adds, do not upend patriarchal authority.[27] The pop-cultural figure of the sexy mature woman channels the same cultural stress brought about by gender paradigm shifts; and significantly, she does not assume cultural visibility until the turn of the twenty-first century when mothers' work force participation rates peaked.[28] Just as postfeminism grew out of a need to reassert sexualized femininities and a polarized gender distinction in response to women's labor-market participation, today's maternal postfeminism speaks to a simultaneous need to appeal to traditional portraits of nurturing motherhood, with fetishized images of luxury domesticity and mommy culture paraphernalia appearing across the cultural field the moment its necessity is threatened.

A full-blown representative of this trend is Fergie's (Stacey Ann Ferguson) music video "M.I.L.F. $." Its maternal spin on postfeminism is reflected in the confident, can-do, sex-positive empowerment of its ensemble, consisting of sexy mothers, the majority of whom are performed by celebrity models who are also real-life mothers. Charged with images of success, competence, attainment, and enjoyment, it promotes the mother as the quintessential independent woman, whose emancipation, as the song title and refrain ("I got that

MILF money") also underscores, is lionized through tokens of wealth and thus economic autonomy. Conflictingly, however, the video only provides sporadic indices of professional working mothers. In its opening scenes, we follow the sizing gaze of an excitable, milk-drooling milkman as he surveys several front yard tableaus with cameos of model mothers, who are gardening, in yoga poses, gathering groceries from a minivan, breastfeeding, and facetiously holding coconuts while providing coconut milk for girl scouts. These are mostly mundane (yet, here fashionably glamorized) housewife leisure activities, excepting the vignette of the supermodel Amber Valletta, primped in a sharp feminine power suit next to a sign advertising: "Amber for mayor of Milfville—she's a Mom I'd Like to Follow."[29] The traditional mother image is suggested not so much by her nurturing qualities (we hardly see any children in the video), but by the campy stylized 1950s Stepford suburbia set design, invoking the clichés of a pre-feminist, patriarchal setting, where housemothers were expected to look irresistible for their husbands while creating a cozy domestic space.[30] However, in line with the postfeminist idea of a contemporary post-patriarchal society, patriarchal husbands are absent, which reinforces the postfeminist claim of a gender-equal society; accordingly, male presences are scarce, non-threatening, and docile as they assume the shape of, for example, the overawed milkman, scantily-clothed beefcake bartenders, and meek masseurs.

The fifties décor transitions to a "Milf Spa," where Fergie and her entourage dance (and are dressed) in a less matronly manner. Here, they receive massages while bathing in tubs of milk, fulfilling the postfeminist woman's self-realization through pampering beauty regimes. The video cuts to scenes of a fifties soda shop, featuring giant milkshakes containing pole-dancing women, where Fergie and her accompanying dancers are dressed as diner waitresses. This then cuts to Fergie as a cornball sexy dominatrix teacher, man(/milf)-handling high-school male teens; images of Fergie and Kim Kardashian enjoying milk showers; and finally, famous hot moms shooting "Got Milf?" ads. With this video, Fergie presents various agential cuts of the sexy mother aiming to reclaim the term milf as a positive self-identifier as well as reform the valence of "mother*cker" (repeated throughout her song) in her move to champion the postfeminist assertion of not only a woman's but a mother's right to sexual self-expression, that is, a mother's volitional objectification, or rather, because it is self-chosen, her "sexual subjectification."[31] Fergie dramatizes the gender-conscious guises of a "post-feminist masquerade" in the video's display of stylized femininities catering to male milf fantasies, as seen in the sexy teacher stereotype, and traditional motherhood roles, as seen in the Milfville residents' maintenance of appearance and home. By adopting a self-consciously flippant, ironic attitude and by emphasizing the artificiality of Milfville's theatrical setting, Fergie signals that her appropriation of sexist stereotypes and unabashed objectification is a "knowing strategy," thereby indicating how its "non-coercive status" is based on free choice.[32] Yet the "choices celebrated in postfeminist inflected media," Rosalind Gill decries, amount to "the freedom to run in heels" and the "right to wear red lipstick,"[33] as opposed to and displacing radical feminist political activism.

Naturally, milf prototypes exist from Phaedra and Jocasta to Mrs. Robinson, but the milf differs from her foremothers who convey the notion that a sexy mom entails danger and poor mothering skills. This subtext of deficient care imbues the determination to dissociate the maternal and sexual (as seen in the yo mama insult: "That's not what yo mama said last night" and "Motherf*cker"), which may stem from the enduring image of the ideal mother, who prioritizes the care of others over herself, which is then difficult to reconcile with the idea of a mother's "self-focused" sexual pleasure. In contrast to the illicit sexuality of her foremothers invariably resulting in tragedy, the milf's motherly aspect is deemed an essential component to her sex appeal; in other words, this sexy-motherly ideal arises as an emergent property. In an increasing number of postfeminist media, such as *I Don't Know How She Does It* (Douglas McGrath, 2011), *Bad Moms* (Jon Lucas, Scott Moore, 2016), and *Modern Family* (Christopher Lloyd, Steven Levitan, 2009–2019) overt gestures of tender mother love do not detract from but heighten a mother's sexual attractiveness. For instance, in *I Don't Know How She Does It*, Jack (Pierce Brosnan) falls in love with the female protagonist, Kate (Sarah Jessica Parker), when he overhears her affectionately singing to her child over the phone. The appearance of this new maternal ideal does not mean, however, that contemporary chick flicks have abandoned the conventional trope of a sexualized irresponsible mother. *Bad Moms*, for example, features the unapologetically promiscuous sidekick, Carla (Kathryn Hahn), whose outrageously careless parenting shocks her gal pals (and the audience for laughs).

Wondering whether the milf moniker is offensive or laudatory, Sarah Maizes in her guide to "MILFdom," *Got Milf?*, arrives at the conclusion that "it was the biggest compliment of all" because it "meant embracing motherhood and sexuality simultaneously."[34] Narrating how the milf ascription was bestowed by a young man witnessing the unflattering tribulations of childminding and her maternal dowdiness, Maizes infers that "being a MILF meant so much more than being 'f@ckable' . . . being a mom didn't hinder my sexiness; it was part of what *made* me sexy!"[35] Being credited as milf-worthy, however, may be regarded as a somewhat backhanded compliment since milfiness implies something remarkable about the idea that a woman who has had a child could still be considered desirable. Although Maizes claims to defy the Madonna-whore dichotomy, she subtly reintroduces this distinction by slut-shaming cougars. While Maizes considers "milf" a compliment, "cougar," in contrast, is "insulting" seeing that "[c]ougars are tightly clad, aggressive, youth-obsessed creatures."[36] In contrast to a cougar, Maizes asserts, "A MILF is pursued and adored. A cougar prowls and conquers. A MILF has children. A cougar dates 'children'. A MILF ages gracefully. A cougar, well . . . it's just sad."[37] The diffraction patterns of these sexual assemblages, however, are affected by the different combinatory intra-actions of, for instance, source and implied target, genre, the reader's situatedness and appropriation. The cougar configuration in Valerie Gibson's cougar guide, for example, shares several overlapping traits with Maizes' cougar portrait and Gibson's reading of the cougar intertextually diffracts date-a-cougar commercials and other media texts suffused with male adolescent fantasies of older women. Yet, Gibson's guide, addressed to fellow cougars, enacts a different agential cut: it is unapologetic about the cougar's assertive sexuality, unashamed of catering to male desires, and the cougar appellation is an accolade rather than an affront: "Today's cougar is full of life, sparkling with joie de vivre, and seemingly ageless (although this may have something to do with major cosmetic surgery)."[38]

Maizes' contradistinction between milfs and cougars is similarly witnessed in the teen sex comedy, *Cougars Inc.*[39] Appealing to male juvenile fantasies of milfs in its premise of male teenagers providing an escort service for older attractive women, the film presents two different versions of the sexy mom: Alison (Kathryn Morris), who, following a tryst with the young male protagonist, Sam (Kyle Gallner), leaves him a check with softhearted intentions as she learns that he cannot pay the tuition for his school (an incident that then escalates into his escort service). She discontinues her liaisons with Sam when she is worried that it will have an adverse effect on her son. In contrast, the milf, Judy (Denise Richardson), is presented as a bored, rich, selfish housewife with an appetite for alcohol, drugs, orgies, and virile young men, which is deemed excessive by the film inasmuch as it casts her as severely unsympathetic. The unfit (sexy) mother figures as the initial catalyst behind Sam's (mis)adventures, since his own mother, a wealthy model, who has ricocheted him from boarding school to boarding school, can no longer pay his tuition. While gratifying a milf fantasy, the film simultaneously indicts failing mothers, whose incompetence, it is implied, is not unrelated to sex-centered and thus self-centered priorities over child-centered ones.

Comparatively, the model mothers in Fergie's music video all share an aloof attitude, suggesting their indifference to the ogling milfman's desiring gaze, especially the breastfeeding mother, whose look of disdain testifies to a disapproval of her objectification: these women are desirable milfs but not actively desiring cougars. According to Gill, "achieving desirability" in a postfeminist context "is explicitly (re-)presented as something to be understood as being done for yourself and not in order to please a man."[40] Yet, the milf's sexual subjectification paradoxically requires the need for an approving male gaze, first, to be desirable, and second, to reject this gaze so as to bolster the idea that her desirability is not intended "to please a man." This is also implied in Fergie's reclamation of the term "mother*cker"; while no longer connoting deficient care, it is still meant as a provocative slur: you want it but can't get it. The milk trope and breastfeeding mother also exemplify how sexual mores are additionally materially conditioned, partially shaped by, and interacting with somatic processes and structures of embodiment. The mammary gland functions as a bodily vector for lactation and nursing, which, in turn, encourages the sticky cultural meanings of comfort and wholesome nurturing, but, as Leder cautions, the uses and interpretations of such body-based vectors are not universal as is also seen in the historically culturally shifting views of nursing in relation to wet nurses and infant formula. Present-day Western culture also codes breasts as erotic body parts. Hence, the shaming of public breastfeeding stems not simply from the sexualization of breasts (naked breasts in other contexts hardly invite the same discomfort), but rather because the lactating breast embodies an inconsistency enveloping the Madonna-whore polarity, whereby the nurturing mother is involuntarily eroticized. Accordingly, it is not coincidental that Fergie's video teasingly plays with "milfshakes" and milk showers, which renders explicit, and at the same time endeavors to undermine, the discord between the Madonna and sexualized woman.

In these examples of maternal sexual assemblages, we see an interesting development of the changing intra-actions shaping the differential bounds of sexual norms, in which the various assemblage components reinforce, clash, or neutralize each other. Where previously the self-sacrificial mother ideal clashed with a mother's sexual appeal, the former now enhances the latter. The prescribed social role of motherhood is not contingent on her sexual desirability, whereby the latter tarries as an unexercised capacity, but a mother's sexual desirability is, in turn, contingent on the perceived skills of her parenting. The interference patterns of these sexual norms may be calibrated further. While milfs can have date nights with milkmen, but only insofar as they prioritize play dates, this nevertheless precariously shades into a continuum shared with the villainized cougar. As a result, they must negotiate the enactments of desirable versus desiring sexualities, preferably gravitating toward the former inasmuch as it reinforces and retains the old Madonna ideal since her focus may still be devoted to domestic care giving in contrast to the desiring (and thus "egocentric") mother. In other words, a diffractive reading shows how the inveterate Madonna-whore binary is not undone but transposed, subtly reinforced, and diffracted according to other intra-active relations of differentiation.

Parental mores are not the only diffracting waves of differentiation for normative and taboo maternal sexualities, inasmuch as they are superimposed with additional waves that partially qualify and intra-act with the diffractive patterns canvassed above. The maternal postfeminist sensibility does not wholly mirror the original vogue of postfeminism because it strikes a conflict at the heart of neoliberal market logic in an entirely new way: how to maximize mothers as laborers without repercussions for the heterosexual reproductive family unit that ensures its continuance. In this respect, an ideal mother is, I propose, "capitalist-elastic,"[41] since she is asked to resolve a tension within capitalism by fulfilling two contradictory demands to safeguard its smooth operation: its need for procreation and caretaking as well as increasing its labor force. Accordingly, a capitalist-elastic mother is one who not only juggles but optimizes home and work life, but not at the expense of each other—and herself and her sanity. Thus, I argue that maternal sexualization, that is, its degrees of celebration and vilification, is also diffractively negotiated along the lines of these women's vocational and domestic lives, so that the intra-active relations between "career-oriented," "breadwinner," and "opt-out" s/mothering become contingencies for maternal sexual norms to the extent that they embody the principle of "capitalist-elasticity." This capitalist-elasticity, however, is, in turn, diffracted by the varying intra-active entanglements between text and individual reader's situatedness.

Bad Moms shares a similar premise to *I Don't Know How She Does It* of the overtaxed working mom pursuing the elusive work-life balance. While our sympathies are with Kate's struggles to advance her career while countering anti-mom bias in the workplace as well as making everyday life ends meet (contrasting her foils, wealthy, pampered stay-at-home moms), the film nevertheless suggests that her situation is barely sustainable. Similarly, *Bad Moms*'s Amy (Mila Kunis) is overburdened and on the verge of burning out, yet the film diverges from *I Don't Know How She Does It* in offering an alternative solution to the modern working mother's predicament. In contrast to the crassly oversexed reckless mother, Carla, *Bad Moms* features the converse cartoonish characters of two different kinds of stay-at-home moms: the mousy, harried, conscientious Kiki (Kristen Bell), whose frazzled appearance and inadequate self-care ensues from her extreme selflessness, and the antagonist, Gwendolyn (Christina Applegate) as the tyrannical, self-aggrandizing, catty queen-bee-PTA-soccer mom. Combined, these three characters showcase what Maizes calls the "MILF Duds": "Moms who prioritize EVERYONE above themselves or—just as sadly—prioritize themselves above all others" and at the expense of their family.[42] Initially, a fastidious supermom like Gwendolyn, the overinvested yet underappreciated lawnmower parent, Amy must learn, it is implied, to navigate the strait between the maternal roles represented by the Scylla of Carla and the Charybdis of Kiki and Gwendolyn.

Amy's new friendship with the hard-drinking party mother, Carla, becomes the occasion not only for her newly chosen life as a "bad mom," but also its accompanying associations of taboo sexualization; yet, here, it is nevertheless diffracted in lighthearted terms. Her self-liberating rebirth as a "bad mom," after dumping her dopey adulterous husband, consists of the self-indulgent pleasures of parties, booze, date nights, and a pampering spa-day with her stressed, overachieving daughter. Capitalizing on the naughty mommies' raunchy and thus inappropriate behavior for comedic purposes, the film signals an increasingly permissive conception of milfs that is nevertheless undercut by a degree of taboo as the humorous aspects arise from her transgressive undertones and the perception of her existence as an incongruity. Amy's sexual self-emancipation is concomitant with a more lax mothering style, exemplified by her substitution of fast-food for healthy, homemade school lunches and by requiring her son to do his *own* homework, challenging his sense of lazy entitlement. Diffracting the cliché scenario of the overzealous school bake sale in *I Don't Know How She Does It*, in contrast to the shaming yet forgivable failings of Kate, who provides a store-purchased cherry pie that she tries to pass off as home-baked, Amy defiantly brings a few measly gas-station-store-bought donut holes to flout Gwendolyn's exorbitant standards for mothers manifested in her dictatorial bake-sale regulations. Amy's rebellion is rewarded with the hot widower dad's flirtatious attentions. Running against Gwendolyn for PTA president, Amy embraces an election platform of lower standards. Her claim that "it's okay to be a bad mom" appeals to the other overworked mothers, who confess their own imperfections: "I give my kids Benadryl every Tuesday night so I can watch 'The Voice'." The film suggests that when mothers relax their idealist expectations, they are ultimately better mothers. Incarnating the chilled, Winnicottian "good enough" mother, Amy is rewarded with all the conventional prizes: a lucrative job, a considerate boyfriend, and socially functioning children. The ending of *Bad Moms* dovetails with Maizes's postfeminist maternal call to arms: "We will nurture our children, we will nurture ourselves and we will all thrive! Say it with me . . . 'I am f@ckable! I am MILF! Hear *me* roar'."[43] Mothers can, it appears, have everything after all, which appeals to the multiple viewing pleasures of the female audience, who witness these heroines enact personal, professional, and sexual desires while fulfilling domestic expectations. Yet, the high degree of closure in *Bad Moms* arguably makes maternal audiences aspire for an unrealistic outcome, whereby disappointment ensues.

The interference patterns of maternal sexual norms are rendered more complex by the superimposition of waves pertaining to mothers' negotiation of occupational and domestic choices, which diffractively nuances the new Madonna-whore dichotomy delineated above. Seeing that the postfeminist call for the revival of traditional forms of motherhood is ostensibly at odds with the call for working mothers, the new sexy Madonna must precariously steer between their extremes, which are typically vilified in the stereotypes of the overcommitted stay-at-home s/mother and the egotistical career-driven mother. Comparatively, despite Fergie's specious glamorization of the fifties housemother, her postfeminist masquerade is equivocal about its idealization: displaying a tongue-in-cheek reflexivity about its constructedness, it excites a deliberate dissonance as viewers know it does not correspond to the real-life working realities of its female performers. The capitalist-elastic optimization of integrating motherhood and work, moreover, leaves little space for accommodating the postfeminist summons for sexualized femininities, which requires a mother's indulgent "self-realization." To resolve these incompatible demands, the working sexy Madonna must carefully temper the patriarchal myth of the self-sacrificial mother and maternal perfectionism, epitomized by Kiki and Gwendolyn, for the reason that "[t]oday's mom," Maizes asserts, "makes her family a priority, but she still finds time to care for herself."[44] Congruently, the film's subtext promotes the feminist and pro-capitalist idea that motherhood cannot, by itself, completely fulfill a woman.

Paradoxically, it is the bad mother assemblage, as represented by Carla, consisting of a self-indulgent sexuality and parental irresponsibility, which is partially integrated in the new ideal of the working sexy Madonna assemblage to buffer and qualify the self-sacrificial helicopter s/mother. The shenanigans of *Bad Mom*'s maternal delinquents, however, are not realized to such a degree that they seriously threaten the status quo of maternal care. The diffraction of traditionally "bad" and "good" mother assemblages thus produces interference processes that not only interact to fortify but also undermine each other. Accordingly, a diagram of the diffractive patterns of contemporary sexualized maternal assemblages cannot simply replace the Madonna-whore dichotomy with a selfless milf versus selfish cougar binary, since its multiple waves diffract in conflicting ways. The contemporary "good enough" maternal ideal must balance not one but many fine lines. Representing a twenty-first-century cultural ideal, the milf promotes a new set of impossible ideals and demands for motherhood: not only must the modern mom balance work with home life, she must also, as the title of Maizes's handbook asserts, learn the art of *"Feeling Fabulous, Looking Great, and Rocking A Minivan."* It is problematic that the responsibility for rectifying a mother's egregious predicament is placed with the individual mother: she should simply let go of her perfectionism, whereby the jarring demands made on her are presumed to be unchangeable. The adversaries of mothers are even depicted as other mothers, such as Gwendolen as an authoritarian enforcer of unrealistic standards, as opposed to the systemic expectations placed on a mother's perfection at home, work, and with her sexual desirability. Like Amy, driving her children to school while late for work, the capitalist-elastic mother is destined to tell them: "I love you kids, get out, get out!"

These diffractive sexualization processes are rendered even more intricate when stratified by age and in respect to the discrepant yet entwined sociohistorical currents facilitating the sexing of maternal and mature bodies. Rising divorce rates have impelled the need to maintain erotic capital since a lifelong partner is no longer a guarantee, and in vitro technologies and the pursuit of educational and career advancement have advanced maternal age. Yet, the sexual perceptions of motherhood and aging femininity depart in other significant respects, naturally also on account of the divergent taboos on sexing maternity and age, in which, for example, the stigma of non-procreative sex undergirds the sexualities of older people. The resexing of aging bodies may be traced to the phenomenon of "successful aging," forging a link between health and sexual desire, wellness and active sexuality. The optimization of life compulsory for an aging population calls for a mediation with the aging of "stubborn" flesh, which is informed by societal-somatic intra-actions: by the ways human practices and technology (such as cosmetic surgery, weight control, judicious dietary habits, fit lifestyle, in vitro fertilization, and hormone replacement therapy) form a response to corporeal changes and processes featuring a life of their own. Conversely, the porosity of corporeal matter absorbs or resists such cultural practices, and thus bodily matter functions as both effect and cause in often unpredictable ways.

Enfolding aforesaid axial waves of occupational and parental merits and exemplifying the reciprocal imbrications of bodies and culture, the sexualization of cougars is diffractively stratified by the ways she negotiates the promise of age evasion in relation to age-related biological changes (for instance, hair loss, age spots, hormone swings, and menopause). Correspondingly, Gibson's cougar guide not only furnishes valuable tips on types of cougar prey and how to survive an introduction to a cub's coeval mother but also provides practical advice on age-defying technology: "Cougars are not afraid to improve upon nature . . . They'll try hormone therapy and photofacials, laser resurfacing and vein removal, Botox and Monobloc. They'll even go under the knife."[45] To be post-menopausal is a profoundly somatic experience: the cessation of menstruation, the shrinking of glandular tissue in the breasts, and lower levels of estrogen. The post-menopausal vector signals a woman's inability to procreate, yet Western cultural myths tend to interpret this vector as the insignia of her (a)sexuality, which makes hormone therapy appealing, as it promises her "resexing." Although hormones do not determine one's gender, using synthetic steroids nevertheless have real effects physically in terms of bodily signs of femaleness and maleness, that is, bodily props considered crucial for many individuals in their performances of gender and sexuality.

Although the sexes may feature similar aging bodily characteristics, they are interpreted in socially different ways, whereby aging sexualities exhibit a double standard. Graying or facial wrinkles on aging male bodies, for example, may connote the silverback or how, Susan Sontag notes, a man's face "records the progressive stages of his life," in contrast to a woman's experience, in which "[e]very wrinkle, every line, every grey hair is a defeat," unlike men who are allowed to look older with little penalty.[46] Unfortunately, as Sontag says, society does not allow in our cultural imagination "a beautiful old woman who does look like an old woman."[47] Therefore, a cougar's worth is dependent on the fact that, although no longer green, she must look young and physically attractive. This demonstrates how bodies do not constitute an infinitely plastic self-identical mass since the perception of disparate bodies engenders different social meanings. What "makes men desirable," Sontag explains, "is by no means tied to their youth. On the contrary, getting older tends . . . to operate in men's favor" since this boosts the likelihood of "fame, money, and, above all, power," which "are sexually enhancing," in contrast to a powerful woman, who is "considered less, rather than more, desirable."[48] Considering the rise of women's socioeconomic power since Sontag's convincing article, however, we are witnessing new gender and sexual norms, as exemplified by Bart Freundlich's *The Rebound* (2009). It depicts an older, strong, professional woman's romance with her young sensitive male nanny. Although the film plays on the awkwardness of how conventional gender roles are upset, which also forms the main obstacle to the couple's union, their May–December relationship is nevertheless deemed acceptable. This reversal of stereotypical gender traits and power also partially colors the cougar's negative valence: as Gibson's guide states, a cougar is typically the subject (not object) of desire, financially independent, not interested in marriage, commitment, or having (more) children, but interested in young male eye-candy, whose social standing or financial stability is irrelevant.[49]

The cougar assemblage illustrates how not only sexual difference but also enactments of social and biological age form intra-acting components shaping her sexualization. The "cut-together apart" differences of age and gender, for example, come into being through their intra-active entangling. How one performs one's age (and how it is interpreted) differs not only between, say, men and women, but the doing of femininity as a twenty-year-old is also different from the normative femininity performed by a sixty-year old. From a diffractive perspective, femininity does not consist of an unchanging essence, to which characteristics of a given age are added; if anything, aging perfectly demonstrates how sociocultural differences are unstable and constantly changing seeing that age and gender mutually inform and modify each other in their ongoing intra-actions mutating throughout one's life course. This shows how entanglements are "highly specific configurations" inasmuch as "they change with each intra-action,"⁵⁰ and are thus locally contingent and subject to changing boundaries, effects, and iterative reconfigurations. Just as gender is a difference that must be continually enacted and remade in relation to particular situations and is lived and ordered in different ways, age is likewise a performative, integrating bodily props, where prescriptive performance is arbitrarily tied to a chronological numeral. Accordingly, given that these enactments are situationally contingent and brought into being within a variety of conditions, practices, and relations, there are plural realizations of femininities and age performances, and thus the particular enactments of these different differences also intra-act in multifarious complex ways.

Just as we should avoid an unnuanced approach to femininity and sexualization, we should heed the diffractions implied in the current expansion of youth culture, whose values are increasingly colonizing the child and adult phases of life. This colonization assumes distinct diffractive shapes. Sexual norms do not dictate that older people should mimic youth; on the contrary, there is an emphasis on youthfulness rather than youth per se. In other words, older people should observe discordant demands by adopting certain youth-based associations (such as a healthy, sexy body) while at the same signaling age-appropriate decorum. In other words, the sexual norms of older people dictate the negotiation of *both* biological and social age, and their intra-active relations. This explains the celebratory sexiness of Helen Mirren in contrast to the ageist trolling of the Queen of Pop, Madonna, on account of her agequeer behavior: despite her biological youthfulness, she does not act the social age corresponding to her chronological age.

While Maizes admits that a woman's sex appeal is linked to youth, in contrast to Gibson's cosmetic surgery advice, she offers primarily diet and exercise advice, emphasizing how a milf "age[s] gracefully" through natural effortlessness and that "[b]eing a MILF isn't about pretending to be young."⁵¹ The subtle distinction between pursuing youth and youthfulness is made evident by Maizes's age policing and disparaging comments: that the cougar blatantly does not act her age, which is reminiscent of the ridicule of older people for wearing clothes meant for the young (as indicated in the expression: "mutton dressed as lamb"). This leaves the cougar in a double-bind since she is encouraged to stay young but is prohibited from revealing that she has made use of any anti-aging measures. She is lauded as sexy insofar as she sustains the illusion of eternal youth, and indicted as contemptible when this illusion is punctured by ineptly forestalling visible signs of physical aging, and moreover, as promiscuous or desperate when age-passing efforts become too transparent inasmuch as she then betrays the imperative of "naturalness" and "authenticity." That is, exposing how she enacts the wrong age, and channels the stigma of non-procreative sexuality tainting the cultural mien of the post-menopausal woman. While the sexual norms of cougars illustrate how social age intra-acts with perceptions of biological age, their alignment does not demonstrate "authenticity" seeing that any enactment of age is a performance. In the words of Oscar Wilde, "being natural is simply a pose, and the most irritating pose I know." Ultimately, however, the cougar (*and* the milf) is condemned to guilt for to age "successfully" involves the impossible demand not to age at all. The importance of a diffractive method is shown by its ability to uncover how sexual norms unevenly emerge and are contingent on the intra-active relations of a given sexual assemblage, in which the distinctive specificities and processes of physiology also refine the sociocultural sensibilities of sexual mores. An understanding of these diffractive processes enables women to better apprehend and maneuver more effectively the forces that would have one betray one's desire, as expressed by Lacan's ethical maxim, by which he meant to resist the seductive internalized impulse to realize a societal ideal and forestall the guilt that arises when failing to conform to its mandate.

NOTES

1. "Mom Jeans," YouTube Video, 00:39–00:41, uploaded by Saturday Night Live, October 9, 2013, https://www.youtube.com/watch?v=2aVxNH6iN9I.
2. Feona Attwood, *Mainstreaming Sex: The Sexualization of Western Culture* (London: I.B. Tauris, 2009).
3. Brian McNair, *Striptease Culture: Sex, Media and the Democratization of Desire* (London: Routledge, 2002).
4. Ariel Levy, *Female Chauvinist Pigs: Women and the Rise of Raunch Culture* (New York: Free Press, 2005).
5. Karen Barad, "Diffracting Diffraction: Cutting Together-Apart," *Parallax* 20, no. 3 (2014): 171, https://doi.org/10.1080/13534645.2014.927623.
6. Karen Barad, *Meeting the Universe Halfway: Quantum Physics and the Entanglement of Matter and Meaning* (Durham: Duke University Press, 2007), 71.
7. Candace West and Sarah Fenstermaker, "Doing Difference," *Gender and Society* 9, no. 1 (1995): 8–37.
8. Manuel DeLanda, *A New Philosophy of Society: Assemblage Theory and Social Complexity* (London: Continuum, 2006), 4.
9. Karen Barad, "Posthumanist Performativity: Toward an Understanding of how Matter Comes to Matter," *Signs: Journal of Women in Culture and Society* 28, no. 3 (2003): 815; *Meeting* 33; "Diffracting," 168.
10. Barad, *Meeting*, 33; "Posthumanist," 815.
11. Barad, *Meeting*, 55.
12. DeLanda, 10.
13. Barad, *Meeting*, 76–79.
14. Ibid., 30.
15. Annemarie Mol, *The Body Multiple: Ontology in Medical Practice* (Durham: Duke University Press, 2002), 25; Barad, "Getting Real: Technoscientific Practices

and the Materialization of Reality," *Differences: A Journal of Feminist Cultural Studies* 10, no. 2 (1998): 116.

16. Jim Gaffigan, "Mr Universe—4 Kids," YouTube Video, 03:15–04:00, uploaded by jimgaffigan, October 9, 2012, https://www.youtube.com/watch?v=GEbZrY0G9PI.

17. Drew Leder, *The Absent Body* (Chicago: The University of Chicago Press, 1990), 150–152.

18. Mol, *The Body Multiple*, 38–40.

19. In this respect, we should also add the posthuman consideration of the constant intra-activity among things-to-things along with the words-*of*-things in light of Vicky Kirby's *Telling Flesh: The Substance of the Corporeal* (New York: Routledge, 1997), which unsettles the body/word divide in a reassessment of the very nature of textuality by extending its circumference to bodily matter, but not as written on, nor as spoken about, but as itself actively articulate and literate. DNA, for instance, is an illustrative example in how "nature scribbles" and "flesh reads."

20. Barad, *Meeting*, 56.

21. Ibid., 91.

22. Annemarie Mol, "Ontological Politics: A Word and Some Questions," *The Sociological Review* 47, no. 1 (1999): 76–77. See also Barad's account, in *Meeting*, of Bohr's two-slit and which-path interference experiment intended to resolve the wave-particle paradox, in which the behavior of the observed phenomenon, light or electron, depends on the given diffraction apparatus used to measure it. This means that not only are ontology and epistemology inextricable, but ontology is also multiple.

23. Mol, *The Body Multiple*, 184.

24. Rosalind Gill, *Gender and the Media* (Cambridge, UK: Polity Press, 2007), 74.

25. Angela McRobbie, *The Aftermath of Feminism: Gender, Culture and Social Change* (London: Sage, 2009), 49.

26. Ibid., 62.

27. Ibid., 65–67.

28. Notably, the term "milf" made its mainstream debut in 1999 in the teen film *American Pie*. On mothers' twenty-first-century participation in the labor market, see Sharon R. Cohany and Emy Sok, "Trends in Labor Force Participation of Married Mothers of Infants," *Monthly Labor Review* 130 (2007): 9–16.

29. Fergie, "M.I.L.F. $." YouTube Video, 00:30, July 1, 2016, https://www.youtube.com/watch?v=bsUWK-fixiA.

30. Congruently, the domestic glamor of this retro-fifties wash also bathes a promotional photoshoot of *Desperate Housewives* on a cover for a U.S. television guide (*TV Guide Magazine*, September 29–October 5, 2008, photograph by Andrew Eccles), in which they are staged in the style of apron-attired, high-heel wearing pin-up models in racy poses, wielding dusters, brooms, and rolling pins.

31. Gill, "Postfeminist Media Culture: Elements of a Sensibility," *European Journal of Cultural Studies* 10, no. 2 (2007).

32. McRobbie, *The Aftermath of Feminism*, 67.

33. Rosalind Gill, "Post-Postfeminism? New Feminist Visibilities in Postfeminist Times," *Feminist Media Studies* 16, no. 4 (2016): 624.

34. Sarah Maizes, *Got Milf?: The Modern Mom's Guide to Feeling Fabulous, Looking Great, and Rocking A Minivan* (New York: Berkley Books, 2011), xv–xvii.

35. Ibid., xvii.

36. Ibid., 11.

37. Ibid., 12.

38. Gibson, *Cougar: A Guide for Older Women Dating Younger Men* (New York: Firefly Books, 2002), 17.

39. Levin Asher, dir, *Cougars Inc* (Sycophant Films, 2011).

40. Gill, "Postfeminist Media."

41. Here, I also nod to the mother figure, "Elastigirl," of *The Incredibles*, dir. Brad Bird (Walt Disney Pictures, 2004), whose mother role is reflected in her superhuman elasticity. Brad Bird chose the particular superpowers of its characters "to comment on roles within the family ... mothers are pulled in ten different directions" "Why *Incredibles 2* Director Brad Bird Says Cartoons Aren't Just for Children," YouTube Video, uploaded by q on cbc, June 14, 2018, https://www.youtube.com/watch?v=cKvgnBnUZ8Y. I thank Gry Faurholt for alerting me to this reference.

42. Maizes, *Got Milf?* 23, 38.

43. Ibid., xxii.

44. Ibid., 6.

45. Gibson, *Cougar: A Guide*, 23.

46. Susan Sontag, "The Double Standard of Aging," *Saturday Review* 55 (September 23, 1972): 35–36.

47. Ibid., 36.

48. Ibid., 32.

49. Gibson, *Cougar: A Guide,* 17.

50. Barad, *Meeting*, 74.

51. Maizes, *Got Milf?* 71.

Chapter 14

Ontoflecting through U2[*]

Nathan D. Frank

First, we hear Bono sing: "I can't believe my existence," which is followed by "I see myself from a distance." Encapsulated in these lyrics from "The Little Things That Give You Away," the ninth track on U2's fourteenth studio EP, *Songs of Experience* (2017), is an ontological insight about the interplay of objectivity and subjectivity, packaged up as a combination of wonder ("I can't believe my existence") and futility ("I can't get back inside"); sandwiched between them is a spatially conceived negotiation ("I see myself from a distance") that allows a subject to register his existence. By getting outside himself, Bono gains "vision over visibility" (as he does in "Moment of Surrender," from 2009's *No Line on the Horizon*) just as, in this moment, he "surrenders" a subjective interiority that he now sees from the distance of an objective exteriority.

Or perhaps it is a vision of *Innocence* that replaces the visibility of *Experience*: perhaps the visions and visibilities in question are less authorially significant and more textually significant, less a product of the songwriter's will and more a function of the songs' own vitalities. In this case, the agency in question belongs to the album as a textual object and not to an authorial Bono, or to U2 collectively. Intentionality relocates such that "textual object" becomes a textual agency[1] with the capacity to intend, and textual intention results ultimately in a reading of its own entanglements

---

[*] I am indebted to, and wish to acknowledge the help of Brandon Walsh, in conjunction with the Robertson Media Center and the Scholars' Lab at the University of Virginia, in collaborating to create Figures 14.1, A–C; Christopher Endrinal and Scott Calhoun (separately) for their private correspondences and guidance in navigating the rich ecology of U2 Studies; and, my musically gifted and otherwise amazing and gracious wife, Nikki, who picked out the notes of "Song for Someone" and "13 (There is a Light)," by ear, on piano. Any agency or intention that I can claim as my own in reading U2 diffractively is entangled with their generous and passionate cuts.

from an exteriority consequent to what Karen Barad calls an "agential cut" (or again, "from a distance"). Traditionally, intention implies *mind*, which, in turn, implies *human* mind. Songs and albums are not human minds, clearly; but, following two previous chapters in which I make a hard case for (nonhuman) textual minds, this essay rounds out a trilogy of theoretical engagement in which minds are, quite simply, objects.[2] In Barad's terminology, minds are *material phenomena*, which denote "the ontological inseparability of objects and apparatuses."[3] I elaborate on my claim below, using U2 lyrics and musicality as text. Meanwhile, I offer a thumbnail defense of Barad's *Meeting the Universe Halfway* against notable detractors as a way of distilling key principles. *MTUH* is my theoretical blueprint for this chapter, and my brief defense of it serves to outline the scope and relevance of Barad's notion of diffractive reading to my own notion of minds-as-objects, which, in turn, extends to—and is an extension of—a ground-figure reversal.[4]

A DISTILLATION OF KEY PRINCIPLES

Kai Merten's introduction to this volume surveys the senses in which reading (or measuring qua reading) co-creates the material phenomena of that which is read(/measured)—that is, in which measurer/reader and material/text become entangled. I gesture here toward several features of my own entanglement with U2. Diffractive reading activates the terms in the lyrics quoted above and corrals them into a methodology, since it takes seriously the desire to "get back inside," even as it effaces all outsides in recognition of *intra*-actions. My theory is thus gathered from the material itself in a way that exemplifies entanglement. Yet, diffractive reading also accounts for agencies that isolate and exclude other agencies, relegating them to objecthood, according to the boundary-making effects of *"specific material engagements that participate in (re)configuring the world."* To appreciate the convergence of these terms as they traverse lyric and theory, it is worth highlighting that "the point" of diffractive reading, and its relevance to the U2 lyric that opens this chapter, is largely to spotlight the assumption that pervades representationalist/non-diffractive modes of reading in which there is a "preexisting distinction between object and subject."[5] Diffractive reading replaces this assumption with another in which "we are part" of "specific materializations," that *"we are part of that nature that we seek to understand."*[6] This Bohr-inspired premise, which Barad takes to be "the heart of the lesson of quantum physics"[7] dovetails with another, which is that everything in the universe is so radically entangled that Timothy Morton's "ecological thought" becomes a puissant touchstone (despite a lack of meaningful dialogue between Barad and some philosophers of the object-oriented stripe) for thinking of minds as nature-culture objects.

A final refinement for clarity's sake: "[D]iffraction does not fix what is the object and what is the subject in advance."[8] This is a crucial cornerstone of my diffractive method. My utilization of this insight is perhaps idiosyncratic in that it involves the reading of each term of a binarism through its presumptive opposite, a move that I practice in my prequels as well. I read subjects and objects, minds and worlds, culture and nature, and ultimately, figures and grounds *through* each other such that they emerge invariably as coequal and reversible. Assumptions regarding minds dissipate when we read them *through* worlds. The result is the realization that seemingly opposite terms are entangled, that they're "one," but they're "not the same," to borrow a line from *Achtung Baby*. To be one but not the same is to be *intra-active*, to *enact* or *perform* exteriorities from within a field of entangled agencies.

Barad's agential realism thus presents a viable and intriguing way of conceptualizing "the entanglement of matter and meaning." My ongoing project benefits from diffractive reading as an ontological method, which is not to say that Barad's ontology is perfectly articulated—far from it. I sometimes think that agential realism raises as many questions as it answers.[9] My own efforts have been to celebrate and cross-pollinate new materialisms, speculative realisms, and contemporary narratologies, all of which contribute to an expansive synthesis that pushes considerations of *textual* ontology forward. My thinking resonates with Ridvan Askin's *Narrative and Becoming*, whose "speculative" or "differential" narratology is driven by the proposal "that any epistemological understanding of narrative needs ontological grounding, that narrative's ontological make-up determines its epistemological value."[10] His approach "casts narrative as expressive rather than representational."[11] Marco Caracciolo makes a similar move "from representation to expression,"[12] albeit without Askin's Deleuzian scaffolding. My prequels to this chapter attempt similarly to move narrative beyond representation. My transition from "the mind of the novel" to "the mind of the lyric"[13] here indicates an endgame that is really a broader attention to textual ontologies, of which narrative and lyric are subsets. Narrative is indeed one kind of textual ontology, but so are lyric and sound art.[14] As thinkers like Heather Dubrow (2006) demonstrate, narrative and lyric frequently cooperate, and narratology proves as effective in lyrical analysis as in narrative analysis insofar as it clarifies instances in which expression supplants representation.[15] Here, we circle back to Barad, since her anti-representationalist agenda is a major feature of *MTUH*. Barad is thus an implicit ally of ontologically minded narratologists such as Askin and Caracciolo.

Yet, misplaced antipathies obfuscate the many compatibilities spanning these intellectual movements and hijack what should be productive affinities.

Some theorists disqualify Barad's agential realism from contemporary realist philosophy on the grounds that its relationism is incompatible with mind-independent realities.[16] Others worry that Barad over-relies on Bohr to the point that her posthumanist thinking is compromised.[17] Still others express a concern that Barad (mis)reads Judith Butler with a reductivity symptomatic of new materialist tendencies—and with the result that agential realism runs essentialist risks.[18] I find that each of these interpretations is so sufficiently addressed by Barad herself as to render them non-problematic. Barad avows quite explicitly that agential realism is committed to the following principles: phenomena *do not* require minds[19]; minds *are* material phenomena[20]; and, Barad's own version of posthumanism—not in the least compromised by Bohr—*affirms each of these tenets while also ousting essentialism from nature*, which is now properly "animated" *and* "isn't the other" of "thinking."[21] In short, Barad's agential realism paves the way for the objectification of subjectivity, and it allows for a realignment of ontology with epistemology. And if "thinking" can be re-natured in posthumanist terms, then so can "mind." Agential realism rearticulates these relationships no matter how badly certain thinkers want inaccessible noumena (and not material phenomena!) as their referents; it is the case despite biases against Bohr's anthropocentricism; and, it is the case despite ideological baggage being read into texts even when those texts explicitly renounce it.

GROUND-FIGURE REVERSIBILITY IN BARAD

The jump from the possibility of nonhuman minds to textual minds is enabled by a reversal of dualisms such as nature-culture, mind-world, and subject-object: not a blurring of lines, not a clearing away of hegemonic structures, not an interrogation, but more radically and straightforwardly, a *reversal* that forcefully and subversively accomplishes what all of these ubiquitous blurrings and clearings-away and interrogations attempt. This reversal, aka diffractive reading, begins with the tendency of contemporary narratology to be as focused on expression over representation—that is, as *ontologically oriented*— as we saw earlier in Askin and Caracciolo. The provocation of this tendency is that a text may assert (/express), rather than reflect (/represent), an originating consciousness. The counterintuitive twist is that *ecological thinking* propels the parallel turns toward ontology in narratology as well as in speculative realist *and* new materialist philosophies. The recent emergence of econarratologies indicates the vast potential for better understanding textual ontologies when ontological narratologies and philosophies converge on ecological grounds. Serpil Oppermann, in *Material Ecocriticism*, stages these grounds as her basecamp from which an explorative synthesis of Baradian entanglement and Mortonian interconnection[22] leads directly to "expressive agencies," many of which reside outside the human.[23] Unlike most explorers of this path, Oppermann draws on Vicki Kirby to make the bold shift from agency to intention:

> The new materialists intrinsically entail a radical trajectory for environmental thought in order to open up the reenchantment of the world in its relationality, heterogeneity, productivity, agency, and vitality. Material ecocriticism adds expressive creativity to the list of capacities, to consider anew the process of reenchantment. This approach invites feeling empathy with all objects, human and nonhuman entities, and forces that constitute the matter of Earth within which human and nonhuman natures intertwine in complex ways. Vicki Kirby, for example, encourages us to "embrace the notion that Nature is articulate, communicative, and in a very real sense—intentional."[24]

Agency is a safe-enough feature of nonhumanist discourse, but rarely does intention get to accompany it. Barad dances gingerly around intention even as her matter intra-acts, teeming with agency and "aliveness," née "vitalism."[25] Oppermann herself pads the boldness of her shift with quotation marks, allowing Kirby to take the heat as the radical who voices something that is still risky even for new materialists. Most theorists hesitate to shift intention from human to nonhuman (let alone textual) grounds.

I keep mentioning "grounds": ecological grounds, nonhuman grounds, textual grounds. Recall too Askin's claim that "that any epistemological understanding of narrative needs ontological grounding." What is a ground? In *On Literary Worlds*, Eric Hayot says that "world is a ground, but it is always the ground of *something*. This something is inseparable from the world as world, and relates to it as content to form."[26] We might as well throw the form-content dualism in with those of nature-culture, mind-world, and subject-object, for they are all about to be reversed, but their reversal begins with a more explicit naming of the *something* for which "world is a ground," and that is *figure*. Ground-figure serves as a top-level dualism in that any reversal of it precipitates further reversals down below. If "world is a ground," then world and ground are interchangeable, and a ground-figure reversal is also a world-figure reversal, and by extension, a mind-world reversal. This makes perfect sense insofar as worlds are conceived traditionally as grounds for figures, some of which are called minds. Likewise, a mind-world reversal implies a subject-object reversal: just as worlds house objects, subjects house minds. And since worlds house objects, then objects are (by definition) contents, so object-subject reversals are form-content reversals.

In *MTUH*, Barad's reversals of subject and object, nature and culture, human and nonhuman, form and content abound. These reversals have everything to do with reading diffractively. Recall that "diffraction does not fix what is the object and what is the subject in advance"—though it is not a reversal per se, the refusal to "fix in advance" allows for and even encourages reversal. The rhetoric of diffraction is not that of subject-object obliteration, elimination, or erasure. Rather, diffractive reading entails subject-object discernibility, just *"not in advance"* and not at the behest of normativity—not with the stacked decks of humanism, individualism, or representationalism; and, not with automatic readings of nature-as-essentialism. And because you don't have to be a new materialist to understand that the universe is not static, it is worth considering the possibility that what is discernible might change.

Our diffractive reading apparatus, which reverses U2's grounds and figures, is nearly ready to go. All it needs is some concrete applicability guided by the qualities of Morton's mesh, and a rock and roll lyric to follow suit. Since Morton's mesh "can mean the holes in a network and the threading between them," and because it "suggests both hardness and delicacy,"[27] diffractive reading gets a lot of mileage out of it. We can read the mesh by reading the network's holes through its threading and its threading through its holes; we can read the mesh by reading its hardness through its delicacy and its delicacy through its hardness. I advocate a meshy way of reading that filters U2's *Songs of Innocence* through its *Songs of Experience* and vice versa.

Roger Clyne's lyric, "there is no more beautiful world," serves as a tutor text to this end, since it is a verbal equivalent to, say, a Rubin F/Vase, or a Necker Cube: a ground-figure image whose competing interpretations are in fact its essence. Clyne's lyric verbally models the mesh, since "there is no more beautiful world" pops to one reader as an image in which the beautiful world *is no more*. Another reader sees Clyne's lyric pop in the competing direction in which there is no more beautiful world *than* the one being referenced, or even *than* some unnamed world outside the sentence's frame of reference. Shifting into a diffractive mode, readers' ability to see Clyne's disappeared world through his most beautiful one, and vice versa, begins first with the detection of the world as being one way or another, and then with the subsequent detection of that same world as being in mutually exclusive relationship to the first mode of detection. The world in question and under observation remains singular while the interpretations of that same world pluralize. These ways of seeing a world cannot happen simultaneously, which took me a long time to figure out,[28] but once observers become aware of mutually exclusive possibilities, they also become capable of reading diffractively. The difference between a world that simply disappears and a world that disappears *after having been observed as the most beautiful* is every bit as profound as the difference between a world whose beauty simply has no equal and a world whose unequaled beauty is observed *after it has ceased to exist*. Diffractive reading is complementary reading that *ontoflects*. We have just ontoflected Clyne's lyric.

To read Clyne's world diffractively is to read it as a ground for whatever figures may occupy that ground, but it is also—necessarily—to let that very reading become a grating for subsequent readings. To say that the discernible realities of Clyne's world emerge differently according to each (diffracted) reading is to understate ontoflection, since what we refer to when we say "world" is *itself* different across each reading. Does this mean that we observe an entirely new entity? The only coherent answer to that question is the diffractive one, since "world" pertains now to *entanglements* of material phenomena over and above objects in isolation. Our recognition that the referent is, by turns, a material phenomenon *and* various entanglements of that first-observed phenomenon with subsequently observed phenomena is different from it being roped into Meillassoux's correlationist circle: a phenomenon (entangled or not) does not transmute into pure thought at the moment of recognition, or conceptualization (which, for Barad, is always embodied), any more than a withdrawn or ancestral object does . . . and even if it does, that thought is real in a way that has yet to be accommodated along what Graham Harman, in a review of *After Finitude*[29] entitled "Meillassoux's Virtual Future," calls "Meillassoux's spectrum,"[30] which is to say that nowhere from naïve realism to subjective idealism, and everything in between—weak and strong correlationism—is a thought accorded the status of materiality.[31]

An entanglement that involves the competing characteristics of meaning and matter may also involve an apparatus involving a mind that, by turns, makes cuts favoring first one side of a given competition, then another, and then, crucially, *each side through the other* (ontoflection). Further, all of this observational practice is itself observable, and that is where Barad derives objectivity and accountability in agential realism. But even if we bracket this observability, a mind-driven apparatus making the cuts *really is* making those cuts—something it wouldn't be able to do without something real upon which to cut; the mind *really is* a part of the apparatus that is itself part of the larger material entanglement. This is how we know that the mind is an object.

DIFFRACTING U2

To my knowledge, nobody claims explicitly to read U2 for their lyrics about water waves,[32] light waves,[33] sound waves,[34] and/or quantum insights,[35] nor would they need to in order to read them diffractively.[36] The closest that I've seen to a diffractive reading of U2 is Christopher Endrinal's "Vocal Layering as Deconstruction and Reinvention in U2," which not only utilizes diagrams of stereo waveforms to examine the superimposed layering of vocal tracks but which follows a sort of ground-figure approach by asking,

> Which sound, then, is the "real" U2? The use of multiple vocal layers challenges the listener's (pre)conceptions of what U2 "should" sound like ... "Even Better Than the Real Thing" not only asks the listener which Bono is the real Bono or which U2 is the real U2 but also urges the listener to contemplate the world as it is being presented by the mass media. In effect, the band is asking, "Is the digital world really better than the real world?"[37]

The questions that vocal layering prompt are rephrasable in ground-figure terminology: Which U2 sound, or which vocal layer, diffracts its other? Which acts as wave and which as grating? In the case of "multiregister layering,"[38] should we read the "doubling voices" against "the main vocal track?" What sort of agential cut determines which is "main" or "doubling" in the first place? In the case of "multivoice layering,"[39] Endrinal deploys the basics of cognitive narratology to sort out characters and narrators in songs ranging from *Pop*'s "Last Night on Earth" to *Zooropa*'s "Numb" to *Achtung Baby*'s "The Fly." In these analyses, attributions of consciousness are bestowed on the songs' figures through a combination of multiple registers and contrasting first-, second-, and third-person voices, as well as through grammatical and syntactical juxtapositions. In other words, verbal content is just as responsible for character/narrator designation as is vocal form. How do we know which occasions the other?

Approaching these questions diffractively means that an inclusive both/and experiment replaces what is otherwise an exclusive either/or decision driven by normative assumptions: read things in one direction, then reverse them and see what happens. The legibility of figures will always depend on their grounds, so any given reading will always be *of figures*. But what counts as a figure need not be fixed in advance. In my first encounter with *Songs of Innocence*, my "reading" (/listening) of it was guided by the assumption that it was the "ground beneath *Songs of Experience*'s feet" (so to speak[40]), that its other half would only be legible as a figure standing on its foundations, as contents molded by its form, and so on. Conventional logic supports this assumption: *Innocence* comes first, both as an album and as a conditional reality of subjective experience. Moreover, *Innocence* tells the U2 origin story more comprehensively than any other album to date. Its songs are about the band's Irish roots, punk-rock tributes, growing up on Dublin's Cedarwood Road, being "raised by wolves," mothers ("Iris"), and the meeting of future wives ("Song for Someone"). As far as origin stories go, *Innocence* ticks a lot of the boxes. By contrast, *Experience* tells the story of the band coming to grips with the passing of *Innocence*. Much of it embraces a nostalgic look *back* at *Innocence*, and it begins with a conclusion: "Love Is All We Have

Left." In addition, *Experience* follows an Obama-era *Innocence* and struggles with its own Trump-era turmoil. *Experience* copes with losses that were unknown in (and to) *Innocence*.

Given these synopses, reading *Innocence* as a ground for *Experience* is tantamount to reading *Experience* through *Innocence*. *Innocence* is the grating to *Experience*'s trajectory, and the ripples that emanate from *Experience* undulate across the surface of *Innocence*, much like the causality emitted through the demonic zones of Morton's temporary autonomous objects. *Experience* is the moon to the world of *Innocence*, whose gravity holds it in legible orbit even as the tides of the world are beholden to the pull of the figure. Elsewhere in literary theory, this may be known simply as influence, and/or intertextuality, but these concepts only allow for unidirectional readings. My default inclination upon hearing *Experience* in the wake of *Innocence*, even—or perhaps especially—in those moments that lyrics from *Innocence* are refurbished for/by *Experience*, is to hear *Experience* as *Innocence*-dependent. The "you are rock and roll" lyric in "American Soul," for instance, seems upon first reading to require the "YOU ARE ROCK N ROLL" lyric from "Volcano" to gain traction. "Volcano" supplies "a piece of ground," volatile and explosive; "American Soul" is an eruption of grief with its "many mothers weeping." The figures of "American Soul" spew violently upward, as their Volcanic ground prepares them to do, so they "Put [their] hands in the air" to "hold up the sky."

According to this view, "Volcano" sets the contextual parameters for "American Soul," shaping its meaning as form shapes content. Overlapping lyrical moments such as these invite experimental ways of reading, and they problematize the conventional view that *Innocence* is *Experience*'s condition of possibility—not just chronologically, but ontologically. They confirm, like "Love Is All We Have Left," that a diffractive method puts us "at the other end of the telescope"; that indeed, there are "so many ways of seeing."

In addition to the lyrical overlap in "Volcano" and "American Soul," I want to explore two other instances in which songs paired across the two albums according to their mutual lyrics provide a way of demonstrating that we can use the pairings to experiment with ground-figure reversal (which I held off doing with "Volcano" and "American Soul"), and that by doing so, new material phenomena emerge. The first of these two other instances is more thematic than verbatim and has to do with the starlight that can be discerned in the eyes of Bono's mother Iris in "Iris (Hold Me Close)," and in the eyes of a third-person "her" in "Love Is All We Have Left." In "Iris (Hold Me Close)," there is a "star" which provides "light"; though it "Has been gone a while," "it's not an illusion." Quite safely, I read this star as the sun; that the sun's light remains a reality despite its source having "been gone a while" is an interesting physical observation (it also resonates with the pervasive thematic refrains throughout both albums about lights going out and the traversals of light across the universe), but it is less interesting than what comes next: that "Something in your eyes" actually "took a thousand years to get here." As with Hayot, U2 leave us to name a certain *something*. It seems that Bono sings here about the wonderment that accompanies realizations that humanity is a byproduct of cosmic dust and radioactivity. Our minds should be blown by such thoughts. But things get weirder: the "something" in Iris's irises is revealed as a light "inside" the singer: "I've got your light inside of me." Bono likes to put poetic aspects of his parents inside himself when he pays homage. He does the same thing in *How to Dismantle an Atomic Bomb*'s "Sometimes You Can't Make it On Your Own," where his father is "the reason why the opera is in [him]." Bono appreciates entanglement. As we know from the first sentence of this chapter, he also appreciates when people can see themselves (preferably from a distance), which is how "Iris (Hold Me Close)" ends: "If only you could see yourself." Bono plays with agential cutting by redrawing the parameters of where his parents end and where he begins; as a result, what emerges as "himself" as a subject is more inclusive of the objects with which he is entangled.

In "Love Is All We Have Left," more ambiguity surrounds the person being referenced than in "Iris (Hold Me Close)," yet there is more clarity about "seven billion stars" as the "something in her eyes." Reading this lyric through the earlier ones from *Innocence*, one might reasonably interpret the "something in her eyes" from the earlier song to be the "seven billion stars" of the later song (instead of the sun). Likewise, a passing familiarity with *Innocence* and its themes lends itself to a reading of the "her" in *Experience* as the "Iris" from *Innocence*—Bono's mother. But if we enact a reversal such that we read *Innocence* through *Experience*, then we end up "at the other end of the telescope," and starlight diffracts differently. Now we read figures against a world in which love is all that remains in what sounds like a futuristic soundscape. No more "Iris playing on the strand," no more boy being buried "beneath the sand." Instead of a past-oriented origin story, *Experience* provides apocalyptic revelation.

It's easy to forget that "Iris (Hold Me Close)" actually begins closer to apocalyptic revelation than to origin story, but indeed, that light-giving star "Has been gone a while." Sounding remarkably like the "extinction event" in "Blackout," in which "the lights go out," "Iris (Hold Me Close)" gains traction against a world in which "Love Is All We Have Left." Here *Innocence* pops as a dark figure against an illuminated (back)ground, evident in the line that "the darkness just lets us see." What is seen, or disclosed, is really the nature of *Experience*. Read this way, *Experience* pops as the world of light and warmth, against which *Innocence*'s silhouetted figure of cold beauty ("The universe is beautiful but cold") emerges.

"Classical" readings would hold that the interaction between these songs to be just that—interaction between two preexisting and individual entities. By contrast, a "quantum" reading entertains the possibility that these songs are intra-actively entangled, and that the boundaries that appear initially to demarcate their differences can be redrawn so that other differences emerge while the first set of differences disappears. Origin fades into apocalypse and a frigid futurism warms to an intimate glow with the reversal of ground and figure. The same ontoflection occurs when we diffract "Song for Someone," the fourth track on *Innocence*, through "13 (There is a Light)," the thirteenth and final track on *Experience*. The refrain from "Song for Someone" is repeated verbatim in "13 (There is a Light)," with the exception that "someone like me" is added to the otherwise identical chorus that ends in "this is a song for someone" in the latter song (see below).

Identical lyrics pose an interesting challenge to the diffractive reader, since ground-figure contrast is more difficult to discern, and therefore, to reverse. The temptation is to read for clues about the indeterminate "someone" "for" whom both "songs" are intended. In the case of "Song for Someone," U2's live performances suggest that the song is "for" Bono's wife, Ali Hewson, and that the song recounts an early chapter in their relationship. The iNNOCENCE + eXPERIENCE Tour included performances of "Song for Someone" in which a catwalk platform, suspended high above the stage and enclosed by a chain-link mesh, was accessed by Bono via a corrugated metal staircase from stage-floor level. Once inside the "cage," the mesh became an opaque screen upon which images were projected. These projections seemed to depict Bono and Ali as teenagers getting to know each other on Cedarwood Road. Thus, the "song" is "for," and the "someone" is, Ali. "13 (There is a Light)" adds a small wrinkle by adding "someone like me" after a chorus shared by both songs, "This is a song / a song for someone." In itself, this does not really provide clear-cut contrast of the sort that might indicate whether the song behaves like a wave or a particle (so to speak), since "someone *like* me" could still be Ali. But this is not to say that no cuts can be made between the two songs. In fact, it is as though "13 (There is a Light)" *wants* to call our attention to contrast itself, letting us know that "darkness always gathers around the light" and imploring readers to maintain the conditions of such contrast: "And there is a light, don't let it go out."

To fully appreciate the newly emergent material phenomena made visible (/audible) to observers when we reverse the grounds and figures of this song pairing, it is helpful to extend the analysis from verbal/lyrical content to musical/sonic dimensions. A remarkably discernible agential cut is enacted by pairing the musical notes of Bono's voice in the chorus of "Song for Someone" with the musical notes of the synthesizer in the chorus of "13 (There is a Light)." Toggling between the chorus of each song, it becomes clear that the synth in "13 (There is a Light)" *matches*, albeit in harmonic transposition (the high and low synth play the harmony in the key of D Major, whereas Bono sings in B Major), the melody from the vocal line in the chorus of "Song for Someone." If the synth were transposed to the same key as the melody in "Song for Someone," in other words, then the synth would be providing a harmony to Bono's melody. Both Bono's voice and the synth swing upward into the same broken chord, albeit in different keys, in time together (see figure 14.1, A–C). Because of the synth's sonic quality, and within the context of the ethereal feel of "13 (There is a Light)" more broadly, this matching of the synth's notes to Bono's vocals at the equivalent spot in the chorus of "Song for Someone" effectuates a sense that the synth shadows or echoes Bono's voice, even though Bono's voice is coming from another album; it is as though the synth "sings back," nostalgically and melancholically, to "Song for Someone:"

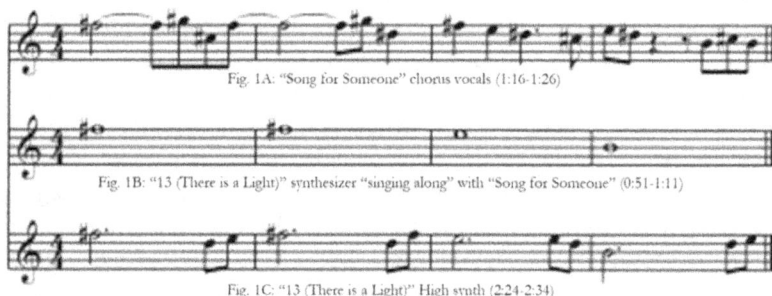

Figure 14.1, A-C: Vocal as instrument and instrument as vocal in "Song for Someone" and "13 (There is a Light)"

I have thought carefully about my language: to describe the sense of a shadow, or of an echo, enacted by the synth is precisely to express the qualities of a ground-dependent figure. In "Shadows and Tall Trees," from the much earlier album *Boy*, the tall trees themselves occasion the scene of "life through a window." Intangible but legible shadows are cut and framed by solid matter that blocks a source of light. Similarly, an echo depends on an originary sound as well as the bouncing of those originary sound waves off of solid objects. Shadows and echoes are the fleeting traces of originary material solidities, and to read the choral synth in "13 (There is a Light)" against the sound of Bono's voice as he belts out the chorus of "Song for Someone" is to read it as the spectral, derivative, figural trace of a solid ground—which is, of course, how it sounds when we read it as the figure to a prior ground.

However, an instrument that "*sings back*" to its source is not merely shadowy or echo-y, but suitably anthropomorphic, and this anthropomorphism is proportional to the sense in which Bono's grounding vocal sounds can be heard as just that—*sounds*, stripped of semiotic content or referential force. That is, to the extent that we can hear the synth sounding out the lyrics of a tune that we already know ("this is a song, a song for someone"), we also, in reverse, hear the *noise* of Bono's vocal chords; we hear ontology over epistemology; we hear being over knowing; we hear the object that is the sound over the subject that intends/makes the sound.

The claim being made here is reversible: an instrument taking on the human characteristics of intention reverses into a human voice taking on the nonhuman and unintentional characteristic of sound-as-object. But what appears to be an inverse relationship, in which Bono's human(itarian) voice corresponds with the nonhuman instrument and in which the nonhuman synth corresponds with the humanity of Bono's voice, is actually a direct relationship. The theoretical legacies that contribute to the objectification of humanness and to the humanizing of objects (texts and sounds included) are united in their emphases both on the independence of texts once they've been severed from authorial control, and on the materiality of humanity and nonhumanity alike.

I asked Christopher Endrinal via email what he thought about the notion of the synth from "13 (There is a Light)" singing along with Bono's voice in the chorus of "Song for Someone." Here is an excerpt of his reply:

> Regarding the "singing along" of the synth, yes it does "sing along" but I'd be cautious using that term unless you really mean to imply the synth is taking on human qualities (not a far-fetched idea in U2's music; see: much of Edge's guitar work). In fact, a colleague of mine, Dr. Martin Blessinger, and I just presented a paper that deals with non-texted vocal lines (we call them "wordless melismas") and how they function formally and narratively and how they relate to the "ineffable" qualities of instrumental music.

I find it fascinating (and impressive) that Endrinal thought to follow his caution against the humanizing of the synth with his concept of wordless melismas; that is, that a statement about anthropomorphization is followed seamlessly by the way that human sounds relate to nonhuman/instrumental sounds. There is no qualification, nor any other indication that the latter only follows from the former in certain cases or according to certain criteria. Instead, the instrument-as-vocal and vocal-as-instrument go hand-in-hand as two agential cuts within the same intra-activity—"*in the dynamics*" of which, as we recall, "*the material and the discursive are mutually implicated.*"[41]

Another fascinating aspect of Endrinal's reply is in its indication that there is already precedent in U2 studies for making the agential cut in both directions. If Edge's guitar work has been studied for its human-like qualities, and if wordless melismas have been observed to "function formally and narratively" like instruments, then the only novelty about my argument is in the pairing of songs across albums, and then in the reversal of the normative way of reading, directionally, across those songs. But to ontoflect properly would not be to stop at a recognition of instrument-as-vocal and vice versa; rather, it would be to filter the instrument *through* the vocal (and vice versa): the difference between a human vocal intended to name Ali as "someone" and a nonhuman sound that can be ontoflected as intending to name Ali as "someone like me" *after* having been observed as the spectral trace of human intention is every bit as profound as a voice with no echo or as a sound with no intention.

But notice now how the ontoflection is no longer the function of Bono's designs and has become instead an emergent property of a double album interfacing with itself. Bono's injunction to keep the light from going out is central to his ongoing quest to see himself, as he finally manages to do in "The Little Things That Give You Away," but it is also central to the artwork's ability to see itself from a distance. We see this accomplished via a double album in which each installment converses with and through its other half. In speaking to itself, it sets itself up such that its grounds and its figures are coequal and reversible. Such textual democracy pulls listeners into the interpretive process: if innocence makes sense of experience, and vice versa, then together they also supply meaning for the listener who, from within the soundscape, hears herself, who understands the impact of her intentions on herself and others, and who recognizes that impact as taking on a material life of its own, changing herself and others in the process; she hears the entanglement of human and nonhuman intention. I believe that U2 hear themselves similarly from within their own sonic creations—or at least that they strive to, as is evident from the chorus to "Love Is Bigger Than Anything In Its Way."

As for my own material situation, I read it (with U2's help) as one of privilege. I see my intentions as figures cut from the ground that I am, from the world of my mind. But I also see these intended and intentional figures turning around to cut me into a figure that I myself have prefigured. I ontoflect. I see that I am entangled with the very thoughts and texts that my mind shapes, and, ontoflecting, I realize these thoughts and texts reshape my mind. It is a realization that gives me pause. These are the little things that give me away.

NOTES

1. I conflate "agency" and "intentionality" with provocation in mind. When Barad severs agency from intentionality, she severs it from *human* intentionality: "Agency is not aligned with human intentionality or subjectivity." *Meeting the Universe Halfway: Quantum Physics and the Entanglement of Matter and Meaning* (Durham: Duke University Press, 2007), 177. Whereas "agency" is sufficiently nonhuman for Barad, "intention" is sufficiently mental for me.

2. Part I of this trilogy is "The Mind of *Then We Came to the End*: A Transmental Approach to Contemporary Metafiction," in *Explorations of Consciousness in Contemporary Fiction*, ed. Grzegorz Maziarczyk and Joanna Teske (Amsterdam: Brill Rodopi, 2017), 225-244; Part II is "Literary Neutrinos and the Hot Dark Matters of Doctorow's City of God." In *E. L. Doctorow: A Reconsideration*, ed. Michael Wutz and Julian Murphet (Edinburgh University Press, January 2020), 179–203.

3. Karen Barad, *Meeting the Universe Halfway: Quantum Physics and the Entanglement of Matter and Meaning* (Durham: Duke University Press, 2007), 133; henceforth cited in text as *MTUH*.

4. See Jol Thoms's photo essay, "Diffractive Aesthetics & Holographic Literacies: Transcoding the Gigaton Volume Detector," in this volume for another articulation of diffractive reading as ground-figure reversal.

5. Both from Barad, *Meeting the Universe Halfway,* 91; emphasis in original.

6. Barad, *Meeting the Universe Halfway,* 26, 67 and passim; emphasis in original.

7. Barad, *Meeting the Universe Halfway,* 67.

8. Barad, *Meeting the Universe Halfway,* 30.

9. For instance, what has agential realism done to media theory? "Rather blasphemously," Barad writes, "agential realism denies the suggestion that our access to the world is mediated, whether by consciousness, experience, language, or any other alleged medium ... Rather like the special theory of relativity, agential realism calls into question the presumption that a medium—an 'ether'—is necessary" (*Meeting*, 409n9). Blasphemy affords creativity: in a passage in which Barad enumerates the qualities of an apparatus, Jussi Parikka suggests replacing "every word 'apparatus' with 'media'—[he finds] it a very good and material-dynamic way to understand the ontology of media technologies" (Parikka, Jussi, "Apparatus Theory of Media á la (or in the wake of) Karen Barad," *Machinology* (blog), July 16, 2009, https://jussiparikka.net/2009/07/16/apparatus-theory-of-media-a-la-or-in-the-wake-of-karen-barad/). Though I appreciate Parikka's ingenuity, agential realism's obliteration of media offers no concrete answers as to whether media are "necessary," or even as to what they might be necessary *for*.

10. Askin, Ridvan, *Narrative and Becoming* (Edinburgh: Edinburgh University Press, 2017), 5.

11. Askin, *Narrative and Becoming,* 21.

12. Marco Caracciolo, *The Experientiality of Narrative: An Enactivist Approach* (Berlin: de Gruyter, 2014), 33–38.

13. And then from "the mind of the lyric" to "the mind of the double-album," inclusive not just of verbal content but also of the artwork's musical/sonic dimensions.

14. See Christoph Cox's *Sonic Flux* (Chicago: University of Chicago Press, 2018) for a contemporary articulation of "sound art," including resistance to use of the phrase.

15. Heather Dubrow, "The Interplay of Narrative and Lyric: Competition, Cooperation, and the Case of the Anticipatory Amalgam," *Narrative* 14, no. 3 (2006): 254–271.

16. Graham Harman, "Agential and Speculative Realism: Remarks On Barad's Ontology," *Rhizomes: Cultural Studies in Emerging Knowledge*, no. 30 (2016):

126–132, https://doi.org/10.20415/rhiz/030.e10; Manuel DeLanda and Graham Harman, *The Rise of Realism* (Cambridge, UK: Polity Press, 2017); Christoph Cox, *Sonic Flux*.

17. Trevor Pinch, "Review Essay: Karen Barad, Quantum Mechanics, and the Paradox of Mutual Exclusivity," *Social Studies of Science* 41, no. 3 (2011): 431–441, https://doi.org/10.1177%2F0306312711400657.

18. Sara Ahmed, "Some Preliminary Remarks on the Founding Gestures of the 'New Materialism'," *European Journal of Women's Studies*, 15, no. 1 (2008): 23–39.

Sara Edenheim, "On the Material Melancholy of Feminist New Materialism," *Australian Feminist Studies* 31, no. 89 (2016): 283–304.

19. Barad, *Meeting the Universe Halfway*, 361.

20. Barad, *Meeting the Universe Halfway*, 133; "material phenomena," for Barad, constitute the objective referents of reality.

21. Barad, *Meeting the Universe Halfway*, 184.

22. I recognize Barad's entanglement and Morton's interconnection as highly developed ontological realisms that operate according to markedly different mechanisms and which are described by suitably different vocabularies. To ventriloquize: the intra-actions of agential realism's components (apparatuses, objects, material phenomena) signify a mutual constitution of entangled agencies, while the components of Morton's ecological ontology entail autonomous objects that emit demonic zones of causality, for instance. C.f. "Objects as Temporary Autonomous Zones," *Continent*. 1, no. 3 (2011): 149–155. But theories of entanglement and interconnection do overlap in significant ways, not least of which is that their ethical implications pose serious problems for "representationalism, metaphysical individualism, and humanism." Barad, *Meeting the Universe Halfway*, 134. Oppermann also mentions Bernard J. Lee's citation (1990) of Meland and Loomer's "relational web" and Andrew Pickering's "mangle" (Chicago: University of Chicago Press, 1995) as sharing in this entanglement-interconnection overlap. "From Ecological Postmodernism to Material Ecocriticism: Creative Materiality and Narrative Agency," in *Material Ecocriticism*, ed Serenella Iovino and Serpil Oppermann (Bloomington: Indiana University Press, 2014), 27-28. See also: Lee, Bernard J. "The Only Survivable World: A Postmodern Systems Approach to a Religious Intuition," Chapter 4, in *Sacred Interconnections: Postmodern Spirituality, Political Economy, and Art*, ed. David Ray Griffin (Albany: SUNY Press, 1990); Andrew Pickering, *The Mangle of Practice: Time, Agency, and Science* (Chicago: University of Chicago Press, 1995).

23. Oppermann, 27–28.

24. Vicki Kirby, *Quantum Anthropologies: Life At Large* (Durham: Duke University Press, 2011), quoted in Opperman, 27.

25. See Barad, *Meeting the Universe Halfway*, n1.

26. Eric Hayot, *On Literary Worlds* (Oxford: Oxford University Press, 2012), 91.

27. Morton, *The Ecological Thought* (Cambridge, MA: Harvard University Press, 2010), 28.

28. Lisa Zunshine refers to Dorrit Cohn's mode of "self-conscious reading . . . to combine two readings by trusting and distrusting [*Lolita*'s] Humbert *at the same time*." Cohn, "Discordant Narration," *Style* 34, no. 2 (2000): 312, quoted in

Zunshine, *Why We Read Fiction: Theory of Mind and the Novel* (Columbus: Ohio State University Press, 2006), 117, emphasis in original). I take Zunshine's point to be metaphorical: both readings of Humbert avail themselves to the self-conscious reader, and a diffractive reader is definitely self-conscious . But just as light cannot be observed as a wave while it is being observed as a particle, so Humbert cannot be observed as trustworthy and *not* trustworthy, simultaneously. I suspect that Zunshine would have no problem restating her point diffractively, but that is speculation.

29. Quentin Meillassoux, *After Finitude: An Essay on the Necessity of Contingency*, trans. (London: Continuum, 2008).

30. Graham Harman, "Meillassoux's Virtual Future," *Continent*. 1, no. 2 (2011): 78–91.

31. Morton comes close when he interprets Husserl's phenomenology to mean "that thoughts are independent of the mind." *Being Ecological* (Cambridge, MA: MIT Press, 2018), 37. But, as Husserl's use of "phenomenon" differs from Barad's use, and as Morton does not relate this insight to correlationism, and as correlationism is, in any case, more concerned about the relationship between reality and thoughts (not minds), then Morton's thought-mind severance amounts to realism without materialism. Similarly, Steven Shaviro argues that "[b]efore it is cognitive, let alone conscious, thought is primordially an affective and aesthetic phenomenon;" speculative realists and allies of OOO thus come the closest to bestowing thought with a mind-independent materiality. *Discognition* (London: Repeater Books, 2016), 16.

32. See, for instance, *Boy*'s "The Ocean" (New York: Island, 1980), *War*'s "Drowning Man" (New York: Island, 1983), *Achtung Baby*'s "Who's Gonna Ride Your Wild Horses" (New York: Island, 1991), *No Line on the Horizon*'s "Fez—Being Born" (Santa Monica, CA: Interscope, 2009), *Songs of Innocence*'s "Every Breaking Wave" (Santa Monica, CA: Interscope, 2014), and *Songs of Experience*'s "Red Flag Day" (Santa Monica, CA: Interscope, 2017).

33. See, for instance: *Boy*'s "Twilight," *War*'s "Red Light," *The Unforgettable Fire*'s "Indian Summer Sky," *Wide Awake in America*'s "The Three Sunrises" (New York: Island, 1985), *The Joshua Tree*'s "Bullet the Blue Sky" (New York: Island, 1987), *Achtung Baby*'s "Ultraviolet (Light My Way)," *Pop*'s "Staring at the Sun" (New York: Island, 1997); *How to Dismantle an Atomic Bomb*'s "City of Blinding Lights" (Santa Monica, CA: Interscope, 2004), and *Songs of Experience*'s "Lights of Home," "Blackout," and "13 (There is a Light)."

34. See, for instance: *No Line on the Horizon*'s "Get On Your Boots."

35. See, for instance, the lyric from "No Line on the Horizon": "She said, 'Time is irrelevant, it's not linear'."

36. Scott Calhoun (who facilitates the U2 Studies Network and directs the U2 Conference) and I agree that "light and water in the U2 canon . . . deserve some extended commentary and analysis of several kinds, for sure. [Calhoun feels] the same way about the talk of silence, sound, and time." Author's private correspondence.

37. Christopher Endrinal, "Vocal Layering as Deconstruction and Reinvention in U2," in *Exploring U2: Essays on the Music, Work, and Influence of U2*, ed. Scott Calhoun (Toronto: Scarecrow Press, 2012), 70.

38. Endrinal, "Vocal Layering as Deconstruction," 68–74.

39. Endrinal, "Vocal Layering as Deconstruction," 74–82.

40. U2 fanatics will recognize the nod here toward the song entitled "The Ground Beneath Her Feet" (a bonus track on *All That You Can't Leave Behind* after appearing on the soundtrack to the film *The Million Dollar Hotel*), while a more literary crowd is likely to recognize Salman Rushdie's 1999 novel of the same name. In fact, Rushdie co-wrote the lyrics to the song with U2 after the release of his novel, and he has made appearances with the band in music videos as well as in live performances. See *The Ground Beneath Her Feet* (New York: Henry Holt, 1999).

41. Barad, *Meeting the Universe Halfway,* 152; emphasis in original.

Chapter 15

Reprogramming Rhetoric

Toward a Diffractive Epistemology of Computer Composition

Sean McCullough

In July 2018, I asked my first (and only) question on Stack Overflow (SO),[1] a popular question and answer forum related to programming. SO is one of many Stack Exchange sites where users pose, answer, and comment on questions related to topics ranging from academia to statistics. Despite clearly stating my problem, providing error reports, and selecting helpful bits of code to contextualize my issue, I received only one answer and two comments. As a user who typically queries Google first about programming quandaries and then navigates to a few of the SO links that Google returns, I know that my question, with the limited interaction it generated, not only failed to help me but also failed to help others. Many SO users, in fact, just look at questions others have asked to find solutions to issues they run across when working on programs.[2] So a question like mine, that does not have adequate answers, feels incomplete in the ways that typical SO users define and interact with questions.

My question pales in comparison to other questions on SO not simply because it does not serve the purposes typical users expect from it though; it also fails to meet the criteria SO uses to define their questions. Through examining and querying SO's Application Programming Interface (API), I have learned that (successful) questions involve much more than clearly defined, researched problems and illuminating code examples.[3] Figure 15.1 highlights some of the forty-three metadata fields SO includes as part of their definition of a question on their site.

When a user submits a question to SO, their software associates a variety of user-submitted and program-generated features with that question in accordance with properties they have determined all questions must have.

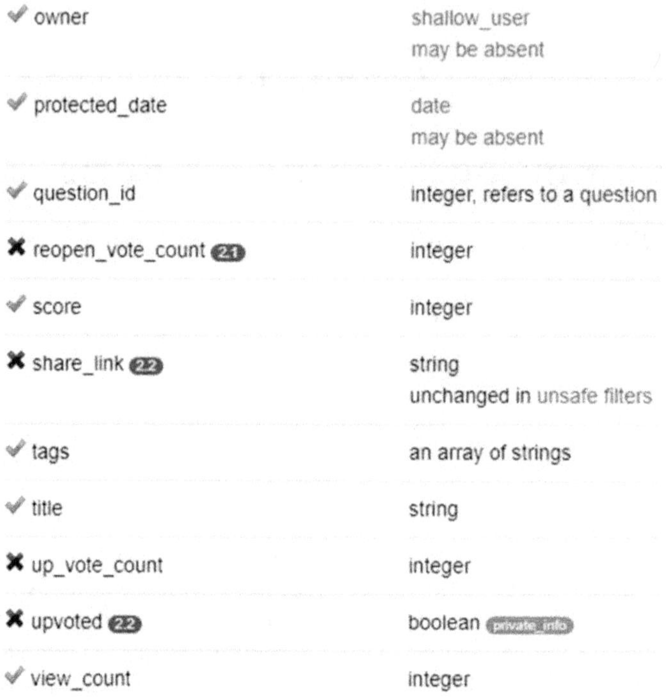

✔ owner	shallow_user may be absent
✔ protected_date	date may be absent
✔ question_id	integer, refers to a question
✘ reopen_vote_count (2.1)	integer
✔ score	integer
✘ share_link (2.2)	string unchanged in unsafe filters
✔ tags	an array of strings
✔ title	string
✘ up_vote_count	integer
✘ upvoted (2.2)	boolean (private_info)
✔ view_count	integer

Figure 15.1 A Subset of Metadata Fields Associated with the Question Object as Defined in SO's API Documentation. See Stack Exchange's API documentation for the Question object, https://api.stackexchange.com/docs/types/question.

A question is, thus, more than its textual features (title and body text); it is also its "tags," "score," "view_count," "up_vote_count," among other things. These metadata features, which are largely hidden from normal users, impact the success of users' questions—just as their textual features do.

Much work addressing technology's impacts on human thought and expression has appeared in English studies disciplines and areas of specialization. Scholars in New Media Studies, Digital Humanities, and New Materialisms have all addressed in some way how computers have altered literate activities. However, as Kevin Brock notes, "[S]uch discussions infrequently focus directly on the software used for particular media and even less frequently on the code that drives that software."[4] A lack of attention to the code that supports software applications and communication on new media platforms elides a key piece of the rhetorical situation that writing and writ*ers* encounter and negotiate in computer composition spaces. Regarding SO, attending to code (within users' questions and that one can glean from SO's object models[5]) illuminates the ways that code, writing, and social media platforms *as* coded programs recursively define and redefine one another.

Rhetoric in a space like SO emerges as a material entanglement, writing *through* programming. Rhetoric cannot be understood apart from its relationship to/within code, discourse, and software. Rhetoric in this space is a diffraction pattern: like ripples that collide in a lake, understanding the relationship between the different rhetorical materials on SO involves reading elements of each "through one another in attending to and responding to the details and specificities of relations of difference and how they matter."[6] By employing Barad's understanding of diffraction as an epistemological tool for viewing these colliding, interacting, and intersecting elements in "dynamic relationality to [one another], being attentive to the iterative production of boundaries, the material-discursive nature of boundary-drawing practices,"[7] I contribute to ongoing discussions of code and/as writing. Ultimately, I claim that viewing rhetoric as it appears in SO's material entanglements *as* a diffraction pattern encourages greater accountability for boundary-drawing practices—particularly between writing and programming. Such an offering is especially significant as more scholars in humanities disciplines continue to analyze software applications and algorithms. My hope is that this research shifts conversations away from attempts to study how programmers, their code, and users argue *separately* in these spaces and moves those discussions toward how rhetorical arguments emerge through their messy collaboration.

In regard to the proposed path of the argument of this essay, forwarding a diffractive reading of rhetoric on SO involves, first, recognizing *as* diffraction patterns the research scholars in humanities and STEM fields have already contributed in their examinations of writing and programming in tandem. Second, such an endeavor also entails demonstrating the ways that those extant patterns "illuminat[e] the indefinite nature of boundaries"[8] scholars establish between writing and programming. Finally, in my reading of rhetorical arguments made through programming on (and *in*) SO, I offer creative reconfigurings of writing and programming that ask us to consider these communicative tasks *through* one another. Specifically, I use programming myself in this study as a tool for querying and understanding SO's object models and data, gathering question and answer metadata features with a Python script. In this study, I analyze SO questions (n = 348,461) sampled from the same three-month period—July to November—over nine years (2009–2018).[9] Using R for data manipulation and analysis, I explore how the code I write interacts with code, discourse, and SO software features to lead to insights about rhetoric that do not fall neatly into categories about writing or programming.

GOD HAS ALREADY BEEN PLAYING DICE: RHETORICAL PROGRAMMING/ PROGRAMMING RHETORIC

Before addressing the ways that scholars have already been reading writing and programming diffractively, I find it helpful to explain how I and others define programming, especially considering that I plan to renegotiate programming's boundaries through my diffractive reading of SO. Programming is one of several terms used to describe the act of communicating to a machine tasks for it to execute: coding, scripting, engineering, designing, and even computer science are often used in place of or in contradistinction to it.[10] In the context of this chapter, I should note that I only deal with high-level programming: languages like Python and R. When a computer runs a Python script, for example, it uses a Python interpreter to convert Python code into machine code. Languages like Python are developed and maintained to make programming more legible for human programmers. Writing in Python, thus, resembles more closely writing in a human language. Words like "for," "in," and "if" are all part of Python's lexicon, and they have meanings for programmers and programs that relate to their English language usage. The SO data I analyze specifically pertains to Python and, therefore, exists for users and most of its developers in the high-level programming space. This fact matters for the ways that users' writing and code and SO's software files engage (or do not appear to engage) with the materiality of the code and technology that support these interactions.

Regarding high-level programming languages, scholars in STEM and humanities fields alike have offered definitions and contextual details that help to explain programming's connection to other forms of human expression and to complicate presumed boundaries. Bjarne Stroustrup, in *Programming: Principles and Practice Using C++*, defines programming as "the design and implementation of programs."[11] Similarly, in her attempt to define programming as a literacy, Annette Vee adumbrates programming's complicated relationship to art and (computer) science: "Programming only emerged as a dominant term in the 1950s," and, because of its "origins with women computers in World War II," it was seen as "the dirty, practical, hands-on work with computers" and "had gained a reputation as an artistic, thoroughly unscientific practice."[12] In our current moment, Vee explains how programming (or, coding as she prefers to call it), because of its perceived use and benefit for an increasing number of industries, has become a literacy, a "cipher for the kind of knowledge a society values."[13] Configured in this way, power differentials have come into play that privilege certain users, bodies, over others. SO reflects much of the material effects of power, serving as a particularly unwelcoming space for groups marginalized in the computer world.[14] While much discussion of programming on SO certainly pertains to Stroustrup's more practical definition, the material entanglements of users, code, program files, and bodies and identities makes programming much more than "the design and implementation of programs."

Diffraction, then, particularly as Barad configures it, becomes a useful tool for cultivating accountability to the boundaries I and other scholars are prone to draw between acts like programming and writing. Much early work exploring connections between the two literate acts emphasizes similarities, moments of amplification between writing and programming. In "Writing and Programming," Thomas Newkirk describes an "Aha!" moment he experienced when overhearing a conversation among computer scientists with whom he carpooled to his university:

> A well written program had the characteristics of good writing. . . . A good program is readable. It proceeds in clearly defined units. It is economical and avoids unnecessary and circuitous steps. Did programmers consider their audience? Of course. . . . Do different programmers have their own "writing" style? Again, the answer was yes.[15]

From the computer science professors' discussion, Newkirk gleaned that knowledge about writing could contribute to knowledge about programming—and vice versa. Similarly, Nancy Hoar examines "data classification and matching" patterns unique to FORTRAN's syntax as a metaphor for helping engineering students to recognize how written sentences categorize and organize data of their own.[16] On SO, users write a hybrid script that meshes human language with code to express their question clearly and to argue for the significance of their topic. Conversations such as those Newkirk and Hoar engage in can be helpful for identifying how rhetoric can be deployed through both writing and programming; however, it is important to remember that no two programming languages are exactly alike and that the systems that support online communication, such as SO, have logics that interfere with users' code and writing in positive and negative ways. Engagement with rhetoric's entanglement within all of these material-discursive systems resists reduction of programming into writing's terms and vice versa.

It can certainly be helpful to apply rhetorical theories to programming practices and situations, as scholars like Robert E. Cummings, Colin Brooke, and Kevin Brock do—Cummings employing the rhetorical triangle,[17] Brooke revisiting rhetoric's five canons in the age of digital technology and new media authoring,[18] and Brock reading programming through the *progymnasmata*.[19] However, much like adapting scientific terms such as diffraction to explore interdisciplinary phenomena, applying theories related to particular modes of human expression to others can run the risk of obviating material manifestations of difference between the elements one compares. For example, as Gerald M. Phillips and Bradley E. Erlwein discover, adapting Kenneth Burke's dramatistic pentad as a heuristic tool for a computer program to "produce a composition" illuminates practically how such creative borrowings can break down: their program's use of Burke's pentad becomes too formulaic, and the computer does not effectively grasp context when composing its arguments.[20] This example is not meant to discourage scholars from conceptualizing rhetoric through the many symbol systems it makes use of and connects; rather, it simply demonstrates the importance of cultivating a Baradian accountability toward boundary-drawing practices.

Cultivating a Baradian accountability, moreover, especially in a time when human materials continue to be "datafied," involves recognizing the already entangled states of writing and programming within networked media and software applications, which I claim becomes apparent when one observes how SO's software and its users negotiate and renegotiate the ways they define communicative objects such as questions. This project, with its emphasis on how SO users construct arguments through discourse and code that is entangled with systems SO programmers develop, employs diffraction as a means of rearticulating the material manifestations of rhetoric within writing *and* programming on this space. Because part of this work involves observing and analyzing computer software, I turn to more recent scholarship in digital humanities and the emerging discipline of rhetorical code studies that has been working to position programming as a necessary area of study for humanists. For Brock, who echoes many other scholars of programming and writing such as Vee, research on the rhetorical aspects of code has been slow and infrequent: "Unfortunately . . . conversations on digital media . . . tend to focus on software as an instrumental tool and thus ignore or otherwise fail to address the role that meaning making, and in particular meaning made in and around code plays in the development and use of software."[21] Similarly, lacking, Brock claims, are conversation and theorization among professional programmers about the meaningful qualities of the code texts they author; however, these professionals "rarely engage in substantive discussion thereof, partly because of a lack of engagement with a humanistic (and specifically rhetorical) vocabulary."[22] The answer is not as simple as cultivating a more technologically rich vocabulary among humanities scholars and similarly enticing programmers to develop a humanistic lens: code is always already an entanglement of material-virtual and humanistic-mechanistic concerns, which is why I argue for a diffractive reading of rhetoric within SO questions' entangled materiality.[23]

Moreover, I analyze SO artifacts through a bundle of computational spaces—a Python script I authored in which I had to figure out how to connect to and converse with SO's API to obtain the communication objects I sought; an Amazon Web Services Lambda Function that executes my Python script on a schedule every day; MongoDB, a cloud database that leverages JavaScript Object Notation to make storage of data simple; and R Studio, an interactive development environment where I manipulate and analyze my medium-sized dataset. Beyond aiding my literal reading and understanding of SO questions, engaging with these various technologies also facilitates my diffractive reading: my reading of SO's API and their data models are filtered through their entanglement with my code and with my own experiences with searching and asking SO questions (some of which I asked to aid in the production of the code used in this analysis).

Many scholars are already doing this type of work, particularly in their analyses of popular internet algorithms that tend to manipulate user-submitted text and other compositional artifacts (such as image and video). Safiya Noble, for example, studies the manner in which Google's page rank algorithm makes discriminatory associations between content and search terms based on race, sexuality, ethnicity, and other factors, identifying "several cases that demonstrate how racism and sexism are part of the architecture and language of technology."[24] Such a careful process of reverse-engineering Google's algorithms by examining the results that appear after a given search brings Google's programs and their developers to the fore, highlighting their material entanglement with users and their material-virtual digital "footprints." "By interacting with computational artifacts," such as Google's search algorithms, James J. Brown, Jr. affirms, "we get a 'feel for the algorithm' at work" and "the machine learns from (and, for Hayles, thinks about) our interventions."[25] Diffraction, as a phenomenon whose outcomes can only ever be modeled probabilistically,[26] helps to differentiate my reading from Noble's and Brown, Jr.'s. Whereas Noble and Brown, Jr. draw clearer boundaries between rhetoric as it emerges within software and from human interaction,[27] my reading demonstrates diffraction's affordances for revealing rhetoric through writing and programming on SO as a phenomenon that was never writing *or* programming, but always writing *and* programming—and also so much more.

QUERYING THE API AS RHETORICAL INQUIRY

When I posed my question to the SO community, I was working under the assumption that clarity of thought and ample code would suffice to secure myself the help I needed. Like many users, I believed that these features were all that a successful question comprised. It was not until I began querying SO's API with a Python script that I began to realize how different many users' definitions of a question are from how SO chooses to define them in their software files. As mentioned, SO associates forty-three metadata features with a question, a question's title, and body text accounting for just two of these properties. Perhaps the two most intriguing metadata elements used to define each SO question though are the "answers" and the "is_answered" fields, which help to define the relationship between questions and answers and how SO displays them to users. In SO's code, Question and Answer classes define how questions and answers will be constructed on their site (i.e., with metadata fields significant to each class). However, because of the way that SO displays questions and answers, on a single page rendered with a unique hypertext link to a specific question, SO's class files for questions and answers invoke one another in their definitions. Thus, the Question class definition contains a field meant to store answers ("answers") that users have submitted in response to a given question. When a user first submits a question, no answers will be found, and the question will emerge with an empty array, a data type with the *potential* to contain one or more answer objects, and an "is_answered" field that, after iterating over the empty list of answers to determine if any of them have been upvoted,[28] evaluates to the default value "False."

Thus, all SO question objects are initially defined as having no answers and being declared unanswered, but these metadata fields are *expected*—by SO's software and its users—to eventually change. While SO certainly suggests that a question can exist without answers (in fact, 12% in this dataset do), moreover, by initially assigning each question an empty array of answer objects, SO *argues* that the standard for questions is to include one or more answers. This argument is made more explicit and apparent when one navigates to a question page that contains no answers. The page states, "Know someone who can answer? Share a link to this question via email, Twitter, or Facebook."[29] Moreover, regardless of whether a page has answers or not, each question's page ends with a space for users to provide their answer, if they so choose. While not seemingly directly coercive, such invitational components, in and of themselves, are rhetorical. Applying Derrida's concept of the "Law of Hospitality" to networked environments, James J. Brown, Jr. suggests that software applications invite and exclude users and uses through enacting "ethical programs," rhetorical procedures for responding to deficiencies in the Law of Hospitality. In general computer use, Brown, Jr. explains, "The Law will always invite packets of information, in whatever form, whether they follow procedure or not. The laws of hospitality must draw lines and sort through what should or should not be allowed to pass."[30] In SO's case, their software always invites one or more answer to questions. The software prepares for each Question object to host multiple answers. However, SO also incorporates ethical programs to determine whether or not any of the answers provided can truly be considered answers. Users, moreover, play a significant role in this determination: Their upvotes decide when a Question object's "is_answered" property becomes "True." In this situation, SO argues, first, that they desire for users to submit multiple answers to questions and, second, that those answers need some filtration mechanism that aid their software and their users in discerning the status of those answers as answers and in determining whether or not the question the original user asked has been adequately answered.

Intriguingly, SO's mechanism for determining whether or not a question has been answered can involve the original poster, but it does not have to. In my case, someone else upvoted the sole answer to my question; I did not perceive the given answer as helpful for the problem I was facing at the time. According to SO's software, though, my question has an answer, and, because that answer was upvoted by someone in the SO community, my question has been adequately answered. While many users may not necessarily be aware of this dynamic, such a determination made automatically by SO's software, without necessarily obtaining an original poster's agreement or consent, bears significantly on the ways other users perceive such questions. Regarding the 348,461 questions in the dataset I collected, 76 percent (263,551) record a "True" value for their "is_answered" field. Of these questions, 81 percent (214,121) have a first answer with a score greater than zero, meaning that their first answer is deemed sufficient for SO considering their question answered.

Practically, it would be difficult to argue that a correlation exists between questions' first answers scoring greater than zero and the presence or absence of more answers. However, this dataset certainly suggests that some diffraction pattern emerging from the collision of users' discourse, code, and visual reading of scores attributed to answers and the arguments SO's software source code makes for classifying questions as answered (and answers as answers) exerts some rhetorical force over users regarding how they define questions, answers, and whether or not a question has been answered. For example, it is interesting that 48 percent (125,267) of questions recording "True" for "is_answered" (n = 263,551) have more than one answer; however, when those questions' first answer happens to have a score greater than zero (enough to classify the question as answered according to SO), this percentage drops to 36 percent (95,753).[31] Even more astounding is that, of all the questions that record "True" for "is_answered," only 19 percent (49,416) have an answer other than the first one provided that leads SO to define that question as answered, and, of these questions, those having more than two answers comprise just 5 percent (12,694) of all questions SO's software considers answered. At least in terms of the dataset I analyze, it would appear that the presence of an answer (that is considered an answer) not only alters the status of a question for SO's software files but for users as well.

At first appearance, the data suggest a marginal inverse relationship between the presence of an "adequate" answer and users' continued engagement with a question: more often than not, questions that receive an adequate answer do not receive more answers. However, figure 15.2, a violin plot of the probability density of the amount of times that a question was viewed, reveals that, although engagement may not take the form of more contributed answers, it can take the shape of a disproportionate distribution of views. The graph positions the probability density of raw number of views for a given question whose first answer "answers" the question ("First") along a wide range of values—high values as well. Conversely, questions whose first answer does not provide a sufficient answer experience view counts probabilistically distributed along a much narrower range of values—lower ones, too. At least on the surface, then, it appears that questions whose first answer SO's users and software consider an answer (signified through a user upvote) are far more likely to be viewed than those whose first answer does not appear to be very good. While a point of uncertainty in search engine optimization marketing conversations, many experts believe that dwell time, the amount of time a user spends on a given search query's results page before heading back to that same list of results, likely factors in some way into the results that appear for given searches. Qi Guo and Eugene Agichtein assert that "page *dwell time* . . . has been proposed as a measure of intrinsic document relevance" and "ha[s] been successfully adapted by the major search engines."[32] Dwell time, along with other search metrics, may offer some explanation as to why questions whose first answer users and SO's software define as an answer receive more

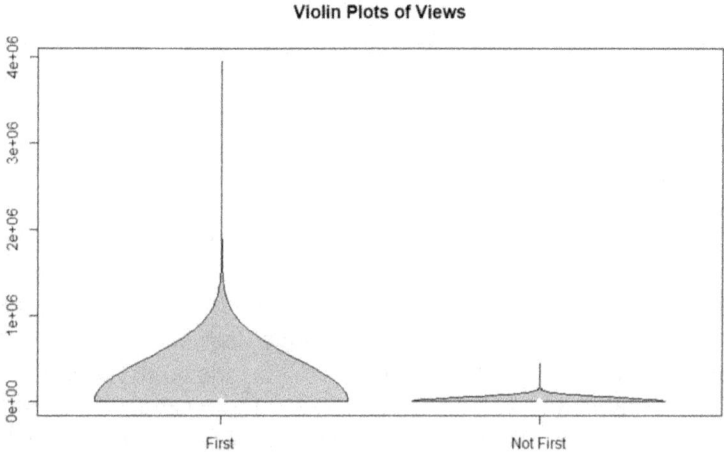

Figure 15.2 Violin Plot of Probability Density of View Count Data from Questions with First Answer vs. Not First.

views: users may be staying on such pages longer than those with weaker first answers, and search engines may be ranking these pages higher, leading to greater numbers of views.[33] Such a finding not only gives insight into how SO's software's metadata and associated functions interact with users, but it also serves to remind readers and users of SO's other function: an archive of programming knowledge that code composers reference through various internet searches. To "read" SO diffractively, then, one must keep track of many intersecting purposes, points of access, and terms of engagement.

Despite the fact that SO's mechanism for defining questions as answered or unanswered appears to collide with users' reading of questions and answers and their own use of code and discourse on SO in a manner that negatively impacts their potential for continued engagement with questions, there may be some "shadows in 'light' regions and bright spots in 'dark' regions"[34] that help to explain why questions that SO deems unanswered seem to persuade users to interact even less than with those they deem to be answered. Among the advice that SO site administrators offer for those seeking to ask questions that will receive helpful responses from other SO members is information pertaining to the use of code in conjunction with more traditional written discourse. In "How do I ask a good question?," the author asserts that, while "not all questions benefit from including code," including some can help, especially if one's "problem is *with* code [they've] written."[35] Regarding how to most effectively make use of code to help contextualize one's question, SO suggests creating a "minimal, reproducible example,"[36] which often entails providing blocks and snippets of code, rather than a whole file. SO's help pages offer a list of "dos and don'ts" for using code when asking a question.

While use of code is marked in a question's "body" metadata field by HTML-like code tags (<code>def foo():</code>), SO's software source code does not necessarily capture inclusion of code within the metadata that developers and administrators argue define a question. Moreover, from analyzing code usage among questions that (A) have answers and SO considers answered, (B) have answers and SO considers unanswered, and (C) have no answers, the raw amount of text characters comprising code in question body text does not serve to differentiate "successful" and "unsuccessful" questions. The first category of questions records a mean (μ) amount of code characters per question of 559 with an amount of characters per question ranging from 0 to 31,718, with outliers emerging with questions that employ 3,709 or more characters of code ($\sigma = 1{,}050$). Similarly, questions that have answers but that SO considers unanswered observe a mean amount of code characters per question of 709, with a range of 0 to 31,970 and outliers existing among questions having 4,576 or more characters of code ($\sigma = 1{,}289$). Finally, questions with no answers employ a mean value of 805 code characters per question, with a range of 0 to 30,769 and outliers occurring in questions containing 5,191 or more characters of code ($\sigma = 1,462$). Significantly, all three categories of questions record a mean percentage of question body text comprising code characters between 44 percent and 46 percent.

Contrary to what some SO users and moderators say, then, simply using code does not appear to correlate to whether or not a question is sufficiently answered according to SO. To ascertain how code users employ interacts with the ways SO's software source code and other users interpret and define their questions, it becomes necessary to determine how code is used to convey the types of problems users wish to address. Reading code at a macro scale is a difficult task. Unlike human language, frequency of words does not necessarily reveal much about particular coding preferences or styles. However, because all code used is written in Python, tailoring a tokenization script to coding conventions typical of Python can help.[37] I tokenized code fragments by bigrams, n-gram units of text with n equaling 2 (ex. "I went," "went to," "to the," "the store"). I then filtered for bigrams starting with "import," a common feature of Python code at the beginnings of files where users declare what packages they will be using in their code.[38] I also filtered for bigrams starting with "class" or "def," two terms Python users employ to denote classes and functions they are defining in their code. When asking a question on SO pertaining to a particular package, moreover, including import statements can help other users to determine if issues questioners encounter may be emerging from how they are importing the packages they use. Class and function declarations can also tell readers the types of objects and methods users are creating and performing. Below (Figure 15.3) is a comparison of the import statements used among the three categories of questions I have defined through SO's software's criteria in their question object model (class and function definitions did not return significant differences):

While each category of question pertains to similar tools (time, sys, requests, re, pandas, os, numpy, matplotlib.pyplot, datetime), there is one noticeable difference. Questions that have answers (A and B) attend to the beautifulsoup package to a greater degree than those that contain no answers (C). Beautifulsoup is a Python package that aids with web scraping, which is becoming an increasingly popular practice as programmers of all skills look to build complex datasets from internet sites and platforms for analysis. The emergence of this one difference between the package import statements and, thus, the types of programs that users write is helpful, but the presence of many similarities across question categories suggests that the rhetorical inclusions (questions receiving answers and, even, helpful ones) and exclusions (questions receiving no answers or a few unhelpful ones) can be attributed to a greater degree to the diffraction patterns that manifest from the many elements of writing and programming on SO.

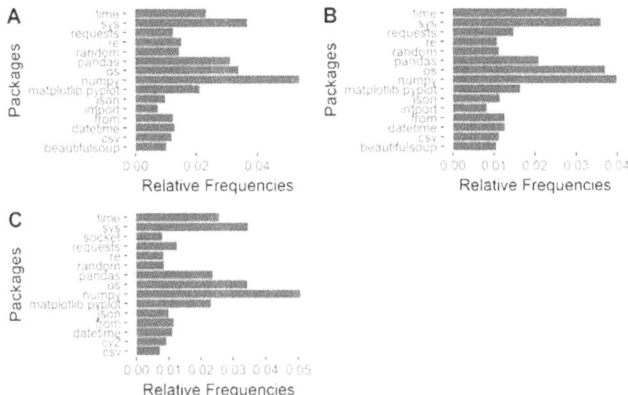

Figure 15.3 Top 15 Package Import Statements Across Each Question Category Measured in Relative Frequencies.

For example, package import statements also correspond to an important metadata field users provide when submitting their questions to SO, that is, "tags." Users provide an array of one or more "tags" to let others in the SO community know what specific technologies related to Python they are engaging with. Tags are an interesting metadata field because, when a user adds a tag to their question, they do so by beginning to type a name for the tag into a search bar and then selecting SO's suggested tag that purportedly best fits their query. Tags are thus a product of collaboration between SO's software, which expands its knowledge of common tags used every time a new user submits a question, and the user. Reducing the topic of a question to a few descriptive tags, however, is a difficult task and can lead to confusion about the question asked, and code used does not always neatly fall into the selected tags. For example, comparing figure 15.3 to figure 15.4, a visualization of the top fifteen tags users choose to categorize their questions, one can notice some crossover, but also some striking dissimilarity:

While questions that have answers and that SO considers to be answered (A) contain many tags that correspond to popular import statements used, a few tags, such as "list," "dictionary," "dataframe," and "arrays," refer to common programming data structures.[39] Actually, regarding just this category (A), users have picked tags that are not necessarily package specific, but that correspond to more general concepts related to Python (and programming in general) that can pose challenges in programs that pertain to flask, django, pandas, or numpy, for instance. Such a phenomenon may in fact be one factor contributing to these questions' success.

Thus far, I have resisted engaging in close reading any SO questions for fear of appearing to "verify" observations made during the quantitative phase

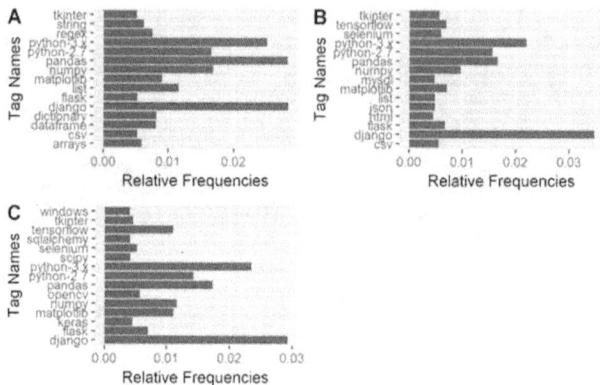

Figure 15.4 Top 15 Selected Tags Across Each Question Category Measured in Relative Frequencies.

of the analysis.[40] Moreover, recognizing this dynamic, I proceed to make observations at a reduced scale briefly and with caution. Identifying one question that interacts interestingly with the categories of questions I have defined according to my own and my quantitative scripts' distant reading with SO, I demonstrate how close and distant findings intersect, diffractively exposing and drawing new boundaries between themselves as they exist in this study.

Regarding the first category of questions, those that have answers and that SO's software considers answered (like the one I posed in July 2018), I decided to choose a question that is an outlier, one that has forty-four answers. As a result of what I have learned in the process of reading rhetoric in and around SO through a variety of technological and material networks, I understand such a question to best exemplify elements of the diffractive reading that I have been trying to demonstrate. The question is simple: "I'm trying to install TensorFlow using pip," the author writes, including one code block detailing the command line error they receive before asking, "What am I doing wrong? So far I've used Python and pip with no issues."[41] This question, earned 470 upvotes ($\mu = 3.7$, $\sigma = 24.9$), 119 favorites ($\mu = 1$, $\sigma = 7.5$), and 522,414 views ($\mu = 3,789.2$, $\sigma = 29,857.4$) on SO. It has forty-four answers, many of which have been upvoted more than ten times. Thus, this question seems to invalidate many of the quantitative relationships observed earlier about SO questions and the ways that SO's classification schemes seem to interact with users and their communication. Apart from perhaps using too much code (159 characters out of 253 consist of code commands, accounting for 63% of the body text) and having a first answer that allows it to be considered answered, this question has attracted plenty of good answers. What does the existence of this anomalous question mean in relation to the diffractive reading of SO questions' rhetorical programs that has been emerging? How did it "slip through" the protocols (vis-à-vis Brown Jr.'s *Ethical Programs*) SO, its users, its code, their code, their writing, and my programs and questions seem to construct?

One conjecture I have aligns with observations made at a larger scale about tag usage. TensorFlow is a popular tag across all categories of questions on SO pertaining to Python. Unlike many questions about TensorFlow implementations, moreover, this SO user's question does not pertain to anything else about Python or programming: only to how to install TensorFlow for use in Python applications. This question is, therefore, purely about something SO data at a large scale demonstrate to be popular already. The question was also asked on August 11, 2016, six months after TensorFlow's initial release. Thus, although this question does not appear to behave as most successful SO questions do, there are contextual details surrounding the manner in which and when it was asked that contribute to its unprecedented attention. Moreover, one SO protocol that users notice and address primarily at the "close reading" level is the existence of duplicate questions. The rhetorical concept of "kairos" may, therefore, play a role in the success of this question: TensorFlow has received many updates and bug patches since its initial release, so a question about how to install the package in a particular language will continue to accrue purchase as new releases come out and new and current TensorFlow users need to figure out how and which versions to install. While many similar questions about installing popular packages like TensorFlow will appear on SO and achieve varying amounts of success, it appears that the ones that do well will not necessarily do so because of anything questioners have done "right" according to SO's administrators' and its community members' standards. Rather, timing may play a role here, as new package updates and releases bring system compatibility headaches for a large number of users at a particular moment.[42] Essentially, this particular question—and, although it is a statistical outlier, there are many such like it on SO—is successful for reasons that require adjustments to observations made about how SO, users, and a variety of programs and coded passages produce a diffractive rhetoric. Significantly, the observations made in close reading neither necessarily support nor refute those made in the distant reading stage, but instead require reconfigurations concerning results and the boundaries I and others draw between the methods themselves.

TOWARD A DIFFRACTIVE EPISTEMOLOGY: FINDINGS AND LIMITATIONS

Examining statements users make in and around code, how those material-discursive elements interact and intersect with SO's software source code, and how my own Python and R programming—as the apparatuses through which I am viewing these entanglements—purport to construct and measure differences leads to a reading of rhetoric as writing *through* programming that only ever manifests in/as this particular collaboration. Such a phenomenon does not diminish the "results" of this analysis; rather, it points to the necessity to continue to challenge one's impulse to isolate writing and programming tasks. In our current historical moment, the two communicative acts are inextricably bound, and working through their entanglement entails moving beyond simply applying theories of writing to programming and vice versa.

While using a Python program to query SO's API helps me gain a better understanding of SO's software source code, I should note that much uncertainty regarding SO's programmed arguments still abounds. Part of this uncertainty is a result of limits companies like SO place on programmers who wish to access their data, but a large portion also stems from my choice to use Python. I would not say that I now *know* the rhetoric of SO's software source code; rather, I know *a* rhetoric *through* my Python program's and SO's source code's entanglement. Were I to have chosen Node.JS as my querying language, I would adjust my characterization of my understanding of rhetoric in this space accordingly. My assessment is still helpful for parsing SO's software's role in influencing the rhetoric of questions and answers on their site, but I assert that it is more helpful for alerting readers to the dynamic relationality of boundaries and boundary-drawing practices in this networked situation. One cannot simply look at each of the described nodes individually to understand how rhetoric moves within SO: one must examine the intersections, the intra-actions, which is what makes diffraction such a valuable theoretical framework for this study.

NOTES

1. Hereafter, referred to in text as (SO).
2. A 2013 study, for example, reveals that only 25 percent of SO users ask more than one question. In my dataset, similarly, 34 percent of users ask more than one question. Shaowei Wang, David Lo and Lingxiao Jiang, "An Empirical Study on Developer Interactions in StackOverflow" (Paper presented at *SAC '13*: *Proceedings of the 28th Annual ACM Symposium on Applied Computing*, Coimbra, Portugal, March 18–22, 2013, https://doi.org/10.1145/2480362.2480557), 1012–1024.
3. See SO's guide to "How do I ask a good question," Help Desk, Stack Overflow, https://stackoverflow.com/help/how-to-ask.
4. Kevin Brock, *Rhetorical Code Studies* (Ann Arbor: University of Michigan Press, 2017), 3.
5. Object models are blueprints that software programmers establish to define properties and functionalities of recurring entities in a program. As shown in Figure 1 above, SO's software outlines properties and methods unique to the Question class: Each question comes with tags, whose data type SO's software asserts to be an array

of character strings, and each question also interfaces with Question class methods that allow each created question to access, store, edit, and delete associated tags. While appearing to be simply functional, these classificatory schemata are rich with rhetoric—SO makes decisions about what fields belong to the Question class and how elements of its program can access and manipulate those fields' data.

6. Karen Barad, *Meeting the Universe Halfway: Quantum Physics and the Entanglement of Matter and Meaning* (Durham: Duke University Press, 2007), 71.

7. Barad, *Meeting*, 94.

8. Karen Barad, "Posthumanist Performativity: Toward an Understanding of How Matter Comes to Matter," *Signs: Journal of Women in Culture and Society* 28, no. 3 (2003): 803.

9. Because SO questions can receive answers only after they have been submitted, I have excluded the most recent years from the analysis to account for time's role in questions receiving answers.

10. See Annette Vee's discussion of these various terms in "Introduction: Computer Programming as Literacy," in *Coding Literacy: How Computer Programming is Changing Writing* (Cambridge, MA: MIT Press, 2017), 1–42.

11. Bjarne Stroustrup, *Programming: Principles and Practice Using C++*. 2nd ed. (Upper Saddle River: Addison-Wesley, 2014), see especially chapter "0.3 Programming and Computer Science."

12. Vee, "Introduction: Computer Programming as Literacy," 12.

13. Ibid., 2.

14. See Jay Hanlon, "Stack Overflow Isn't Very Welcoming. It's Time for That to Change," *The Overflow* (blog), *Stack Overflow*, April 26, 2018, https://stackoverflow.blog/2018/04/26/stack-overflow-isnt-very-welcoming-its-time-for-that-to-change/.

15. Thomas Newkirk, "Writing and Programming: Two Modes of Composing," *Computers, Reading, and Language Arts* 2, no. 2 (1984): 40.

16. Nancy Hoat, "Conquering the Myth: Expository Writing and Computer Programming," *CCC* 38, no. 1 (1987): 94, https://www.jstor.org/stable/357591 /.

17. Robert E. Cummings, "Coding with Power: Toward a Rhetoric of Computer Coding and Composition," *Computers and Composition* 23, no. 4 (2006): 442.

18. Collin Gifford Brooke, *Lingua Fracta: Toward a Rhetoric of New Media* (Creskill: Hampton Press, 2009).

19. Brock, *Rhetorical Code Studies*, 152.

20. Gerald M. Phillips, and Bradley R. Erlwein. Phillips, Gerald M. and Bradley R. Erlwein. "Composition of the Computer: Simple Systems and Artificial Intelligence," *Communication Quarterly* 36, no. 4 (1988): 250, https://doi.org/10.1080/01463378809369729.

21. Brock, *Rhetorical Code Studies*, 2.

22. Brock, *Rhetorical Code Studies*, 186.

23. In future work, I plan to more thoroughly analyze the relationships between all communication objects (questions, answers, and comments) on SO; however, such work is beyond the scale of the current project.

24. Safiya Noble, *Algorithms of Oppression: How Search Engines Reinforce Racism* (New York: New York University Press, 2018), 10.

25. James J. Brown Jr., "Crossing State Lines: Rhetoric and Software Studies," in *Rhetoric and the Digital Humanities*, ed. Jim Ridolfo and William Hart-Davidson (Chicago: University of Chicago Press, 2015), 22.

26. For an accessible discussion of particle-wave relationships and calculations, see Mark E. Tuckerman's "Electron diffraction, postulates of quantum mechanics, the Bohr model, and the Beer-Lambert law" from his Advanced Chemistry 1 online course text. Because particles exhibit wave and particle behaviors in diffraction, "the outcome of [a] position measurement will not be the same in each realization even if it is performed in the same way . . . Thus, if the result of a position measurement can yield different outcomes, then *the only thing we can predict is the probability that a given measurement of the position yields a particular value. The quantum world is not deterministic but rather intrinsically probabilistic.*"

27. I should note that Noble's indictment of Google's algorithms is a timely rhetorical argument for Google and its developers to attend more carefully to the code they write and the voices and perspectives they allow to have a say in the direction they take with their products. In this case, drawing definitive boundaries between users, algorithms, and other communicative acts (such as textual search input) serves Noble's explicit purpose much more effectively.

28. Rather than declare "is_answered" to be "True" based on the presence of answers provided to a particular question, the method SO employs checks to see if any answers a question may or may not contain have been upvoted. According to Stack Overflow Web Developer m0sa, "[is_answered] is the flag we use for the unanswered tab. It's just named badly. Consider thinking about it as 'hasAnswerWithScoreGreaterThanZero.'" Reply to "The Search parameter isanswered [sic] ignores acceptance," StackExchange, February 25, 2015, https://meta.stackexchange.com/questions/250109/the-search-parameter-isanswered-ignores-acceptances?rq=1

29. See [Debajoy Das], "How to make a coherence Map Listener asynchronous in my Java Application," Stack Overflow, November 16, 2019, https://stackoverflow.com/questions/58892632/how-to-make-a-coherence-map-listener-asynchronous-in-my-java-application.

30. James J. Brown Jr., *Ethical Programs: Hospitality and the Rhetorics of Software* (Ann Arbor: University of Michigan Press, 2015), 10.

31. Of these types of questions, whose first answer SO's software considers sufficient to mark the question "answered" (214,121), moreover, 45 percent (95,753) have multiple answers.

32. Qui Guo and Eugene Agichtein, "Beyond Dwell Time: Estimating Document Relevance from Cursor Movements and other Post-Click Searcher Behavior," *WWW '12: Proceedings of the 21st International Conference on World Wide Web*, Association for Computing Machinery (April 2012): 569, https://doi.org/10.1145/2187836.2187914.

33. Exploring search engines' roles in further complicating the diffractive relationality described in this project is currently being pursued for future work on this topic.

34. Barad, *Meeting*, 93.

35. "How Do I Ask a Good Question?," Stack Overflow, https://stackoverflow.com/help/how-to-ask.

36. "How to create a Minimal, Reproducible, Example," Stack Overflow.

37. In text mining, tokenization refers to the act of determining the units for analysis, be they all individual words contained in a corpus, any form of n-gram (bigrams, trigrams, etc.), or whole sentences or paragraphs.

38. Packages are collections of classes and functions users write and reference within their code. If I create a program that defines a "Student" class, for example, I can import that class into another program file, say a file meant to display all student evaluation information. Moreover, if someone has written and shared a package of code files that can help me display this information in a visually appealing way, I can import that package and use their classes and methods as needed.

39. Data structures offer methods of organizing information into collections of data types (character string, integers, Booleans) that can be accessed in different ways depending on the mode that would be most effective for a given process. For example, arrays, called "lists" in Python, are indexed and ordered data structures. In a given program, it may be most convenient to store a series of temporary values in an indexable structure like an array so that I can access values by their position within the array.

40. See two conflicting theories on how close and distant reading relate to one another. Frontini, Francesca, Mohamed Amine Boukhaled and Jean-Gabriel Ganascia, "Mining for Characterising Patterns in Literature Using Correspondence Analysis: An Experiment on French Novels," *Digital Humanities Quarterly* 11, no. 2 (2017): hal-01527780, https://hal.archives-ouvertes.fr/hal-01527780/document; Andrew Piper, "Novel Devotions: Conversional Reading, Computational Modeling, and the Modern Novel," *New Literary History,* 46, no. 1 (2015): 68.

41. Christos Iraklis Tsatsoulis [desertnaut], "TensorFlow not found using pip." Stack Overflow, February 8, 2019, https://stackoverflow.com/questions/38896424/tensorflow-not-found-using-pip.

42. This phenomenon is being explored in future work on this expanding dataset.

Bibliography

Adams, Stephen J. *Poetic Designs: An Introduction to Meters, Verse Forms and Figures of Speech*. 1979; repr. Peterborough: Broadview Press, 2003.
Adnan, Etel. *Journey to Mount Tamalpais*. Sausalito: The Post-Apollo Press, 1986.
———. "The Cost of Love We Are Not Willing to Pay." In *dOCUMENTA (13)*. Catalogue 1/3, *The Books of Books*, 94–96. Ostfildern: Hatje Cantz, 2012. Exhibition Catalog.
Ahmed, Sara. "Open Forum Imaginary Prohibitions: Some Preliminary Remarks on the Founding Gestures of the 'New Materialism.'" *European Journal of Women's Studies* 15, no. 1 (2008): 23–39.
———. "Some Preliminary Remarks on the Founding Gestures of the 'New Materialism.'" *European Journal of Women's Studies*, 15, no. 1 (2008): 23–39.
Alaimo, Stacey and Susan J. Hekman, eds. *Material Feminisms*. Bloomington: Indiana University Press, 2008.
Althusser, Louis. "The Underground Current of the Materialism of the Encounter." In *Philosophy of the Encounter: Later Writings, 1978–87*, translated by G. M. Goshgarian. London: Verso, 2006.
Andermahr, Sonya. "Both /And Aesthetics: Gender, Art, and Language in Brigid Brophy's *In Transit* and Ali Smith's *How to Be Both*." *Contemporary Women's Writing* 12, no. 2 (July 2018): 248–263. https://doi.org/10.1093/cww/vpy001.
Anderson, Dianna E. *Problematic: How Toxic Callout Culture is Destroying Feminism*. Lincoln: University of Nebraska Press, 2018.
Anker, Elizabeth S. "Postcritical Reading, the Lyric, and Ali Smith's *How to Be Both*." *Diacritics* 45, no. 4 (2017): 16–42. https://doi.org/10.1353/dia.2017.0018.
Anker, Elizabeth S., and Rita Felski, eds. *Critique and Postcritique*. Durham: Duke University Press, 2017.
Apter, Emily. *The Translation Zone*. Princeton: Princeton University Press, 2004.
Aristotle. *On Rhetoric: A Theory of Civic Discourse*. Translated by George Alexander Kennedy. New York: Oxford University Press, 1991.

Askin, Ridvan. *Narrative and Becoming*. Edinburgh: Edinburgh University Press, 2017.

Attridge, Derek. *J.M. Coetzee and the Ethics of Reading: Literature in the Event*. Chicago: University of Chicago Press, 2004.

———. *The Singularity of Literature*. New York: Routledge, 2004.

Attwood, Feona. *Mainstreaming Sex: The Sexualization of Western Culture*. London: I.B. Tauris, 2009.

Avanessian, Armen and Björn Quiring, eds. *Abyssus Intellectualis: Spekulativer Horror*. Berlin: Merve, 2013.

Bad Moms. Directed by Jon Lucas, Scott Moore, STX Entertainment, *Netflix*, 2016.

Barad, Karen. "Diffracting Diffraction: Cutting Together-Apart." In Kaiser and Thiele, *Diffracted Worlds*, 4–23. First published in *Parallax* 20, no. 3 (2014): 168–187. https://doi.org/10.1080/13534645.2014.927623.

———. "Erasers and Erasures: Pinch's Unfortunate 'Uncertainty Principle.'" *Social Studies of Science* 41, no. 3 (2011): 443–454. https://doi.org/10.1177%2F0306312711406317.

———. "Getting Real: Technoscientific Practices and the Materialization of Reality." *Differences: A Journal of Feminist Cultural Studies* 10, no. 2 (1998): 87–128.

———. "'Matter Feels, Converses, Suffers, Desires, Yearns and Remembers': Interview with Karen Barad." In *New Materialism: Interviews & Cartographies*, edited by Rick Dolphijn and Iris van der Tuin, 48–70. Ann Arbor: Open Humanities Press, an imprint of Michigan Publishing, University of Michigan Library, 2012. http://dx.doi.org/10.3998/ohp.11515701.0001.001.

———. "Posthumanist Performativity: Toward an Understanding of How Matter Comes to Matter." *Signs: Journal of Women in Culture and Society* 28, no. 3 (2003): 801–831.

———. "Quantum Entanglements and Hauntological Relations of Inheritance: Dis/continuities, Spacetime Enfoldings, and Justice-to-Come." *Derrida Today* 3, no. 2 (2010): 240–268.

———. "Troubling Time/s and Ecologies of Nothingness: Re-turning, Re-membering, and Facing the Incalculable." *New Formations* 92 (2017): 56–86.

———. "Verschränkungen und Politik: Karen Barad im Gespräch mit Jennifer Sophia Theodor." In *Verschränkungen*, translated by Jennifer Sophia Theodor, 174–212. Berlin: Merve Verlag, 2015.

———. *Meeting the Universe Halfway: Quantum Physics and the Entanglement of Matter and Meaning*. Durham: Duke University Press, 2007.

Barber, Dorothy Elizabeth Klein. "The Structure of *The Lord of the Rings*." PhD diss., University of Michigan, 1965.

Barthes, Roland. "The Death of the Author." Translated by Richard Howard. *Aspen: The Magazin in a Box*, no. 5+6 (Fall-Winter 1967): item 3 (web documentation). http://www.ubu.com/aspen/aspen5and6/threeEssays.html#barthes.

Bataille, George. "Base Materialism and Gnosticism." In *Visions of Excess: Selected Writings, 1927–1939*. Minneapolis: University of Minnesota Press, 1985.

Batens, Diderik, and Jean-Paul van Bendegem, eds. *Theory and Experiment: Recent Insights and New Perspectives on their Relation*. Vol. 195. Dordrecht: Springer, 2012.
Batterman, Robert, ed. *The Oxford Handbook of Philosophy of Physics*. Oxford: Oxford University Press, 2013.
Beck, John. *Writing the Radical Center: William Carlos Williams, John Dewey, and American Cultural Politics*. Albany: State University of New York Press, 2001.
Bell, Peter. "Regent unter dem Himmel: Die Sala dei Mesi des Palazzo Schifanoia in Ferrara als Modell eines astrologischen Weltbildes." In *Weltbilder im Mittelalter: Perceptions of the World in the Middle Ages*, edited by Philipp Billion, Nathanael Busch, Dagmar Schlüter and Xenia Stolzenburg, 1–27. Bonn: Bernstein, 2009. https://doi.org/10.11588/artdok.00002074.
Bennett, Jane. *Vibrant Matter: A Political Ecology of Things*. Durham: Duke University Press, 2010.
Bennett, Michael James. "Deleuze and the Epicurean Philosophy: Atomic Speed and Swerve Speed." *Journal of French and Francophone Philosophy – Revue de la philosophie française et de la langue française* XXI, no. 2 (2013): 131–157.
Bertschik, Julia. "Literatur als Gehäuse der 'nächsten Dinge' im 19. Jahrhundert." In *Magie der Geschichten: Weltverkehr, Literatur und Anthropologie in der zweiten Hälfte des 19. Jahrhunderts*, edited by Michael Neumann und Kerstin Stüssel, 321–347. Constance: Konstanz University Press, 2011.
Best, Stephen and Sharon Marcus. "Surface Reading: An Introduction." *Representations* 108, no. 1 (2009): 1–21.
Binning, G. and H. Rohrer. "Scanning Tunneling Microscopy." *IBM Journal of Research and Development*, n.s., 44, no. 1.2 (2000): 279–93.
Blas, Zach. "Queerness, Openness." In Keller, Masciandaro, and Thacker, *Leper Creativity*, 101–114.
Blumenberg, Hans. *Die Lesbarkeit der Welt*. Frankfurt am Main: Suhrkamp, 1981.
Bock von Wülfingen, Bettina. "Das Genom als Text: Die Schriftmetapher Revisited." *Metaphorik* 26 (2016): 117–153. https://www.metaphorik.de/de/journal/26/das-genom-als-text-die-schriftmetapher-revisited.html.
Borges, Jorge Luis. "El libro de arena." In *Obras Completas*, edited by Carlos Frías, 68–71. Vol. 3, *1975–1985*. Barcelona: Emecé, 2011.
Bozalek, Vivienne and Michalinos Zembylas. "Diffraction or Reflection? Sketching the Contours of Two Methodologies in Educational Research." *International Journal of Qualitative Studies in Education* 30, no. 2 (2017): 111–127.
Braidotti, Rosi and Simone Bingall, eds. *Posthuman Ecologies: Complexity and Process after Deleuze*. London: Rowman and Littlefield International, 2019.
Braidotti, Rosi. "Affirmation versus Vulnerability: On Contemporary Ethical Debates." In *Ethics After Poststructuralism: A Critical Reader*, edited by Lee Olsen, Brendan Johnston, and Ann Keniston, 248–265. Jefferson: McFarland, 2020.
———. *Transpositions on Nomadic Ethics*. Cambridge: Polity, 2012.
Breslin, Ann, and Alex Montwill. *Let There Be Light: The Story of Light from Atoms to Galaxies*. 2nd ed. London: Imperial College Press, 2013.

Breyfogle, Nicholas B. "At the Watershed: 1958 and the Beginnings of Lake Baikal Environmentalism." *Slavonic & East European Review* 93, no. 1 (2015): 147–180.

———. "Sacred Waters: The Spiritual World of Lake Baikal." In *Meanings and Values of Water in Russian Culture*, 48–66. Abingdon, Oxon: Routledge, 2016.

Brock, Kevin. *Rhetorical Code Studies*. Ann Arbor: University of Michigan Press, 2017.

Brooke, Collin Gifford. *Lingua Fracta: Toward a Rhetoric of New Media*. Creskill: Hampton Press, 2009.

Brosch, Renate. "Ekphrasis in Recent Popular Novels: Reaffirming the Power of Art Images." *Poetics Today* 39, no. 2 (June 2018): 403–23. ProQuest.

Brown, James J. Jr. "Crossing State Lines: Rhetoric and Software Studies." In *Rhetoric and the Digital Humanities*, edited by Jim Ridolfo and William Hart-Davidson. 20–32. Chicago: University of Chicago Press, 2015.

———. *Ethical Programs: Hospitality and the Rhetorics of Software*. Ann Arbor: University of Michigan Press, 2015.

Bunz, Mercedes. "Facing Our New Monster: on Critique in the Era of Affirmation." Position Paper for "Terra Critica: Re-visioning the Critical Task of the Humanities in a Globalized World." December 7/8, 2012, Utrecht University.

Butler, Catherine. "Tolkien and Worldbuilding." In *J. R. R. Tolkien: The Hobbit and The Lord of the Rings*." New Casebooks, edited by Peter Hunt, 106–120. New York: Palgrave, 2013.

Campagna, Federico. *Technic and Magic: The Reconstruction of Reality*. London: Bloomsbury Academic, 2018.

Campe, Rüdiger. "Die Schreibszene: Schreiben." In *Paradoxien, Dissonanzen, Zusammenbrüche: Situationen offener Epistemologie*, edited by Hans Ulrich Gumbrecht and Karl Ludwig Pfeiffer, 759–772. Frankfurt am Main: Suhrkamp, 1991.

Canavan, Gerry. "From 'A New Hope' to no hope at all: 'Star Wars,' Tolkien and the Sinister and Depressing Reality of Expanded Universes." *Salon*, December 24, 2015.

Caracciolo, Marco. *The Experientiality of Narrative: An Enactivist Approach*. Berlin: de Gruyter, 2014.

Carpenter, Humphrey and Christopher Tolkien, eds. *The Letters of J. R. R. Tolkien*. Boston: Houghton Mifflin, 2000; London: Allen and Unwin, 1981.

Carpenter, Humphrey. *J. R. R. Tolkien: The Authorized Biography*. Boston: Houghton Mifflin Company, 1977.

Carrington, Damian. "'Extraordinary Thinning' of Ice Sheets Revealed Deep Inside Antarctica." *The Guardian*, May 16, 2019. https://www.theguardian.com/environment/2019/may/16/thinning-of-antarctic-ice-sheets-spreading-inland-rapidly-study.

Caws, Mary Anne. *Reading Frames in Modern Fiction*. Princeton: Princeton University Press, 1985.

Chance, Jane. *Tolkien, Self and Other: "This Queer Creature."* New York: Palgrave, 2016.

Cohany, Sharon R., and Emy Sok. "Trends in Labor Force Participation of Married Mothers of Infants." *Monthly Labor Review* 130 (2007): 9–16.

Coole, Diana H. and Samantha Frost, eds. *New Materialisms: Ontology, Agency, and Politics*. Durham: Duke University Press, 2010.

Coppola, Maria Micaela. "'A whole spectrum of colours new to the eye': Gender Metamorphoses and Identity Frescoes in *Girl Meets Boy* and *How to Be Both* by Ali Smith." *Textus: English Studies in Italy* 28, no. 1 (January-April 2015): 169–185.

Cox, Christoph. *Sonic Flux: Sound, Art, and Metaphysics*. Chicago: University of Chicago Press, 2018.

Cummings, Robert E. "Coding with Power: Toward a Rhetoric of Computer Coding and Composition." *Computers and Composition* 23, no. 4 (2006): 430–443.

Curry, Patrick. *Defending Middle-Earth: Tolkien, Myth and Modernity*. Edinburgh: Floris Books, 1997.

Damrosch, David. *How to Read World Literature?* Hoboken: Wiley-Blackwell, 2008.

de la Cadena, Marisol. *Earth Beings: Ecologies of Practice Across Andean Worlds*. Durham: Duke University Press, 2015.

de Man, Paul. "Autobiography as De-facement." In *The Rhetoric of Romanticism*, 93–123. New York: Columbia University Press, 1984.

DeLanda, Manuel and Graham Harman. *The Rise of Realism*. Cambridge, UK: Polity Press, 2017.

DeLanda, Manuel. *A New Philosophy of Society: Assemblage Theory and Social Complexity*. London: Continuum, 2006.

Deleuze, Gilles and Félix Guattari. *A Thousand Plateaus*. Translated by Brian Massumi. London: Continuum, 2004.

Deleuze, Gilles. "Faces and surfaces." In *Desert Islands and other Texts 1953–1974*, edited by David Lapoujade, translated by Mike Taormina, 281–284. Los Angeles: Semiotext, 2004. Originally published as a booklet by Karl Flinker as *Mélanges: Pouvoir et surface. Avec six surface de Gilles Deleuze*, with illustrations by Gilles Deleuze and Stéfan Czerkinsky, Paris 1973.

———. *Bergsonism*. Translated by Hugh Tomlinson and Barbara Habberjam. New York: Zone Books, 1988.

———. *Difference and Repetition*. Translated by Paul Patton. London: Continuum, 2001.

———. *Différence et Répétition*. Paris: Presses Universitaires de France, 1968.

———. *Logique du Sense*. Paris: Édicion de Minuit, 2005.

———. *Negotiations 1972 – 1990*. Translated by Martin Joughin. New York: Columbia University Press, 1995.

———. *What is Philosophy?* Translated by Hugh Tomilson and Graham Burchell. New York: Columbia University Press, 1991.

Derrida, Jacques. *Dissemination*. Translated, with introduction and notes by Barbara Johnson. London: Athlone, 1981.

———. *Margins of Philosophy*. Chicago: Chicago University Press, 1982.

Deutscher, Penelope. *How to Read Derrida*. London: Granta Books, 2005.

Doherty, Melanie. "Non-Oedipal Networks and the Inorganic Unconcious." In Keller, Masciandaro, and Thacker, *Leper Creativity*, 115–129.

Dolphijn, Rick. "Undercurrents and the Desert(ed): Negarestani, Tournier and Deleuze Map the Polytics of a 'New Earth'." In *Postcolonial Literatures and Deleuze. Colonial Pasts, Differential Futures*, edited Lorna Burns and Birgit M. Kaiser, 199–216. London: Palgrave MacMillan, 2012.

Domínguez, Carlos María. *Casa de Papel*. Montevideo: Ediciones de la Banda Oriental, 2002.

Dorrit, Cohn. "Discordant Narration." *Style* 34, no. 2 (2000): 307–316.

Drout, Michael D.C., ed. *J. R. R. Tolkien Encyclopedia: Scholarship and Critical Assessment*. New York: Routledge, 2007.

Dubrow, Heather. "The Interplay of Narrative and Lyric: Competition, Cooperation, and the Case of the Anticipatory Amalgam." *Narrative* 14, no. 3 (2006): 254–271.

Edenheim, Sara. "On the Material Melancholy of Feminist New Materialism." *Australian Feminist Studies* 31, no. 89 (2016): 283–304.

Edmond, Jacob. "Diffracted Waves and World Literature." In Kaiser and Thiele, *Diffracted Worlds*, 81–93. London: Routledge, 2018. Previously published in *Parallax* 20, no. 3 (2014): 245–257. https://doi.org/10.1080/13534645.2014.927632.

Edwards, Caroline, and Tony Venezia, eds. *China Miéville: Critical Essays*. Canterbury: Gylphi, 2015.

Ekman, Stefan. *Here Be Dragons: Exploring Fantasy Maps and Settings*. Middletown: Wesleyan University Press, 2013.

Endrinal, Christopher. "Vocal Layering as Deconstruction and Reinvention in U2." In *Exploring U2: Essays on the Music, Work, and Influence of U2*, edited by Scott Calhoun, 67–83. Toronto: Scarecrow Press, 2012.

Fergie. "M.I.L.F. $." YouTube Video, uploaded by Fergie, July 1, 2016. https://www.youtube.com/watch?v=bsUWK-fixiA.

Feynman, Richard. *The Character of Physical Law*. Cambridge: MIT Press, 2017.

Fischer-Lichte, Erika. *The Semiotics of the Theater*. Bloomington: Indiana University Press, 1994.

Flieger, Verlyn. "But What Did He Really Mean?" *Tolkien Studies* 11 (2014): 149–166.

———. *A Question of Time: J. R. R. Tolkien's Road to Faërie*. Kent: Kent State University Press, 1997.

———. *Splintered Light: Logos and Language in Tolkien's World*. Rev. ed. London: Kent State University Press, 2002. First published 1983 by William B. Erdmans Publishing.

Fonstad, Karen Wynn. *The Atlas of Middle-Earth*. Rev. ed. Boston: Houghton Mifflin Company, 1991.

Foucault, Michel. "The Confession of the Flesh." A Conversation with Alain Grosrichard, Gerard Wajeman, Jaques-Alain Miller, Guy Le Gaufey, Dominique Celas, Gerard Miller, Catherine Millot, Jocelyne Livi and Judith Miller. In *Power/Knowledge: Selected Interviews and Other Writings 1972–1977*, edited by Colin Gordon, translated by Colin Gordon, Leo Marshall, John Mepham, and Kate Soper, 194–228. New York: Pantheon Books 1980.

———. *Archaeology of Knowledge*. Translated by A. M. Sheridan Smith. London: Routledge, 2004.

Fox Keller, Evelyn. *Refiguring Life: Metaphors of Twentieth-Century Biology.* Columbia: Columbia University Press, 1995.

Frank, Nathan D. "Literary Neutrinos and the Hot Dark Matters of Doctorow's *City of God.*" In *E. L. Doctorow: A Reconsideration*, edited by Michael Wutz and Julian Murphet, 179–203. Edinburgh University Press, January 2020.

———. "The Mind of *Then We Came to the End*: A Transmental Approach to Contemporary Metafiction." In *Explorations of Consciousness in Contemporary Fiction*, edited by Grzegorz Maziarczyk and Joanna Teske, 225–244. Amsterdam: Brill Rodopi, 2017.

Freedman, Carl. *Art and Idea in the Novels of China Miéville.* Canterbury: Gylphi, 2015.

Friebe, Cord, Meinard Kuhlmann, Holger Lyre, Paul M. Näger, Oliver Passon, Manfred Stöckler. *The Philosophy of Quantum Physics.* Translated by William D. Brewer. Cham: Springer, 2018.

Frontini, Francesca, Mohamed Amine Boukhaled and Jean-Gabriel Ganascia. "Mining for Characterising Patterns in Literature Using Correspondence Analysis: An Experiment on French Novels." *Digital Humanities Quarterly* 11, no. 2 (2017): hal-01527780. https://hal.archives-ouvertes.fr/hal-01527780/document.

Gaffigan, Jim. "Mr Universe – 4 Kids." YouTube Video, uploaded by jimgaffigan, 9 Oct. 2012. http://www.youtube.com/watch?v=GEbZrY0G9PI.

Galloway, Alexander R. "What is Hermeneutic Light?" In Keller, Masciandaro, and Thacker, *Leper Creativity:* Cyclonopedia *Symposium*, 159–172. New York: punctum books 2012.

Garner, Benjamin Maxwell. "Far Over the Misty Mountains Cold: An Ecocritical Reading of J. R. R. Tolkien's *The Hobbit.*" Honor Theses, Bucknell University, 2015.

Gasché, Rodolphe. "The Scene of Writing." *Glyph* 1, no. 1 (March 1, 1977): 150–171.

Gelder, Ken, ed. *New Directions in Popular Fiction: Genre, Distribution, Reproduction.* London: Palgrave Macmillan, 2016.

Gelder, Ken. "The Fields of Popular Fiction." In *New Directions in Popular Fiction: Genre, Distribution, Reproduction*, edited by Ken Gelder, 1–19. London: Palgrave Macmillan, 2016.

Gerlich, Stefan, Sandra Eibenberger, Mathias Tomandl, Stefan Nimmrichter, Klaus Hornberger, Paul J. Fagan, Jens Tüxen, Marcel Mayor and Markus Arndt. "Quantum Interference of Large Organic Molecules." *Nature Communications* 2 (2011): 1–5. https://doi.org/10.1038/ncomms1263.

Gibson, Valerie. *Cougar: A Guide for Older Women Dating Younger Men.* New York: Firefly Books, 2002.

Gill, Rosalind. "Postfeminist Media Culture: Elements of a Sensibility." *European Journal of Cultural Studies* 10, no. 2 (2007): 147–166.

———. "Post-Postfeminism? New Feminist Visibilities in Postfeminist Times." *Feminist Media Studies* 16, no. 4 (2016): 610–630.

———. *Gender and the Media.* Cambridge, UK: Polity Press, 2007.

Gillis, Stacey, Gillian Howie, and Rebecca Munford, eds. *Third Wave Feminism: A Critical Exploration.* Basingstoke: Palgrave Macmillan, 2004.

Gillis, Stacy and Rebecca Munford. "Genealogies and Generations: The Politics and Praxis of Third Wave Feminism." *Women's History Review* 13, no. 2 (2004): 165–182.

Golovchenko, J. A. "Tunneling Microscopy." In *Solvay Conference on Surface Science: Invited Lectures and Discussions*, edited by Frederik W. DeWette, 198–215. Berlin: Springer, 1988.

Gómez-Barris, Macarena. *The Extractive Zone: Social Ecologies and Decolonial Perspectives*. Durham: Duke University Press, 2017.

Gratton, Peter. *Speculative Realism: Problems and Prospects*. London: Bloomsbury, 2014.

Grossman, Lev. "Literary Revolution in the Supermarket Aisle: Genre Fiction Is Disruptive Technology." *TIME*, May 23, 2012. http://entertainment.time.com/2012/05/23/genre-fiction-is-disruptive-technology/.

Grosz, Elizabeth. *Time Travels: Feminism, Nature, Power*. Durham: Duke University Press, 2005.

Guattari, Félix. "The Three Ecologies." Translated by Chris Turner. *New Formations*, no. 8 (1989): 131–147.

Guo, Qi and Eugene Agichtein. "Beyond Dwell Time: Estimating Document Relevance from Cursor Movements and other Post-Click Searcher Behavior." *WWW '12: Proceedings of the 21st International Conference on World Wide Web*, Association for Computing Machinery (April 2012): 569–578. https://doi.org/10.1145/2187836.2187914.

Hanlon, Jay. "Stack Overflow Isn't Very Welcoming. It's Time for That to Change." *The Overflow* (blog). Stack Overflow, April 26, 2018. https://stackoverflow.blog/2018/04/26/stack-overflow-isnt-very-welcoming-its-time-for-that-to-change/.

Hansma, Paul K. and Jerry Tersoff. "Scanning Tunneling Microscopy." *Journal of Applied Physics* 61, no. 2 (1987): R1–R24.

Haraway, Donna. *Modest_Witness@Second_Millenium.FemaleMan©_Meets_OncoMouse™: Feminism and Technoscience*. New York: Routledge, 1997.

———. "Modest_Witness@Second_Millennium." In *The Haraway Reader*, 223–250. New York: Routledge, 2004.

———. "Reading Buchi Emecheta: Contests for Women's Experience in Women's Studies." *Women: A Cultural Review* 1, no. 3 (1990): 240–255. https://doi.org/10.1080/09574049008578043.

———. "The Promises of Monsters: A Regenerative Politics for Inappropriate/d Others." In *Cultural Studies*, edited by Lawrence Grossberg, Cary Nelson, and Paula A. Treichler, 295–337. New York; Routledge, 1992.

———. *How Like a Leaf: An Interview with Thryza Nicholas Goodeve*. New York: Routledge, 1998.

———. *Staying with the Trouble: Making Kin in the Chthulucene*. Durham: Duke University Press, 2016.

Harman, Graham. "Agential and Speculative Realism: Remarks On Barad's Ontology." *Rhizomes: Cultural Studies in Emerging Knowledge*, no. 30 (2016): 126–132. https://doi.org/10.20415/rhiz/030.e10.

———. "Meillassoux's Virtual Future." *Continent* 1, no. 2 (2011): 78–91.

———. *The Quadruple Object*. Winchester, UK: Zero Books, 2011.

———. *Weird Realism: Lovecraft and Philosophy*. Winchester: Zero Books, 2012.

Harris, Gareth. "Etel Adnan: 'This is the summit of my career'." *The Art Newspaper*, June 13, 2018. https://www.theartnewspaper.com/interview/etel-adnan-this-is-the-summit-of-my-career.

Hartmann, Johanna, Christine Marks, and Hubert Zapf, eds. *Zones of Focused Ambiguity in Siri Hustvedt's Works: Interdisciplinary Essays*. Berlin: De Gruyter, 2016.

Hawkesworth, Mary. "The Semiotics of Premature Burial: Feminism in a Postfeminist Age." *Signs: Journal of Women in Culture and Society* 29, no. 4 (2004): 961–985.

Hayot, Eric. *On Literary Worlds*. Oxford: Oxford University Press, 2012.

Heidegger, Martin. *Heraklit*, edited by Martin S. Frings. Vol. 55 of *Gesamtausgabe*, edited by Martin S. Frings. Frankfurt am Main: Vittorio Klostermann, 1994.

Heisenberg, Werner. *Physics and Beyond: Encounters and Conversations*. New South Wales: Allen and Unwin, 1971.

Hekman, Susan. "Constructing the Ballast: An Ontology for Feminism." In *Material Feminisms*, ed. Stacey Alaimo and Susan J. Hekman, 85–119. Bloomington: Indiana University Press, 2008.

———. *The Material of Knowledge: Feminist Disclosures*. Bloomington: Indiana University Press, 2010.

Helms, Randel. *Tolkien's World*. London: Thames and Hudson, 1974.

Hemmings, Clare. "Invoking Affect: Cultural Theory and the Ontological Turn." *Cultural Studies* 19, no. 5 (2005): 548–567. https://doi.org/10.1080/09502380500 365473.

———. *Why Stories Matter: The Political Grammar of Feminist Theory*. Durham: Duke University Press, 2011.

Hicks, Dan and Mary C. Beaudry, eds. *The Oxford Handbook of Material Culture Studies*. Oxford: Oxford University Press, 2010.

Hill, Rebecca. "Phallocentrism in Bergson: Life and Matter." In *Deleuze and Gender*, edited by Claire Colebrook and Jami Weinstein, 123–136. Edinburgh: Edinburgh University Press, 2011.

Hinton, Peta and Iris van der Tuin, eds. "Feminist Matters: The Politics of New Materialism." Special issue, *Women: A Cultural Review* 25, no. 1 (2014): 1–122.

Hinton, Peta, and Xin Liu. "The Im/possibility of Abandonment in New Materialist Ontologies." *Australian Feminist Studies* 30, no. 84 (2015): 128–145.

Hoat, Nancy. "Conquering the Myth: Expository Writing and Computer Programming." *CCC* 38, no. 1 (1987): 93–95. https://www.jstor.org/stable/357591 /.

Honegger, Thomas. "More Light than Shadow? Jungian Approaches to Tolkien and the Archetypical Image of the Shadow." *Tolkiendil* (fansite). Last modified April 6, 2020, 16:47. http://www.tolkiendil.com/essais/tolkien_1892–2012/thomas_honegger.

Hornung, Alfred. "*The Shaking Woman* in the Media: Life Writing and Neuroscience." In Hartmann, Marks and Zapf, *Zones of Focused Ambiguity in Siri Hustvedt's Works*, 67–82.

Houellebecq, Michel. *H.P. Lovecraft: Against the World, Against Life*. Translated by Dorna Khazeni. n. p.: Believer Magazine, 2005.
Hume, Angela and Gillian Osborne, eds. *Ecopoetics: Essays in the Field*. Iowa City: University of Iowa Press, 2018.
Hustvedt, Siri. "Philosophy Matters in Brain Matters." In *A Woman Looking at Men Looking At Women*, 473–486. London: Sceptre 2016.
———. "Playing, Wild Thoughts, and A Novel's Underground." In *Living, Thinking, Looking*, 37–41. London: Sceptre, 2012.
———. "The Real Story." In *Living, Thinking, Looking*, 93–115. London: Sceptre, 2012.
———. *A Woman Looking at Men Looking at Women*. London: Sceptre, 2016.
———. *The Blazing World: A Novel*. New York: Simon and Schuster, 2014.
———. *The Shaking Woman or A History of My Nerves*. New York: Henry Holt, 2010.
Hyde, Emily. "Eyes, Camera. Camera, Eyes." *Post45*, October 10, 2015. http://post45.research.yale.edu/2015/11/eyes-camera-camera-eyes/.
———. "Point, Line and Counterpoint: From Environment to Fluid Space." In *Neurobiology of "Umwelt," How Living Beings Perceive the World*, edited by A. Berthoz and Yves Christen, 141–155. Berlin: Springer, 2009.
Iovino, Serenella and Serpil Oppermann, eds. *Material Ecocriticism*. Bloomington: Indiana University Press, 2014.
Irni, Sari. "The Politics of Materiality: Affective Encounters in a Transdisciplinary Debate." *European Journal of Women's Studies* 20, no. 4 (2013): 347–360.
Iser, Wolfang. *The Implied Reader: Patterns of Communication in Prose Fiction from Bunyan to Beckett*. Baltimore: John Hopkins University Press, 2011.
Jansen, Franz Klaus. "Revisiting Quantum Mechanical Weirdness from a Bio-Psychological Perspective." *Philosophy Study* 8, no. 8 (August 2018): 343–354.
Jarvis, Timothy. "The Weird, the Posthuman, and the Abjected World-in-itself: Fidelity to the 'Lovecraft Event' in the Work of Caitlín R. Kiernan and Laird Barron." *Textual Practice* 31, no. 6 (2017): 1133–1148.
Jauss, Hans-Robert. *Toward an Aesthetic of Reception*. Translated by Timothy Bahti. Minneapolis: University of Minnesota Press, 2013.
Johnson, Ryan. "The Theory of Ideas in Ancient Atomism and Gilles Deleuze." PhD diss., Duquesne University, 2013. https://dsc.duq.edu/etd/706/.
Jordanova, Ludmilla J. *Sexual Visions: Images of Gender in Science and Medicine between the Eighteenth and Twentieth Centuries*. Madison: University of Wisconsin Press, 1993.
Jung, Carl Gustav. *Archetypen*. Edited by Lorenz Jung. Munich: Deutscher Taschenburg Verlag, 2001.
Kahn, Charles. *The Art and Thought of Heraclitus: An Edition of the Fragments with Translation and Commentary*. Cambridge: Cambridge University Press, 2001.
Kaiser, Birgit Mara and Kathrin Thiele, eds. *Diffracted Worlds – Diffractive Readings: Onto-Epistemologies and the Critical Humanities*. London: Routledge, 2018.

Kaiser, Birgit Mara and Kathrin Thiele. "Diffraction: Onto-Epistemology, Quantum Physics and the Critical Humanities." *Parallax* 20, no. 3 (2014): 165–167. https://doi.org/10.1080/13534645.2014.927621.

Kaiser, Birgit Mara. "A New German, Singularly Turkish: Reading Emine Sevgi Özdamar with Derrida's *Monolingualism of the Other*." *Textual Practice* 28, no. 6 (2014): 969–987. https://doi.org/10.1080/0950236X.2014.925492.

———. "Worlding CompLit: Diffractive Reading with Barad, Glissant and Nancy." In Kaiser and Thiele, *Diffracted Worlds*, 110–123. London: Routledge, 2018. Previously published in *Parallax* 20, no. 3 (2014): 274–287. https://doi.org/10.1080/13534645.2014.927634.

Kant, Immanuel. *Critique of Pure Reason*. Translated Norman Kemp Smith. Boston: Bedford, 1965.

Kay, Lily E. *Who Wrote the Book of Life? A History of the Genetic Code*. Stanford: Stanford University Press, 2000.

Keller, Daniela. "Germany and Physics in English Fiction after 1960: A Diffractive Reading of Anglo-German Entanglements." PhD diss., University of Basel, 2019.

Keller, Ed, Nicola Masciandaro, and Eugene Thacker, eds. *Leper Creativity: Cyclonopedia Symposium*. New York: punctum books, 2012.

Keller, Evelyn Fox. "Gender and science." In *Discovering Reality: Feminist Perspectives on Epistemology, Metaphysics, Methodology, and Philosophy of Science*, edited by Merrill B. Hintikka and Sandra G. Harding, 187–205. Dordrecht: Springer, 2003.

Kerry, Paul E. *The Ring and the Cross: Christianity and the Lord of the Rings*. Lanham: Fairleigh Dickinson University Press, 2011.

Kirby, Vicki. *Telling Flesh: The Substance of the Corporeal*. New York: Routledge, 1997.

———. *Quantum Anthropologies: Life At Large*. Durham: Duke University Press, 2011.

Kitto, H.D.F. "The Polis." In *The City Reader*, edited by Richard T. LeGates and Frederic Stout, 40–45. London: Routledge, 1996.

Klappert, Annina. *Sand als Metaphorisches Modell für Virtualität*. Berlin: de Gruyter 2020.

Kleinman, Adam. "Intra-actions." *Mousse Magazine* 34, Summer 2012, 76–81.

Kluge, Alexander. "Heraklit der Dunkle." Interview by Oskar Negt. *Ten to Eleven*, Alexander Kluge: Kulturgeschichte im Dialog, April 1, 1996. https://kluge.library.cornell.edu/de/conversations/negt/film/2119.

Kocher, Paul H. *Master of Middle-Earth: The Fiction of J. R. R. Tolkien*. Boston: Houghton Mifflin, 1972.

Korpua, Jyrki. "Constructive Mythopoetics in J. R. R. Tolkien's Legendarium," Phd. diss, University of Oulu Graduate School, 2015. http://jultika.oulu.fi/files/isbn9789526209289.pdf.

Kusek, Robert, and Wojciech Szymański. "Ali Smith's *How to Be Both* and the *Nachleben* of Aby Warburg: 'Neither Here nor There.'" *Hungarian Journal of English and American Studies* 23, no. 2 (2017): 263–284. ProQuest.

Lachmann, Renate. "Die Parenthese und ihre Umklammerung." In *Satzzeichen: Szenen der Schrift*, edited by Helga Lutz, Nils Plath, and Dietmar Schmidt, 36–39. Berlin: Kadmos, 2017.

Lampert, Jay. *Deleuze and Guattari's Philosophy of History*. New York: The Free Press, 1978.

Langbaum, Robert. "The Epiphanic Mode in Wordsworth and Modern Literature." *New Literary History* 14, no. 2 (Winter 1983): 335–358. https://www.jstor.org/stable/468689.

Latour, Bruno. *Reassembling the Social: An Introduction to Actor-Network-Theory*. Oxford: Oxford University Press, 2005.

———. *Science in Action: How to Follow Scientists and Engineers through Society*. Cambridge: Harvard University Press, 1987.

———. "Why Has Critique Run Out of Steam? From Matters of Facts to Matters of Concern." *Critical Inquiry* 30, no. 2 (2004): 225–248. http://www.jstor.org/stable/10.1086/421123.

Leder, Drew. *The Absent Body*. Chicago: The University of Chicago Press, 1990.

Lee, Bernard J. "The Only Survivable World: A Postmodern Systems Approach to a Religious Intuition." Chapter 4 in *Sacred Interconnections: Postmodern Spirituality, Political Economy, and Art*, edited by David Ray Griffin. Albany: SUNY Press, 1990.

Lennard, John. *But I Digress: The Exploitation of Parentheses in English Printed Verse*. Oxford: Oxford University Press, 1992.

Levy, Ariel. *Female Chauvinist Pigs: Women and the Rise of Raunch Culture*. New York: Free Press, 2005.

Lewis, Cara L. "Beholding: Visuality and Postcritical Reading in Ali Smith's *How to Be Both*." *Journal of Modern Literature* 42, no. 3 (Spring 2019): 129–150. Project MUSE.

Lezra, Jacques. *Untranslating Machines: A Genealogy for the Ends of Global Thought*. London: Rowman & Littlefield International, 2017.

Lillywhite, Austin. "Relational Matters: A Critique of Speculative Realism and a Defense of Non-Reductive Materialism." *Chiasma* 4, no. 4 (2017): 13–39.

Livesey, Graham. "Assemblage." In *The Deleuze Dictionary*, edited by Adrian Parr, 18–19. Edinburgh: Edinburgh University Press, 2010.

Long, Mark. "William Carlos Williams, Ecocriticism, and Contemporary American Poetry." In *Ecopoetry: An Introduction*, edited by J. Scott Bryson, 58–74. Salt Lake City: University of Utah Press, 2002.

Lotman, Jurij. *The Structure of the Artistic Text*. Translated by Ronald Vroon. Ann Arbor: Michigan University, 1977.

Luckhurst, Roger. "American Weird." In *The Cambridge Companion to American Science Fiction*, edited by Gerry Canavan and Eric Carl Link, 194–205. New York: Cambridge University Press, 2015.

———. "The Weird: A Dis/orientation." *Textual Practice* 31, no. 6 (2017): 1041–1061.

Lynch, Michael and Steve Woolgar, eds. *Representation in Scientific Practice*. Cambridge: MIT, 1990.

Mackay, Robin. "Introduction: Laruelle Undivided." In *From Decision to Heresy: Experiments in Non-Standard Thought*, by François Laruelle, edited by Robin Mackay and, 1–32. Falmouth: Urbanomic/Sequence Press, 2012.

Maddox, Brenda. *Rosalind Franklin: The Dark Lady of DNA*. London: Harper Collins, 2002.

Maizes, Sarah. *Got Milf?: The Modern Mom's Guide to Feeling Fabulous, Looking Great, and Rocking A Minivan*. New York: Berkley Books, 2011.

Mansfeld, Jaap. "Der erste Systematiker: Anaximander." In *Die Vorsokratiker I; Griechisch/Deutsch*, edited by Jaap Mansfeld, 56–81. Stuttgart: Philipp Reclam jun. GmbH & Co., 1999.

———. "Der Wegbereiter: Thales." In *Die Vorsokratiker I*, edited by Jaap Mansfeld, 39–55. Stuttgart: Philipp Reclam jun. GmbH & Co., 1999.

Maran, Timo. "Biosemiotic Criticism." In *The Oxford Handbook of Ecocriticism*, 260–275. Oxford: Oxford University Press, 2014.

———. "Biosemiotic Criticism: Modelling the Environment in Literature." *Green Letters* 18, no. 3 (2014): 297–311.

Marshall, Kate. "*Cyclonopedia* as Novel (a Meditation on Complicity as Inauthenticity)." In Keller, Masciandaro, and Thacker, *Leper Creativity*, 147–157.

———. "The Old Weird." *Modernism / Modernity* 23, no. 3 (2016): 631–649.

Martin, Emily. "The Egg and the Sperm: How Science Has Constructed a Romance Based on Stereotypical Male-female Roles." *Signs: Journal of Women in Culture and Society* 16, no. 3 (1991): 485–501.

Masciandaro, Nicola and Edia Connole. *Floating Tomb: Black Metal Theory*. Milan, Mimesis International, 2015.

Masciandaro, Nicola. "Gourmandized in the Abattoir of Openness." In Keller, Masciandaro, and Thacker, *Leper Creativity*, 181–191.

Maudlin, Tim. *Philosophy of Physics: Quantum theory*. Princeton: Princeton University Press, 2019.

McHale, Brian. *Postmodernist Fiction*. London: Routledge, 1987.

McLaurin, Allen. *Virgina Woolf: The Echoes Enslaved*, New York: Cambridge University Press, 1973.

McNair, Brian. *Striptease Culture: Sex, Media and the Democratization of Desire*. London: Routledge, 2002.

McNeil, Maureen. "Post-Millennial Feminist Theory: Encounters with Humanism, Materialism, Critique, Nature, Biology and Darwin." *Journal for Cultural Research* 14, no. 4 (2010): 427–437.

McRobbie, Angela. The Aftermath of Feminism: Gender, Culture and Social Change. London: Sage, 2009.

Meillassoux, Quentin. *After Finitude: An Essay on the Necessity of Contingency*. Translated by Ray Brassier. London: Continuum, 2008.

Mellamphy, Dan and Biswas Mellamphy, Nandita. "Phileas Fogg, or the Cyclonic Passepartout: On the Alchemical Elements of War." In Keller, Masciandaro, and Thacker, *Leper Creativity*, 193–211.

Merten, Kai. "Undermining Masculinity: Psychoanalysis, the 'Weak Man' and the 'Caring Woman,' in Rebecca West's *The Return of the Soldier* and Willa Muir's

Imagined Corners." In *Psychoanalyticism: Uses of Psychoanalysis in Novels, Poems, Plays and Films*, edited by Anton Kirchhofer and Ingrid Hotz-Davis, 32–52. Trier: WVT, 2000.

Metz, Christian. *Film Language: A Semiotics of the Cinema.* Chicago: University of Chicago Press, 1974.

Meyer, Holt. "Durch den Regenbogen." In *Den Rahmen sprengen: Anmerkungspraktiken in Literatur, Kunst und Film,* edited by Bernhard Metz and Sabine Zubarik, 64–89. Berlin: Kadmos, 2012.

Miéville, China. "Gothic Politics: A Discussion with China Miéville." *Gothic Studies* 10, no. 1 (2008): 61–70.

———. "Long Live the New Weird." *The 3rd Alternative* 35 (2003): 3.

———. "M.R. James and the Quantum Vampire Weird; Hauntological: Versus and/or and and/or or?" *Collapse* 4 (2008): 105–128.

———. "Weird Fiction." In *The Routledge Companion to Science Fiction*, edited by Mark Bould, Andrew M. Butler, Adam Roberts, and Sherryl Vint, 510–516. London: Routledge, 2009.

———. *Perdido Street Station.* London: Pan Books, 2011. First published in 2000 by Macmillan (London).

———. *The City and the City.* London: Pan Books, 2010.

———. *The Scar.* London: Pan Books, 2011. First published in 2002 by Macmillan (London).

Mol, Annemarie and John Law. "Regions, Networks and Fluids: Anaemia and Social Topology." *Social Studies of Science* 24, no. 4 (1994): 641–71.

Mol, Annemarie. "Ontological Politics. A Word and Some Questions." *The Sociological Review* 47, no. 1 (1999): 74–89.

———. *The Body Multiple: Ontology in Medical Practice.* Durham: Duke University Press, 2002.

"Mom Jeans." YouTube Video, 1:27, uploaded by Saturday Night Live, October 9, 2013. http://www.youtube.com/watch?v=2aVxNH6iN9I.

Moran, Stacey. "Quantum Decoherence." *Philosophy Today* 63, no. 4 (Fall 2019): 1051–1068.

Moretti, Franco. "'Operationalizing': Or, the Function of Measurement in Literary Theory." *New Left Review* 84 (November/December 2013): 103–119.

Moretti, Franco. "Conjectures on World Literature." *New Left Review* 1 (January/February 2000): 54–68.

———. *Distant Reading.* London: Verso, 2013.

———. "Patterns and Interpretation." *Stanford Literary Lab*, Pamphlet 15 (September 2017): 4, https://litlab.stanford.edu/pamphlets/.

Morton, Timothy. *Being Ecological.* Cambridge, MA: MIT Press, 2018.

———. "Deconstruction and/as Ecology." In *The Oxford Handbook of Ecocriticism*, edited by Greg Garrard, 291–304. Oxford: Oxford University Press, 2014.

———. "Objects as Temporary Autonomous Zones." *Continent.* 1, no. 3 (2011): 149–155.

———. *The Ecological Thought.* Cambridge, MA: Harvard University Press, 2010.

Moslund, Sten Pulz. *Literature's Sensuous Geographies: Postcolonial Matters of Place*. New York: Palgrave Macmillan, 2015.
Moten, Fred and Wu Tsang. "'Who Touched Me?' If I Can't Dance, I Don't Want To Be Part Of Your Revolution." Edited by Frédérique Bergholtz and Susan Gibb. Amsterdam: If I Can't Dance, I Don't Want To Be Part Of Your Revolution, 2016.
Murphy, Berenice M. *Key Concepts in Contemporary Popular Fiction*. Edinburgh: Edinburgh University Press, 2017.
Negarestani, Reza. *Cyclonopedia: Complicity with Anonymous Materials*. Melbourne: re.press, 2008.
Neimanis, Astrida. "Bodies of Water, Human Rights and the Hydrocommons." *TOPIA: Canadian Journal of Cultural Studies* 21 (2009): 161–182.
Nerdinger, Winfried, ed. *Architektur wie sie im Buche steht: Fiktive Bauten und Städte in der Literatur*. Salzburg: Anton Pustet, 2006.
Neumann, Gerhard and Sigrid Weigel, eds. *Die Lesbarkeit der Kultur: Literaturwissenschaften zwischen Kulturtechnik und Ethnographie*. München: Fink Verlag, 2000.
Newkirk, Thomas. "Writing and Programming: Two Modes of Composing." *Computers, Reading, and Language Arts* 2, no. 2 (1984): 40–43.
Noble, Safiya. *Algorithms of Oppression: How Search Engines Reinforce Racism*. New York: New York University Press, 2018.
Noys, Benjamin and Timothy S. Murphy. "Introduction: Old and New Weird." *Genre* 49, no. 2 (July 2016): 117–134.
Noys, Benjamin. "Georges Bataille's Base Materialism." *Cultural Values* 4, no. 2 (1998): 499–517. https://doi.org/10.1080/14797589809359312.
Olkowski, Dorothea. "The Cogito and the Limits of Neo-materialism and Naturalized Objectivity." *Rhizomes: Cultural Studies in Emerging Knowledge* 30 (2016). https://doi.org/10.20415/rhiz/030.e09.
Oppermann, Serpil. "From Ecological Postmodernism to Material Ecocriticism: Creative Materiality and Narrative Agency." In *Material Ecocriticism*, edited by Serenella Iovino and Serpil Oppermann, 21–36. Bloomington: Indiana University Press, 2014.
Parikka, Jussi. "Apparatus Theory of Media á la (or in the Wake of) Karen Barad." *Machinology* (blog), July 16, 2009, https://jussiparikka.net/2009/07/16/apparatus-theory-of-media-a-la-or-in-the-wake-of-karen-barad/.
Peeren, Esther. "Specters." In *Symptoms of the Planetary Condition*, edited by Mercedes Bunz, Birgit Mara Kaiser, and Kathrin Thiele, 167–171. Lüneburg: meson press, 2017.
Phillips, Gerald M. and Bradley R. Erlwein. "Composition of the Computer: Simple Systems and Artificial Intelligence." *Communication Quarterly* 36, no. 4 (1988): 243–261. https://doi.org/10.1080/01463378809369729.
Pickering, Andrew. *The Mangle of Practice: Time, Agency, and Science*. Chicago: University of Chicago Press, 1995.
Pinch, Trevor. "Review Essay: Karen Barad, Quantum Mechanics, and the Paradox of Mutual Exclusivity." *Social Studies of Science* 41, no. 3 (2011): 431–441. https://doi.org/10.1177%2F0306312711400657.

Piper, Andrew. "Novel Devotions: Conversional Reading, Computational Modeling, and the Modern Novel." *New Literary History* 46, no. 1 (2015): 63–98.

Plath, Nils. *Hier und Anderswo: Zum Stellenlesen bei Franz Kafka, Samuel Beckett, Theodor W. Adorno und Jacques Derrida*. Berlin: Kadmos, 2017.

Plato. "Cratylus." In *Complete Works*, edited, with introduction and notes by John M. Cooper, and translated by C.D.C. Reeve, 101–156. Indianapolis: Hackett Publishing Company, 1997.

Pollmann, Inga. "Invisible Worlds, Visible: Uexküll's Umwelt, Film and Film Theory." *Critiqual Inquiry* 39, no. 4 (2013): 777–816.

Pope, Rob. *Textual Intervention: Critical and Creative Strategies for Literary Studies*. London: Routledge, 1995.

Rankin, Sandy. "AGASH AGASP AGAPE: The Weaver as Immanent Utopian Impulse in China Miéville's *Perdido Street Station* and *Iron Council*." *Extrapolation* 50, no. 2 (June 2009): 239–257.

Reger, Jo. *Different Wavelengths Studies of the Contemporary Women's Movement*. London: Routledge, 2014.

Rheinberger, Hans-Jörg. "Forming and being informed: Hans-Jörg Rheinberger in conversation with Michael Schwab." In *Experimental Systems: Future Knowledge in Artistic Research*, edited by Michael Schwab, 198–219. Leuven: Leuven University Press, 2013.

———. *Toward a History of Epistemic Things: Synthesizing Proteins in the Test Tube*. Stanford: University of Stanford Press, 1997.

Rittel, Horst W. and Melvin M. Webber. "2.3 planning problems are wicked." *Polity* 4, no. 155 (1973): e169.

Roger Clyne and the Peacemakers. *No More Beautiful World*. Tuscon: EmmaJava, 2007.

Rohr, Susanne. "'The Image Makers': Reality Constitution in the Role of Autism in Siri Hustvedt's *The Blazing World*." In Hartmann, Marks and Zapf, *Zones of Focused Ambiguity*, 249–261.

Roof, Judith. *The Poetics of DNA*. Minneapolis: University of Minnesota Press, 2007.

Rosa, Hartmut. *Resonance: A Sociology of Our Relationship to the World*. Translated by James C. Wagner. Cambridge: Polity Press, 2019.

Rosebury, Brian. *Tolkien: A Critical Assessment*. New York: St. Martin's, 1992.

———. *Tolkien: A Cultural Phenomen*. New York: Palgrave, 2003.

Rosenkranz, Pamela. "Cyclonopedia." *Artforum International: Best of 2009* (blog), January 1, 2010. https://re-press.org/cyclonopedia-artforum-international-best-of-2009/.

Rothman, Joshua. "A Better Way to Think about the Genre Debate." *The New Yorker*, November 6, 2014. https://www.newyorker.com/books/joshua-rothman/better-way-think-genre-debate.

Rouse, Joseph. "Barad's Feminist Naturalism." *Hypatia* 19, no. 1 (2004): 142–161.

———. *Engaging Science: How to Understand its Practices Philosophically*. Ithaca: Cornell University Press, 2018.

Rücker, Jens. Afterword to *Heraklit: Urworte,* edited by Jürgen von der Wense, 39–56. Berlin, Blauwerke, 2016.

Ruhmer, Eberhard. *Francesco del Cossa*. Munich: F. Bruckmann, 1959.
Ruschowski, Klaudia. "The Many Worlds of Etel Adnan." *PAJ: A Journal of Performance & Art* 117 (2017): 77–81.
Rushdie, Salman. *The Ground Beneath Her Feet*. New York: Henry Holt, 1999.
Ryan, Marie-Laure. *Possible Worlds, Artificial Intelligence, and Narrative Theory*. Bloomington: Indiana University Press, 1991.
Sabo, Deborah. "Archeology and the Sense of History in J. R. R. Tolkien's Middle-Earth." *Mythlore* 26, no. 1/2 (Fall/Winter 2007): 91–112.
Said, Edward. *Culture & Imperialism*. London: Vintage, 1994.
———. "Opponents, Audiences, Constituencies, and Community." In *The Politics of Interpretation*, edited by W. J. T. Mitchell, 7–32. Chicago: University of Chicago Press, 1982.
Saint-Amour, Paul K. "Weak Theory, Weak Modernism." *Modernism/Modernity* 27, no. 3 (September 2018): 437–459. https://doi.org/10.1353/mod.2018.0035.
Sanzo, Kameron. "New Materialism(s)." *Critical Posthumanism: Genealogy of the Posthuman* (blog), April 25, 2018. http://criticalposthumanism.net/new-materialisms/.
Schlosshauer, Maximilian. "Decoherence, the Measurement Problem, and Interpretations of Quantum Mechanics." *Reviews of Modern Physics* 76, no. 4 (2005): 1267–1305.
———. *Decoherence and the Quantum-to-Classical Transition*. Berlin: Springer, 2007.
Scholz, Susanne and Ulrike Vedder eds. *Handbuch Literatur & Materielle Kultur*. Berlin: De Gruyter, 2019.
Schrödinger, Erwin. "An Undulatory Theory of the Mechanics of Atoms and Molecules." *Physical Review* 28, no. 6 (1926): 1049–70.
Schweber, Silvan S. Review of *Meeting the Universe Halfway: Quantum Physics and the Entanglement of Matter and Meaning*, by Karen Barad. *Isis* 99, no. 4 (2008): 879–882. https://doi.org/10.1086/597741.
Sciscione, Anthony. "Symptomatic Horror: Lovecraft's 'The Colour Out of Space.'" In Keller, Masciandaro, and Thacker, *Leper Creativity*, 131–146.
Scribner, F. Scott: "Towards a Material Imaginary: Bataille, Nonlogical Difference, and the Language of Base Materialism." *Pli* no. 13 (2002): 209–220.
Sebeok, Thomas. *A Sign Is Just a Sign*. Bloomington: Indiana University Press, 1991.
Sederholm, Carl H. and Jeffrey Andrew Weinstock, eds. *The Age of Lovecraft*. Minnesota: University Press, 2016.
Sehgal, Melanie. "Diffractive Propositions: Reading Alfred North Whitehead with Donna Haraway and Karen Barad." In Kaiser and Thiele, *Diffracted Worlds*, 24–37. London: Routledge, 2018. Previously published in *Parallax* 20, no. 3 (2014): 188–201. https://doi.org/10.1080/13534645.2014.927625.
Sellberg, Karin, and Peta Hinton. "Introduction: The Possibilities of Feminist Quantum Thinking." *Rhizomes: Cultural Studies in Emerging Knowledge* 30 (2016). https://doi.org/10.20415/rhiz/030.i01.
Shaviro, Steven. *Discognition* (London: Repeater Books, 2016).

Shippey, T. A. *The Road to Middle-Earth*. London: Allen and Unwin, 1982.
Shklovsky, Viktor. "Art, as Device." Translated, with an introduction, by Alexandra Berlina. *Poetics Today* 36, no. 3 (September 2015): 151–174.
Siewers, Alfred K. "Tolkien's Cosmic-Christian Ecology: The Medieval Underpinnings." In *Tolkien's Modern Middle Ages*, edited by Jane Chance and Alfred K. Siewers. 139–153. New York: Palgrave, 2005.
Sikelianos, Eleni. "Refuse/Refuge: Be Longing." *Poetry Foundation*, February 12, 2018. https://www.poetryfoundation.org/harriet/2018/02/refuse-refuge-be-longing
Smith, Ali. *Artful*. London: Penguin, 2013. First published 2012 by Hamish Hamilton (London).
———. "Brighton Festival 2015 Trailer." YouTube Video, 2:07. April 15, 2015. https://youtu.be/7CW3CsVNcyQ.
———. *How to Be Both*. London: Penguin, 2015. First published 2014.
Solopova, Elizabeth. *Languages, Myths and History: An Introduction to the Linguistic and Literary Background of J. R. R. Tolkien's Fiction*. Oxford: North Landing, 2009.
Sonesson, Göran. "Methods and Models in Pictorial Semiotics." Report 3 from the Project Pictorial Meanings in the Society of Information, Lund University, 1988.
Sontag, Susan. "The Double Standard of Aging." *Saturday Review* 55 (September 23, 1972): 29–38.
Spivak, Gayatri Chakravorty. "Bonding in Difference. Interview with Alfred Arteaga." In *The Spivak Reader*, edited by Donna Landry and Gerald Maclean, 15–28. London: Routledge, 1996.
———. *An Aesthetic Education in the Era of Globalization*. Cambridge: Harvard University Press, 2012.
———. *Death of a Discipline*. New York: Columbia University Press, 2003.
———. *Readings*. London: Seagull Books, 2014.
Stamp, Philip C. E. "The Decoherence puzzle." *Studies in History and Philosophy of Science Part B: Studies in History and Philosophy of Modern Physics* 37, no. 3 (2006): 467–497.
Stengers, Isabelle. "Introductory Notes on an Ecology of Practices." *Cultural Studies Review* 11, no. 1 (2005): 183–196.
Stephan, Matthias. *Defining Literary Postmodernism for the Twenty-First Century*. Cham: Palgrave, 2019.
Stroustrup, Bjarne. *Programming: Principles and Practice Using C++*. 2nd ed. Upper Saddle River: Addison-Wesley, 2014.
Sullivan, Nikki. "The Somatechnics of Perception and the Matter of the Non/Human: A Critical response to the New Materialism." *European Journal of Women's Studies* 19, no. 3 (2012): 299–313.
Tagushi, Lenz. "A Diffractive and Deleuzian Approach to Analyzing Interview Data." *Feminist Theory* 13 (2012): 265–281.
Tally Jr., Robert T. "Tolkien's Geopolitical Fantasy: Spatial Narrative in *Lord of the Rings* in Popular Fiction and Spatiality." In *Popular Fiction and Spatiality*:

Reading Genre Settings, edited by Lisa Fletcher, 125–140. New York: Palgrave, 2016.
Tappen-Scheuermann, Diana. "Reality Bites: Fractured Narrative and Author-Reader Interaction." In Hartmann, Marks and Zapf, *Zones of Focused Ambiguity*, 39–50.
Taylor, Carol A. "Close Encounters of a Critical Kind: A Diffractive Musing In/Between New Material Feminism and Object-Oriented Ontology." *Cultural Studies? Critical Methodologies* 16, no. 2 (2016): 201–212.
Teare, Brian. *Companion Grasses*. Richmond, CA: Omnidawn Publishing, 2013.
Testi, Claudio A. "Tolkien's Work: Is it Christian or Pagan? A Proposal for a 'Synthetic' Approach." *Tolkien Studies* 10 (2013): 1–47.
Thacker, Eugene. "Black Infinity; or, Oil discovers Humans." In Keller, Masciandaro, and Thacker, *Leper Creativity*, 173–180.
Thacker, Eugene. *In the Dust of this Planet*. Vol. 1, *Horror of Philosophy*. Winchester: Zero Books, 2011.
Thiele, Kathrin. "Ethos of Diffraction: New Paradigms for a (Post)humanist Ethics." In Kaiser and Thiele, *Diffracted Worlds*, 38–52. London: Routledge, 2018. Previously published in *Parallax* 20, no. 3 (2014): 202–216. https://doi.org/10.1080/13534645.2014.927627.
Thompson, Lucas. "Method Reading." *New Literary History* 50, no. 2 (2019): 293–321.
Tilley, Christopher. *Interpreting Landscapes: Geologies, Topographies, Identities*. Walnut Creek: Left Coast Press, 2012.
———. *Material Culture and Text: The Art of Ambiguity*. London: Routledge, 1991.
Tilley, Christopher. *Metaphor and Material Culture*. Oxford: Blackwell, 2000.
Timofeeva, Oxana. "Ultra-Black: Towards a Materialist Theory of Oil." *E-Flux Journal* 84 (September 2017), https://www.e-flux.com/journal/84/149335/ultra-black-towards-a-materialist-theory-of-oil/.
Todd, Zoe. "An Indigenous Feminist's Take on the Ontological Turn: 'Ontology' is just another Word for Colonialism." *Journal of Historical Sociology* 29, no. 1 (2016): 4–22.
Tolkien, J. R. R. "On Fairy-Stories." In *Tree and Leaf*. 109–161. Boston: Houghton Mifflin, 1965. First published in 1939.
———. "The New Shadow." In *The Peoples of Middle-Earth*, edited by Christopher Tolkien. Vol. 12 of *The History of Middle-Earth*. London: Harper Collins, 1996.
———. *Beowulf: The Monsters and the Critics*. Sir Isreal Gollancz Memorial Lecture. In *Proceedings of the British Academy*, Vol. XXII, 245–95. London: Oxford University Press, 1936.
———. *Morgoth's Ring*. Vol. 10 of *The History of Middle-Earth*, edited by Christopher Tolkien. London: Harper Collins, 1993.
———. *Silmarillion*. London: Harper and Collins, 1977.
———. *The Book of Lost Tales, Part I*. Vol. 1 of *The History of Middle-Earth*, edited by Christopher Tolkien. London: Harper Collins, 2015. First published in 1983.
———. *The Fellowship of the Ring*. London: Houghton Mifflin, 1965. First published in 1954.

———. *The Return of the King*. London: Houghton Mifflin, 1965. First published in 1954.

———. *The Return of the Shadow*. In *The History of* The Lord of the Rings, *Part I*, edited by Christopher Tolkien. London: Harper Collins, 2000. First published in 1988.

———. *The Shaping of Middle-Earth*. Vol. 4 of *The History of Middle-Earth*, edited by Christopher Tolkien. London: Harper Collins, 2015. First published in 1986.

———. *The Two Towers*. London: Houghton Mifflin, 1965. First published in 1954.

———. *Unfinished Tales*. London: Houghton Mifflin, 1980.

Tougaw, Jason. "The Self is a Moving Target: The Neuroscience of Siri Hustvedt's Artists." In Hartmann, Marks and Zapf, *Zones of Focused Ambiguity*, 113–132.

Tranter, Kirsten. "An Interview with China Miéville." *Contemporary Literature* 53, no. 3 (September 2012): 417–436.

Tsing, Anna Lowenhaupt, Heather Anne Swanson, Elaine Gan, and Nils Bubandt, eds. *Arts of Living on a Damaged Planet: Ghosts and Monsters of the Anthropocene*. Minneapolis: University of Minnesota Press, 2017.

Tuana, Nancy, ed. *Feminism and Science*. Indiana: Indiana University Press, 1989.

Tuckerman, Mark E. "5: Electron Diffraction, Postulates of Quantum Mechanics, the Bohr model, and the Beer-Lambert law." (online course). Chemistry LibreTexts. Updated June 5, 2019. https://chem.libretexts.org/.

U2. *Achtung Baby*. New York: Island, 1991.

———. *Boy*. New York: Island, 1980.

———. *How to Dismantle an Atomic Bomb*. Santa Monica, CA: Interscope, 2004.

———. *Pop*. New York: Island, 1997.

———. *Songs of Experience*. Santa Monica, CA: Interscope, 2017.

———. *Songs of Innocence*. Santa Monica, CA: Interscope, 2014.

———. *The Joshua Tree*. New York: Island, 1987.

———. *The Unforgettable Fire*. New York: Island, 1984.

———. *War*. ILPS 9733. New York: Island, 1983.

———. *Wide Awake in America*. New York: Island, 1985.

———. *No Line On the Horizon*. Santa Monica, CA: Interscope, 2009.

———. *Zooropa*. New York: Island, 1993.

van der Tuin, Iris. "'A Different Starting Point, a Different Metaphysics': Reading Bergson and Barad Diffractively." *Hypatia* 26, no. 1 (2011): 22–42.

———. "Deflationary Logic: Response to Sara Ahmed." *European Journal of Women's Studies* 15, no. 4 (2008): 412.

———. "Diffraction as a Methodology for Feminist Onto-Epistemology: On Encountering Chantal Chawaf and Posthuman Interpellation." In Kaiser and Thiele, *Diffracted Worlds*, 67–80. London: Routledge, 2018. Previously published in *Parallax* 20, no. 3 (2014): 231–244. https://doi.org/10.1080/13534645.2014.927631.

van Elferen, Isabella. "Techno-Gothics of the Early-Twenty-First Century." In *The Cambridge Companion to the Modern Gothic*, edited by Jerrold E. Hogle, 138–154. Cambridge: Cambridge University Press, 2014.

VanderMeer, Ann, and Jeff VanderMeer, eds. *The New Weird*. San Francisco: Tachyon Publications, 2008.
———. *The Weird: A Compendium of Strange and Dark Stories*. New York: Tor, 2011.
Vee, Annette. "Introduction: Computer Programming as Literacy." In *Coding Literacy: How Computer Programming is Changing Writing*. 1–42. Cambridge: MIT Press, 2017.
von Contzen, Eva. "'Both close and distant': Experiments of Form and the Medieval in Contemporary Literature." Special issue, *Frontiers of Narrative Studies* 3, no. 2 (2017): 289–303. https://doi.org/10.1515/fns-2017-0019.
von Uexküll, Jakob and Georg Kriszat. *Streifzüge durch die Umwelten von Tieren und Menschen: Ein Bilderbuch unsichtbarer Welten –Bedeutungslehre*. Reinbek: Rowohlt, 1951.
von Uexküll, Thure. "The Sign Theory of Jakob von Uexküll." In *Classics of Semiotics*, edited by Martin Krampen, Klaus Oehler, Roland Posner, Thomas A. Sebeok, and Thure von Uexküll, 147–180. New York: Plenum Press, 1987.
Wagner, Roy. *An Anthropology of the Subject: Holographic Worldview in New Guinea and its Meaning and Significance for the World of Anthropology*. Berkeley: University of California Press, 2001.
Wallin, Mark Rowell. "Myth, Monsters and Markets: Ethos, Identification, and the Video Game Adaptations of *The Lord of the Rings*." *Game Studies* 7, no. 1 (August 2007). http://gamestudies.org/0701/articles/wallin.
Walter, Benjamin. "Ich packe meine Bibliothek aus." In *Denkbilder*, 88–96. Frankfurt am Main: Suhrkamp 1974.
———. "Unpacking My Library: A Talk about Book Collecting." In *Illuminations: Essays and Reflections*, edited by Hannah Arendt, translated by Harry Zohn, 59–67. New York: Schocken Books 1968.
———. *Illuminations*. Edited by Hannah Arendt. New York: Schocken, 1968.
Walther, Bo Kampmann. "Big Theory – Strong Theory: The Ontological Ghost of Post-Ontological Epistemology." *Cybernetics and Human Knowing* 11, no. 3 (2004): 30–55.
———. "Lights Behind Thick Curtains: Images of Fear and Familiarity in Tolkien." *Tolkien Studies* 17 (in press).
Wang, Shaowei, David Lo and Lingxiao Jiang. "An Empirical Study on Developer Interactions in StackOverflow." Paper presented at *SAC '13: Proceedings of the 28th Annual ACM Symposium on Applied Computing*, Coimbra, Portugal, March 18–22, 2013. 1012–1024. https://doi.org/10.1145/2480362.2480557.
Warburg, Aby. "Italienische Kunst und internationale Astrologie im Palazzo Schifanoja zu Ferrara." 1912. In *Die Erneuerung der heidnischen Antike: Kulturwissenschaftliche Beiträge zur Geschichte der europäischen Renaissance*, edited by Horst Bredekamp and Michael Diers, 459–81. Vol. 1.2 of *Aby Warburg: Gesammelte Schriften; Studienausgabe*. Berlin: Akademie Verlag, 1998.
Warminski, Andrzej. "Parenthesis. Hegel by Heidegger." In *Readings in Interpretation: Hölderlin, Hegel, Heidegger*, Introduction by Rodolphe Gasché, 112–162. Minneapolis: University of Minnesota Press, 1987.

Wasko, Janet and Govind Shanadi. "More than Just Rings: Merchandise for Them All." In *The Lord of the Rings: Popular Culture in Global Context*, edited by Ernest Mathijs, 23–42. London: Wallflower Press, 2006.

Wasson, Sara. "China Miéville's *Perdido Street Station* (2000) – Gothic Literary Science Fiction." In *The Gothic: A Reader*, edited by Simon Bacon, 203–210. Oxford: Peter Lang, 2018.

Watson, James D. *The Double Helix. A Personal Account of the Discovery of the Structure of DNA*. London: Weidenfeld and Nicolson, 1968.

Weaver, Milly. "Reading Words Alongside Images: Ali Smith and Visual Portraiture." *Interdisciplinary Literary Studies* 20, no. 4 (2018): 527–548. Project MUSE.

Weinstock, Jeffrey Andrew. "Jeff VanderMeer's *Annihilation* (2014) – Gothic and the New Weird." In *The Gothic*, edited by Simon Bacon, 211–217. Oxford: Peter Lang, 2018.

———. "The New Weird." In *New Directions in Popular Fiction: Genre, Distribution, Reproduction*, edited by Ken Gelder, 177–199. London: Palgrave Macmillan, 2016.

Wenders, Wim, dir. *The Million Dollar Hotel*. Studio Home Entertainment, 2001.

West, Candace and Sarah Fenstermaker. "Doing Difference." *Gender and Society* 9, no. 1 (1995): 8–37.

Wetdell, Noura. "Etel Adnan: Responsibility to That Green." *Flash Art* 324/52 (2019): 89.

Wheeler, John Archibald and Wojciech Hubert Zurek, eds. *Quantum Theory and Measurement*. Vol. 49 of *Princeton Series in Physics*. Princeton: Princeton University Press, 2014.

Wheeler, Wendy. "Postscript on Biosemiotics: Reading Beyond Words – and Ecocritcism." *New Formations* 64 (2008): 137–154.

———. "The Lightest Burden: The Aesthetic Abductions of Biosemiotics." In *Handbook of Ecocriticism and Cutural Ecology*, edited by Hubert Zapf, 19–44. Berlin, Boston: De Gruyter, 2016.

Whitehead, Alfred North. *Process and Reality: An Essay in Cosmology*. New York: The Free Press, 1978.

———. *Science and the Modern World*. New York: Macmillan, 1954.

———. *The Concept of Nature: The Tarner Lectures Delivered in Trinity College November 1919*. Ann Arbor: University of Michigan Press, 1957.

"Why *Incredibles 2* Director Brad Bird Says Cartoons Aren't Just for Children." YouTube Video, uploaded by q on cbc, June 14, 2018. http://www.youtube.com/watch?v=cKvgnBnUZ8Y.

Williams, William Carlos. "Paterson." The Dial: A Semi-monthly Journal of Literary Criticism, Discussion and Information, February 1927.

———. *Imaginations*. New York: New Directions, 1971.

———. *Paterson*. Edited by Christopher MacGowan. New York: New Directions, 1992.

———. *The Autobiography of William Carlos Williams*. New York: New Directions, 1967.

Wirth, Uwe. "(In Klammern)." In *Satzzeichen: Szenen der Schrift*, edited by Helga Lutz, Nils Plath, and Dietmar Schmidt, 31–35. Berlin: Kadmos, 2017.
Woodward, Ben. "Untimely (and Unshapely) Decomposition of Onto-Epistemological Solidity: Negarestani's *Cyclonopedia* as Metaphysics." In Keller, Masciandaro, and Thacker, *Leper Creativity*, 213–224.
Wurth, Kiene Brillenburg. "Diffraction, Handwriting and Intra-Mediality in Louise Paille's *Livres-livres*." In Kaiser and Thiele, *Diffracted Worlds*, 94–109. London: Routledge, 2018. Previously published in *Parallax* 20, no. 3 (2014): 258–273. https://doi.org/10.1080/13534645.2014.927633.
Young, Tory. "Invisibility and Power in the Digital Age: Issues for Feminist and Queer Narratology." *Textual Practice* 32, no. 6 (2018): 991–1006. https://doi.org/10.1080/0950236X.2018.1486546.
Zeh, Hans Dieter. "Roots and Fruits of Decoherence." In *Quantum Decoherence*, 151–175. Basel: Birkhäuser, 2006.
———. "What is Achieved by Decoherence?" In *New Developments on Fundamental Problems in Quantum Physics*, 441–451. Dordrecht: Springer, 1997.
Zertuche, Hayley. "A Humanimal Rhetorics of Biological Materiality." In *Rhetorical Animals: Boundaries of the Human in the Study of Persuation*, edited by Kristian Bjørkdahl and Alex C. Parrish, 23–40. Lanham: Lexington Books, 2018.
Zunshine, Lisa. *Why We Read Fiction: Theory of Mind and the Novel*. Columbus: Ohio State University Press, 2006.

Index

Abram, David, 139; *The Spell of the Sensuous*, 139
actor-network theory (ANT), 54–55; meaning-making in, 55
Adnan, Etel, 17; *Journey to Mount Tamalpais*, 32–44
Adorno, Theodor W., 105–6, 137
affirmative engagement, 80–83
agencement, 213, 215, 217, 218
agencies, 53, 269, 270, 282n1; expressive, 273; nonhumanist discourse, 273
agential cuts, 195, 217, 270; Cartesian cut *versus*, 251; entanglements, 4; intra-actions, 4; mutually exclusive, 4
agential realism, 73, 125, 271, 272, 283n9, 284n22; essentialist risks, 272; principles, 272; relationism, 272
agential separability, 64, 215
aging: cultural markers, 255; cultural myths and, 249; youth-based standards, 255. *See also* Mothers and older women
Ahmed, Sara, 79
aletheia, 148
Althusser, Louis, 54, 56
Alvanson, Kristen, 95
Amazon Web Services Lambda Function, 293

American poetry, 125–26
amniotic onto-logic, 240
Andermahr, Sonya, 156
Anker, Elizabeth S., 155, 168n13; *Critique and Postcritique*, 168n13
ANT. *See* Actor-network theory
anthropocentrism, 54
anthropomorphization, 281
Anzaldùa, Gloria, 99, 100
apartheid type of difference, 64
API. *See* Application Programming Interface
a-poria, 104, 105, 106
apparatuses, 99, 213–17; agential cuts, 4; author/reader/text, 35, 40, 48n38, 212–13; diffractive, 12, 80, 274; material-discursive, 205; measurement, 77, 79–80; mind, 276; two-slit, 105–6
Application Programming Interface (API), 287, 293–302
artifactuality, 73
artistic text, 16–17
Askin, Ridvan, 271, 272, 273; *Narrative and Becoming*, 271
assemblages, 56; Deleuzian, 250–51; eco-techno-cosmo-logical, 244; enunciative, 235; linguistic, 125;

relations and relationality, 56; sexual, 250–66
astronomy, 124
atom(s), 54, 56–57; clinamen, 57; immanent self-determination of, 57; relata as, 56; STM, 71–72
atomic collision, 57
Attridge, Derek, 17, 32, 35, 44–45, 50n63; *Coetzee and the Ethics of Reading*, 44; *The Singularity of Literature*, 45
Attwood, Feona, 250
Avanessian, Armen, 94

Bad Moms, 260–61
Baikal, 238, 240
Barad, Karen, 1–13, 16, 18–23, 35, 37–39, 42, 43, 51–54, 58, 64–65, 71–75, 77–85, 93, 94, 96, 98–101, 104–5, 107, 110n55, 117–27, 129, 130, 131n7, 133n33, 134n47, 135–40, 145, 148, 168n14, 170n40, 173n80, 177, 194, 195, 205, 213–17, 226, 228, 229n16, 237, 239, 245n7, 250–53, 270–75, 283n9, 289, 291; agential realism, 73, 125, 271, 272, 283n9, 284n22; anti-representationalist agenda, 271; critics, 78; diffractive reading, 2–7; ground-figure reversibility, 272–75; infinitesimal entities, 239; interpretation of Stern-Gerlach experiment, 79–80; inventive provocations, 195; *Meeting the Universe Halfway*, 1, 71, 124–25, 133n26, 133n33, 136, 138, 177, 270, 271, 273; queer quantum world, 74; two-system dilemma and, 120
Barthes, Roland, 53, 61
Bataille, George, 60, 135, 136, 139–40, 148; base materialism, 136, 139–40
Beck, John, 122
Beck, Ulrich, 249–50
becoming, 56, 61–62; ethical dimension, 64; ontology of, 55

Bell, Peter, 167
Benjamin, Walter, 20, 41, 105–6; *Ich packe meine Bibliothek aus*, 217–28
Bennett, Jane, 18, 56, 57, 59; *Vibrant Matter*, 59
Bennett, Michael James, 56
Bergson, Henri, 81–82, 83
Bertschik, Julia, 8
Best, Stephen, 41–42, 212; "Surface Reading: An Introduction," 41–42
Beyond the Standard Model (BSM), 239
bifurcation of nature, 236, 241
binary light-darkness story, 65
Binning, Gerd, 71
biosemiotics, 11, 12–13; diffractive reading and, 14–16
black illumination, 97, 99–100, 102; (non-)simultaneity as, 105–6
blackness and darkness, 98–100
Blanchot, Maurice, 60
blobjectivity, 95–96
Blumenberg, Hans, 9–11, 14, 25n35, 123; *Die Lesbarkeit der Welt*, 9
bodily praxis, 252
body, 252–53; materially distinctive/specific, 252, 253; media texts, 253–54; phenomenological vectors, 252; reading, 254
Bohr, Niels, 43, 54, 64–65, 76, 78, 216, 226, 270, 272; concept of complementarity, 79, 89n61, 122, 124; quantum physics (Copenhagen Interpretation), 76, 137
Bono, 269, 276–82
books, materiality of, 218–26; freedom, 224; history, 224; imagination, 220–26; memories, 222, 223; processuality, 224–26; regularity of access, 221–22. *See also specific book titles*
A Borderline Conception Lying at The Extreme Edge of the World of Appearances, 22
braille system, 71
breasts, sexualization of, 259

Brock, Kevin, 288, 291, 292
Brooke, Colin, 291
Brophy, Brigid, 156; *In Transit*, 156
Brosch, Renate, 172n65
Brown, James J., Jr., 293
Butler, Judith, 272

Calhoun, Scott, 285n35
Campagna, Federico, 241
Campe, Rüdiger, 101
capacious methodology, 119
capitalist-elastic mother, 260
Caracciolo, Marco, 271, 272
carbon: footprint, 31; spending, 31
care, 82
Carson, Rachel, 246n19; *Silent Spring*, 246n19
Caws, Mary Anne, 107
Christov-Bakargiev, Carolyn, 33, 34, 35
classical bodies, 75
classical realm, 3, 78
Clement of Alexandria, 62
clinamen, 57
Clyne, Roger, 274–75
CO_2 emissions, 31
code (software), 22–23
Code Studies, 22
Cohn, Dorrit, 284–85n28
co-in-habitation, 46, 50n68
collapse, 76, 77; Barad on, 77; notion of, 76
computational criticism, 42, 43
Connole, Edia, 112n97
contrapuntal reading, 45
Coppola, Maria Micaela, 171–72n61, 172n63
cougar-cub dating, 249
cougars, 249, 250; Maizes on, 265; milfs compared with, 258; sexualization of, 263; sexual norms of, 265–66. *See also* Mothers and older women
Cougars Inc., 258
critical consciousness, 154
critical interferometry, 237, 243

critique as a weapon, 80–81
cultural markers of age, 255
cultural power of feminism, 254–55
cultural texts, 22, 253
cultural textuality, 10
Cummings, Robert E., 291
Curie, Marie, 126
Czerkinsky, Stéphane, 229n22

D'Aguilon, François, 98
D'Ardenne, Simone, 147; "The Man and the Scholar," 147
darkness and blackness, 98–100
data structures, 305n39
dead matter, 139
decoherence, 18, 73–74; Barad using, 77; concept, 76–77; controversy, 77–79; Zeh on, 76
deconstruction, 5
DeLanda, Manuel, 250–51
del Cossa, Francesco, 156, 157, 160, 163
Deleuze, Gilles, 20, 54, 55, 64, 135, 136, 211–16, 218, 226; atomic collision, 57; *Bergsonism*, 146, 147; "conceptual personae," 68n35; *Difference and Repetition*, 56, 67–68n18, 146; encounter, 56–57; Epicurean atomism, 56–57; la rencontre, 56; philosophical time, 65; philosophy of becoming, 56, 65; "theory of ideas," 67–68n18; virtual/virtuality, 20, 136, 145–47, 213; *What is Philosophy*, 56, 67n2
Deleuzian materialism, 20
de Man, Paul, 60
Democritus, 53, 57
Denkbilder, 217
Derrida, Jacques, 24n15, 49n56, 53, 60, 94, 106, 113n102, 139, 228, 294
Dickinson, Emily, 125
Didymus, Arius, 64
difference: apartheid type of, 64; resonance, 82–83; thinking and reading differently, 64–65; Western philosophy, 64, 65

Diffracted Worlds – Diffractive Readings (Kaiser and Thiele), 1
diffraction, 1, 93, 137–40, 194–95, 291; as an affirmative method of relating, 82–83; Cartesian epistemology, 137; concept, 2–5, 245n2; entangled relationalities, 58; as a feminist "optics," 72–73; as fictive model, 3; mutually exclusive agential cuts, 4; obstructions/obstacles, 3; patterns, 119–20; posthuman(ist) theorization of, 82; real and metaphorical, 3–4; reflection *versus*, 5; as "re-turning," 96; rhetoric of, 274; Taylor on, 82; waves, 2–3
diffraction experiments, 75–76. *See also* Double-slit diffraction experiment
diffraction gratings, 3
diffractive aesthetics, 242–43
diffractive intertextuality. *See* Intertextuality
diffractive reading, 1, 194; as affirmative engagement, 80–83; Baradian approach, 5–7; biosemiotics and, 14–16; Haraway's metaphorical analogy, 118; interventionist literary-critical approaches, 5–6; Literary and Cultural Studies, 5; literary texts, 6; materialist reading theories, 2, 7–14; overview, 2; politics of, 17, 44–46; reflexive reading *versus*, 5; reworking, 81–82; scientific notion, 6
dispositif, 213–14, 215
distant reading, 41, 42–43
divorce rates, 263
DNA, 160–61
dOCUMENTA, 33, 35
Doherty, Melanie, 96, 97
Domínguez, Carlos María, 20, 217; *Casa de papel*, 217–28
double helix sculpture, 160–61
double-slit diffraction experiment, 75–76; interference pattern, 75–76; non-scientists on, 75; refined versions, 76; two-slit experiment, 99

dualism, 272, 273
Dubrow, Heather, 271
Duchamp, Marcel, 246n16

Eastern philosophy *versus* Western philosophy, 69n49
eco-criticism, 123
ecological thought/thinking, 270–71, 272
econarratologies, 272
eco-poetics, 118
Edge, 281
eidola, 57
Einstein, Albert, 76
encounter, 56–57
Endrinal, Christopher, 275–76, 281
entanglement: agential cuts, 4; Barad on, 74, 77; givenness of, 77; intra-activity, 59; organisms, 11; as quantum mechanical, 77; relational ontology, 57–59; repetition, 77
enunciative assemblages, 235
Epicurus, 56, 57
eponyms, 148
Erfurt Network on New Materialism, 1
ethics, 64; ethical maxim, 266; ethical thinking, 59; ethico-onto-epistemological approach, 195; ethics of care, 73; ethics of reading, 17, 32, 35, 44–45
Ettinger, Bracha L., 50n68, 82, 83
evil, 136
expressive agencies, 273
extradimensional object, 240

fantasy, 136
fashionista, 255
Felski, Rita, 168n13; *Critique and Postcritique*, 168n13
female sexualities, 22, 249–66. *See also* Mothers and older women
feminism: cultural power of, 254–55; sexual assemblages, 250–66
Fenstermaker, Sarah, 250
Fergie, 255–59, 262

Feynman, Richard, 75
figurative language, 38–39
Flieger, Verlyn, 147
flowing holes, 102–4, 112n97
Floyd, George, 110n55
Foucault, Michel, 20, 80, 211–16, 226, 229n16, 250; *Archaeology of Knowledge*, 212
fragment, 60
frame narrative, 107
Franklin, Rosalind, 160
Freundlich, Bart, 264

Gaffigan, Jim, 252
Galloway, Alexander, 98–99
Gasché, Rodolphe, 101
gate hysteria, 104, 105, 106
gender, 252–53; performance, 252–53, 263; socioeconomic equality, 255
gender disparity, 255
gene editing, 9
genome, 8–9
Gibson, Valerie, 258, 263
Giddens, Anthony, 249–50
Gigaton Volume Detector (GVD), 235–45
Gill, Rosalind, 257, 258
Ginsberg, Allen, 126
glamour, 147
Gómez-Barris, Macarena, 241–42
Gratton, Peter, 106
Grimaldi, Francesco, 99
Grosz, Elizabeth, 80
Guattari, Félix, 55, 56, 211–12
Gulf oil spill, 100, 101

Haraway, Donna, 1, 5, 43, 58, 64, 73, 75, 79, 80, 83, 86, 93, 117–21, 123, 125–27, 129, 131n5, 134n47, 136, 137, 154, 194; *Modest Witness*, 130; "The Promises of Monsters," 130
Harman, Graham, 138–39, 275; "Meillassoux's Virtual Future," 275
Hayot, Eric, 273, 278; *On Literary Worlds*, 273

Heckman, Susan, 125
Heidegger, Martin, 66, 68–69n40, 107–8, 139
Heisenberg, Werner, 122, 137–38
Hemmings, Clare, 79
Heraclitus, 18, 51–52, 53, 59–66; as a/the theorist of diffraction *avant la lettre*, 61; fragments of work, 51; knowledge production, 62–63; philosophy/theory, 51–52, 61–66; Plato on, 61; river fragments, 63–64
Hermogenes, 61
Hidden Writing, 94, 96, 98, 101
Hoar, Nancy, 291
( )hole complex, 94, 96, 100–108
hologram, 240
hormone therapy, 263
horror and speculation, 93–108. *See also* Speculative horror/texts
How to Be Both (Smith): Anker on, 155; diffractive structure, 157–63; extra-textual entanglements, 163–67; Lewis on, 154–55; as a material-discursive book, 155
human diffractions, 14
human language. *See* Language
human reading, 8, 11
human subjects, 53
Humphrey, John, 38
Husserl, Edmund, 139
Hustvedt, Siri, 21; *The Blazing World*, 193–207; *Living, Thinking, Looking*, 206; *The Shaking Woman or a History of My Nerves*, 193, 194; *A Woman Looking At Men Looking At Women*, 193, 206–7
Hyde, Emily, 167n4
Hydraglyph, 101
hydrocommons, 240
hypermasculine theory of life, 81, 83
Hyperstition, 95, 96

IBM, 71
I Don't Know How She Does It, 260, 261

images. *See* Photographic images
immutable and combinable mobiles, 55–56
inclusivity, 82–83
Incognitum Hactenus, 106–7
indeterminacy, 79, 80
ineffability, 241, 243
infinitesimal entities, 239
in-forming, 60
Ingold, Tim, 55–56; *Making: Anthropology, Archaeology, Art and Architecture*, 55; *Point, Line, Counterpoint: From Environment to Fluid Space*, 55
intangibility, 241, 243
intentionality, 269–70, 282n1
interference patterns, 75–76; critical interferometry, 243; maternal sexual norms, 261–62
interferences, 236
interferometry, 236, 237, 243
intertextuality, 5–6, 96; nonhierarchizing interculturality, 6
intra-actions/intra-activity/intra-active, 4, 10, 46, 53, 54, 57–61, 66, 97, 103, 136, 138, 154, 236, 250, 251, 253, 259, 260, 264, 265, 267n19, 271, 281; words and things, 253
inventive provocations, 195
isomorphic projection, 242
It-I worlds (It-I-self), 66

JavaScript Object Notation, 293

Kafka, Franz, 94, 105–6
Kaiser, Birgit, 1, 6, 16, 17, 19, 51, 59, 93, 97, 98, 178, 194–95; *Diffracted Worlds – Diffractive Readings*, 1
Kirby, Vicky, 58, 267n19, 273
Klein, Melanie, 80
Kluge, Alexander, 63
knowledge-making practice, 5
knowledge production, 62–63
knowledge production in ANT, 55

Lake Baikal. *See* Baikal
landscape laboratories, 235–45; cosmologics, 243; diffractive aesthetics, 241–42; intra-active operations, 235–36; isomorphic projection, 242; multidimensionality, 236
language, 14–16; written language, 23
la rencontre, 56
Latour, Bruno, 20, 54, 55–56, 80–81, 123, 134n47, 213, 216, 226
Law, John, 56
Leder, Drew, 252, 259
legendarium, 140
legibility of the world, 9
Leiber, Fritz, 94, 97, 98, 102; "Black Gondolier," 94, 97, 98, 101
Lennard, John, 100
Leper Creativity, 96–100; "Leper Creativity" (*Cyclonopedia* symposium), 96
Lewis, Cara L., 154–55, 162–63, 166, 168n13, 169n21, 171n59
Lillywhite, Austin, 94
Long, Michael, 123
Lotman, Yuri, 13, 15, 16–17
Lovecraft, H. P., 93, 96, 97, 102, 180; "The Festival," 102
Lovecraftian worm-ridden space, 96
Lucretius, 56, 57
lumen, 98–100
lunulae, 100, 103, 106
lux, 98–100
lyrical analysis, 271

Maddox, Brenda, 160
Madonna-whore dichotomy, 254, 257, 261–62
Maizes, Sarah, 257–58, 260, 261, 262, 265; "*Feeling Fabulous, Looking Great, and Rocking A Minivan*," 262
Maran, Timo, 11
Marcus, Sharon, 41–42, 212; "Surface Reading: An Introduction," 41–42
Marshall, Kate, 95

Marx, Karl, 80
Masciandaro, Nicola, 99–100, 103, 107, 112n82, 112n97
material culture, 7–8
material imaginary, 136, 139
materialist ecocriticism, 11, 272–73
materialistic thinking, 53–54
materialist reading theories, 2, 7–14
materiality, 139, 155; books, 218–26
materialization, 59, 74
material objects: literary texts on, 8
maternal and female midlife sexual assemblages. *See* Mothers and older women
matter reading, 2
McHale, Brian, 166
McLaurin, Allen, 103
McNeil, Maureen, 80
McRobbie, Angela, 254, 255
Meillassoux, Quentin, 18, 22, 275; *After Finitude*, 275; "Meillassoux's spectrum," 275
Merleau-Ponty, Maurice, 94, 139
Merten, Kai, 123, 270
meshworks, 55–56. *See also* Networks
metafiction, 95
metaphorical diffraction, 3–4
metonymic metaphor, 127
Meyer, Holt, 100
Miéville, China, 21; *The Scar*, 21, 175–88
"M.I.L.F. $." (music video), 255–57
milfs, 249, 250, 257–59, 267n28; cougars compared with, 258; Maizes on, 257–58; sexual subjectification, 258–59. *See also* Mothers and older women
mind, 270
misanthropic subtraction, 97
modelling, 13
modest witness, 43
Mol, Annemarie, 56, 252–54
monsters/monstrosity, 181–83
Moran, Stacey, 3; "Decoherent Reading," 129, 131n7

Moretti, Franco, 42–43; "Patterns and Interpretation," 42
Morton, Timothy, 139, 270–71, 274, 277, 284n22; "Deconstruction and/as Ecology," 139
motherhood, 249; sexual perceptions of, 263; social role of, 259
mothers and older women: capitalist-elastic mother, 260; cultural myths, 249; mainstream media, 249; normative and taboo sexualities, 259–60; pop-cultural figure, 255; raunch culture (Levy), 250; sexualization, 249–50; sexualized images, 249, 255; transversal-sensitive analysis, 254. *See also* Cougars; Milfs
multiregister layering, 276
music, 21, 22. *See also* U2 (rock band)
myclimate, 31
mysterious interactions, 18

Nancy, Jean-Luc, 94
narratives: epistemological understanding, 271; frames, 107; Kantian reasoning, 139; textual ontology, 271
narratology, 271
National Gallery, 167, 173n87
nature, bifurcation of, 236, 241
naturecultures, 121
Negarestani, Reza, 18, 93–94; *Cyclonopedia*, 94–98, 100–108
Negt, Oskar, 63
Neimanis, Astrida, 240, 246n21
nemat-space, 96
Netherlands, 31
networks, 54–56. *See also* Meshworks
neutrinos, 235, 237, 238, 246nn12–13
New American poetry. *See* American poetry
Newkirk, Thomas, 291
New Materialism, 19, 94, 118, 138
Newtonian physics, 83, 120
Nietzsche, Friedrich, 64, 66, 80

nonlogical difference, 139
non-retinal, 239, 246n16

objective observer, 62
object models, 289, 302n5
O'Hanlon, Ann, 38
O'Hanlon, Dick, 38
oil, 95, 97, 102–5; crypto-ontology, 98; darkness and blackness, 98–100; diffractive idea, 98–99; flow of, 96; Tiamaterialistic differentiation, 96, 103–4
older women. *See* Mothers and older women
Olkowski, Dorothea, 78
onto-epistemological entanglement, 1, 3–4, 7
onto-epistemological thinking, 194
onto-logic, 240, 247n22
onto-story, 18, 59–66; concept, 59; fragmentary texts, 60; intra-active, 60
open dialogue, 60
operative ontology of Latour, 55
Oppermann, Serpil, 272–73, 284n22; *Material Ecocriticism*, 272–73
optical illusions, 72
organisms: entanglement with the world, 11; sign structure, 11
othering, 183
The Oxford Handbook of Material Culture Studies, 8

packages, 305n38
parenthesis/parenthetical pattern, 103–8; as diffractive pattern, 104; lunulae of, 101; as plot hole, 100–101; quantum tunneling, 104–5; typographical, 103; Warminski on, 107–8
Parikka, Jussi, 283n9
Parmenides, 62
Parsani, Hamid, 95–96, 101, 102
particles: collapse of wave into, 76; wave behaviour/nature of, 3
Passaic Falls, 127–29

patterns, 41–44; agential realist perspective, 43; modest witness, 43
Peirce, Charles, 13
Perception Workshop, 38
Pereen, Esther, 228
petropolitical undercurrents, 95, 104
phantazein, 20, 136
phenomenological vectors of body, 252
philosophical time, 65
photographic images, 21–22
physical matter, 8
physics: diffractive entanglement in, 6; measurement problem, 73, 76–79; twenty-first-century, 124
Pinch, Trevor, 78
planetary bodies, 238
Plath, Nils, 94, 98, 105–6, 107, 112n84
Plato, 51, 61, 62; *Cratylus*, 61
Plutarch, 64
political formalism, 130
Pollmann, Inga, 11, 26n55
Polybius, 62
postfeminism, 250, 254–56; achieving desirability, 258. *See also* Mothers and older women
programming, 290–91; defined, 290, 291; languages, 290, 291; writing and, 291
Protagoras, 122
Python (programming language), 290, 302; TensorFlow, 301

quantum bodies, 74–79
quantum realm, 3, 75, 78
quantum tunneling, 104–5
queer quantum world, 74
Quiring, Björn, 94

R (programming language), 290, 301
radical outside, 94
radioactive properties, 126
reading, 1; modern science and, 9, 123; relationality, 52–54; as taking measurements, 6; as world understanding, 9

real diffraction, 3–4
The Rebound, 264
reflexive reading, 5
reflexivity, 5, 130, 137, 154, 173n80
relational ontology, 52–59, 138–39
resonance, 82–83
respect, 82
reversal of dualisms, 272–74
Rheinberger, Hans-Jörg, 8
rhetoric, 23
riddle, 60
river fragments/readings, 63–64
Rohrer, Heinrich, 71
Romanticism, 117
Rosenkranz, Pamela, 95
Rushdie, Salman, 285n39

Said, Edward, 45
Saint-Amour, Paul, 130
Salone dei Mesi, 157, 162, 163, 167
Sanzo, Kameron, 94
scanning tunneling microscope (STM), 71–72
"The Scene of Writing," 101
Scholz, Susanne, 8
Schweber, Silvan S., 78
scientific measurement, 6
Scribner, F. Scott, 139
Sedgwick, Eve, 66, 80
Sehgal, Melanie, 6, 83, 94–95, 104
self-awareness, 216
self-reflection, 216
sexual assemblages, 250–66. *See also* Mothers and older women
sexual formations, 251
sexual identities, 249
sexualities, 22, 249–66; age-differentiated, 254–55; diffractive notion of, 251. *See also* Mothers and older women
sexualization, 249–50; breasts, 259; culture, 250; diffractive processes, 263; postmodern power, 250
sexual norms, 249
sexual objectification, 250

Shklovsky, Viktor, 21, 178, 179, 182–88
sign systems, 13
Sikelianos, Eleni, 118–19
Smith, Ali, 20; *Artful*, 153; *How to Be Both*, 20, 153–67, 169n25, 170n32, 170n38
snake writing, 101–2
social constructivism, 53
socioeconomic gender equality, 255
Socrates, 61
Sontag, Susan, 264
Space Race, 38–40
spacetimemattering, 35, 46, 106
speculative horror/texts, 18–19, 93–108; "Black Infinity; or, Oil discovers Humans" (Thacker), 94, 97–102, 105, 106; "*Caltiki*" (Thacker), 94, 98, 100, 102, 105, 106, 107; *Cyclonopedia* (Negarestani), 94–98, 100–108
speculative realism, 18, 94, 109n12, 271
Spinoza, Baruch de, 64, 132n18
Spivak, Gayatri Chakravorty, 33, 35, 44, 47n5, 50n66
Stack Exchange sites, 287
Stack Overflow (SO), 287–302; API, 287, 293–302; classification schemes, 300; metadata fields, 287, *288*; programming, 291; rhetoric, 289; software source code, 297–98, 302; tags, 299–300, *300*; TensorFlow, 301
"Standard Model of Particle Physics," 238
Stern-Gerlach experiment, 79–80
Stevenson, Robert Louis, 206
still images, 21–22
STM. *See* Scanning tunneling microscope
Stroustrup, Bjarne, 290; *Programming: Principles and Practice Using C++*, 290
sub-creation, 140
supercelestial creature, 243

superposition, 120
surfacing/surface reading, 41–43, 211–28; *agencement*, 213, 215, 217, 218; apparatuses, 213–17; *Casa de papel* (Domínguez), 217–28; *dispositif*, 213–15. See also Foucault, Michel; *Ich packe meine Bibliothek aus* (Benjamin), 217–28
sweepings, 62
symptomatic reading, 42

tags, 299–300
Tagushi, Lenz, 138
Tappen-Scheuermann, Diana, 207
Taylor, Carol, 82
Teare, Brian, 118–19
TensorFlow, 300, 301
text reading, 2
texts, 253; agency, 253; as creative resources, 253; cultural, 253; media, 253–54; ontologies, 253, 271
textual democracy, 282
textual intention, 269–70
textual minds, 270
Thacker, Eugene, 18, 94, 97–107; "Black Infinity; or, Oil discovers Humans," 94, 97–102, 105, 106; "Caltiki," 94, 98, 100, 102, 105, 106, 107; *In the Dust of this Planet*, 94; *Horror of Philosophy*, 94. See also Parenthesis/parenthetical pattern
Theophrastus, 62
Thiele, Kathrin, 1, 6, 50n68, 58, 64, 81, 82, 93, 98, 194, 237; *Diffracted Worlds – Diffractive Readings*, 1
things-to-words, 253
Thwaites glacier basin of Antarctica, 31
Tiamaterialistic differentiation, 96, 103–5
Tilley, Christopher, 7–8
time and temporality, 65
Timofeeva, Oxana, 110–11n55
Tolkien, J. R. R., 20, 135–36, 140–49, 150n20, 151n37; affection for *eponyms*, 148; *The Lord of the Rings*, 135, 136,
140; *The New Shadow*, 135, 136, 137, 140–46, 148; "On Fairy-Stories," 140, 148; *The Peoples of Middle-Earth*, 136, 143; *The Return of the King*, 142; *The Silmarillion*, 136, 145; "Tal-Elmar," 136, 137, 143–45, 148
transcoding, 236
Trinh Minh-ha, 64
Tsing, Anna, 41
tunneling current, 71
twist, concept of, 159–60
two-system dilemma, 120

U2 (rock band), 22, 269–82; *Achtung Baby*, 271, 276; diffracting, 275–82; "The Fly," 276; "Iris (Hold Me Close)", 277–78; "Last Night on Earth," 276; "The Little Things That Give You Away," 269, 282; "Love Is All We Have Left," 276–78; *No Line on the Horizon*, 269; "Numb," 276; *Pop*, 276; "Shadows and Tall Trees," 280; "Song for Someone," 276, 279–81; *Songs of Experience*, 269, 274, 276–81; *Songs of Innocence*, 269, 274, 276–81; "13 (There is a Light)," 279–80, 281; *Zooropa*, 276
Umwelt/Umwelten, 11–14
uncertainty principle, 122, 137–38
UNESCO World Heritage site, 240
"The Unnamable," 102, 112n82
unseeing, 83, 85
uranium, 126

van der Tuin, Iris, 6, 81–82, 83, 89n61
Vedder, Ulrike, 8
Vee, Annette, 290, 292
Venturi, Adolfo, 157
von Contzen, Eva, 167n3, 170n38
von Uexküll, Jakob, 11–14, 26n55, 26n57

Warminski, Andrzej, 107–8
water/water bodies, 240–41; hydrocommons, 241

Watson, James D., 160; *The Double Helix*, 160
Weaver, Milly, 172n65
Wense, Hans Jürgen von der, 66
West, Candace, 250
West Antarctic Ice Sheet, 31
Western philosophy: difference, 64, 65; Eastern philosophy *versus*, 69n49
Wheeler, Wendy, 11, 13, 15
Whitehead, Alfred North, 80, 83, 104, 106, 235–36, 238; *Science and the Modern World*, 238
Wilde, Oscar, 266
"William Carlos Williams, Ecocriticism, and Contemporary American Poetry," (Long), 123
Williams, William Carlos, 19; *Kora in Hell*, 125; *Paterson*, 19, 117–31; scientific analogy, 126; *Spring and All*, 118, 121

Wirth, Uwe, 100
Woodward, Ben, 106
Woolf, Virginia, 103
words-to-things, 253
words-to-words, 253
world: as agential intra-activity, 58; materialization, 59; organic, 11; reading/writing nature, 9–10; sweepings, 62; Williams on, 124
worlding, 59
world-text-reader relationship, 19

X-ray diffraction, 160

Zeh, Hans Dieter, 76
Zeitgenossenschaft, 52, 65, 66, 67n2
Zertuche, Hayley, 11, 12
Žižek, Slavoj, 250
Zunshine, Lisa, 284–85n28

About the Contributors

Nathan D. Frank is a doctoral candidate at the University of Virginia. His dissertation explores contemporary doubt through the work of novelists who invoke, reimagine, and emulate scripture, a project underwritten by critical techniques ranging from speculative realisms to narrative theory. He is a co-organizer of the U2 Conference (http://u2conference.com/) and can be found writing and cycling around the world-class vineyards of central Virginia, outside Charlottesville, that he, his family, and his dogs call home.

Brendan Johnston is a PhD candidate in English Literature at the University of Nevada, Reno. His work focuses on twentieth-century American literature, modernist poetry, and materialist theory. He has recently co-edited and written the introduction for an edited collection entitled *Ethics After Poststructuralism: A Reader* (2020), which considers the ethics of Emmanuel Levinas in light of twenty-first-century issues in feminism, biopolitics, decolonialism, and ecology.

Birgit Mara Kaiser is an associate professor of Comparative Literature and Transcultural Aesthetics at Utrecht University, The Netherlands. Her research spans late eighteenth- to twenty-first-century literatures in English, French, and German, with special interest in aesthetics, affect, and subject formation. She also works on postcolonial literature (esp. French North-African and Caribbean) and critical cultural studies. Recently, publications appeared in *Comparative Literature*, *Interventions*, *Parallax*, *Textual Practice* and *PhiloSOPHIA: A Journal of Continental Feminism*. More @ https://www.uu.nl/medewerkers/BMKaiser and www.terracritica.net.

Daniela Keller is a postdoctoral teaching and research fellow at the Department of English in Basel, Switzerland. She successfully defended her PhD thesis with the title *Germany and Physics in English Fiction after 1960: A Diffractive Reading of Anglo-German Entanglements* in 2019 and has coedited the essay collections *English Topographies in Literature and Culture: Space, Place, and Identity* (2016) as well as *Brexit and Beyond: Nation and Identity* (2021) with Ina Habermann.

Annina Klappert is a private lecturer (*Habilitation*) for Literary Studies and has held two endowed professorships at the Humboldt University of Berlin and several interim professorships at the Universities of Erfurt and Cologne. Currently, she is Max Kade Visiting Professor at the Johns Hopkins University. Her research interests are theories of virtuality, mediality, and textuality; contemporary literature, literature around 1800, and the "femmes de lettres" of the seventeenth and eighteenth century; literary houses, New Materialism and the material order of knowledge. Her latest book is *Sand als metaphorisches Modell für Virtualität* (2020).

Agnieszka Kotwasińska is an assistant professor at the American Studies Center, the University of Warsaw. She specializes in Gothic and horror studies, gender studies, queer theory, and feminist new materialism(s). Her research interests center on embodiment in the so-called low genres, death, illness, and mourning in horror, and schizoanalysis. She has published articles in *Somatechnics*, *Praktyka Teoretyczna*, and *Humanities*, among others. She is currently working on her first monograph exploring horror fiction by American women writers.

Sean McCullough is a PhD candidate in Texas Christian University's Rhetoric and Composition program. His dissertation research focuses on the intersections between digital social spaces, software, and literacies. While finishing his PhD, Sean is also working as a technology consultant, developing software solutions for clients from various industries.

Kai Merten is a professor of British Literary Studies at the University of Erfurt, where he has founded the Erfurt Network on New Materialism. His research interests include British literature of the Romantic age and of the twentieth century, literature and media studies, literature and theatricality and New Materialism. He has also edited collections on postcolonial media theory, cultural alterity around 1800 and on literature and knowledge. An edited collection on New Materialist literary theory is forthcoming.

Stacey Moran is an assistant professor in the School of Arts, Media and Engineering and the Department of English at Arizona State University. Her work lies at the intersections of feminist theory and technoscience, design studies, and critical pedagogy. Moran is the associate director of the Center for Philosophical Technologies (CPT), focused on critical and speculative research on philosophy, technology, and design. Moran's research informs her creative practice, which explores the relation between mythology and material practices.

Peter Schuck teaches German literature at the University of Erfurt. He studied Comparative Literature and Philosophy at the University of Erfurt and the Ruhr-Universität Bochum. In Erfurt, he completed his PhD with a thesis on zombies. His current research and teaching interests include twentieth- and twenty-first-century fiction and poetry, posthumanism, queer studies, and the theatricality of the written text.

Susan Yi Sencindiver, PhD, holds research and teaching appointments at the School of Communication and Culture, Aarhus University, Denmark. She teaches and publishes in the fields of age, motherhood, and gender studies. She is a coordinator for the Centre for Studies in Otherness (www.otherness.dk) and an associate editor of the journal *Otherness: Essays and Studies*. Recent publications include "New Materialism." *Oxford Bibliographies in Literary and Critical Theory*, edited by Eugene O'Brien, 2017.

Matthias Stephan (Aarhus University, Denmark) researches postmodernism, and its implications in Gothic, science fiction, and crime fiction, and has recently begun to explore Ecocriticism and New Materialism. His work has appeared in *Scandinavian Studies*, *Coolabah* and the edited collections *Netflix Nostalgia* and *Transcending the Postmodern*. His monograph *Defining Literary Postmodernism for the Twenty-First Century* is available at Palgrave. He is general editor for *Otherness: Essays and Studies*, and a coordinator of the *Centre for Studies in Otherness*.

Jol Thoms is an internationally active artist and researcher based in London, UK working at the forefront of experimental physics, environmental humanities, and feminist science studies. Working with agential realism, counterallegory, and practices of situating his work aims towards an understanding of physics as an ethical and cultural practice of story-telling that matters. He is a PhD candidate in the School of Arts at the University of Westminster, where he is also an organizer of the Deep Field Project.

Bo Kampmann Walther, PhD, is an associate professor at the Institute for Cultural Sciences, University of Southern Denmark. Has written, taught, and lectured extensively on new media, computer games, new media philosophy, and sports and media (football). He is also a football columnist and consultant. He is currently writing two books; one on ludification, and another on Tolkien.

Max Walther, literary critic, is a PhD candidate in the department of Media Studies at Bauhaus-Universität Weimar. As part of the post-graduate program on Media Anthropology, he is working on a project on Simone Weil, Chris Kraus, Kathy Acker, and Annie Ernaux. At the manifold intersections between mysticism and French Theory, the project seeks to uncover experimental modes of (non-)expression and within that an alternative epistemology.

www.ingramcontent.com/pod-product-compliance
Lightning Source LLC
Chambersburg PA
CBHW070011010526
44117CB00011B/1519